CHAPTERS INTO VERSE

CHAPTERS INTO VERSE

A Selection of Poetry in English Inspired by the Bible
from Genesis through Revelation

Assembled and edited by

ROBERT ATWAN
and LAURANCE WIEDER

OXFORD
UNIVERSITY PRESS

2000

OXFORD
UNIVERSITY PRESS

Oxford   New York
Athens   Auckland   Bangkok   Bogotá   Buenos Aires   Calcutta   Cape Town
Dar es Salaam   Delhi   Florence   Hong Kong   Istanbul   Karachi   Kuala Lumpur
Madras   Madrid   Melbourne   Mexico City   Mumbai   Nairobi   Paris   Singapore
Taipei   Tokyo   Toronto   Warsaw

and associated companies in
Berlin   Ibadan

Published by Oxford University Press, Inc.
198 Madison Avenue, New York, New York 10016

Oxford is a registered trademark
of Oxford University Press

Cataloging-in-Publication Data
Chapters into verse : a selection of poetry in English inspired by the Bible from
Genesis through Revelation / assembled and edited by Robert Atwan & Laurance
Wieder.
        p.   cm.
    Includes indexes.
    ISBN 0-19-513676-4
    1. Bible—History of Biblical events—Poetry. 2. Religious poetry, English. 3.
Religious poetry, American. I. Atwan, Robert. II. Wieder, Laurance, 1946–
PR1191 .C45 2000
821.008'03822—dc21

                                                                                99-056691

Book design by Susan Day

Pages 481–485 constitute a continuation of the copyright page

1 3 5 7 9 8 6 4 2
Printed in the United States of America
on acid-free paper

CONTENTS

Part II: Gospels through Revelation

The Beloved ෴

The Crucified ෴

PREFACE

This edition of *Chapters into Verse* is the latest response to the question Robert Atwan asked Laurance Wieder in 1989: How about a collection of poetry inspired by the Bible? Research for the books that grew from the question became a three-year grand tour of an undiscovered country: scriptural poetry in English. The definitive, two-volume hardcover edition of *Chapters into Verse: Poetry in English Inspired by the Bible*, published in 1993, offered a stately progress through the reclaimed territory. Wieder's second answer to the question of the Bible in English poetry, *The Poets' Book of Psalms: The Complete Psalter as Rendered by Twenty-five Poets from the Sixteenth to the Twentieth Centuries*, first appeared in 1995. Casting a wider net along a single shore, Atwan, George Dardess, and Peggy Rosenthal saw their *Divine Inspiration: The Life of Jesus in World Poetry* released in 1998.

This one-volume paperback, *Chapters into Verse: A Selection of Poetry in English Inspired by the Bible from Genesis through Revelation*, has the same origins but other ambitions and a swifter pace than its multivolume parent. Where the hardcover is inclusive, this edition is exemplary. Individual poets whose extensive contributions appear in the comprehensive survey here may be represented by one or a few poems. Minor poems, and items of historical curiosity only, were left out to quicken the flow. Where a single biblical passage inspired many poems, fewer works were retained to give the best reading.

We believe this epitomized version makes another spirited argument for the strength, variety, and continued vitality of the scriptural tradition. It is a generous introduction to many of the voices song and faith and reason have assumed responding to what made Elijah tremble, "the still, small voice."

Thanks to Elda Rotor, our editor at Oxford University Press, for making this new, one-volume edition of *Chapters into Verse* possible.

We again want to express our gratitude to the many friends and colleagues for the help they gave us throughout the stages of a vast undertaking: George Dardess, Rev. Lawrence E. Frizzell, Glen Hartley, Michael Heyward, Ron Horning, Gen Kanai, Kenneth Koch,

Christina Moustakis, Joyce Carol Oates, Charles O'Neill, Alicia Ostriker, Jon Roberts, Peggy Rosenthal, David Shapiro, J. O. Tate, and Edward W. Tayler. We appreciate the help and guidance we received from the staff at Oxford University Press, particularly from T. Susan Chang. Finally, we dedicate this book to our families: for Helene, Gregory, and Emily Atwan; for Andrea and Aiah Wieder.

Robert Atwan and Laurance Wieder
2000

INTRODUCTION

There are no songs comparable to the songs of Zion;
no orations equal to those of the prophets;
and no politics like those which the Scriptures teach.

— JOHN MILTON

Ezra Pound once tweaked T. S. Eliot for preferring Moses to the
Muses. Pound's witty remark reminds us of English poetry's two great
heritages: the classical and the scriptural or (as Matthew Arnold
named them) the Hellenic and the Hebraic. Poetry inspired by classi-
cal Greek and Latin models has dominated the poetic landscape for
so many centuries that most readers now consider it the only literary
tradition. Although the scriptural tradition in English poetry is every
bit as venerable as the classical, it has never received the attention
accorded its chosen twin. Like Ishmael and Esau, it has led a shadow
existence. We hope that this collection will finally bring the scriptural
tradition out of the shadows and into the light.

Chapters into Verse, therefore, is more than just another anthology
of English-language poetry. The original, two-volume edition was the
first collection ever assembled of poems inspired by the Bible. It sur-
veys and defines a literary legacy that has lived and at times flourished
in the wilderness, unremarked by the reigning literary culture. All of
the poems selected for both the editions respond to specific passages of
Scripture. Arranged in Biblical order, from Genesis to Revelation,
every poem is preceded by at least the kernel of the appropriate chap-
ter and verse. Whenever possible, we print a poem's Biblical source in
full; at other times, to save space, we have excerpted chapter and verse
so that readers will have in front of them the salient passage(s) for con-
text and comparison. Whenever a poet responds to an extensive
Biblical episode, we provide as much text as is convenient, expecting
that readers will turn to their own Bibles for further illumination.

We think that this arrangement lets the reader experience not
merely an isolated poem or favorite Biblical quotation; it places the
dialogue between individual poet and sacred text in plain view. Each
poem, as it retells, contemplates, expands, debates with, praises, voices,
or reimagines the language and events of the Bible, becomes as
well an exegesis of the text. *Chapters into Verse* can thus be read as
a poetic commentary upon the scriptures. The authority of this com-
mentary derives from the individual poet's imaginative insight—from
an intuitive precision and expressive vitality—rather than from schol-
arship or sectarian politics or established religion.

The collection covers an enormous range of literary styles, histori-

cal periods, and religious backgrounds. Poets from much of the
English-speaking world are present, representing a diversity of coun-
tries, cultures, communities, and idioms—from the English meta-
physical poets of the seventeenth century to the African-American
voices of the Harlem Renaissance, from the Scots dialect of Robert
Burns to the jaunty music of Australian Victor Daley. Whether writ-
ing in the King's English, another English, or their own invented lan-
guage, the poets of the scriptural tradition also employ the whole
range of verse forms and personal tones familiar to readers of English
literature: from lyric to dramatic, from blank verse to highly-wrought
rhyme, from ridicule to reverence, from the majestic to the demotic,
from epic to epigrammatic.

The Old and New Testaments have stimulated different poetic
responses to the sacred texts. The Old Testament presents a special
challenge to poets because of the extraordinary poetry it already con-
tains; poets responding to the Hebrew Scriptures need to be fearless—
as was William Blake—about competition. Walt Whitman, truly one
of the fearless, claimed that he was "a thorough believer in the
Hebrew Scriptures." Boldly intending his *Leaves of Grass* to be a
"new Bible" for a new era, Whitman nevertheless prophesied that
"No true Bard will ever contravene the Bible." Recognizing a scrip-
tural tradition, he saw the unspoken covenant that existed between
the books of the Bible and the work of poets. "If the time ever
comes," he wrote, "when iconoclasm does its extremest in one direc-
tion against the books of the Bible in its present form, the collection
must still survive in another, and dominate just as much as hitherto,
or more than hitherto, through its divine and primal poetic structure."

To be included in *Chapters into Verse*, a poem had to meet two
criteria: it had to possess real literary merit (as distinct from admirable
sentiment, or propriety, or didactic fervor) and it had to derive from a
specific scriptural source. As a result, some prominent figures who
never or rarely partook of poetic inspiration from scripture are missing
from this anthology, among them Geoffrey Chaucer, William
Shakespeare, Andrew Marvell, Percy Bysshe Shelley, Edgar Allan Poe,
and Wallace Stevens. In their place will be found such less familiar
names as Francis Quarles, Thomas Stanley, Anne Finch Countess of
Winchilsea, Christopher Smart, P. Hately Waddell, and, starting in
the twentieth century, such Jewish poets as Charles Reznikoff and
Delmore Schwartz.

The decision to use the King James Bible was not so much ours as
it was the authors we included. So many important poets since the
seventeenth century have relied on this Bible's resonant style, regard-
less of their religious or historical backgrounds, that it made no liter-
ary or editorial sense for us to use any other version or translation.
Aside from its theological importance, the King James Bible is itself

a monumental literary achievement. Built on a foundation laid by William Tyndale, Miles Coverdale, and the learned committee in Geneva, its language informs both the literature and the everyday chatter of the English-speaking world, an influence rivalled by no other vernacular bible. Thomas Macaulay called the King James Version "a book which, if everything else in our language should perish, would alone suffice to show the whole extent of its beauty and power." Much of that beauty and power emerges in this collection.

The history of the Bible in English runs parallel to the development of English poetry. John Wycliffe, who made an English Bible from the Latin Vulgate, was a contemporary of Friar Herebert. The first translation from the original tongues into English was undertaken by the unfortunate English Catholic priest, William Tyndale. He perished at the stake after falling into the hands of the Inquisition in the 1540s, the same decade that saw the deaths of the first English sonneteers, Sir Thomas Wyatt and Henry Howard Earl of Surrey. Besides Englishing Petrarch, Wyatt also translated the Seven Penitential Psalms before his execution for leading a rebellion against the Catholic Queen Mary Tudor; Surrey verse-paraphrased Ecclesiastes. The Geneva Bible, issued by a committee of Calvinists in 1560, was for almost a century the Bible of English Protestants, whose cause found a champion and martyr in the ideal courtier and poet, Sir Philip Sidney. Sidney and his sister Mary Herbert Countess of Pembroke are mostly remembered for the crypto-virgilian pastoral, *The Countess of Pembroke's Arcadia*. But as Sidney noted in his *An Apologie for Poetrie*, the Psalmist David was first a shepherd, then a king, and so the original pastoral poet. Before he died, Sidney translated the first forty-three Psalms; his sister took up the task and triumphantly completed the Sidney Psalter. Other Renaissance poets, perhaps uncertain which camp (England or Rome, high or low, Hellenic or Hebraic) would prevail, pursued the double career: Sir John Davies and Thomas Campion, among many, made Psalms; Edmund Spenser epitomized the Book of Revelation in unrhymed sonnets; Michael Drayton translated the songs of the Patriarchs and Prophets, and John Donne the "Lamentations of Jeremy." By the time James I's committee dedicated the official English Bible in 1611, Shakespeare's life was nearly over and John Milton's had just begun.

By the eighteenth century, literature and scripture had pretty much parted company. The Augustan poets, for the most part, eschewed religious themes, while the religious poets either used verse as sectarian propaganda or aimed it at a popular and sentimental audience. Isaac Watts, John Keble, and Charles Wesley, the most popular religious poets of their time, are largely remembered now for their contributions to the Protestant Hymnal. Of the eighteenth-century literary poets, both Christopher Smart, author of "A Song to

David" and a translator of the Psalms, and William Cowper, who
wrote the Olney Hymns, suffered bouts of depression and religious
mania which gave a pretext for literary criticism to dismiss their reli-
gious verse.

Even William Blake, perhaps the last great poet to take the work-
ings of the divine as his whole theme, has sometimes been prey to
unconvinced readers' suspicions that his inspiration partakes more of
madness than of the sacred breath. Oddly, the worldly Lord Byron
actively engaged the scriptural tradition: his *Hebrew Melodies* are
psalms in the Scots ballad tradition of Robert Burns and Thomas
Moore. In the 1870s, P. Hately Waddell, a disciple of Robert Burns,
published *The Psalms: frae Hebrew intil Scottis*, a work every bit the
equal of the Scots Chaucerian Gawin Douglas' *Thirteen Books of the
Aeneid* which Ezra Pound called "a better book than Virgil's."

It may surprise readers who regard the twentieth century as all
Muses and no Moses to find so many modern poets in this collection.
Not all literary modernists threw away their Bibles, as Wallace Stevens
did in 1907 ("I'm glad the silly thing is gone," he wrote). Some, such
as Charles Reznikoff, arranged and paraphrased the Jewish Bible.
Perhaps the greatest heir of the poets of the New England Puritans
(who called themselves Israel), Robert Frost wrote plain-style poetry
that responded to scripture in profound and moral music. D. H.
Lawrence knew his King James intimately (he wrote a book on
Revelation), and quarreled with the New Testament intensely. Many
of his poems read as though they were written directly in the margins
of his Bible. Every bit as feisty as Lawrence, Laura (Riding) Jackson
regarded herself as "religious in my devotion to poetry. But in saying
this I am thinking of religion as it is a dedication to, a will to know
and make known, the ultimate knowledge, a will to think, to be, with
truth, to voice, to live articulately by, the essentialities of existence."
In her Biblical poems, she continued that ongoing debate with the
creation which informs the lyric dissents of Anne Bradstreet, Emily
Dickinson, and Marianne Moore.

The past fifty years have seen at least three entirely new transla-
tions of the Bible from original tongues, and poets' versions of
Genesis, Job, and the Book of Psalms. Sparked by a renewed interest
in Biblical scholarship, especially recent research into the Hebrew
Bible, many contemporary poets are rediscovering the scriptural tradi-
tion. That tradition is also being reinvigorated by the work of women
poets from many religious backgrounds who are viewing the Bible
from new perspectives.

The range of literary styles and historical periods covered in *Chapters
into Verse* compelled us to make several editorial decisions regarding
the texts of older poems. At first we thought we should retain the fla-

vor of the archaic spelling, punctuation, and typographical conventions of sixteenth, seventeenth, and eighteenth century poetry, but upon reflection that notion struck us as fussy. We wanted the poetry to be as clear as possible, to present the fewest barriers to direct, unmediated reading. So we decided to exhibit the older poetry entirely in contemporary dress, with no quaint frills or peculiar decoration or typographic bombast. We found that outright modernization transforms many inaccessible-looking texts into poems that seem breathtakingly fresh. To avoid clutter on the page, we kept notes and glosses to a minimum.

Because the New Testament relates the life of Jesus in four (often overlapping) accounts, we decided it would be more efficient to "harmonize" the gospels into a single narrative. Events told in common were represented by what we considered the most direct and clearest version; details peculiar to each account were fitted into the mosaic whenever possible; obscurities and contradictions, such as where and when Peter denied Christ, were left standing.

CHAPTERS INTO VERSE

PART ONE

GENESIS THROUGH MALACHI

Immediate are the Acts of God, more swift
Than time or motion, but to human ears
Cannot without process of speech be told,
So told as earthly notion can receive.

JOHN MILTON
Paradise Lost, Bk VII
ll. 176–79

EXTRACTS

The Bible is an antique Volume ✌ EMILY DICKINSON

The Bible is an antique Volume –
Written by faded Men
At the suggestion of Holy Spectres –
Subjects – Bethlehem –
Eden – the ancient Homestead –
Satan – the Brigadier –
Judas – the Great Defaulter –
David – the Troubadour –
Sin – a distinguished Precipice
Others must resist –
Boys that "believe" are very lonesome –
Other Boys are "lost" –
Had but the Tale a warbling Teller –
All the Boys would come –
Orpheus' Sermon captivated –
It did not condemn –

The H. Scriptures I ✌ GEORGE HERBERT

Oh Book! infinite sweetness! let my heart
    Suck every letter, and a honey gain,
    Precious for any grief in any part;
To clear the breast, to mollify all pain.

Thou art all health, health thriving till it make
    A full eternity: thou art a mass
    Of strange delights, where we may wish and take.
Ladies, look here; this is the thankful glass,

That mends the lookers' eyes: this is the well
    That washes what it shows. Who can endear
    Thy praise too much? thou art heaven's ledger here,
Working against the states of death and hell.

    Thou art joy's handsell: heaven lies flat in thee,
    Subject to every mounter's bended knee.

The Book of Books ∾ SIR WALTER SCOTT

Within this ample volume lies
The mystery of mysteries.
Happiest they of human race
To whom their God has given grace
To read, to fear, to hope, to pray,
To lift the latch, to force the way;
But better had they ne'er been born
That read to doubt or read to scorn.

Taste ∾ CHRISTOPHER SMART

O guide my judgment and my taste,
    Sweet Spirit, author of the book
Of wonders, told in language chaste
    And plainness, not to be mistook.

O let me muse, and yet at sight
    The page admire, the page believe;
'Let there be light, and there was light,
    Let there be Paradise and Eve!'

Who his soul's rapture can refrain?
    At Joseph's ever-pleasing tale,
Of marvels, the prodigious train,
    To Sinai's hill from Goshen's vale.

The Psalmist and proverbial Seer,
    And all the prophets' sons of song,
Make all things precious, all things dear,
    And bear the brilliant word along.

O take the book from off the shelf,
    And con it meekly on thy knees;
Best panegyric on itself,
    And self-avouched to teach and please.

Respect, adore it heart and mind.
    How greatly sweet, how sweetly grand,

Who reads the most, is most refined,
    And polished by the Master's hand.

On the Bible   ᴔ   THOMAS TRAHERNE

When thou dost take this sacred book into thy hand
Think not that thou the included sense dost understand.

It is a sign thou wantest sound intelligence
If that thou think thyself to understand the sense.

Be not deceived thou then on it in vain mayst gaze;
The way is intricate that leads into a maze.

Here's naught but what's mysterious to an understanding eye;
Where reverence alone stands ope, and sense stands by.

GENESIS

1:1–1:2   In the beginning God created the heaven and the earth.
    And the earth was without form, and void; and darkness was upon the
face of the deep. And the Spirit of God moved upon the face of the waters.

from *Paradise Lost, Bk VII*   ᴔ   JOHN MILTON
ll. 205–216; 224–242

               Heaven opened wide
Her ever-during gates, harmonious sound
On golden hinges moving, to let forth
The King of Glory in his powerful word
And spirit coming to create new worlds.
On heavenly ground they stood, and from the shore
They viewed the vast immeasurable abyss
Outrageous as a sea, dark, wasteful, wild,
Up from the bottom turned by furious winds
And surging waves, as mountains to assault
Heaven's height, and with the center mix the pole.
         Silence, ye troubled waves, and thou Deep, peace. . . .

Then stayed the fervid wheels, and in his hand
He took the golden compasses, prepared
In God's eternal store, to circumscribe
This universe, and all created things:
One foot he centered, and the other turned
Round through the vast profundity obscure,
And said, Thus far extend, thus far thy bounds,
This be thy just circumference, O World.
Thus God the Heaven created, thus the Earth,
Matter unformed and void: Darkness profound
Covered the abyss: but on the watery calm
His brooding wings the spirit of God outspread,
And vital virtue infused, and vital warmth
Throughout the fluid mass, but downward purged
The black tartareous cold infernal dregs
Adverse to life; then founded, then conglobed
Like things to like, the rest to several place
Disparted, and between spun out the air,
And Earth self-balanced on her center hung.

1:3   And God said, Let there be light:

Let There Be Light!   ᢖ   D. H. LAWRENCE

If ever there was a beginning
there was no god in it
there was no Verb
no Voice
no Word.

There was nothing to say:
Let there be light!
All that story of Mr God switching on day
is just conceit.

Just man's conceit!
—Who made the sun?
—My child, I cannot tell a lie,
I made it!

George Washington's Grandpapa!

All we can honestly imagine in the beginning
is the incomprehensible plasm of life, of creation
struggling
and *becoming* light.

1:3–1:8   and there was light. And God saw the light, that it was good: and
God divided the light from the darkness. And God called the light Day, and
the darkness he called Night. And the evening and the morning were the
first day.

And God said, Let there be a firmament in the midst of the waters, and
let it divide the waters from the waters. And God made the firmament, and
divided the waters which were under the firmament from the waters which
were above the firmament: and it was so. And God called the firmament
Heaven. And the evening and the morning were the second day.

There is No Land Yet   ↵   LAURA (RIDING) JACKSON

The long sea, how short-lasting,
From water-thought to water-thought
So quick to feel surprise and shame.
Where moments are not time
But time is moments.
Such neither yes nor no,
Such only love, to have to-morrow
By certain failure of now and now.

On water lying strong ships and men
In weakness skilled reach elsewhere:
No prouder places from home in bed
The mightiest sleeper can know.
So faith took ship upon the sailor's earth
To seek absurdities in heaven's name—
Discovery but a fountain without source,
Legend of mist and lost patience.

The body swimming in itself
Is dissolution's darling.

With dripping mouth it speaks a truth
That cannot lie, in words not born yet
Out of first immortality,
All-wise impermanence.

And the dusty eye whose accuracies
Turn watery in the mind
Where waves of probability
Write vision in a tidal hand
That time alone can read.

And the dry land not yet,
Lonely and absolute salvation—
Boasting of constancy
Like an island with no water round
In water where no land is.

1:14–1:19   And God said, Let there be lights in the firmament of the heaven to divide the day from the night; and let them be for signs, and for seasons, and for days, and years: And let them be for lights in the firmament of the heaven to give light upon the earth: and it was so. And God made two great lights; the greater light to rule the day, and the lesser light to rule the night: he made the stars also. . . . And the evening and the morning were the fourth day.

Ode ✌ JOSEPH ADDISON

The spacious firmament on high
With all the blue ethereal sky,
And spangled heavens, a shining frame,
Their great original proclaim:
The unwearied sun, from day to day,
Does his creator's power display,
And publishes to every land
The work of an almighty hand.

Soon as the evening shades prevail,
The moon takes up the wondrous tale,
And nightly to the listening earth

Repeats the story of her birth:
Whilst all the stars that round her burn,
And all the planets in their turn,
Confirm the tidings as they roll,
And spread the truth from pole to pole.

What though, in solemn silence, all
Move round the dark, terrestrial ball?
What though nor real voice nor sound
Amid their radiant orbs be found?
In reason's ear they all rejoice,
And utter forth a glorious voice,
For ever singing, as they shine,
'The hand that made us is divine'.

1:24–1:25   And God said, Let the earth bring forth the living creature after
his kind, cattle, and creeping thing, and beast of the earth after his kind:
and it was so. And God made the beast of the earth after his kind, and cat-
tle after their kind, and every thing that creepeth upon the earth after his
kind: and God saw that it was good.

The Animals ↣ EDWIN MUIR

They do not live in the world,
Are not in time and space.
From birth to death hurled
No word do they have, not one
To plant a foot upon,
Were never in any place.

For with names the world was called
Out of the empty air,
With names was built and walled,
Line and circle and square,
Dust and emerald;
Snatched from deceiving death
By the articulate breath.

But these have never trod
Twice the familiar track,
Never never turned back
Into the memoried day.
All is new and near
In the unchanging Here
Of the fifth great day of God,
That shall remain the same,
Never shall pass away.

On the sixth day we came.

1:26   And God said, Let us make man in our image, after our likeness: and
let them have dominion over the fish of the sea, and over the fowl of the air,
and over the cattle, and over all the earth, and over every creeping thing
that creepeth upon the earth.

Fill and Illumined   ᘒ   JOSEPH CERAVOLO

God created his image.
I love him like the door.
Speak to me now.
Without god there is no god.
Forget everything!
Lie down and be circumscribed
                and circumcised.
Yet there is no pain.
Yet there is no joy.

1:27   So God created man in his own image, in the image of God created
he him; male and female created he them.

A Divine Image   ᘒ   WILLIAM BLAKE

Cruelty has a Human Heart,
And Jealousy a Human Face;
Terror the Human Form Divine,
And Secrecy the Human Dress.

The Human Dress is forged Iron,
The Human Form a fiery Forge,
The Human Face a Furnace sealed,
The Human Heart its hungry Gorge.

The Image o' God ᔓ JOE CORRIE

Crawlin' aboot like a snail in the mud,
    Covered wi' clammy blae
ME, made after the image o' God —
    Jings! but it's laughable, tae.

Howkin' awa' 'neath a mountain o' stane,
    Gaspin' for want o' air,
The sweat makin' streams doon my bare back-bane
    And my knees a' hauckit and sair.

Strainin' and cursin' the hale shift through,
    Half-starved, half-blin', half-mad;
And the gaffer he says, 'Less dirt in that coal
    Or ye go up the pit, my lad!'

So I gi'e my life to the Nimmo squad
    For eicht and fower a day;
Me! made after the image o' God —
    Jings! but it's laughable, tae.

1:28–1:30 And God blessed them, and God said unto them, Be fruitful, and multiply, and replenish the earth, and subdue it: and have dominion over the fish of the sea, and over the fowl of the air, and over every living thing that moveth upon the earth. . . .

The Pulley ᔓ GEORGE HERBERT

    When God at first made man,
Having a glass of blessings standing by,
'Let us' (said he) 'pour on him all we can;
Let the world's riches, which dispersed lie,
        Contract into a span.'

So strength first made a way;
Then beauty flowed, then wisdom, honor, pleasure.
When almost all was out, God made a stay,
Perceiving that alone of all his treasure
    Rest in the bottom lay.

'For if I should' (said he)
'Bestow this jewel also on my creature,
He would adore my gifts instead of me,
And rest in nature, not the God of nature:
    So both should losers be.

'Yet let him keep the rest,
But keep them with repining restlessness;
Let him be rich and weary, that at least,
If goodness lead him not, yet weariness
    May toss him to my breast.'

1:31–2:1   And God saw every thing that he had made, and, behold, it was
very good. And the evening and the morning were the sixth day.
    Thus the heavens and the earth were finished, and all the host of them.

Genesis   ᘒ   GEOFFREY HILL

I
Against the burly air I strode
Crying the miracles of God.

And first I brought the sea to bear
Upon the dead weight of the land;
And the waves flourished at my prayer,
The rivers spawned their sand.

And where the streams were salt and full
The tough pig-headed salmon strove,
Ramming the ebb, in the tide's pull,
To reach the steady hills above.

II

The second day I stood and saw
The osprey plunge with triggered claw,
Feathering blood along the shore,
To lay the living sinew bare.

And the third day I cried: "Beware
The soft-voiced owl, the ferret's smile,
The hawk's deliberate stoop in air,
Cold eyes, and bodies hooped in steel,
Forever bent upon the kill."

III

And I renounced, on the fourth day,
This fierce and unregenerate clay,
Building as a huge myth for man
The watery Leviathan,

And made the long-winged albatross
Scour the ashes of the sea
Where Capricorn and Zero cross,
A brooding immortality –
Such as the charmed phoenix has
In the unwithering tree.

IV

The phoenix burns as cold as frost;
And, like a legendary ghost,
The phantom-bird goes wild and lost,
Upon a pointless ocean tossed.

So, the fifth day, I turned again
To flesh and blood and the blood's pain.

V

On the sixth day, as I rode
In haste about the works of God,
With spurs I plucked the horse's blood.

By blood we live, the hot, the cold,
To ravage and redeem the world:
There is no bloodless myth will hold.

And by Christ's blood are men made free
Though in close shrouds their bodies lie
Under the rough pelt of the sea;

Though Earth has rolled beneath her weight
The bones that cannot bear the light.

2:8–2:9   And the LORD God planted a garden eastward in Eden; and there
he put the man whom he had formed. And out of the ground made the
LORD God to grow every tree that is pleasant to the sight, and good for
food; the tree of life also in the midst of the garden, and the tree of knowl-
edge of good and evil.

When Adam Walked in Eden Young   ⌇   A. E. HOUSMAN

When Adam walked in Eden young,
    Happy, 'tis writ, was he,
While high the fruit of knowledge hung
    Unbitten on the tree.

Happy was he the livelong day;
    I doubt 'tis written wrong:
The heart of man, for all they say,
    Was never happy long.

And now my feet are tired of rest,
    And here they will not stay,
And the soul fevers in my breast
    And aches to be away.

2:10–2:18   And a river went out of Eden to water the garden; and from
thence it was parted, and became into four heads. . . .
    And the LORD God took the man, and put him into the garden of Eden
to dress it and to keep it. And the LORD God commanded the man, saying,
Of every tree of the garden thou mayest freely eat: But of the tree of the
knowledge of good and evil, thou shalt not eat of it: for in the day that thou
eatest thereof thou shalt surely die.

Eden ⁓ THOMAS TRAHERNE

A learned and a happy ignorance
            Divided me
        From all the vanity,
From all the sloth, care, pain and sorrow that advance
    The madness and the misery
Of men. No error, no distraction I
Saw soil the Earth, or overcloud the sky.

I knew not that there was a serpent's sting,
            Whose poison shed
        On men did overspread
The world: nor did I dream of such a thing
    As sin, in which mankind lay dead.
They all were brisk and living weights to me,
Yea pure, and full of immortality.

Joy, pleasure, beauty, kindness, glory, love
            Sleep, day, life, light,
        Peace, melody, my sight,
My ears and heart did fill, and freely move.
    All that I saw did me delight:
The *Universe* was then a world of treasure,
To me an universal world of pleasure.

Unwelcome penitence was then unknown;
            Vain costly toys,
        Swearing and roaring boys,
Shops, markets, taverns, coaches were unshown:
    So all things were that drowned my joys.
No thorns choked up my path, nor hid the face
Of bliss and beauty, nor eclipsed the place.

Only what Adam in his first estate,
            Did I behold;
        Hard silver and dry gold
As yet lay under ground: my blessed fate
    Was more acquainted with the old
And innocent delights which he did see
In his Original Simplicity.

Those things which first his Eden did adorn
                    My infancy
              Did crown: simplicity
Was my protection when I first was born.
     Mine eyes those treasures first did see
Which God first made: the first effects of love
My first enjoyments upon Earth did prove;

And were so great, and so divine, so pure;
                    So fair and sweet,
              So true; when I did meet
Them here at first, they did my soul allure
     And drew away my infant feet
Quite from the works of men; that I might see
The glorious wonders of the Deity.

Sonnet IV   ᴈ   E.E. CUMMINGS

this is the garden: colors come and go
frail azures fluttering from night's outer wing
strong silent greens serenely lingering,
absolute lights like baths of golden snow.

This is the garden: pursed lips do blow
upon cool flutes within wide glooms, and sing
(of harps celestial to the quivering string)
invisible faces hauntingly and slow.

This is the garden. Time shall surely reap
and on Death's blade lie many a flower curled,
in other lands where other songs be sung;
yet stand They here enraptured, as among
the slow deep trees perpetual of sleep
some silver-fingered fountain steals the world.

2:18–2:20   And the LORD God said, It is not good that the man should be
alone; I will make him an help meet for him. And out of the ground the LORD
God formed every beast of the field, and every fowl of the air; and brought
them unto Adam to see what he would call them: and whatsoever Adam
called every living creature, that was the name thereof. And Adam gave names
to all cattle, and to the fowl of the air, and to every beast of the field;

Naming the Animals ঌ ANTHONY HECHT

Having commanded Adam to bestow
Names upon all the creatures, God withdrew
To empyrean palaces of blue
That warm and windless morning long ago,
And seemed to take no notice of the vexed
Look on the young man's face as he took thought
Of all the miracles the Lord had wrought,
Now to be labelled, dubbed, yclept, indexed.

Before an addled mind and puddled brow,
The feathered nation and the finny prey
Passed by; there went biped and quadruped.
Adam looked forth with bottomless dismay
Into the tragic eyes of his first cow,
And shyly ventured, "Thou shalt be called 'Fred.' "

2:20–2:22   but for Adam there was not found an help meet for him. And
the LORD God caused a deep sleep to fall upon Adam, and he slept: and he
took one of his ribs, and closed up the flesh instead thereof; And the rib,
which the LORD God had taken from man, made he a woman, and brought
her unto the man.

The Recognition of Eve ঌ KARL SHAPIRO

Whatever it was she had so fiercely fought
Had fled back to the sky, but still she lay
With arms outspread, awaiting its assault,
Staring up through the branches of the tree,
The fig tree. Then she drew a shuddering breath
And turned her head instinctively his way.
She had fought birth as dying men fight death.

Her sigh awakened him. He turned and saw
A body swollen, as though formed of fruits,
White as the flesh of fishes, soft and raw.
He hoped she was another of the brutes
So he crawled over and looked into her eyes,

The human wells that pool all absolutes.
It was like looking into double skies.

And when she spoke the first word (it was *thou*)
He was terror-stricken, but she raised her hand
And touched his wound where it was fading now,
For he must feel the place to understand.
Then he recalled the longing that had torn
His side, and while he watched it whitely mend,
He felt it stab him suddenly, like a thorn.

He thought the woman had hurt him. Was it she
Or the same sickness seeking to return;
Or was there any difference, the pain set free
And she who seized him now as hard as iron?
Her fingers bit his body. She looked old
And involuted, like the newly-born.
He let her hurt him till she loosed her hold.

Then she forgot him and she wearily stood
And went in search of water through the grove.
Adam could see her wandering through the wood,
Studying her footsteps as her body wove
In light and out of light. She found a pool
And there he followed shyly to observe.
She was already turning beautiful.

2:23   And Adam said, This is now bone of my bones, and flesh of my
flesh: she shall be called Woman, because she was taken out of Man.

The Follies of Adam   ᷱ   THEODORE ROETHKE

1
Read me Euripides,
Or some old lout who can
Remember what it was
To jump out of his skin.

Things speak to me, I swear;
But why am I groaning here,
Not even out of breath?

2

What are scepter and crown?
No more than what is raised
By a naked stem:
The rose leaps to this girl;
The earthly lives in her;
A thorn does well in the wind,
At ease with all that flows.

3

I talked to a shrunken root;
Ah, how she laughed to see
Me staring past my foot,
One toe in eternity;
But when the root replied,
She shivered in her skin,
And looked away.

4

Father and son of this death,
The soul dies every night;
In the wide white, the known
Reaches of common day,
What eagle needs a tree?
The flesh fathers a dream;
All true bones sing alone.

5

Poseidon's only a horse,
Laughed a master of hump and snort;
He cared so much for the sport,
He rode all night, and came
Back on the sea-foam;
And when he got to the shore,
He laughed, once more.

2:25 And they were both naked, the man and his wife, and were not ashamed.

The Fall   ✥   JOHN WILMOT, EARL OF ROCHESTER

How blessed was the created state
   Of man and woman, ere they fell,
Compared to our unhappy fate:
   We need not fear another hell.

Naked beneath cool shades they lay;
   Enjoyment waited on desire;
Each member did their wills obey,
   Nor could a wish set pleasure higher.

But we, poor slaves to hope and fear,
   Are never of our joys secure;
They lessen still as they draw near,
   And none but dull delights endure.

Then, Chloris, while I duly pay
   The nobler tribute of my heart,
Be not you so severe to say
   You love me for the frailer part.

As Adam Early in the Morning   ✥   WALT WHITMAN

As Adam early in the morning,
Walking forth from the bower refreshed with sleep,
Behold me where I pass, hear my voice, approach,
Touch me, touch the palm of your hand to my body as I pass,
Be not afraid of my body.

3:1–3:6 Now the serpent was more subtil than any beast of the field which the LORD God had made. And he said unto the woman, Yea, hath God said, Ye shall not eat of every tree of the garden?

   And the woman said unto the serpent, We may eat of the fruit of the trees of the garden: But of the fruit of the tree which is in the midst of the garden, God hath said, Ye shall not eat of it, neither shall ye touch it, lest ye die.

And the serpent said unto the woman, Ye shall not surely die: For God doth know that in the day ye eat thereof, then your eyes shall be opened, and ye shall be as gods, knowing good and evil.

And when the woman saw that the tree was good for food, and that it was pleasant to the eyes, and a tree to be desired to make one wise, she took of the fruit thereof, and did eat,

Eve ᧒ RALPH HODGSON

Eve, with her basket, was
Deep in the bells and grass,
Wading in bells and grass
Up to her knees,
Picking a dish of sweet
Berries and plums to eat,
Down in the bells and grass
Under the trees.

Mute as a mouse in a
Corner the cobra lay,
Curled round a bough of the
Cinnamon tall. . . .
Now to get even and
Humble proud heaven and—
Now was the moment or
Never at all.

"Eva!" Each syllable
Light as a flower fell,
"Eva!" he whispered the
Wondering maid,
Soft as a bubble sung
Out of a linnet's lung,
Soft and most silverly
"Eva!" he said.

Picture that orchard sprite,
Eve, with her body white,
Supple and smooth to her
Slim finger tips,

Wondering, listening,
Listening, wondering,
Eve with a berry
Half-way to her lips.

Oh, had our simple Eve
Seen through the make-believe!
Had she but known the
Pretender he was!
Out of the boughs he came,
Whispering still her name,
Tumbling in twenty rings
Into the grass.

Here was the strangest pair
In the world anywhere,
Eve in the bells and grass
Kneeling, and he
Telling his story low. . . .
Singing birds saw them go
Down the dark path to
The Blasphemous Tree.

Oh, what a clatter when
Titmouse and Jenny Wren
Saw him successful and
Taking his leave!
How the birds rated him!
How they all hated him!
How they all pitied
Poor motherless Eve.

Picture her crying
Outside in the lane,
Eve, with no dish of sweet
Berries and plums to eat,
Haunting the gate of the
Orchard in vain. . . .
Picture the lewd delight
Under the hill tonight—
"Eva!" the toast goes round,
"Eva!" again.

3:6   and gave also unto her husband with her; and he did eat.

Sharing Eve's Apple   ᔭ   JOHN KEATS

O blush not so! O blush not so!
   Or I shall think you knowing;
And if you smile the blushing while,
   Then maidenheads are going.

There's a blush for won't, and a blush for shan't,
   And a blush for having done it:
There's a blush for thought and a blush for nought,
   And a blush for just begun it.

O sigh not so! O sigh not so!
   For it sounds of Eve's sweet pippin;
By these loosened lips you have tasted the pips
   And fought in an amorous nipping.

Will you play once more at nice-cut-core,
   For it only will last our youth out,
And we have the prime of the kissing time,
   We have not one sweet tooth out.

There's a sigh for yes, and a sigh for no,
   And a sigh for I can't bear it!
O what can be done, shall we stay or run?
   O cut the sweet apple and share it!

3:8   And they heard the voice of the LORD God walking in the garden in
the cool of the day: and Adam and his wife hid themselves from the pres-
ence of the LORD God amongst the trees of the garden.

Songs of Experience   ᔭ   WILLIAM BLAKE
Introduction

Hear the voice of the Bard!
Who Present, Past, and Future, sees;
Whose ears have heard

The Holy Word
That walked among the ancient trees,

Calling the lapsed Soul,
And weeping in the evening dew;
That might control
The starry pole,
And fallen, fallen light renew!

"O Earth, O Earth, return!
"Arise from out the dewy grass:
"Night is worn,
"And the morn
"Rises from the slumberous mass.

"Turn away no more;
"Why wilt thou turn away?
"The starry floor,
"The watery shore,
"Is given thee till the break of day."

3:9–3:10   And the LORD God called unto Adam, and said unto him,
Where art thou?
    And he said, I heard thy voice in the garden, and I was afraid, because I
was naked; and I hid myself.

Earth's Answer ⟋   WILLIAM BLAKE

Earth raised up her head
From the darkness dread and drear.
Her light fled,
Stony dread!
And her locks covered with grey despair.

"Prisoned on watery shore,
"Starry Jealousy does keep my den:
"Cold and hoar,
"Weeping o'er,
"I hear the Father of the ancient men.

"Selfish father of men!
"Cruel, jealous, selfish fear!
"Can delight,
"Chained in night,
"The virgins of youth and morning bear?

"Does spring hide its joy
"When buds and blossoms grow?
"Does the sower
"Sow by night,
"Or the plowman in darkness plow?

"Break this heavy chain
"That does freeze my bones around.
"Selfish! vain!
"Eternal bane!
"That free Love with bondage bound."

3:11–3:13   And he said, Who told thee that thou wast naked? Hast thou eaten of the tree, whereof I commanded thee that thou shouldest not eat?
    And the man said, The woman whom thou gavest to be with me, she gave me of the tree, and I did eat.
    And the LORD God said unto the woman, What is this that thou hast done? And the woman said, The serpent beguiled me, and I did eat.

Original Sequence ∿ PHILIP BOOTH

Time was the apple Adam ate.
Eve bit, gave seconds to his mouth.
and then they had no minute left
to lose. Eyes opened in mid-kiss,
they saw, for once, raw nakedness,
and hid that sudden consequence
behind an hour's stripped leaves.

This is one sequence in the plot,
the garden where God came, that time,
to call. Hands behind him, walking
to and fro, he counted how

the fruit fell, bruised on frozen sod.
This was his orchard, his to pace;
the day was cool, and he was God.

Old Adam heard him humming, talking
to himself:
      Winesap, King,
      ripen in sun,
      McIntosh and
      Northern Spy
      fall one by one,
      ripen to die.

Adam heard him call his name,
but Adam, no old philosopher,
was not sure what he was after.
We're naked, Lord, and can't come out.
Eve nudged him with the bitter fruit.
God paused. *How do you know? Where is
that woman that I sprung from you?*

Eve held the twisted stem, the pulp;
she heard the low snake hiss, and let fly
blindly with a woman arm, careless
where her new-won anger struck.
The fodder for that two-fold flock
fell, an old brown core, at God's
stopped feet. He reached, and wound the clock.

3:14–3:20   . . . And unto Adam he said, Because thou hast hearkened unto
the voice of thy wife, and hast eaten of the tree, of which I commanded thee,
saying, Thou shalt not eat of it: cursed is the ground for thy sake; in sorrow
shalt thou eat of it all the days of thy life; Thorns also and thistles shall it
bring forth to thee; and thou shalt eat the herb of the field; In the sweat of
thy face shalt thou eat bread, till thou return unto the ground; for out of it
wast thou taken: for dust thou art, and unto dust shalt thou return. And
Adam called his wife's name Eve; because she was the mother of all living.

The Cloud ॐ DEREK WALCOTT

And, laterally,
to Adam's pulsing eye,
the erect ridges would throb and recede.

a sigh under the fig tree and a sky
deflating to the serpent's punctured hiss,
repeating you will die.

The woman lay still as the settling mountains.
There was another silence,
all was thick with it;

the clouds given a mortal destination,
the silent shudder from the broken branch
where the sap dripped

from the torn tree.
When she, his death,
turned on her side and slept,
the breath he drew was his first real breath.

What left the leaves,
the phosphorescent air,
was both God and the serpent leaving him.
Neither could curse or bless.

Pollen was drifting to the woman's hair,
his eye felt brighter,
a cloud's slow shadow slowly covered them,

and, as it moved, he named it Tenderness.

3:21   Unto Adam also and to his wife did the LORD God make coats of
skins, and clothed them.

Adam Posed ᴐ   ANNE FINCH, COUNTESS OF WINCHILSEA

Could our first father, at his toilsome plough,
Thorns in his path, and labor on his brow,
Clothed only in a rude, unpolished skin,
Could he a vain fantastic nymph have seen,
In all her airs, in all her antic graces,
Her various fashions, and more various faces;
How had it posed that skill, which late assigned
Just appellations to each several kind!
A right idea of the sight to frame;
T'have guessed from what new element she came;
T'have hit the wavering form, or given this thing a name.

3:22–3:23   and now, lest he put forth his hand, and take also of the tree of
life, and eat, and live for ever: Therefore the LORD God sent him forth from
the garden of Eden, to till the ground from whence he was taken.

Eden is that old-fashioned House ᴐ   EMILY DICKINSON

Eden is that old-fashioned House
We dwell in every day
Without suspecting our abode
Until we drive away.

How fair on looking back, the Day
We sauntered from the Door –
Unconscious our returning,
But discover it no more.

3:24   So he drove out the man; and he placed at the east of the garden of
Eden Cherubims, and a flaming sword which turned every way, to keep the
way of the tree of life.

To the Garden the World ↝ WALT WHITMAN

To the garden the world anew ascending,
Potent mates, daughters, sons, preluding,
The love, the life of their bodies, meaning and being,
Curious here behold my resurrection after slumber,
The revolving cycles in their wide sweep having brought me again,
Amorous, mature, all beautiful to me, all wondrous,
My limbs and quivering fire that ever plays through them, for reasons,
        most wondrous,
Existing I peer and penetrate still,
Content with the present, content with the past,
By my side or back of me Eve following,
Or in front, and I following her just the same.

They Wondered Why the Fruit had Been Forbidden ↝
W. H. AUDEN

They wondered why the fruit had been forbidden;
It taught them nothing new. They hid their pride,
But did not listen much when they were chidden;
They knew exactly what to do outside.

They left: immediately the memory faded
Of all they'd learnt; they could not understand
The dogs now who, before, had always aided;
The stream was dumb with whom they'd always planned.

They wept and quarrelled: freedom was so wild.
In front, maturity, as he ascended,
Retired like a horizon from the child;

The dangers and the punishments grew greater;
And the way back by angels was defended
Against the poet and the legislator.

4:1   And Adam knew Eve his wife; and she conceived, and bare Cain, and
said, I have gotten a man from the LORD.

Imperial Adam   ᧒   A. D. HOPE

Imperial Adam, naked in the dew,
Felt his brown flanks and found the rib was gone.
Puzzled he turned and saw where, two and two,
The mighty spoor of Jahweh marked the lawn.

Then he remembered through mysterious sleep
The surgeon fingers probing at the bone,
The voice so far away, so rich and deep:
"It is not good for him to live alone."

Turning once more he found Man's counterpart
In tender parody breathing at his side.
He knew her at first sight, he knew by heart
Her allegory of sense unsatisfied.

The pawpaw drooped its golden breasts above
Less generous than the honey of her flesh;
The innocent sunlight showed the place of love;
The dew on its dark hairs winked crisp and fresh.

This plump gourd severed from his virile root,
She promised on the turf of Paradise
Delicious pulp of the forbidden fruit;
Sly as the snake she loosed her sinuous thighs,

And waking, smiled up at him from the grass;
Her breasts rose softly and he heard her sigh—
From all the beasts whose pleasant task it was
In Eden to increase and multiply

Adam had learned the jolly deed of kind:
He took her in his arms and there and then,
Like the clean beasts, embracing from behind,
Began in joy to found the breed of men.

Then from the spurt of seed within her broke
Her terrible and triumphant female cry,
Split upward by the sexual lightning stroke.
It was the beasts now who stood watching by:

The gravid elephant, the calving hind,
The breeding bitch, the she-ape big with young
Were the first gentle midwives of mankind;
The teeming lioness rasped her with her tongue;

The proud vicuña nuzzled her as she slept
Lax on the grass; and Adam watching too
Saw how her dumb breasts at their ripening wept,
The great pod of her belly swelled and grew,

And saw its water break, and saw, in fear,
Its quaking muscles in the act of birth,
Between her legs a pigmy face appear,
And the first murderer lay upon the earth.

4:3–4:10   . . . And the LORD said unto Cain, Where is Abel thy brother?
And he said, I know not: Am I my brother's keeper?
    And he said, What hast thou done? the voice of thy brother's blood
crieth unto me from the ground.

Eve ⁊ CHRISTINA ROSSETTI

'While I sit at the door,
Sick to gaze within,
Mine eye weepeth sore
For sorrow and sin:
As a tree my sin stands
To darken all lands;
Death is the fruit it bore.

'How have Eden bowers grown
Without Adam to bend them!
How have Eden flowers blown,
Squandering their sweet breath,

Without me to tend them!
The Tree of Life was ours,
Tree twelvefold-fruited,
Most lofty tree that flowers,
Most deeply rooted:
I chose the Tree of Death.

'Hadst thou but said me nay,
Adam, my brother,
I might have pined away;
I, but none other:
God might have let thee stay
Safe in our garden
By putting me away
Beyond all pardon.

'I, Eve, sad mother
Of all who must live,
I, not another,
Plucked bitterest fruit to give
My friend, husband, lover.
O wanton eyes run over;
Who but I should grieve?—
Cain hath slain his brother:
Of all who must die mother,
Miserable Eve!'

Thus she sat weeping,
Thus Eve our mother,
Where one lay sleeping
Slain by his brother.
Greatest and least
Each piteous beast
To hear her voice
Forgot his joys
And set aside his feast.
The mouse paused in his walk
And dropped his wheaten stalk;
Grave cattle wagged their heads
In rumination;
The eagle gave a cry

From his cloud station:
Larks on thyme beds
Forbore to mount or sing;
Bees drooped upon the wing;
The raven perched on high
Forgot his ration;
The conies in their rock,
A feeble nation,
Quaked sympathetical;
The mocking-bird left off to mock;
Huge camels knelt as if
In deprecation;
The kind hart's tears were falling;
Chattered the wistful stork;
Dove-voices with a dying fall
Cooed desolation
Answering grief by grief.
Only the serpent in the dust,
Wriggling and crawling,
Grinned an evil grin, and thrust
His tongue out with its fork.

4:17–5:4   . . . This is the book of the generations of Adam. In the day that
God created man, in the likeness of God made he him; Male and female
created he them; and blessed them, and called their name Adam, in the day
when they were created. . . .

Ancient History ᔈ SIEGFRIED SASSOON

Adam, a brown old vulture in the rain,
Shivered below his wind-whipped olive-trees;
Huddling sharp chin on scarred and scraggy knees,
He moaned and mumbled to his darkening brain;
'He was the grandest of them all – was Cain!
'A lion laired in the hills, that none could tire:
'Swift as a stag: a stallion of the plain,
'Hungry and fierce with deeds of huge desire.'

Grimly he thought of Abel, soft and fair –
A lover with disaster in his face,
And scarlet blossom twisted in bright hair.
'Afraid to fight; was murder more disgrace?. . .
'*God always hated Cain*'. . . He bowed his head –
The gaunt wild man whose lovely sons were dead.

5:25–6:2   . . . And it came to pass, when men began to multiply on the face of the earth, and daughters were born unto them, That the sons of God saw the daughters of men that they were fair; and they took them wives of all which they chose.

The Woman and the Angel   ジ   ROBERT SERVICE

An angel was tired of heaven, as he lounged in the golden street;
His halo was tilted side-ways, and his harp lay mute at his feet;
So the Master stooped in His pity, and gave him a pass to go,
For the space of a moon, to the earth-world, to mix with the
          men below.

He doffed his celestial garments, scarce waiting to lay them straight;
He bade good-bye to Peter, who stood by the golden gate;
The sexless singers of heaven chanted a fond farewell,
And the imps looked up as they pattered on the red-hot flags of hell.

Never was seen such an angel—eyes of heavenly blue,
Features that shamed Apollo, hair of a golden hue;
The women simply adored him; his lips were like Cupid's bow;
But he never ventured to use them—and so they voted him slow.

Till at last there came One Woman, a marvel of loveliness,
And she whispered to him: "Do you love me?" And he answered that
          woman, "Yes."
And she said: "Put your arms around me, and kiss me, and hold me—
          so—"
But fiercely he drew back, saying: "This thing is wrong, and I know."

Then sweetly she mocked his scruples, and softly she him beguiled:
"You, who are verily man among men, speak with the tongue
          of a child.

We have outlived the old standards; we have burst, like an
      over-tight thong,
The ancient, outworn, Puritanic traditions of Right and Wrong."

Then the Master feared for His angel, and called him again to
      His side,
For oh, the woman was wondrous, and oh, the angel was tried!
And deep in his hell sang the Devil, and this was the strain of
      his song:
"The ancient, outworn, Puritanic traditions of Right and Wrong."

7:11–7:14 . . . And the rain was upon the earth forty days and forty nights.
In the selfsame day entered Noah, and Shem, and Ham, and Japheth, the
sons of Noah, and Noah's wife, and the three wives of his sons with them,
into the ark; They, and every beast after his kind, and all the cattle after their
kind, and every creeping thing that creepeth upon the earth after his kind,
and every fowl after his kind, every bird of every sort.

Author's Prologue ✌ DYLAN THOMAS

This day winding down now
At God speeded summer's end
In the torrent salmon sun,
In my seashaken house
On a breakneck of rocks
Tangled with chirrup and fruit,
Froth, flute, fin and quill
At a wood's dancing hoof,
By scummed, starfish sands
With their fishwife cross
Gulls, pipers, cockles, and sails,
Out there, crow black, men
Tackled with clouds, who kneel
To the sunset nets,
Geese nearly in heaven, boys
Stabbing, and herons, and shells
That speak seven seas,
Eternal waters away
From the cities of nine

Days' night whose towers will catch
In the religious wind
Like stalks of tall, dry straw,
At poor peace I sing
To you strangers (though song
Is a burning and crested act,
The fire of birds in
The world's turning wood,
For my sawn, splay sounds),
Out of these seathumbed leaves
That will fly and fall
Like leaves of trees and as soon
Crumble and undie
Into the dogdayed night.
Seaward the salmon, sucked sun slips,
And the dumb swans drub blue
My dabbed bay's dusk, as I hack
This rumpus of shapes
For you to know
How I, a spinning man,
Glory also this star, bird
Roared, sea born, man torn, blood blest.
Hark: I trumpet the place,
From fish to jumping hill! Look:
I build my bellowing ark
To the best of my love
As the flood begins,
Out of the fountainhead
Of fear, rage red, manalive,
Molten and mountainous to stream
Over the wound asleep
Sheep white hollow farms
To Wales in my arms.
Hoo, there, in castle keep,
You king singsong owls, who moonbeam
The flickering runs and dive
The dingle furred deer dead!
Huloo, on plumbed bryns,
O my ruffled ring dove
In the hooting, nearly dark
With Welsh and reverent rook,
Coo rooing the woods' praise,

Who moons her blue notes from her nest
Down to the curlew herd!
Ho, hullaballoing clan
Agape, with woe
In your beaks, on the gabbing capes!
Heigh, on horseback hill, jack
Whisking hare! who
Hears, there, this fox light, my flood ship's
Clangour as I hew and smite
(A clash of anvils for my
Hubbub and fiddle, this tune
On a tongued puffball)
But animals thick as thieves
On God's rough tumbling grounds
(Hail to His beasthood!).
Beasts who sleep good and thin,
Hist, in hogsback woods! The haystacked
Hollow farms in a throng
Of waters cluck and cling,
And barnroofs cockcrow war!
O kingdom of neighbours, finned
Felled and quilled, flash to my patch
Work ark and the moonshine
Drinking Noah of the bay,
With pelt, and scale, and fleece:
Only the drowned deep bells
Of sheep and churches noise
Poor peace as the sun sets
And dark shoals every holy field.
We will ride out alone, and then,
Under the stars of Wales,
Cry, Multitudes of arks! Across
The water lidded lands,
Manned with their loves they'll move,
Like wooden islands, hill to hill.
Huloo, my prowed dove with a flute!
Ahoy, old, sea-legged fox,
Tom tit and Dai mouse!
My ark sings in the sun
At God speeded summer's end
And the flood flowers now.

7:15   And they went in unto Noah into the ark, two and two of all flesh, wherein is the breath of life.

Parley of Beasts   ᧷   HUGH MACDIARMID

Auld Noah was at hame wi' them a',
The lion and the lamb,
Pair by pair they entered the Ark
And he took them as they cam'.

If twa o' ilka beist there is
Into this room sud come,
Wad I cud welcome them like him
And no' staun' gowpin' dumb!

Be chief wi' them and they wi' me
And a' wi' ane anither
As Noah and his couples were
There in the Ark thegither.

It's fain I'd mell wi' tiger and tit,
Wi' elephant and ell,
But noo-a-days e'en wi' ain's se
At hame it's hard to feel.

8:4–8:7   . . . And it came to pass at the end of forty days, that Noah opened the window of the ark which he had made: And he sent forth a raven, which went forth to and fro, until the waters were dried up from off the earth.

Noah's Raven   ᧷   W. S. MERWIN

Why should I have returned?
My knowledge would not fit into theirs.
I found untouched the desert of the unknown,
Big enough for my feet. It is my home.
It is always beyond them. The future
Splits the present with the echo of my voice.
Hoarse with fulfillment, I never made promises.

9:8–9:11   And God spake unto Noah, and to his sons with him, saying, . . .
I will establish my covenant with you, neither shall all flesh be cut off any
more by the waters of a flood; neither shall there any more be a flood to
destroy the earth.

Holy Sonnet V   ᢣ   JOHN DONNE

I am a little world made cunningly
Of elements, and an angelic sprite,
But black sin hath betrayed to endless night
My world's both parts, and (oh) both parts must die.
You which beyond that heaven which was most high
Have found new spheres, and of new lands can write,
Pour new seas in mine eyes, that so I might
Drown my world with my weeping earnestly,
Or wash it if it must be drowned no more:
But oh it must be burnt! alas the fire
Of lust and envy have burnt it heretofore,
And made it fouler; Let their flames retire
And burn me ô Lord, with a fiery zeal
Of thee and thy house, which doth in eating heal.

9:12–9:13   And God said, . . . I do set my bow in the cloud, and it shall be
for a token of a covenant between me and the earth.

The Rainbow: or Curious Covenant   ᢣ
ROBERT HERRICK

Mine eyes, like clouds, were drizzling rain,
And as they thus did entertain
The gentle beams from Julia's sight
To mine eyes levelled opposite:
O thing admired! there did appear
A curious rainbow smiling there;
Which was the Covenant, that she
No more would drown mine eyes, or me.

9:14–9:21   . . . And Noah began to be an husbandman, and he planted a vineyard: And he drank of the wine, and was drunken; and he was uncovered within his tent.

Wine and Water   ↜   G. K. CHESTERTON

Old Noah he had an ostrich farm and fowls on the largest scale,
He ate his egg with a ladle in an egg-cup big as a pail,
And the soup he took was Elephant Soup, and the fish he took
        was Whale,
But they all were small to the cellar he took when he set out to sail,
And Noah he often said to his wife when he sat down to dine,
"I don't care where the water goes if it doesn't get into the wine."

The cataract of the cliff of heaven fell blinding off the brink
As if it would wash the stars away as suds go down the sink,
The seven heavens came roaring down for the throats of hell to drink,
And Noah he cocked his eye and said, "It looks like rain, I think,
The water has drowned the Matterhorn as deep as a Mendip mine,
But I don't care where the water goes if it doesn't get into the wine."

But Noah he sinned, and we have sinned; on tipsy feet we trod,
Till a great big black teetotaller was sent us for a rod,
And you can't get wine at a P. S. A., or chapel, or Eisteddfod,
For the Curse of Water has come again because of the wrath of God,
And water is on the Bishop's board and the Higher Thinker's shrine,
But I don't care where the water goes if it doesn't get into the wine.

10:8–11:9   . . . And the whole earth was of one language, and of one speech. And it came to pass, as they journeyed from the east, that they found a plain in the land of Shinar; and they dwelt there. And they said one to another, Go to, let us make brick, and burn them thoroughly. And they had brick for stone, and slime had they for mortar. And they said, Go to, let us build us a city and a tower, whose top may reach unto heaven; and let us make us a name, lest we be scattered abroad upon the face of the whole earth. . .

The Tower of Babel ↝ LAURANCE WIEDER

Nimrod gazed across the plain
About the city he had made,
From the horizon to his feet,
The valley where two rivers meet,
And sighed, and stared into the heavens:
A polished stone of mirror blue
By day, an inky pool by night
That flickered in the milky light
Of living stars, and changing moon:
The open pupil of God's eye?
Beyond the city's walls, dunes walked
The earth in scattered generations.
How could he keep these people one?
All Babel came to Nimrod's summons
From the ramparts: "Let's be done
With building cities in the sun,
For none among us has the power
To stop the wind, or stay the hour.
Go to, come, take brick and slime
To raise a tower up to heaven,
To make ourselves a name, one nation,
People, not dispersed or crushed
By storm, or time, or death." A hush,
Then, "Yes," they answered in one voice,
(For they were all of Adam's line
And tongue, and when a thing was named
They could imagine it entire)
"Come, let us stoke the kiln and fire
Bricks. Go to the river, gather
Ooze for mortar, and together
We will build this signal tower."
Donkeys strained, yoked oxen groaned,
Masons trued each handmade brick.
They did not need an architect;
A thousand thousand ziggurats
Stacked each upon the other, left
Mountains, thunderstorms below:
So high rose the first great story.
Spiral ramps gyred up the sides,
With little cities at the edge

For animal and traveler
To rest, as they ascended, ledge
By ledge. "Brick on brick," the hunter
Muttered to the mass, "and soon
We'll reach the porches of the moon
Where heaven and the angels are."
The Lord looked down, and saw the Tower
Rear above its mortar city
And said: "Behold, this human many
Are as one. They speak one tongue,
And this thing they begin to do.
Now no thing will be beyond them,
Nothing they imagine. Go to,"
The Lord said to his angels, "Come,
Let us go down and there confound
Their language and their speech,
That they not understand nor reach
Us, others." But said, then done.
On Shinar's plain once burst
Confusion from the sky, a whirlwind
Hurtling whistled, swamped, dispersed
The people into many nations.
Language lost, a weighty thud
And screech of men in hail of bricks
Puffed dust upon the plain as thick
As polar snow, as fall monsoon.

Where once prayers said were unison,
And conversations harmony,
We now mistake our dearest loves;
Crowds muddle in cacophony.
So far from being of one name
We clash, strive, swindle, beat, and blame
The other for not being nearer
To ourselves, or speaking clearer.
Nimrod's grave magnificence
Redounds as naked arrogance
And God, that made of Babel rubble,
We call in many tongues a father,
Light, indifferent, shepherd, mild,
Stern, an absence, or a bubble.

12:1–13:18   . . . But the men of Sodom were wicked and sinners before the
LORD exceedingly. And the LORD said unto Abram, after that Lot was sepa-
rated from him, Lift up now thine eyes, and look from the place where thou
art northward, and southward, and eastward, and westward: For all the land
which thou seest, to thee will I give it, and to thy seed for ever. And I will
make thy seed as the dust of the earth: so that if a man can number the
dust of the earth, then shall thy seed also be numbered. Arise, walk through
the land in the length of it and in the breadth of it; for I will give it unto
thee. Then Abram removed his tent, and came and dwelt in the plain of
Mamre, which is in Hebron, and built there an altar unto the LORD.

Retirement ❧ HENRY VAUGHAN

Fresh fields and woods! the Earth's fair face,
God's foot-stool, and man's dwelling-place.
I ask not why the first Believer
Did love to be a country liver?
Who to secure pious content
Did pitch by groves and wells his tent;
Where he might view the boundless sky,
And all those glorious lights on high:
With flying meteors, mists and showers,
Subjected hills, trees, meads and flowers:
And every minute bless the King
And wise creator of each thing.
    I ask not why he did remove
To happy Mamre's holy grove,
Leaving the cities of the plain
To Lot and his successless train?
All various lusts in cities still
Are found; they are the thrones of ill.
The dismal sinks, where blood is spilled,
Cages with much uncleanness filled.
But rural shades are the sweet fence
Of piety and innocence.
They are the meek's calm region, where
Angels descend, and rule the sphere:
Where heaven lies leiguer, and the dove
Duly as dew, comes from above.
If Eden be on Earth at all,
'Tis that, which we the country call.

17:1–18:15   . . . Now Abraham and Sarah were old and well stricken in age; and it ceased to be with Sarah after the manner of women. Therefore Sarah laughed within herself, saying, After I am waxed old shall I have pleasure, my lord being old also?

And the LORD said unto Abraham, Wherefore did Sarah laugh, saying, Shall I of a surety bear a child, which am old? Is any thing too hard for the LORD? At the time appointed I will return unto thee, according to the time of life, and Sarah shall have a son.

Then Sarah denied, saying, I laughed not; for she was afraid. And he said, Nay; but thou didst laugh.

Sarah   ∽   DELMORE SCHWARTZ

The angel said to me: "Why are you laughing?"
"Laughing! Not me! Who was laughing? I did not laugh. It was
A cough. I was coughing. Only hyenas laugh.
It was the cold I caught nine minutes after
Abraham married me: when I saw
How I was slender and beautiful, more and more
Slender and beautiful.
                    I was also
Clearing my throat; something inside of me
Is continually telling me something
I do not wish to hear: A joke: A big joke:
But the joke is always just on me.
He said: you will have more children than the sky's stars
And the seashore's sands, if you just wait patiently.
Wait: patiently: ninety years? You see
The joke's on me!"

18:16–18:27   . . . And the LORD said, If I find in Sodom fifty righteous within the city, then I will spare all the place for their sakes.

And Abraham answered and said, Behold now, I have taken upon me to speak unto the LORD, which am but dust and ashes:

Oaks and Squirrels   ∽   ANNE PORTER

"I speak to my Lord though I am dust and ashes,"
A handful of ashes the wind will soon send flying

Into the drifted oak-leaves under the hedge.
No gardener ever rakes there
Only the squirrels gather bedding there
When they stack up their rustling nests.

You have granted me more time
On earth than the squirrels, less time than the oak,
Whose secret takes a hundred years to tell.
Out of the acorn in the dirt
Its wooden sticks come up
Already knowing how to grow their leaves
And when to spend them all.
Knowing exactly
How to thread up into a winter sky
A dark-veined map like that of a great river
Spun out in tapering streams,
Twig by twig ascending and unfolding
Until at night its topmost buds
Enter the country of the stars.
By day
The squirrels run like script along its boughs
And write their lives with their light bodies.
They are afraid of us
We can never hold them
And there's no room for us in their invisible ark.
Our home is warring disobedient history.

18:28–19:25   . . . The sun was risen upon the earth when Lot entered into
Zoar. Then the LORD rained upon Sodom and upon Gomorrah brimstone and
fire from the LORD out of heaven; And he overthrew those cities, and all the
plain, and all the inhabitants of the cities, and that which grew upon the ground.

The Destruction of Sodom   ᷣ   DARYL HINE

One would never suspect there were so many vices.
It is, I think, a tribute to the imagination
Of those who in these eminently destructible cities
Have made an exact science of perversion
That they, like us, limited by their bodies,
Could put those bodies to such various uses.

Before now men have been punished for their uses
Contrary to nature, though some, indulging phantom vices
Secretly in the brothels of the imagination,
Have escaped so far a condemnation like these cities'
Which were rebuked for innocent perversion
Through the spirit's envy of too simple bodies.

Do not suppose that I intend to praise their bodies,
Though I admit that bodies have their uses,
Nor is my purpose to defend their vices.
Simply as a pervert of the imagination
I pronounce the funeral oration of two cities
Famous for acts of unimaginable perversion.

All love deserves the epitaph 'Perversion',
Being unnaturally concerned, like physics, with foreign bodies,
Inseparable from their uses and abuses.
To those who care for nothing but their vices
Love is the faculty of the imagination.
Fantasy, I say, debauches cities.

Discreetly, Lord, show mercy to these cities,
Not for the sake of their, but your, perversion
That contradicts its own created bodies.
These are precisely the instruments grace uses,
Alchemically reforming virtues of their vices,
To raise a heaven from the imagination.

O, where is that heaven of the imagination,
The first and least accessible of cities,
If not in the impossible kingdom of perversion?
Its angels have no sexes and no bodies,
Its speech, no words, its instruments, no uses.
None enter there but those who know their vices.

Number your vices in imagination:
Would they teach whole cities of perversion?
Forgive us our bodies, forgive our bodies' uses.

19:26–19:32 . . . And Lot went up out of Zoar, and dwelt in the mountain, and his two daughters with him; for he feared to dwell in Zoar: and he dwelt in a cave, he and his two daughters. And the firstborn said unto the younger, Our father is old, and there is not a man in the earth to come in unto us after the manner of all the earth: Come, let us make our father drink wine, and we will lie with him, that we may preserve seed of our father.

On the two Great Floods ૐ FRANCIS QUARLES

Two floods I read of; water, and of wine;
The first was Noah's; Lot, the last was thine:
The first was the effect; the last, the cause
Of that foul sin, against the sacred laws
Of God and nature, incest: Noah found
An ark to save him, but poor Lot was drowned:
Good Noah found an ark; but Lot found none:
We're safer in God's hands then in our own:
The former flood of waters did extend
But some few days; this latter has no end;
They both destroyed, I know not which the worst:
The last is even as general, as the first:
The first being ceased, the world began to fill;
The last depopulates, and wastes it still:
Both floods o'erwhelmed both man and beast together;
The last is worst, if there be best of either:
The first are ceased: Heaven vowed it by a sign;
When shall we see a rainbow after wine?

19:33–19:35 And they made their father drink wine that night: and the firstborn went in, and lay with her father; and he perceived not when she lay down, nor when she arose. And it came to pass on the morrow, that the firstborn said unto the younger, Behold, I lay yesternight with my father: let us make him drink wine this night also; and go thou in, and lie with him, that we may preserve seed of our father. And they made their father drink wine that night also: and the younger arose, and lay with him; and he perceived not when she lay down, nor when she arose.

Lot and his Daughters I ᴗ A. D. HOPE

The ruddy fire-glow, like her sister's eyes,
Flickered on her bare breasts and licked along
The ripeness of her savage flanks; a tongue
Of darkness curled between her restless thighs.

Black as the Syrian night, on her young head
Clustered the tendrils of their ancient vine;
The cave gaped with its drunken mouth; the wine
Babbled, unceasing, from the old man's bed:

'I have two daughters . . . let them serve your need
. . . virgins . . . but these, my guests . . . you understand'—
She crept in and lay down. Her Promised Land
Lay waiting for the sower with his seed.

She felt him stir; she felt herself embraced;
The tough old arms bit hard on loin and breast;
The great beard smothered her. She was possessed.
A lioness roared abruptly in the waste.

But Lot's grim heart was far away. Beside
The Jordan stream, in other days, he stood
And kept the great beast, raging, from her brood,
And drove his javelin through her tawny hide.

19:36–19:38   Thus were both the daughters of Lot with child by their
father. And the firstborn bare a son, and called his name Moab: the same is
the father of the Moabites unto this day. And the younger, she also bare a
son, and called his name Benammi: the same is the father of the children of
Ammon unto this day.

Lot and his Daughters II ᴗ A. D. HOPE

The sun above the hills raged in the height.
Within Lot's cave, his vine-stock's living screen
Filtered the noon-day glare to a dim green
And hung the fat grapes bunched against the light.

The rascal patriarch, the bad old man,
Naked and rollicking on his heap of straw,
Scratching his hairy cods—one drunken paw
Spilled the red liquor from its silver can.

His beard, white as a blossoming branch, gaped wide;
Out flew a laugh: 'By God, the wine is out!
More wine!'
                    The cavern rumbled to his shout.
Brown fingers pushed the leafy screen aside.

And, padding broadly with their bare-foot tread,
Calm-eyed, big-bellied, purposeful and slow,
Lot's delicate daughters, in the bloom and glow
Of their fulfilment stood beside his bed.

Crafty from fear, reckless with joy and greed,
The old man held them in his crapulous eye:
Mountains of promise bulging in his sky;
Ark of his race; God's covenant to his seed.

They stooped to take his cup, tilted and poured;
The must rose mantling to the glittering rim;
And, as the heart of Lot grew bold in him,
It boasted and exulted in the Lord.

'The one Just Man from Sodom saved alive!
Did not His finger point me to this cave?
Behold His hand once more stretched out to save!
For Jahweh too is just. My seed shall thrive.

'Shall not the Judge of all the earth do right?
Why did his angels take me by the hand?
My tribe shall yet be numbered with the sand
Upon the shore and with the stars of night.

'With me it shall be as with Abraham.
Dark are His ways, but sure and swift to bless—
How should my ewes breed in the wilderness?
And lo, the Lord himself provides a ram!'

But Lot's resourceful daughters, side by side,
Smiled back, inscrutable, patient and content;
Their slender bodies, ripe and eloquent,
Swayed like the standing corn at harvest-tide.

And, conscious of what trouble stirred below
His words and flickered in his shrewd old eyes,
They placed the cup that kept their father wise
In that best wisdom, which is not to know.

21:1–22:13   . . . And it came to pass after these things, that God did tempt
Abraham, and said unto him, Abraham: and he said, Behold, here I am.

And he said, Take now thy son, thine only son Isaac, whom thou lovest,
and get thee into the land of Moriah; and offer him there for a burnt offer-
ing upon one of the mountains which I will tell thee of.

And Abraham rose up early in the morning, and saddled his ass, and
took two of his young men with him, and Isaac his son, and clave the wood
for the burnt offering, and rose up, and went unto the place of which God
had told him.

Then on the third day Abraham lifted up his eyes, and saw the place afar
off. And Abraham said unto his young men, Abide ye here with the ass; and I
and the lad will go yonder and worship, and come again to you. And Abraham
took the wood of the burnt offering, and laid it upon Isaac his son; and he
took the fire in his hand, and a knife; and they went both of them together.

And Isaac spake unto Abraham his father, and said, My father: and he
said, Here am I, my son. And he said, Behold the fire and the wood: but
where is the lamb for a burnt offering?

And Abraham said, My son, God will provide himself a lamb for a burnt
offering: so they went both of them together.

And they came to the place which God had told him of; and Abraham
built an altar there, and laid the wood in order, and bound Isaac his son,
and laid him on the altar upon the wood. And Abraham stretched forth his
hand, and took the knife to slay his son.

And the angel of the LORD called unto him out of heaven, and said,
Abraham, Abraham: and he said, Here am I. And he said, Lay not thine hand
upon the lad, neither do thou any thing unto him: for now I know that thou
fearest God, seeing thou hast not withheld thy son, thine only son from me.

And Abraham lifted up his eyes, and looked, and behold behind him a
ram caught in a thicket by his horns: and Abraham went and took the ram,
and offered him up for a burnt offering in the stead of his son.

Abraham to kill him ✌ EMILY DICKINSON

Abraham to kill him
Was distinctly told –
Isaac was an urchin –
Abraham was old –

Not a hesitation –
Abraham complied –
Flattered by obeisance –
Tyranny demurred –

Isaac – to his children
Lived to tell the tale –
Moral – with a mastiff
Manners may prevail.

The Parable of the Old Man and the Young ✌
WILFRED OWEN

So Abram rose, and clave the wood, and went,
And took the fire with him, and a knife.
And as they sojourned both of them together,
Isaac the first-born spake and said, My Father,
Behold the preparations, fire and iron,
But where the lamb for this burnt offering?
Then Abram bound the youth with belts and straps,
And builded parapets and trenches there,
And stretched forth the knife to slay his son.
When lo! an angel called him out of heaven,
Saying, Lay not thy hand upon the lad,
Neither do anything to him. Behold,
A ram, caught in a thicket by its horns;
Offer the Ram of Pride instead of him.
But the old man would not so, but slew his son,
And half the seed of Europe, one by one.

24:1–24:63   . . . And Isaac went out to meditate in the field at the eventide:
and he lifted up his eyes, and saw, and, behold, the camels were coming.

Isaac's Marriage ∽ HENRY VAUGHAN

Praying and to be married? It was rare,
But now 'tis monstrous; and that pious care
Though of our selves, is so much out of date,
That to renew't were to degenerate.
But thou a chosen sacrifice wert given,
And offered up so early unto heaven
Thy flames could not be out; religion was
Rayed into thee, like beams into a glass,
Where, as thou grewst, it multiplied and shined
The sacred constellation of thy mind.
But being for a bride, prayer was such
A decried course, sure it prevailed not much.
Hadst ne'er an oath, nor compliment? thou wert
An odd dull suitor; hadst thou but the art
Of these our days, thou couldst have coined thee
New several oaths, and compliments (too) plenty;
O sad, and wild excess! and happy those
White days, that durst no impious mirth expose!
When conscience by lewd use had not lost sense,
Nor bold-faced custom banished innocence;
Thou hadst no pompous train, nor antic crowd
Of young, gay swearers, with their needless, loud
Retinue; all was here smooth as thy bride
And calm like her, or that mild evening-tide:
Yet, hadst thou nobler guests: Angels did wind
And rove about thee, guardians of thy mind,
These fetched thee home thy bride, and all the way
Advised thy servant what to do, and say;
These taught him at the well, and thither brought
The chaste, and lovely object of thy thought;
But here was ne'er a compliment, not one
Spruce, supple cringe, or studied look put on,
All was plain, modest truth: Nor did she come
In rolls and curls, mincing and stately dumb,
But in a virgin's native blush and fears
Fresh as those roses, which the day-spring wears.
O sweet, divine simplicity! O grace
Beyond a curled lock, or painted face!
A pitcher too she had, nor thought it much
To carry that, which some would scorn to touch;

With which in mild, chaste language she did woo
To draw him drink, and for his camels too.
   And now thou knewest her coming, it was time
To get thee wings on, and devoutly climb
Unto thy God, for marriage of all states
Makes most unhappy, or most fortunates;
This brought thee forth, where now thou didst undress
Thy soul, and with new pinions refresh
Her wearied wings, which so restored did fly
Above the stars, a track unknown, and high,
And in her piercing flight perfumed the air
Scattering the myrrh, and incense of thy prayer.
So from Lahai-roi's well some spicy cloud[1]
Wooed by the sun swells up to be his shroud,
And from his moist womb weeps a fragrant shower,
Which, scattered in a thousand pearls, each flower
And herb partakes, where having stood awhile
And something cooled the parched, and thirsty isle,
The thankful Earth unlocks her self, and blends,
A thousand odors, which (all mixed,) she sends
Up in one cloud, and so returns the skies
That dew they lent, a breathing sacrifice.
   Thus soared thy soul, who (though young,) didst inherit
Together with his blood, thy father's spirit,
Whose active zeal, and tried faith were to thee
Familiar ever since thy infancy.
Others were timed, and trained up to't but thou
Didst thy swift years in piety out-grow,
Age made them reverend, and a snowy head,
But thou wert so, ere time his snow could shed;
Then, who would truly limn thee out, must paint
First, a young Patriarch, then a married Saint.

27:1–28:12   . . . And Jacob went out from Beersheba, and went toward
Haran. And he lighted upon a certain place, and tarried there all night,
because the sun was set; and he took of the stones of that place, and put
them for his pillows, and lay down in that place to sleep. And he dreamed,
and behold a ladder set up on the earth, and the top of it reached to heaven: and behold the angels of God ascending and descending on it.

---

1 A *well in the South Country where Jacob dwelt, between* Cadesh, & Bered; Heb. *the well of him*
   that liveth, and seeth me. [Vaughan's note]

The Jacob's Ladder ☙ DENISE LEVERTOV

The stairway is not
a thing of gleaming strands
a radiant evanescence
for angels' feet that only glance in their tread, and need not
touch the stone.

It is of stone.
A rosy stone that takes
a glowing tone of softness
only because behind it the sky is a doubtful, a doubting
night gray.

A stairway of sharp
angles, solidly built.
One sees that the angels must spring
down from one step to the next, giving a little
lift of the wings:

and a man climbing
must scrape his knees, and bring
the grip of his hands into play. The cut stone
consoles his groping feet. Wings brush past him.
The poem ascends.

29:1–30:13   . . . And when Rachel saw that she bare Jacob no children,
Rachel envied her sister; and said unto Jacob, Give me children, or else I
die. And Jacob's anger was kindled against Rachel: and he said, Am I in
God's stead, who hath withheld from thee the fruit of the womb? And she
said, Behold my maid Bilhah, go in unto her; and she shall bear upon my
knees, that I may also have children by her. And she gave him Bilhah her
handmaid to wife: and Jacob went in unto her. . . .

The Patriarch ☙ ROBERT BURNS

As honest Jacob on a night,
    Wi' his beloved beauty,
Was duly laid on wedlock's bed,

And noddin' at his duty
   Tal de dal, & c.

'How lang, she says, ye fumblin' wretch,
 'Will ye be f— —g at it?
'My eldest wean might die of age,
 'Before that ye could get it.

'Ye pegh, and grane, and groazle there,
 'And mak an unco splutter,
'And I maun ly and thole you here,
 'And fient a hair the better.'

Then he, in wrath, put up his graith,
 'The deevil's in the hizzie!
'I m–w you as I m–w the lave,
 'And night and day I'm bisy.

'I've bairn'd the servant gypsies baith,
 'Forbye your titty Leah;
'Ye barren jad, ye put me mad,
 'What mair can I do wi' you.

'There's ne'er a m–w I've gi'en the lave,
 'But ye ha'e got a dizzen;
'And d—n'd a ane ye 'se get again,
 'Altho' your c—t should gizzen.'

Then Rachel calm, as ony lamb,
 She claps him on the waulies,
Quo' she, 'ne'er fash a woman's clash,
 'In trowth, ye m–w me braulies.

'My dear 'tis true, for mony a m–w,
 'I'm your ungratefu' debtor;
'But ance again, I dinna ken,
 'We'll aiblens happen better.'

Then honest man! wi' little wark,
 He soon forgot his ire;
The patriarch, he coost the sark,
 And up and till 't like fire!!!

32:11–32:29   . . . And Jacob was left alone; and there wrestled a man with him until the breaking of the day. And when he saw that he prevailed not against him, he touched the hollow of his thigh; and the hollow of Jacob's thigh was out of joint, as he wrestled with him. And he said, Let me go, for the day breaketh. And he said, I will not let thee go, except thou bless me. And he said unto him, What is thy name? And he said, Jacob. And he said, Thy name shall be called no more Jacob, but Israel: for as a prince hast thou power with God and with men, and hast prevailed. And Jacob asked him, and said, Tell me, I pray thee, thy name. And he said, Wherefore is it that thou dost ask after my name? And he blessed him there.

A little East of Jordan   ✌   EMILY DICKINSON

A little East of Jordan,
Evangelists record,
A Gymnast and an Angel
Did wrestle long and hard –

Till morning touching mountain –
And Jacob, waxing strong,
The Angel begged permission
To Breakfast – to return –

Not so, said cunning Jacob!
"I will not let thee go
Except thou bless me" – Stranger!
The which acceded to –

Light swung the silver fleeces
"Peniel" Hills beyond,
And the bewildered Gymnast
Found he had worsted God!

35:9–37:3   . . . Now Israel loved Joseph more than all his children, because he was the son of his old age: and he made him a coat of many colours.

Joseph's Coat ♪ GEORGE HERBERT

Wounded I sing, tormented I indite,
Thrown down I fall into a bed, and rest:
Sorrow hath changed its note: such is his will,
Who changeth all things, as him pleaseth best.
For well he knows, if but one grief and smart
Among my many had his full career,
Sure it would carry with it even my heart,
And both would run until they found a bier
To fetch the body; both being due to grief.
But he hath spoiled the race; and given to anguish
One of joy's coats, ticing it with relief
To linger in me, and together languish.
I live to show his power, who once did bring
My joys to weep, and now my griefs to sing.

37:4–37:11   And when his brethren saw that their father loved him more
than all his brethren, they hated him, and could not speak peaceably unto
him. And Joseph dreamed a dream, and he told it his brethren: and they
hated him yet the more. . . .

Jacob ♪ DELMORE SCHWARTZ

All was as it is, before the beginning began, before
We were bared to the cold air, before
Pride. Fullness of bread. Abundance of idleness.
No one has ever told me what now I know:
Love is unjust, justice is loveless.

So, as it was to become, it was, in the black womb's ignorance
Coiled and bound, under the mother's heart.
There in the womb we wrestled, and writhed, hurt
Each other long before each was other and apart,
Before we breathed: who then committed greed,
Impersonation, usurpation? So, in the coming forth,
In the noose and torment of birth, Esau went first,
He was red all over. I followed him, clutching his heel,
And we were named: Esau, the one of the vivid coat,

Jacob, the one who clutches the heel of the one
Who has a vivid coat. The names were true
As the deceptive reality into which we were thrown.
For I did not know what clutching was, nor had I known
Would I have known whose heel I clutched, my brother's or my own!

So, the world we entered then and thus was one
In which the second must be second that the first may be first.
The world of precedence, order, other, under and above,
The darkness, sweetness, confusion and unity of love!
How the truth of our names became, as we grew, more true,
Growing like truth. How could it be otherwise? For truth abides
Hidden in the future, in the ambush of the marvellous,
Unknown and monstrous, at the very heart of surprise.

The gift was mind. The gift was eminence. The gift
Like every gift, was guilt. The guilt began
In the darkness and dark mystery where all begins.
The mystery of the perpetual invisible fires whence flow
The very beasts and woods where—
                                    with what happiness!
                                    what innocence!—
Esau my brother hunted, cantering like the horses of summer.
And sleeping, when he returned, the sleep of winter farms,
Spontaneous and blessed, like energy itself, sleeping or awake.
Until the hour when the angel struck!

So it was: so:
O angel of the unspeakable,
Why must a gift be guilt and hurt the gifted one?
O angel of the unspeakable, power of powers,
Locking my reins, my arms, my heart all night
So that my body was burdened as with the load of all stones
Dost thou remember what, in the darkness, I cried,
During the desperation in which I died
The last death of hope and the little deaths of the heart
Wrestling and writhing between two rivers—on one bank,
Esau, awaiting me, like a river slept—beneath me once more.
"Hast thou not seen," I cried aloud, to the unspeakable.
"Esau my brother: his handsome hunting heart upon a horse?"
How should it seem so strange that I should win,

Since victory was my gift? Unjust, like every gift,
A something neither deserved, nor gained by toil . . .
How else could it be gift and given?
Favor: favored: favorite:
Gold hair: great strength: Esau was very tall,
Possessed by the supple grace of the sea's waves, breaking.

Now Joseph is, as I was: in Egypt's pit,
In that accustomed depth and isolated height
The solitude of eminence, the exiled intelligence,
Which separated me even as it created me:
Estranged and unloved, gifted and detested,
Denied the love of the servants and the dogs.
Joseph a stranger in Egypt may only know
What I have known: my gifts, my victory, my guilt.
For Egypt is a country like a gift.
The gift is loved but not the gifted one.
The coat of many colors is much admired
By everyone, but he who wears the coat
Is not made warm. Why should the gift be the cause of pain,
O thou unspeakable? Must the vivid coat
Of eminence elect the favored favorite
As scapegoat or turncoat, exile or fugitive,
The loved of mother and God, and by all others
Shunned in fear or contempt?
                                        I knew what it was,
When Joseph became my favorite: knew the sympathy
Of the long experience of the unasked-for gift:
Knew the nature of love: how many colors
Can a coat have? What should we wish, if
We could choose? What should I desire
—Not to have loved my son, the best of sons?
Rejected the choice of love? Should I have hidden
My love of him? Or should he have concealed the self
I loved, above all others, wearing the coat
Which is customary, the coats his brothers wore?
To how many coats can a color give vividness?
How can the heart know love, and not love one the more?
Love is unjust: justice is loveless.

40:1–41:45   . . . And Pharaoh called Joseph's name Zaphnathpaaneah; and he gave him to wife Asenath the daughter of Potipherah priest of On. And Joseph went out over all the land of Egypt.

Asenath   DIANA HUME GEORGE

Why did you choose me for your wife, Joseph?
You could have had any woman,
but you asked Pharoah for me.
When you lived in our house,
you never looked on me at all,
though I tried to catch your eye.

I know what my mother said you did, Joseph.
You say it isn't true,
and I believe you.
But you broke her.
She never was herself again.
She couldn't sleep at night.
Even the potions did her no good.
She woke up staring every night,
dreaming she was drowning,
sea creatures pulling at her feet,
dreaming she was strangled
by snakes wound about her throat,
dreaming she was dead.
When she did die,
she died in slow sleep,
unconscious for weeks.
I stood over her breathing body,
watching her eyes crawling
under their lids.

She wailed on our wedding night.
I know it.
I could hear her miles away
from our bed.
I can hear her years away now.
She paid for her desire with her soul,
Joseph, with the curse of the ages
upon her nameless head.

I stare at your sleeping face.
You are a good man, Joseph,
wise and true and chosen.
Your eyes are running in their lids.
Where are you going?
What do you want?
What are you dreaming,
diviner of dreams?

41:46–45:11   . . . Then Joseph could not refrain himself before all them that stood by him; and he cried, Cause every man to go out from me. And there stood no man with him, while Joseph made himself known unto his brethren. And he wept aloud: and the Egyptians and the house of Pharaoh heard. And Joseph said unto his brethren, I am Joseph; doth my father yet live? And his brethren could not answer him; for they were troubled at his presence. And Joseph said unto his brethren, Come near to me, I pray you. And they came near. And he said, I am Joseph your brother, whom ye sold into Egypt. . .

Israel II ℘ CHARLES REZNIKOFF

Since Potiphar made you his overseer,
he has been blessed in house and field;
all that he has is in your hand,
and he knows of nothing but the bread that he eats.
And you in our house have become comely—
you were nothing but a bag of bones.
Come here!
Your cheeks were sunken so,
your eyes staring and your hair
dishevelled like this, like this.
Are not my hands soft?
You stepped as lightly as a deer,
as slim and graceful as a deer,
and held your head as proudly.
Sit here.
Kiss me.
Not so.
Oh, you don't know how to kiss.
Kiss me so.

Wet your lips and kiss me so.
Kiss my eyes, my throat,
now my mouth—
oh, you fool! You fool!

You are magicians and wise men at my feasts;
now, what is the meaning of my dreams?

"Have me in mind when it shall be well with you,
make mention of me to Pharaoh, and bring me out of this house;
for I was stolen from the land of the Hebrews;
and here also I have done nothing that they should put me into the
        dungeon."
Since then, two full years have passed, and until this day I have
        forgotten Joseph.

Therefore, let Pharaoh set a man, discreet and wise,
to appoint overseers, and these gather in the cities from the fields
        about them
grain in the good years against the years of famine.
Where can we find such a man?
I have no one discreet and wise as you.
You shall be over my house, and according to your word shall my
        people be ruled;
only I, on the throne, will be greater.
Clothe him in fine linen and put a gold chain about his neck,
he shall ride in the second chariot and all cry out before him,
        Bend the knee!

You are spies, you come to see the nakedness of the land.
No, my lord, we are not spies, we have come to buy food.
We are brothers, the sons of one man in Canaan.
And is your father yet alive?
He is.
Have you another brother?
We have.
We were twelve,
the youngest is with our father,
and one is no more.

My lord, we have brought you a present of the fruit of our land:
A little balm, a little honey, spicery and myrrh, pistachios and
    almonds.
Is your father well, the old man of whom you spoke? Is he yet alive?
Is this your youngest brother of whom you spoke?

Why have you rewarded evil for good? Where is the cup from which
    my lord drinks?
The man in whose hand the cup was found shall be my bondsman.

Now when I come to the servant your father and the lad is not
    with us—
his brother is dead, and he alone is left of his mother, and his father
    loves him—
let me remain instead of the lad, a bondsman to my lord.

Let every man go out but these.
I am Joseph.
Come nearer.
I am Joseph, your brother, whom you sold into Egypt.
And now be not grieved, nor angry with yourselves,
for I was sent before you to save us all alive;
you meant evil against me, but it was meant for good.
Go up to our father and say to him,
your son Joseph has become head of all Egypt;
without Joseph no man, except Pharaoh on the throne, lifts hand or
    foot throughout Egypt.
You have not thought to see his face and you shall see his sons also.
Come to him and you shall dwell in the land of Goshen—
and he shall be near me and his children and his children's children
and bring all your flocks and herds and all that you have;
for there are yet five years of famine.
You shall tell my father of all my glory in Egypt;
you shall take wagons out of Egypt for your little ones and your wives,
    and bring our father and come;
and I will give you all the good of the land of Egypt.
I will establish my people like a pyramid,
no longer to be blown along like sand.

47:27–49:33   . . . And the time drew nigh that Israel must die: and he called his son Joseph, and said unto him, If now I have found grace in thy sight, put, I pray thee, thy hand under my thigh, and deal kindly and truly with me; bury me not, I pray thee, in Egypt: But I will lie with my fathers, and thou shalt carry me out of Egypt, and bury me in their buryingplace. And he said, I will do as thou hast said. And he said, Swear unto me. And he sware unto him. And Israel bowed himself upon the bed's head. . . . And Israel said unto Joseph, Behold, I die: but God shall be with you, and bring you again unto the land of your fathers.

And Jacob called unto his sons, and said, Gather yourselves together, that I may tell you that which shall befall you in the last days. Gather yourselves together, and hear, ye sons of Jacob; and hearken unto Israel your father. . . . And he charged them, and said unto them, I am to be gathered unto my people: bury me with my fathers in the cave that is in the field of Ephron the Hittite, In the cave that is in the field of Machpelah, which is before Mamre, in the land of Canaan. . . .

Muse in Late November   ↗

JONATHAN HENDERSON BROOKS

I greet you, son, with joy and winter rue:
For you the fatted calf, the while I bind
Sackcloth against my heart for siring you
At sundown and the twilight. Child, you find
A sire sore tired of striving with the winds;
Climbing Mount Nebo with laborious breath
To view the land of promise through blurred lens,
Knowing he can not enter, feeling death.

And, as old Israel called his dozen sons
And placed his withered hands upon each head
Ere he was silent with the skeletons
In Mamre of the cold, cave-chambered dead,
So would I bless you with a dreamer's will:
The dream that baffles me, may you fulfill.

EXODUS

1:6–1:19 And Joseph died, and all his brethren, and all that generation. . . .

Now there arose up a new king over Egypt, which knew not Joseph. And he said unto his people, Behold, the people of the children of Israel are more and mightier than we: Come on, let us deal wisely with them; . . . Therefore they did set over them taskmasters to afflict them with their burdens. . . . But the more they afflicted them, the more they multiplied and grew. . . .

And the king of Egypt spake to the Hebrew midwives, of which the name of the one was Shiphrah, and the name of the other Puah: And he said, When ye do the office of a midwife to the Hebrew women, and see them upon the stools; if it be a son, then ye shall kill him: but if it be a daughter, then she shall live. But the midwives feared God, and did not as the king of Egypt commanded them, but saved the men children alive. And the king of Egypt called for the midwives, and said unto them, Why have ye done this thing, and have saved the men children alive? And the midwives said unto Pharaoh, Because the Hebrew women are not as the Egyptian women; for they are lively, and are delivered ere the midwives come in unto them. . . .

The Midwives CELIA GILBERT

Low huts, groans muffled,
babes slide to waiting arms
and afterbirth's
the buried plumage
of angels fallen
in travail,
but the mothers,
dazzled, tend
clandestine liberty
at hand—
sweet new bodies,
every one redeemer.

2:5–2:6 And the daughter of Pharaoh came down to wash herself at the river; and her maidens walked along by the river's side; and when she saw the ark among the flags, she sent her maid to fetch it. And when she had opened it, she saw the child:

Pharao's Daughter ⤳ MICHAEL MORAN—'ZOZIMUS'

In Agypt's land contaygious to the Nile,
Old Pharao's daughter went to bathe in style,
She tuk her dip and came unto the land,
And for to dry her royal pelt she ran along the strand:

A bull-rush tripped her, whereupon she saw
A smiling babby in a wad of straw,
She took it up and said in accents mild,
'Tare-an-ages, girls, which o'yees own the child?'

Epitaph ⤳ ELEANOR WILNER

Though only a girl,
the first born of the Pharaoh,
I was the first to die.
Young then,
we were bored already,
rouged pink as oleanders
on the palace grounds, petted
by the eunuchs, overfed
from gem-encrusted bowls, barren
with wealth, until the hours of the afternoon
seemed to outlast even
my grandmother's mummy, a perfect
little dried apricot
in a golden skin. We would paint
to pass the time, with delicate
brushes dipped in char
on clay, or on our own blank lids.
So it was that day we found him
wailing in the reeds, he seemed
a miracle to us, plucked
from the lotus by the ibis' beak,
the squalling seed of the sacred
Nile. He was permitted
as a toy; while I pretended play
I honed him like a sword.
For him, I was as polished and as perfect

as a pebble in a stutterer's mouth.
While the slaves' fans beat
incessantly as insect wings,
I taught him how to hate
this painted Pharoah's tomb
this palace built of brick
and dung, and gilded like a poet's
tongue; these painted eyes.

3:1–3:6   Now Moses kept the flock of Jethro his father in law, the priest of Midian: and he led the flock to the backside of the desert, and came to the mountain of God, even to Horeb. And the angel of the LORD appeared unto him in a flame of fire out of the midst of a bush: and he looked, and, behold, the bush burned with fire, and the bush was not consumed. And Moses said, I will now turn aside, and see this great sight, why the bush is not burnt.

And when the LORD saw that he turned aside to see, God called unto him out of the midst of the bush, and said, Moses, Moses. And he said, Here am I. And he said, Draw not nigh hither: put off thy shoes from off thy feet, for the place whereon thou standest is holy ground. Moreover he said, I am the God of thy father, the God of Abraham, the God of Isaac, and the God of Jacob. And Moses hid his face; for he was afraid to look upon God.

Sitting by a Bush in Broad Daylight ᴥ ROBERT FROST

When I spread out my hand here today
I catch no more than a ray
To feel of between thumb and fingers;
No lasting effect of it lingers.

There was one time and only the one
When dust really took in the sun;
And from that one intake of fire
All creatures still warmly suspire.

And if men have watched a long time
And never seen sun-smitten slime
Again come to life and crawl off,
We must not be too ready to scoff.

God once declared he was true
And then took the veil and withdrew,
And remember how final a hush
Then descended of old on the bush.

God once spoke to people by name.
The sun once imparted its flame.
One impulse persists as our breath.
The other persists as our faith.

9:13–14   And the LORD said unto Moses, Rise up early in the morning, and stand before Pharaoh, and say unto him, Thus saith the LORD God of the Hebrews, Let my people go, that they may serve me. For I will at this time send all my plagues upon thine heart, and upon thy servants, and upon thy people; that thou mayest know that there is none like me in all the earth.

The Coming of the Plague   ♫   WELDON KEES

September was when it began.
Locusts dying in the fields; our dogs
Silent, moving like shadows on a wall;
And strange worms crawling; flies of a kind
We had never seen before; huge vineyard moths;
Badgers and snakes, abandoning
Their holes in the field; the fruit gone rotten;
Queer fungi sprouting; the fields and woods
Covered with spiderwebs; black vapors
Rising from the earth— all these,
And more, began that fall. Ravens flew round
The hospital in pairs. Where there was water,
We could hear the sound of beating clothes
All through the night. We could not count
All the miscarriages, the quarrels, the jealousies.
And one day in a field I saw
A swarm of frogs, swollen and hideous,
Hundreds upon hundreds, sitting on each other,
Huddled together, silent, ominous,
And heard the sound of rushing wind.

13:17–22   And it came to pass, when Pharaoh had let the people go, that God led them not through the way of the land of the Philistines, . . . But God led the people about, through the way of the wilderness of the Red sea: and the children of Israel went up harnessed out of the land of Egypt. And Moses took the bones of Joseph with him: for he had straitly sworn the children of Israel, saying, God will surely visit you; and ye shall carry up my bones away hence with you. . . . And the LORD went before them by day in a pillar of a cloud, to lead them the way; and by night in a pillar of fire, to give them light; to go by day and night: He took not away the pillar of the cloud by day, nor the pillar of fire by night, from before the people.

The Pillar of the Cloud   ᔜ
JOHN HENRY, CARDINAL NEWMAN

Lead, Kindly Light, amid the circling gloom,
   Lead Thou me on!
The night is dark, and I am far from home—
   Lead Thou me on!
Keep Thou my feet; I do not ask to see
The distant scene,—one step enough for me.

I was not ever thus, nor prayed that Thou
   Shouldst lead me on!
I loved to choose and see my path; but now
   Lead Thou me on!
I loved the garish day, and, spite of fears,
Pride ruled my will: remember not past years.

So long Thy power hath blest me, sure it still
   Will lead me on,
O'er moor and fen, o'er crag and torrent, till
   The night is gone;
And with the morn those angel faces smile
Which I have loved long since, and lost awhile.

14:24–14:29   And it came to pass, that in the morning watch the LORD looked unto the host of the Egyptians through the pillar of fire and of the cloud, and troubled the host of the Egyptians, And took off their chariot wheels, that they drave them heavily: so that the Egyptians said, Let us flee from the face of Israel; for the LORD fighteth for them against the Egyptians.

And the LORD said unto Moses, Stretch out thine hand over the sea, that the waters may come again upon the Egyptians, upon their chariots, and upon their horsemen. And Moses stretched forth his hand over the sea, and the sea returned to his strength when the morning appeared; and the Egyptians fled against it; and the LORD overthrew the Egyptians in the midst of the sea. And the waters returned, and covered the chariots, and the horsemen, and all the host of Pharaoh that came into the sea after them; there remained not so much as one of them. But the children of Israel walked upon dry land in the midst of the sea; and the waters were a wall unto them on their right hand, and on their left.

Exodus ᴕ GEORGE OPPEN

Miracle of the children   the brilliant
Children   the word
Liquid as woodlands   Children?

When she was a child I read Exodus
To my daughter   'The children of Israel. . . '

Pillar of fire
Pillar of cloud

We stared at the end
Into each other's eyes   Where
She said hushed

Were the adults   We dreamed to each other
Miracle of the children
The brilliant children   Miracle

Of their brilliance   Miracle
of

14:30–14:31   Thus the LORD saved Israel that day out of the hand of the Egyptians; and Israel saw the Egyptians dead upon the sea shore. And Israel saw that great work which the LORD did upon the Egyptians: and the people feared the LORD, and believed the LORD, and his servant Moses.

Mock on, Mock on Voltaire, Rousseau ⌇

WILLIAM BLAKE

Mock on, Mock on Voltaire, Rousseau:
Mock on, Mock on: 'tis all in vain!
You throw the sand against the wind,
And the wind blows it back again.

And every sand becomes a Gem
Reflected in the beams divine;
Blown back they blind the mocking Eye,
But still in Israel's paths they shine.

The Atoms of Democritus
And Newton's Particles of light
Are sands upon the Red sea shore,
Where Israel's tents do shine so bright.

15:22–15:23   So Moses brought Israel from the Red sea, and they went out
into the wilderness of Shur; and they went three days in the wilderness, and
found no water. And when they came to Marah, they could not drink of the
waters of Marah, for they were bitter: therefore the name of it was called Marah.

The Jewish Cemetery at Newport ⌇

HENRY WADSWORTH LONGFELLOW

How strange it seems! These Hebrews in their graves,
    Close by the street of this fair seaport town,
Silent beside the never-silent waves,
    At rest in all this moving up and down!

The trees are white with dust, that o'er their sleep
    Wave their broad curtains in the southwind's breath,
While underneath these leafy tents they keep
    The long, mysterious Exodus of Death.

And these sepulchral stones, so old and brown,
    That pave with level flags their burial-place,
Seem like the tablets of the Law, thrown down
    And broken by Moses at the mountain's base.

The very names recorded here are strange,
    Of foreign accent, and of different climes;
Alvares and Rivera interchange
    With Abraham and Jacob of old times.

"Blessed be God! for he created Death!"
    The mourners said, "and Death is rest and peace;"
Then added, in the certainty of faith,
    "And giveth Life that nevermore shall cease."

Closed are the portals of their Synagogue,
    No Psalms of David now the silence break,
No Rabbi reads the ancient Decalogue
    In the grand dialect the Prophets spake.

Gone are the living, but the dead remain,
    And not neglected, for a hand unseen,
Scattering its bounty, like a summer rain,
    Still keeps their graves and their remembrance green.

How came they here? What burst of Christian hate,
    What persecution, merciless and blind,
Drove o'er the sea—that desert desolate—
    These Ishmaels and Hagars of mankind?[2]

They lived in narrow streets and lanes obscure,
    Ghetto and Judenstrass, in mirk and mire;
Taught in the school of patience to endure
    The life of anguish and the death of fire.

All their lives long, with the unleavened bread
    And bitter herbs of exile and its fears,
The wasting famine of the heart they fed,
    And slaked its thirst with marah of their tears.

Anathema maranatha![3] was the cry
    That rang from town to town, from street to street;
At every gate the accursed Mordecai[4]
    Was mocked and jeered, and spurned by Christian feet.

2 GEN 21:9–21
3 1CO 16:22
4 EST 2:15–3:6

Pride and humiliation hand in hand
    Walked with them through the world where'er they went;
Trampled and beaten were they as the sand
    And yet unshaken as the continent.

For in the background figures vague and vast
    Of patriarchs and of prophets rose sublime,
And all the great traditions of the Past
    They saw reflected in the coming time.

And thus forever with reverted look
    The mystic volume of the world they read,
Spelling it backward, like a Hebrew book,
    Till life became a Legend of the Dead.

But ah! what once has been shall be no more!
    The groaning earth in travail and in pain
Brings forth its races, but does not restore,
    And the dead nations never rise again.

19:9–20:6   And the LORD said unto Moses, Lo, I come unto thee in a thick cloud, that the people may hear when I speak with thee, and believe thee for ever. And Moses told the words of the people unto the LORD. . . . And it came to pass on the third day in the morning, that there were thunders and lightnings, and a thick cloud upon the mount, and the voice of the trumpet exceeding loud; so that all the people that was in the camp trembled. . . .

And God spake all these words, saying,
I am the LORD thy God, which have brought thee out of the land of Egypt,
    out of the house of bondage.
Thou shalt have no other gods before me.
Thou shalt not make unto thee any graven image,
    or any likeness of any thing that is in heaven above,
    or that is in the earth beneath, or that is in the water under the earth.
    Thou shalt not bow down thyself to them, nor serve them:
    for I the LORD thy God am a jealous God,
    visiting the iniquity of the fathers upon the children
    unto the third and fourth generation of them that hate me;
    And shewing mercy unto thousands of them that love me,
    and keep my commandments.

Thou shalt not take the name of the LORD thy God in vain;

for the LORD will not hold him guiltless that taketh his name in vain.

Remember the sabbath day, to keep it holy.

Six days shalt thou labour, and do all thy work:

But the seventh day is the sabbath of the LORD thy God:

in it thou shalt not do any work, thou, nor thy son, nor thy daughter,

thy manservant, nor thy maidservant, nor thy cattle, nor thy stranger

that is within thy gates:

For in six days the LORD made heaven and earth, the sea,

and all that in them is, and rested the seventh day: wherefore the LORD

blessed the sabbath day, and hallowed it.

Honour thy father and thy mother:

that thy days may be long upon the land which the LORD thy God

giveth thee.

Thou shalt not kill.

Thou shalt not commit adultery.

Thou shalt not steal.

Thou shalt not bear false witness against thy neighbour.

Thou shalt not covet thy neighbour's house, thou shalt not covet thy

neighbour's wife, nor his manservant, nor his maidservant, nor his ox,

nor his ass, nor any thing that is thy neighbour's.

The Law Given at Sinai ∽ ISAAC WATTS

Arm thee with thunder, heavenly muse,
And keep th' expecting world in awe;
Oft hast thou sung in gentler mood
The melting mercies of thy God;
Now give thy fiercest fires a loose,
And sound his dreadful law:
To Israel first the words were spoke,
To Israel freed from Egypt's yoke,
Inhuman bondage! the hard galling load
Over-pressed their feeble souls,
Bent their knees to senseless bulls,
And broke their ties to God.

Now had they passed the Arabian bay,
   And marched between the cleaving sea;
The rising waves stood guardians of their wondrous way,
    But fell with most impeteous force
       On the pursuing swarms
       And buried Egypt all in arms.
Blending in watery death the rider and the horse:
O'er struggling Pharoah rolled the mighty tide,
And saved the labors of a pyramid.
    Apis and Ore in vain he cries,
    And all his horned gods beside,
    He swallows fate with swimming eyes,
    And cursed the Hebrews as he died.

    Ah! foolish Israel, to comply
    With Memphian idolatry!
    And bow to brutes, (a stupid slave)
    To idols impotent to save!
Behold thy God, the sovereign of the sky,
    Has wrought salvation in the deep,
    Has bound thy foes in iron sleep,
       And raised thine honors high;
    His grace forgives thy follies past,
    Behold he comes in majesty,
    And Sinai's top proclaims his law:
    Prepare to meet thy God in haste!
    But keep an awful distance still:
    Let Moses round the sacred hill
       The circling limits draw.

Hark! the shrill echoes of the trumpet roar,
    And call the trembling armies near;
    Slow and unwilling they appear,
Rails kept them from the mount before,
    Now from the rails their fear:
'Twas the same herald, and the trump the same
    Which shall be blown by high command,
    Shall bid the wheels of nature stand,
    And heaven's eternal will proclaim,
       That 'time shall be no more.'

Thus while the laboring angel swelled the sound,
And rent the skies, and shook the ground,
Up rose th' Almighty; round his sapphire seat
    Adoring thrones in order fell;
    The lesser powers at distance dwell,
And cast their glories down successive at his feet:
    Gabriel the great prepares his way,
'Lift up your heads, eternal doors,' he cries;
    Th' eternal doors his word obey,
    Open and shoot celestial day
        Upon the lower skies.
    Heaven's mighty pillars bowed their head,
        As their Creator bid,
And down Jehovah rode from the superior sphere,
A thousand guards before, and myriads in the rear.

    His chariot was a pitchy cloud,
    The wheels beset with burning gems;
    The winds in harness with the flames
    Flew o'er th' ethereal road:
Down through his magazines he past
    Of hail, and ice, and fleecy snow,
Swift rolled the triumph, and as fast
    Did hail, and ice, in melted rivers flow.
    The day was mingled with the night,
His feet on solid darkness trod,
His radiant eyes proclaimed the God,
    And scattered dreadful light;
He breathed, and sulphur ran, a fiery stream:
He spoke, and (though with unknown speed he came)
Chid the slow tempest, and the lagging flame.

        Sinai received his glorious flight,
    With axle red, and glowing wheel,
        Did the wingéd chariot light,
    And rising smoke obscured the burning hill.
        Lo, it mounts in curling waves,
        Lo, the gloomy pride out-braves
    The stately pyramids of fire
    The pyramids to heaven aspire,
And mix with stars, but see their gloomy offspring higher.

So you have seen ungrateful ivy grow
Round the tall oak that six score years has stood,
    And proudly shoot a leaf or two
  Above its kind supporter's utmost bough,
And glory there to stand the loftiest of the wood.

  Forbear, young muse, forbear;
  The flowery things that poets say,
    The little arts of simile
    Are vain and useless here;
  Nor shall the burning hills of old
    With Sinai be compared,
  Nor all that lying Greece has told,
    Or learnéd Rome has heard;
Ætna shall be named no more,
    Ætna, the torch of Sicily;
        Not half so high
        Her lightnings fly,
Not half so loud her thunders roar
Cross the Sicanian sea, to fright th' Italian shore.
  Behold the sacred hill: Its trembling spire
  Quakes at the terrors of the fire,
  While all below its verdant feet
  Stagger and reel under th' almighty weight:
Pressed with a greater than feigned Atlas' load
  Deep groaned the mount; it never bore
    Infinity before,
It bowed, and shook beneath the burden of a God.

  Fresh horror seize the camp, despair
  And dying groans, torment the air,
And shrieks, and swoons, and deaths were there;
The bellowing thunder, and the lightning's blaze,
  Spread through the host a wild amaze;
Darkness on every soul, and pale was every face:
  Confused and dismal were the cries,
  'Let Moses speak, or Israel dies:'
  Moses the spreading terror feels,
  No more the man of God conceals
  His shivering and surprise:

Yet, with recovering mind, commands
Silence, and deep attention, through the Hebrew bands.
   Hark! from the center of the flame,
   All armed and feathered with the same,
Majestic sounds break through the smoky cloud:
   Sent from the all-creating tongue
   A flight of cherubs guard the words along,
And bear their fiery law to the retreating crowd.

   'I am the Lord: 'tis I proclaim
   'That glorious and that fearful name,
   'Thy God and King: 'twas I, that broke
   'Thy bondage, and th' Egyptian yoke;
   'Mine is the right to speak my will,
   'And thine the duty to fulfil.

'Adore no God beside me, to provoke mine eyes:
'Nor worship me in shapes and forms that men devise;
'With reverence use my name, nor turn my words to jest;
'Observe my sabbath well, nor dare profane my rest;
'Honor, and due obedience, to thy parents give;
'Nor spill the guiltless blood, nor let the guilty live:
'Preserve thy body chaste, and flee th' unlawful bed;
'Nor steal thy neighbour's gold, his garment, or his bread:
'Forbear to blast his name with falsehood, or deceit;
'Nor let thy wishes loose upon his large estate.'

26:30–27:20   And thou shalt rear up the tabernacle according to the fashion thereof which was shewed thee in the mount. . . . All the vessels of the tabernacle in all the service thereof, and all the pins thereof, and all the pins of the court, shall be of brass. And thou shalt command the children of Israel, that they bring thee pure oil olive beaten for the light, to cause the lamp to burn always.

The Jew ∿ ISAAC ROSENBERG

Moses, from whose loins I sprung,
Lit by a lamp in his blood

Ten immutable rules, a moon
For mutable lampless men.

The blond, the bronze, the ruddy,
With the same heaving blood,
Keep tide to the moon of Moses.
Then why do they sneer at me?

32:1–32:34   . . . And the LORD said unto Moses, Go, get thee down; for
thy people, which thou broughtest out of the land of Egypt, have corrupted
themselves: They have turned aside quickly out of the way which I com-
manded them: they have made them a molten calf, and have worshipped it,
and have sacrificed thereunto, and said, These be thy gods, O Israel, which
have brought thee up out of the land of Egypt. . . .

And it came to pass on the morrow, that Moses said unto the people, Ye
have sinned a great sin: and now I will go up unto the LORD; peradventure
I shall make an atonement for your sin. And Moses returned unto the
LORD, and said, Oh, this people have sinned a great sin, and have made
them gods of gold. Yet now, if thou wilt forgive their sin—; and if not, blot
me, I pray thee, out of thy book which thou hast written.

And the LORD said unto Moses, Whosoever hath sinned against me,
him will I blot out of my book. . . .

The Book of the World ᨆ
WILLIAM DRUMMOND OF HAWTHORNDEN

Of this fair volume which we World do name,
If we the sheets and leaves could turn with care,
Of Him who it corrects, and did it frame,
We clear might read the art and wisdom rare?
Find out his Power which wildest powers doth tame,
His Providence extending everywhere,
His Justice which proud rebels doth not spare.
In every page, no, period of the same:
But silly we (like foolish children) rest
Well pleased with colored vellum, leaves of gold,
Fair dangling ribbons, leaving what is best,

On the great Writer's sense ne'er taking hold;
    Or if by chance our minds do muse on ought,
    It is some picture on the margin wrought.

34:21–34:28 ... And the LORD said unto Moses, Write thou these words:
for after the tenor of these words I have made a covenant with thee and
with Israel. And he was there with the LORD forty days and forty nights; he
did neither eat bread, nor drink water. And he wrote upon the tables the
words of the covenant, the ten commandments.

The Latest Decalogue ꝏ ARTHUR HUGH CLOUGH

Thou shalt have one God only; who
Would be at the expense of two?
No graven images may be
Worshipped, except the currency:
Swear not at all; for, for thy curse
Thine enemy is none the worse:
At church on Sunday to attend
Will serve to keep the world thy friend:
Honour thy parents; that is, all
From whom advancement may befall:
Thou shalt not kill; but needst not strive
Officiously to keep alive:
Do not adultery commit;
Advantage rarely comes of it:
Thou shalt not steal; an empty feat
When it's so lucrative to cheat:
Bear not false witness; let the lie
Have time on its own wings to fly:
Thou shalt not covet; but tradition
Approves all forms of competition.
The sum of all is, thou shalt love,
If any body, God above:
At any rate shall never labour
More than thyself to love thy neighbor.[5]

5 LEV 19:18 Thou shalt not avenge, nor bear any grudge against the children of thy people, but
    thou shalt love thy neighbour as thyself: I am the LORD.

LEVITICUS

11:1–11:4   And the LORD spake unto Moses and to Aaron, saying unto them, Speak unto the children of Israel, saying, These are the beasts which ye shall eat among all the beasts that are on the earth. Whatsoever parteth the hoof, and is clovenfooted, and cheweth the cud, among the beasts, that shall ye eat. Nevertheless these shall ye not eat of them that chew the cud, or of them that divide the hoof: as the camel, because he cheweth the cud, but divideth not the hoof; he is unclean unto you.

The Chewing the Cud ⟿ ROBERT HERRICK

When well we speak, and nothing do that's good,
We not divide the hoof, but chew the cud:
But when good words, by good works, have their proof,
We then both chew the cud, and cleave the hoof.

11:13–11:20   And these are they which ye shall have in abomination among the fowls; they shall not be eaten, they are an abomination: the eagle, and the ossifrage, and the ospray, And the vulture, and the kite after his kind; Every raven after his kind; And the owl, and the night hawk, and the cuckow, and the hawk after his kind, And the little owl, and the cormorant, and the great owl, And the swan, and the pelican, and the gier eagle, And the stork, the heron after her kind, and the lapwing, and the bat. All fowls that creep, going upon all four, shall be an abomination unto you.

A Paraphrase on . . . Leviticus Chap. XI. Vers. 13, &c.
Fashioned after the Manner of Master Geoffery Chaucer
in his Assembly of Fowls ⟿ THOMAS WARTON THE ELDER
Containing the Reasons of the several Prohibitions

Of feathered fowls, that fan the buxom air,
Not all alike were made for food to men;
For, these thou shalt not eat, doth God declare,
Twice ten their number, and their flesh unclean:
First the great eagle, bird of feigned Jove,
Which Thebans worship, and diviners love:

Next ossifrage, and osprey, (both one kind)
Of luxury, and rapine, emblems meet,
That haunt the shores, the choicest prey to find,
And burst the bones, and scoop the marrow sweet:
The vulture, void of delicace, and fear,
Who spareth not the pale dead man to tear:

The tall-built swan, fair type of pride confessed;
The pelican, whose sons are nursed with blood,
Forbid to man! — She stabbeth deep her breast,
Self murderess through fondness to her brood:
They too that range the thirsty wilds among,
The ostriches, unthoughtful of their young:

The raven ominous, (as Gentiles hold)
What time she croaketh hoarsely *A la Morte*;
The hawk, aerial hunter, swift, and bold,
In feats of mischief trained for disport;
The vocal cuckoo, of the falcon race,
Obscene intruder in her neighbor's place:

The owl demure, who loveth not the light,
(Ill semblance she of wisdom to the Greek)
The smallest fowls dread foe, the coward kite,
And the still her'n, arresting fishes meek;
The glutton cormorant, of sullen mood:
Regarding no distinction in her food.

The stork, which dwelleth on the fir tree-top,
And trusteth that no Power shall her dismay,
As kings on their high stations place their hope,
Nor wist that there be higher far than they:
The gay ger-eagle, beautiful to view,
Bearing within a savage heart untrue:

The ibis whom in Egypt Israel found,
Fell bird! that living serpents can digest;
The crested lapwing, wailing shrill around,
Solicitous, with no contentment blessed:
Last the foul bat, of bird, and beast first bred,
Flitting, with little leathern sails dispread.

16:1–16:24   . . . And Aaron shall lay both his hands upon the head of the
live goat, and confess over him all the iniquities of the children of Israel,
and all their transgressions in all their sins, putting them upon the head of
the goat, and shall send him away by the hand of a fit man into the wilder-
ness: And the goat shall bear upon him all their iniquities unto a land not
inhabited: and he shall let go the goat in the wilderness. And Aaron shall
come into the tabernacle of the congregation, and shall put off the linen
garments, which he put on when he went into the holy place, and shall
leave them there: And he shall wash his flesh with water in the holy place,
and put on his garments, and come forth, and offer his burnt offering, and
the burnt offering of the people, and make an atonement for himself, and
for the people.

Day of Atonement   ᘺ   CHARLES REZNIKOFF

The great Giver has ended His disposing;
the long day
is over and the gates are closing.
How badly all that has been read
was read by us,
how poorly all that should be said.

All wickedness shall go in smoke.
It must, it must!
The just shall see and be glad.
The sentence is sweet and sustaining;
for we, I suppose, are the just;
and we, the remaining.

If only I could write with four pens between five fingers
and with each pen a different sentence at the same time —
but the rabbis say it is a lost art, a lost art.
I well believe it. And at that of the first twenty sins that we confess,
five are by speech alone;
little wonder that I must ask the Lord to bless
the words of my mouth and the meditations of my heart.

Now, as from the dead, I revisit the earth and delight
in the sky, and hear again
the noise of the city and see

earth's marvelous creatures—men.
Out of nothing I became a being,
and from a being I shall be
nothing—but until then
I rejoice, a mote in Your world,
a spark in Your seeing.

NUMBERS

13:17–13:27   And Moses sent them to spy out the land of Canaan. . . .
Now the time was the time of the first ripe grapes. So they went up, and
searched the land from the wilderness of Zin unto Rehob, as men come to
Hamath. And they ascended by the south, and came unto Hebron; where
Ahiman, Sheshai, and Talmai, the children of Anak, were. (Now Hebron was
built seven years before Zoan in Egypt.) And they came unto the brook of
Eshcol, and cut down from thence a branch with one cluster of grapes, and
they bare it between two upon a staff; and they brought of the pomegran-
ates, and of the figs. The place was called the brook Eshcol, because of the
cluster of grapes which the children of Israel cut down from thence. And
they returned from searching of the land after forty days. And they went and
came to Moses, and to Aaron, and to all the congregation of the children of
Israel, . . . and shewed them the fruit of the land. And they told him, and
said, We came unto the land whither thou sentest us, and surely it floweth
with milk and honey; and this is the fruit of it.

The Bunch of Grapes   ᕱ   GEORGE HERBERT

Joy, I did lock thee up: but some bad man
            Hath let thee out again:
And now, me thinks, I am where I began
       Seven years ago: one vogue and vein,
       One air of thoughts usurps my brain.
I did toward Canaan draw; but now I am
Brought back to the Red sea, the sea of shame.

For as the Jews of old by God's command
            Traveled, and saw no town:
So now each Christian hath his journeys spanned:

Their story pens and sets us down.
A single deed is small renown.
God's works are wide, and let in future times;
His ancient justice overflows our crimes.

Then have we too our guardian fires and clouds;
        Our Scripture-dew drops fast:[6]
We have our sands and serpents, tents and shrouds;
    Alas! our murmurings come not last.
    But where's the cluster? where's the taste
Of mine inheritance? Lord, if I must borrow,
Let me as well take up their joy, as sorrow.

But can he want the grape, who hath the wine?
        I have their fruit and more.
Blessed be God, who prospered Noah's vine,
    And made it bring forth grapes good store.
    But much more him I must adore,
Who of the law's sour juice sweet wine did make,
Even God himself, being pressed for my sake.

14:28–14:35   Say unto them, As truly as I live, saith the LORD, . . . your
children shall wander in the wilderness forty years, and bear your whore-
doms, until your carcases be wasted in the wilderness. After the number of
the days in which ye searched the land, even forty days, each day for a year,
shall ye bear your iniquities, even forty years, and ye shall know my breach
of promise. I the LORD have said, I will surely do it unto all this evil congre-
gation, that are gathered together against me: in this wilderness they shall
be consumed, and there they shall die.

Golden Calf ᴐ NORMAN MACCAIG

If all the answer's to be the Sinai sort
The incorruptible lava of the word
Made alphabetic in a stormspout, what
Mere human vocables you've ever heard,

---

6 NUM 11:9; DEU 32:1

Poor golden calf, could overbear, I wonder,
    The magniloquence of thunder?

You're for another flame. The Moses in me
Looks with a stone face on our gaudy lives.
His fingers, scorched with godhead, point, and loose
An influence of categorical negatives
That make an image of love, a trope of lover.
    Our dancing days are over.

The buckles tarnish at the thought of it.
The winecup shatters. The bragging music chokes
To the funeral silence it was awkward in.
And before the faggot of salvation smokes,
Your knees are loosed, your wreathed neck bows lowly
    In presence of the holy.

What's a disgruntled cloud to you or me?
Listen to my multitudes, and beam for them,
Making a plinth of this dark wilderness.
Utter such rigmaroles an apothegm,
Doing its head-stroke, drowns in such wild water
    And proves itself no matter.

Or where's the desert cat, or hunching shade
That ambles hugely in the dark outside,
Or hospitable anguish beckoning
To its foul ceremony a sorry bride
Could bear the darts struck from your hide by torches
    That guard our pleasure's marches?

Forty years. Small wilderness to unravel
Such an unknotted thread of wandering.
The desert is in Moses' skull, the journey
To the white thalamus whose cradling
Enfolds the foetus of the law—gestation
    Of Moses as a nation.

A chosen people, since they have no choice.
The doors are locked, the flesh-pots on the shelves,
And a long line of lamentation moves

Led by the nose through their own better selves
To buy with blood a land of milk and honey
    Where's no need of money.

The smoke and thunder die. And here I stand
Smelling of gunpowder and holiness.
The great fire does its belly-dance and in it
You shine unharmed, not knowing what's to confess;
And the desert, seeing the issue grows no clearer,
    Takes one long slow step nearer.

DEUTERONOMY

16:19 Thou shalt not wrest judgment; thou shalt not respect persons, nei-
ther take a gift: for a gift doth blind the eyes of the wise, and pervert the
words of the righteous.

To his Conscience ∽ ROBERT HERRICK

Can I not sin, but thou wilt be
My private Protonotary?
Can I not woo thee to pass by
A short and sweet iniquity?
I'll cast a mist and cloud, upon
My delicate transgression,
So utter dark, as that no eye
Shall see the hugged impiety:
Gifts blind the wise, and bribes do please,
And wind all other witnesses:
And wilt not thou, with gold, be tied
To lay thy pen and ink aside?
That in the murk and tongueless night,
Wanton I may, and thou not write?
It will not be: And, therefore, now,
For times to come, I'll make this vow,
From aberrations to live free;
So I'll not fear the Judge, or thee.

30:11–30:14   For this commandment which I command thee this day, it is not hidden from thee, neither is it far off. It is not in heaven, that thou shouldest say, Who shall go up for us to heaven, and bring it unto us, that we may hear it, and do it? Neither is it beyond the sea, that thou shouldest say, Who shall go over the sea for us, and bring it unto us, that we may hear it, and do it? But the word is very nigh unto thee, in thy mouth, and in thy heart, that thou mayest do it.

from A *Song for Occupations*   ⌁   WALT WHITMAN

6

Will you seek afar off? you surely come back at last,
In things best known to you finding the best, or as good as the best,
In folks nearest to you finding the sweetest, strongest, lovingest,
Happiness, knowledge, not in another place but this place, not for
      another hour but this hour,
Man in the first you see or touch, always in friend, brother, nighest
      neighbor— woman in mother, sister, wife,
The popular tastes and employments taking precedence in poems or
      anywhere,
You workwomen and workmen of these States having your own
      divine and strong life,
And all else giving place to men and women like you.

When the psalm sings instead of the singer,
When the script preaches instead of the preacher,
When the pulpit descends and goes instead of the carver that carved
      the supporting desk,
When I can touch the body of books by night or by day, and when
      they touch my body back again,
When a university course convinces like a slumbering woman and
      child convince,
When the minted gold in the vault smiles like the night-watchman's
      daughter,
When warrantee deeds loaf in chairs opposite and are my friendly
      companions,
I intend to reach them my hand, and make as much of them as I do
      of men and women like you.

34:1–34:4   And Moses went up from the plains of Moab unto the mountain of Nebo, to the top of Pisgah, that is over against Jericho. And the LORD shewed him all the land of Gilead, unto Dan, And all Naphtali, and the land of Ephraim, and Manasseh, and all the land of Judah, unto the utmost sea, And the south, and the plain of the valley of Jericho, the city of palm trees, unto Zoar. And the LORD said unto him, This is the land which I sware unto Abraham, unto Isaac, and unto Jacob, saying, I will give it unto thy seed: I have caused thee to see it with thine eyes, but thou shalt not go over thither.

Pisgah-Sights. I & II ❧   ROBERT BROWNING

I
Over the ball of it,
    Peering and prying,
How I see all of it,
    Life there, outlying!
Roughness and smoothness,
    Shine and defilement,
Grace and uncouthness:
    One reconcilement.

Orbed as appointed,
    Sister with brother
Joins, ne'er disjointed
    One from the other.
All's lend-and-borrow;
    Good, see, wants evil,
Joy demands sorrow,
    Angel weds devil!

'Which things must – *why* be?'
    Vain our endeavour!
So shall things aye be
    As they were ever.
'Such things should *so* be!'
    Sage our desistence!
Rough-smooth let globe be,
    Mixed – man's existence.

Man – wise and foolish,
　　Lover and scorner,
Docile and mulish –
　　Keep each his corner!
Honey yet gall of it!
　　There's the life lying,
And I see all of it,
　　Only, I'm dying!

II
Could I but live again,
　　Twice my life over,
Would I once strive again?
　　Would I not cover
Quietly all of it –
　　Greed and ambition –
So, from the pall of it,
　　Pass to fruition?

'Soft!' I'd say, 'Soul mine!
　　Three-score and ten years,
Let the blind mole mine
　　Digging out deniers!
Let the dazed hawk soar,
　　Claim the sun's rights too!
Turf 'tis thy walk's o'er,
　　Foliage thy flight's to.'

Only a learner,
　　Quick one or slow one,
Just a discerner,
　　I would teach no one.
I am earth's native:
　　No rearranging it!
I be creative,
　　Chopping and changing it?

March, men, my fellows!
　　Those who, above me,
(Distance so mellows)
　　Fancy you love me:

Those who, below me,
   (Distance makes great so)
Free to forego me,
   Fancy you hate so!

Praising, reviling,
   Worst head and best head,
Past me defiling,
   Never arrested,
Wanters, abounders,
   March, in gay mixture,
Men, my surrounders!
   I am the fixture.

So shall I fear thee,
   Mightiness yonder!
Mock-sun – more near thee,
   What is to wonder?
So shall I love thee,
   Down in the dark, – lest
Glowworm I prove thee,
   Star that now sparklest!

34:5–34:10   So Moses the servant of the LORD died there in the land of
Moab, according to the word of the LORD. And he buried him in a valley in
the land of Moab, over against Bethpeor: but no man knoweth of his sepul-
chre unto this day. And Moses was an hundred and twenty years old when
he died: his eye was not dim, nor his natural force abated. And the children
of Israel wept for Moses in the plains of Moab thirty days: so the days of
weeping and mourning for Moses were ended. . . . And there arose not a
prophet since in Israel like unto Moses, whom the LORD knew face to face,

The Death of Moses ⤳   GEORGE ELIOT

Moses, who spake with God as with his friend,
And ruled his people with the twofold power
Of wisdom that can dare and still be meek,
Was writing his last word, the sacred name
Unutterable of that Eternal Will
Which was and is and evermore shall be.

Yet was his task not finished, for the flock
Needed its shepherd and the life-taught sage
Leaves no successor; but to chosen men,
The rescuers and guides of Israel,
A death was given called the Death of Grace,
Which freed them from the burden of the flesh
But left them rulers of the multitude
And loved companions of the lonely. This
Was God's last gift to Moses, this the hour
When soul must part from self and be but soul.

God spake to Gabriel, the messenger
Of mildest death that draws the parting life
Gently, as when a little rosy child
Lifts up its lips from off the bowl of milk
And so draws forth a curl that dipped its gold
In the soft white—thus Gabriel draws the soul.
"Go bring the soul of Moses unto me!"
And the awe-stricken angel answered, "Lord,
How shall I dare to take his life who lives
Sole of his kind, not to be likened once
In all the generations of the earth?"

Then God called Michaël, him of pensive brow,
Snow-vest and flaming sword, who knows and acts:
"Go bring the spirit of Moses unto me!"
But Michaël with such grief as angels feel,
Loving the mortals whom they succor, pled:
"Almighty, spare me; it was I who taught
Thy servant Moses; he is part of me
As I of thy deep secrets, knowing them."

Then God called Zamaël, the terrible,
The angel of fierce death, of agony
That comes in battle and in pestilence
Remorseless, sudden or with lingering throes
And Zamaël, his raiment and broad wings
Blood-tinctured, the dark lustre of his eyes
Shrouding the red, fell like the gathering night
Before the prophet. But that radiance
Won from the heavenly presence in the mount

Gleamed on the prophet's brow and dazzling pierced
Its conscious opposite: the angel turned
His murky gaze aloof and inly said:
"An angel this, deathless to angel's stroke."

But Moses felt the subtly nearing dark:
"Who art thou? and what wilt thou?" Zamaël then:
"I am God's reaper; through the fields of life
I gather ripened and unripened souls
Both willing and unwilling. And I come
Now to reap thee." But Moses cried,
Firm as a seer who waits the trusted sign:
"Reap thou the fruitless plant and common herb—
Not him who from the womb was sanctified
To teach the law of purity and love."
And Zamaël baffled from his errand fled.

But Moses, pausing, in the air serene
Heard now that mystic whisper, far yet near,
The all-penetrating Voice, that said to him,
"Moses, the hour is come and thou must die."
"Lord, I obey; but thou rememberest
How thou, Ineffable, didst take me once
Within thy orb of light untouched by death."
Then the Voice answered, "Be no more afraid:
With me shall be thy death and burial."
So Moses waited, ready now to die.

And the Lord came, invisible as a thought,
Three angels gleaming on his secret track,
Prince Michaël, Zamaël, Gabriel, charged to guard
The soul-forsaken body as it fell
And bear it to the hidden sepulchre
Denied forever to the search of man.
And the Voice said to Moses: "Close thine eyes."
He closed them. "Lay thine hand upon thine heart,
And draw thy feet together." He obeyed.
And the Lord said, "O spirit! child of mine!
A hundred years and twenty thou hast dwelt
Within this tabernacle wrought of clay.
This is the end: come forth and flee to heaven."

But the grieved soul with plaintive pleading cried,
"I love this body with a clinging love:
The courage fails me, Lord, to part from it."

"O child, come forth! for thou shalt dwell with me
About the immortal throne where seraphs joy
In growing vision and in growing love."

Yet hesitating, fluttering, like the bird
With young wing weak and dubious, the soul
Stayed. But behold! upon the death-dewed lips
A kiss descended, pure, unspeakable—
The bodiless Love without embracing Love
That lingered in the body, drew it forth
With heavenly strength and carried it to heaven.

But now beneath the sky the watchers all,
Angels that keep the homes of Israel
Or on high purpose wander o'er the world
Leading the Gentiles, felt a dark eclipse:
The greatest ruler among men was gone.
And from the westward sea was heard a wail,
A dirge as from the isles of Javanim,
Crying, "Who now is left upon the earth
Like him to teach the right and smite the wrong?"
And from the East, far o'er the Syrian waste,
Came slowlier, sadlier, the answering dirge:
"No prophet like him lives or shall arise
In Israel or the world forevermore."

But Israel waited, looking toward the mount,
Till with the deepening eve the elders came
Saying, "His burial is hid with God.
We stood far off and saw the angels lift
His corpse aloft until they seemed a star
That burnt itself away within the sky."

The people answered with mute orphaned gaze
Looking for what had vanished evermore.
Then through the gloom without them and within
The spirit's shaping light, mysterious speech,

Invisible Will wrought clear in sculptured sound,
The thought-begotten daughter of the voice,
Thrilled on their listening sense: "He has no tomb.
He dwells not with you dead, but lives as Law."

JOSHUA

3:9–3:11   And Joshua said unto the children of Israel, Come hither, and
hear the words of the LORD your God. And Joshua said, Hereby ye shall
know that the living God is among you, and that he will without fail drive
out from before you the Canaanites, and the Hittites, and the Hivites, and
the Perizzites, and the Girgashites, and the Amorites, and the Jebusites.
Behold, the ark of the covenant of the Lord of all the earth passeth over
before you into Jordan.

The Story of Joshua   ᘛ   ALICIA OSTRIKER

The New Englanders are a people of God settled
in those which were once the devil's territories.
   —Cotton Mather, *The Wonders of the Invisible World,* 1692

We reach the promised land
Forty years later
The original ones who were slaves
Have died
The young are seasoned soldiers
There is wealth enough for everyone and God
Here at our side, the people
Are mad with excitement.
Here is what to do, to take
This land away from the inhabitants:
Burn their villages and cities
Kill their men
Kill their women
Consume the people utterly.
God says: is that clear?
I give you the land, but
You must murder for it.
You will be a nation

Like other nations,
Your hands are going to be stained like theirs
Your innocence annihilated.
Keep listening, Joshua.
Only to you among the nations
Do I also give knowledge
The secret
Knowledge that you are doing evil
Only to you the commandment:
Love ye therefore the stranger, for you were
Strangers in the land of Egypt, a pillar
Of fire to light your passage
Through the blank desert of history forever.
This is the agreement.
Is it entirely
Clear, Joshua,
Said the Lord.
I said it was. He then commanded me
To destroy Jericho.

6:2–6:25 . . . So the people shouted when the priests blew with the trumpets: and it came to pass, when the people heard the sound of the trumpet, and the people shouted with a great shout, that the wall fell down flat, so that the people went up into the city, every man straight before him, and they took the city. And they utterly destroyed all that was in the city, both man and woman, young and old, and ox, and sheep, and ass, with the edge of the sword. . . .

Women of Jericho   ↜   PHYLLIS MCGINLEY

Though seven times, or seventy times seven,
Your armies circle our beleaguered town,
Not with their clamor may our gates be riven;
O, not by trumpets shall the walls go down!
Send out your troops to trample the fresh grasses
With horns and banners! They shall find defeat.
These walls can bear the insolence of brasses
Sounded at noonday in the dust and heat.

It is the whisper, only, that we dread:
The hushed and delicate murmur like low weeping

Which shall assail us, when, as do the dead,
The warders sleep and all the town lies sleeping.
That holy word is whispered which can fell
These armored walls, and raze the citadel.

10:1–10:13 . . . Then spake Joshua to the LORD in the day when the LORD
delivered up the Amorites before the children of Israel, and he said in the
sight of Israel, Sun, stand thou still upon Gibeon; and thou, Moon, in the
valley of Ajalon. And the sun stood still, and the moon stayed, until the peo-
ple had avenged themselves upon their enemies. Is not this written in the
book of Jasher? So the sun stood still in the midst of heaven, and hasted
not to go down about a whole day.

Joshua ◡ X. J. KENNEDY

Earth stopped. The Holy City hit a mountain
As a tray of dishes meets a swinging door.
Oceans lunged to converge, one with another.
He who had called that halt stood bemused there.

Who would have thought a simple invocation. . . ?
As brazen leaves, troops fell. His walking stick
Tapped as he limped across a foiled battalion.
Sun and moon hung stone still, their axles stuck.

No cricket sprang from upright walls of grass.
Clouds swung in bunches, wingless. Who could look
Long on so high a carnage: all creation
Crushed like a sprig of heather in a book?

Futile to wail, wear sackcloth, tear his tongue out—
How could he feel commensurate remorse?
At last the sun, God resting noncommittal,
Rose in confusion and resumed its course.

24:1–24:13 . . . And I have given you a land for which ye did not labour,
and cities which ye built not, and ye dwell in them; of the vineyards and
oliveyards which ye planted not do ye eat.

Joshua at Schechem ∾ CHARLES REZNIKOFF

You Hebrews are too snug in Ur,
said God; wander about waste places,
north and south leave your dead;
let kings fight against you,
and the heavens rain fire and brimstone
on you. And it was so.
And God looked again and saw
the Hebrews with their sons and daughters
rich in flocks and herds,
with jewels of silver
and jewels of gold.
And God said, Be slaves
to Pharaoh. And it was so.
And God looked again and saw
the Hebrews at the fleshpots,
with fish to eat,
cucumbers and melons.
And God said, Be gone
into the wilderness by the Red Sea
and the wilderness of Shur and the wilderness
of Shin; let Amalek come upon you,
and fiery serpents bite you. And it was so.
And God looked again and saw in a land of brooks and springs
        and fountains,
wheat and barley,
the Hebrews, in a land on which they did not labor,
in cities which they did not build,
eating of vineyards and olive trees which they did not plant.
And God scattered them—
through the cities of the Medes, beside the waters of Babylon;
they fled before Him into Egypt and went down to the sea in ships;
the whales swallowed them,
the birds brought word of them to the king;
the young men met them with weapons of war,
the old men with proverbs—
and God looked and saw the Hebrews
citizens of the great cities,
talking Hebrew in every language under the sun.

24:19–24:27   And Joshua said unto the people, Ye cannot serve the LORD: for he is an holy God; he is a jealous God; he will not forgive your transgressions nor your sins. If ye forsake the LORD, and serve strange gods, then he will turn and do you hurt, and consume you, after that he hath done you good. . . . And Joshua wrote these words in the book of the law of God, and took a great stone, and set it up there under an oak, that was by the sanctuary of the LORD. And Joshua said unto all the people, Behold, this stone shall be a witness unto us; for it hath heard all the words of the LORD which he spake unto us: it shall be therefore a witness unto you, lest ye deny your God.

The Stone   ﾐ   HENRY VAUGHAN

I have it now:
But where to act, that none shall know,
Where I shall have no cause to fear
    An eye or ear,
        What man will show?
If nights, and shades, and secret rooms,
    Silent as tombs,
Will nor conceal nor assent to
My dark designs, what shall I do?
Man I can bribe, and woman will
Consent to any gainful ill,
But these dumb creatures are so true,
No gold nor gifts can them subdue.
'Hedges have ears,' said the old sooth,
'And every bush is something's booth;'
This cautious fools mistake, and fear
Nothing but man, when ambushed there.

        But I (Alas!)
Was shown one day in a strange glass
That busy commerce kept between
God and his creatures, though unseen.

        They hear, see, speak,
And into loud discoveries break,
As loud as blood. Not that God needs
Intelligence, whose spirit feeds

All things with life, before whose eyes,
Hell and all hearts stark naked lies.
But[7] he that judgeth as he hears,
He that accuseth none, so steers
His righteous course, that though he knows
All that man doth, conceals or shows,
Yet will not he by his own light
(Though both all-seeing and all right,)
Condemn men; but will try them by
A process, which even man's own eye
Must needs acknowledge to be just.

    Hence sand and dust
Are shaked for witnesses, and stones
Which some think dead, shall all at once
With one attesting voice detect
Those secret sins we least suspect.
For know, wild men, that when you err
Each thing turns scribe and register,
And in obedience to his Lord,
Doth your most private sins record.

    The Law delivered to the Jews,
Who promised much, but did refuse
Performance, will for that same deed
Against them by a stone proceed;
Whose substance, though 'tis hard enough,
Will prove their hearts more stiff and tough.
But now, since God on himself took
What all mankind could never brook,
If any (for he all invites)
His easy yoke rejects or slights,
The *Gospel* then (for 'tis his word
And not himself[8] shall judge the world)
Will by loose dust that man arraign,
As one than dust more vile and vain.

7 John chap. 5. ver. 30, 45. [Vaughan's note]
8 St. John, chap. 12. ver. 47, 48. [Vaughan's note]

JUDGES

11:29–11:39   Then the Spirit of the LORD came upon Jephthah, and he passed over Gilead, and Manasseh, and passed over Mizpeh of Gilead, and from Mizpeh of Gilead he passed over unto the children of Ammon. And Jephthah vowed a vow unto the LORD, and said, If thou shalt without fail deliver the children of Ammon into mine hands, Then it shall be, that whatsoever cometh forth of the doors of my house to meet me, when I return in peace from the children of Ammon, shall surely be the LORD'S, and I will offer it up for a burnt offering. So Jephthah passed over unto the children of Ammon to fight against them; and the LORD delivered them into his hands. . . . Thus the children of Ammon were subdued before the children of Israel. And Jephthah came to Mizpeh unto his house, and, behold, his daughter came out to meet him with timbrels and with dances: and she was his only child; beside her he had neither son nor daughter. And it came to pass, when he saw her, that he rent his clothes, and said, Alas, my daughter! thou hast brought me very low, and thou art one of them that trouble me: for I have opened my mouth unto the LORD, and I cannot go back.

And she said unto him, My father, if thou hast opened thy mouth unto the LORD, do to me according to that which hath proceeded out of thy mouth; forasmuch as the LORD hath taken vengeance for thee of thine enemies, even of the children of Ammon. And she said unto her father, Let this thing be done for me: let me alone two months, that I may go up and down upon the mountains, and bewail my virginity, I and my fellows. And he said, Go. And he sent her away for two months: and she went with her companions, and bewailed her virginity upon the mountains. And it came to pass at the end of two months, that she returned unto her father, who did with her according to his vow which he had vowed:

Jephtha's Daughter ᢤ
GEORGE NOEL GORDON, LORD BYRON

Since our country, our God—Oh, my sire!
Demand that thy daughter expire;
Since thy triumph was bought by thy vow—
Strike the bosom that's bared for thee now!

And the voice of my mourning is o'er,
And the mountains behold me no more:
If the hand that I love lay me low,
There cannot be pain in the blow!

And of this, oh, my father! be sure —
That the blood of thy child is as pure
As the blessing I beg ere it flow,
And the last thought that soothes me below.

Though the virgins of Salem lament,
Be the judge and the hero unbent!
I have won the great battle for thee,
And my father and country are free!

When this blood of thy giving hath gushed,
When the voice that thou lovest is hushed,
Let my memory still be thy pride,
And forget not I smiled as I died!

13:2–16:9   And there was a certain man of Zorah, of the family of the Danites, whose name was Manoah; and his wife was barren, and bare not. And the angel of the LORD appeared unto the woman, and said unto her, Behold now, thou art barren, and bearest not: but thou shalt conceive, and bear a son. Now therefore beware, I pray thee, and drink not wine nor strong drink, and eat not any unclean thing: For, lo, thou shalt conceive, and bear a son; and no razor shall come on his head: for the child shall be a Nazarite unto God from the womb: and he shall begin to deliver Israel out of the hand of the Philistines. . . . And the woman bare a son, and called his name Samson. . . .

And it came to pass afterward, that he loved a woman in the valley of Sorek, whose name was Delilah. And the lords of the Philistines came up unto her, and said unto her, Entice him, and see wherein his great strength lieth, and by what means we may prevail against him, that we may bind him to afflict him; and we will give thee every one of us eleven hundred pieces of silver. And Delilah said to Samson, Tell me, I pray thee, wherein thy great strength lieth, and wherewith thou mightest be bound to afflict thee. And Samson said unto her, If they bind me with seven green withs that were never dried, then shall I be weak, and be as another man. Then the lords of the Philistines brought up to her seven green withs which had not been dried, and she bound him with them. Now there were men lying in wait, abiding with her in the chamber. And she said unto him, The Philistines be upon thee, Samson. And he brake the withs, as a thread of tow is broken when it toucheth the fire. So his strength was not known.

Angry Samson ⟋ ROBERT GRAVES

Are they blind, the lords of Gaza
    In their strong towers,
Who declare Samson pillow-smothered
    And stripped of his powers?

O stolid Philistines
    Stare now in amaze
At my foxes running in your cornfields
    With their tails ablaze,

At swung jaw-bone, at bees swarming
    In the stark lion's hide,
At these, the gates of well-walled Gaza
    A-clank to my stride.

16:17–16:21   That he told her all his heart, and said unto her, There hath
not come a razor upon mine head; for I have been a Nazarite unto God
from my mother's womb: if I be shaven, then my strength will go from me,
and I shall become weak, and be like any other man. And when Delilah saw
that he had told her all his heart, she sent and called for the lords of the
Philistines, saying, Come up this once, for he hath shewed me all his heart.
Then the lords of the Philistines came up unto her, and brought money in
their hand. And she made him sleep upon her knees; and she called for a
man, and she caused him to shave off the seven locks of his head; and she
began to afflict him, and his strength went from him. And she said, The
Philistines be upon thee, Samson. And he awoke out of his sleep, and said,
I will go out as at other times before, and shake myself. And he wist not
that the LORD was departed from him. But the Philistines took him, and
put out his eyes, and brought him down to Gaza, and bound him with fet-
ters of brass; and he did grind in the prison house.

Samson to his Delilah ⟋ RICHARD CRASHAW

Could not once blinding me, cruel, suffice?
When first I looked on thee, I lost mine eyes.

16:22   Howbeit the hair of his head began to grow again after he was shaven.

from *Samson Agonistes*   ~   JOHN MILTON
ll. 53–114

But what is strength without a double share
Of wisdom, vast, unwieldy, burdensome,
Proudly secure, yet liable to fall
By weakest subtleties, not made to rule,
But to subserve where wisdom bears command.
God, when he gave me strength, to show withal
How slight the gift was, hung it in my hair.
But peace, I must not quarrel with the will
Of highest dispensation, which herein
Haply had ends above my reach to know:
Suffices that to me strength is my bane,
And proves the source of all my miseries;
So many, and so huge, that each apart
Would ask a life to wail, but chief of all,
O loss of sight, of thee I most complain!
Blind among enemies, O worse than chains,
Dungeon, or beggary, or decrepit age!
Light the prime work of God to me is extinct,
And all her various objects of delight
Annulled, which might in part my grief have eased,
Inferior to the vilest now become
Of man or worm; the vilest here excel me,
They creep, yet see, I dark in light exposed
To daily fraud, contempt, abuse, and wrong,
Within doors, or without, still as a fool,
In power of others, never in my own;
Scarce half I seem to live, dead more than half.
O dark, dark, dark, amid the blaze of noon,
Irrecoverably dark, total eclipse
Without all hope of day!
O first created Beam, and thou great Word,
"Let there be light, and light was over all";
Why am I thus bereaved thy prime decree?
The sun to me is dark
And silent as the moon,
When she deserts the night

Hid in her vacant interlunar cave.
Since light so necessary is to life,
And almost life itself, if it be true
That light is in the soul,
She all in every part; why was the sight
To such a tender ball as th' eye confined?
So obvious and so easy to be quenched,
And not as feeling through all parts diffused,
That she might look at will through every pore?
Then had I not been thus exiled from light;
As in the land of darkness yet in light,
To live a life half dead, a living death,
And buried; but O yet more miserable!
My self, my sepulcher, a moving grave,
Buried, yet not exempt
By privilege of death and burial
From worst of other evils, pains and wrongs,
But made hereby obnoxious more
To all the miseries of life,
Life in captivity
Among inhuman foes.
But who are these?

16:23–16:30   Then the lords of the Philistines gathered them together for to
offer a great sacrifice unto Dagon their god, and to rejoice: for they said, Our
god hath delivered Samson our enemy into our hand. And when the people
saw him, they praised their god: for they said, Our god hath delivered into our
hands our enemy, and the destroyer of our country, which slew many of us.
And it came to pass, when their hearts were merry, that they said, Call for
Samson, that he may make us sport. And they called for Samson out of the
prison house; and he made them sport: and they set him between the pillars.
And Samson said unto the lad that held him by the hand, Suffer me that I may
feel the pillars whereupon the house standeth, that I may lean upon them. . . .

The Warning   ৵   HENRY WADSWORTH LONGFELLOW

Beware! The Israelite of old, who tore
    The lion in his path,—when, poor and blind,
He saw the blessed light of heaven no more
    Shorn of his noble strength and forced to grind

In prison, and at last led forth to be
A pander to Philistine revelry,—

Upon the pillars of the temple laid
    His desperate hands, and in its overthrow
Destroyed himself, and with him those who made
    A cruel mockery of his sightless woe;
The poor, blind slave, the scoff and jest of all,
Expired, and thousands perished in the fall!

There is a poor, blind Samson in this land,
    Shorn of his strength and bound in bonds of steel,
Who may, in some grim revel, raise his hand,
    And shake the pillars of this Commonweal,
Till the vast temple of our liberties
A shapeless mass of wreck and rubbish lies.

FIRST SAMUEL

1:1–1:20   Now there was a certain man of Ramathaimzophim, of mount
Ephraim, and his name was Elkanah, the son of Jeroham, the son of Elihu,
the son of Tohu, the son of Zuph, an Ephrathite: And he had two wives; the
name of the one was Hannah, and the name of the other Peninnah: and
Peninnah had children, but Hannah had no children. . . . And she was in
bitterness of soul, and prayed unto the LORD, and wept sore. And she
vowed a vow, and said, O LORD of hosts, if thou wilt indeed look on the
affliction of thine handmaid, and remember me, and not forget thine hand-
maid, but wilt give unto thine handmaid a man child, then I will give him
unto the LORD all the days of his life, and there shall no razor come upon
his head. . . . Wherefore it came to pass, when the time was come about
after Hannah had conceived, that she bare a son, and called his name
Samuel, saying, Because I have asked him of the LORD.

Hope   ↭   CHRISTOPHER SMART

Ah! Hannah, why shouldst thou despair,
    Quick to the tabernacle speed;
There on thy knees prefer thy prayer,
    And there thy cause to mercy plead.

Her pious breathings now ascend,
    As from her heart the sighs she heaves;
And angels to her suit attend,
    Till strong in hope she now conceives.

Then Samuel soon was brought to light
    To serve the Lord, as yet a child—
O what a heart-reviving sight!
    Sure cherubims and seraphs smiled.

Thus yet a child may I begin
    To serve the Lord with all my heart;
To shun the wily lures of sin,
    And claim the prize, or e'er I start.

16:19–17:50   Wherefore Saul sent messengers unto Jesse, and said, Send
me David thy son, which is with the sheep. . . . And David came to Saul, and
stood before him: and he loved him greatly; and he became his armour-
bearer. And Saul sent to Jesse, saying, Let David, I pray thee, stand before me;
for he hath found favour in my sight. And it came to pass, when the evil spirit
from God was upon Saul, that David took an harp, and played with his hand:
so Saul was refreshed, and was well, and the evil spirit departed from him.

Now the Philistines gathered together their armies to battle. . . . And
there went out a champion out of the camp of the Philistines, named
Goliath, of Gath, whose height was six cubits and a span. . . .

And David said to Saul, Let no man's heart fail because of him; thy ser-
vant will go and fight with this Philistine. . . . And he took his staff in his
hand, and chose him five smooth stones out of the brook, and put them in a
shepherd's bag which he had, even in a scrip; and his sling was in his hand:
and he drew near to the Philistine. And the Philistine came on and drew near
unto David; and the man that bare the shield went before him. And when the
Philistine looked about, and saw David, he disdained him: for he was but a
youth, and ruddy, and of a fair countenance. And the Philistine said unto
David, Am I a dog, that thou comest to me with staves? And the Philistine
cursed David by his gods. And the Philistine said to David, Come to me, and
I will give thy flesh unto the fowls of the air, and to the beasts of the field.

Then said David to the Philistine, Thou comest to me with a sword, and
with a spear, and with a shield: but I come to thee in the name of the LORD
of hosts, the God of the armies of Israel, whom thou hast defied. This day
will the LORD deliver thee into mine hand; and I will smite thee, and take
thine head from thee; and I will give the carcases of the host of the

Philistines this day unto the fowls of the air, and to the wild beasts of the earth; that all the earth may know that there is a God in Israel. And all this assembly shall know that the LORD saveth not with sword and spear: for the battle is the LORD'S, and he will give you into our hands.

And it came to pass, when the Philistine arose, and came, and drew nigh to meet David, that David hasted, and ran toward the army to meet the Philistine. And David put his hand in his bag, and took thence a stone, and slang it, and smote the Philistine in his forehead, that the stone sunk into his forehead; and he fell upon his face to the earth. So David prevailed over the Philistine with a sling and with a stone, and smote the Philistine, and slew him; but there was no sword in the hand of David.

I took my Power in my Hand – 〜 EMILY DICKINSON

I took my Power in my Hand –
And went against the World –
'Twas not so much as David – had –
But I – was twice as bold –

I aimed my Pebble – but Myself
Was all the one that fell –
Was it Goliath – was too large –
Or was myself – too small?

17:51   Therefore David ran, and stood upon the Philistine, and took his sword, and drew it out of the sheath thereof, and slew him, and cut off his head therewith. And when the Philistines saw their champion was dead, they fled.

David and Goliath 〜 P. HATELY WADDELL

This bit lilt o' his ain till David's Praise,
Whan he fought again Goliath,
Stan's like a to-fa' till the Psalms
                    [Quo' the LXX.]

Sma' was I, amang brether o' mine;
An' the bairn was I, i' my faither's ha';

My faither's fe I was hirdin:
My han's, they wrought the organ fine;
An' my fingers, wi' thairms, the harp an' a'
    They war girdin.

An' wha was 't tell'd the Lord o' me?
The Lord himsel, he hearken'd till me;
An' his rinner he sent, an' he cried me awa—
    Cried me awa frae my faither's fe;
An' wi' chrystin oyle o' his ain an' a',
    He chrystit me:
Brether o' mine, they war brave an' braw;
    An' the Lord o' them wad hae nought ava'.

Furth gaed I, till fecht wi' the frem;
    Syne by his eidols he swure at me:
Bot that swurd o' his ain, I claught it frae him;
An' I sned his head frae his shouthirs trim;
An' the skaith an' the scorn I carried it a',
    Frae the folk o' Israel, hame wi' me!

18:14   And David behaved himself wisely in all his ways; and the LORD
was with him.

I do not believe that David killed Goliath ✒
CHARLES REZNIKOFF

I do not believe that David killed Goliath.
It must have been—
you will find the name in the list of David's captains.
But, whoever it was, he was no fool
when he took off the helmet
and put down the sword and the spear and the shield
and said, The weapons you have given me are good,
but they are not mine:
I will fight in my own way
with a couple of pebbles and a sling.

31:1   Now the Philistines fought against Israel: and the men of Israel fled
from before the Philistines, and fell down slain in mount Gilboa.

Song of Saul Before his Last Battle ᴣ
GEORGE NOEL GORDON, LORD BYRON

Warriors and chiefs! should the shaft or the sword
Pierce me in leading the host of the Lord,
Heed not the corse, though a king's, in your path:
Bury your steel in the bosoms of Gath!

Thou who art bearing my buckler and bow,
Should the soldiers of Saul look away from the foe,
Stretch me that moment in blood at thy feet!
Mine be the doom which they dared not to meet!

Farewell to others, but never we part,
Heir to my royalty, son of my heart!
Bright is the diadem, boundless the sway,
Or kingly the death, which awaits us to-day!

31:2–31:6   And the Philistines followed hard upon Saul and upon his sons;
and the Philistines slew Jonathan, and Abinadab, and Melchishua, Saul's
sons. And the battle went sore against Saul, and the archers hit him; and he
was sore wounded of the archers. Then said Saul unto his armourbearer,
Draw thy sword, and thrust me through therewith; lest these uncircumcised
come and thrust me through, and abuse me. But his armourbearer would
not; for he was sore afraid. Therefore Saul took a sword, and fell upon it.
And when his armourbearer saw that Saul was dead, he fell likewise upon
his sword, and died with him. So Saul died, and his three sons, and his
armourbearer, and all his men, that same day together.

The Death of Saul ᴣ   PHILIP LEVINE

"Is Saul also among the prophets?"
                    1 Samuel 10

The sleeping armies of the living God
Embraced the King who could not wake or sleep.

Their faith in him who had no will to faith
Or faith but theirs was more than he could bear.
Hearing their leader scream, they roused, unarmed,
Unsure of what they heard—the needs of terror
Calling through sleep—nor did they understand
When, later, beside a stream, they strapped on armour,
Blessed and buckled halters, received their vows,
The soldier's vows which they would not fulfill
Until they clasped the final lack of peace.

All roads led upward to the mountain top
Where he would flush the partridge of the hills,
David the stave with which God whipped his fury:
A fury that was love, a love of self.
He thought he saw him riding next to him,
Turned on his mount, thrilling the wayward flanks
That stretched below. This time he could not speak,
And when they leaned to touch he saw his son.
Not for the loss of David did he weep,
But for the knowledge gained: the fear of death
Was but a shadow of the power of love,
Though death had fixed those eyes which turned toward his.
Beyond the olive line, on sun-bleached rocks,
The Philistines were closing ranks to charge.
Violent, Godless, their prayer for strength at arms
Descended like the driving words of God
On those below, aching for certitude.
The archers done, the first waves met and broke;
The flanks closed in and locked; both forces joined,
Their differences obscured in smoke and dust.
Habit or need? His dead and dying troops
Would never know what drove King Saul to kneel,
A penitent upon those burning slopes,
Finding, too late, in every Godless act
And every act of will the will of God.

And Jonathan was dead; the hope of Saul
A trophy wrapped in scarlet, lovingly;
His brothers slain, their armour-bearers fled
And crouched and wept by Saul, who knew too well
The messages they lacked the strength to give.

A King of God in death, he persevered;
Pride against pride deployed until it failed.
His wounded ceased their cries. He was alone.
The sword by which he lived was all he had,
And so he turned to it, knowing the act
Would end his name and heritage forever,
Knowing the way, far from his living love,
Far from the shepherd boy conceived in grace,
And further still from Him he could not name.

SECOND SAMUEL

3:1–6:15   . . . Then came all the tribes of Israel to David unto Hebron, . . .
and king David made a league with them in Hebron before the LORD: and
they anointed David king over Israel. David was thirty years old when he
began to reign, and he reigned forty years. . . .

Again, David gathered together all the chosen men of Israel, thirty thou-
sand. And David arose, and went with all the people that were with him
from Baale of Judah, to bring up from thence the ark of God, whose name
is called by the name of the LORD of hosts that dwelleth between the cheru-
bims. And they set the ark of God upon a new cart, and brought it out of
the house of Abinadab that was in Gibeah: and Uzzah and Ahio, the sons of
Abinadab, drave the new cart. . . .

And David danced before the LORD with all his might; and David was
girded with a linen ephod. So David and all the house of Israel brought up
the ark of the LORD with shouting, and with the sound of the trumpet.

David ꝏ   CHARLES REZNIKOFF

The shadow does not leave my feet,
how shrunken now it lies;
with sunshine I am anointed king,
I leap before the ark, I sing;
I seem to walk but I dance about,
you think me silent but I shout.

6:16–20   And as the ark of the LORD came into the city of David, Michal
Saul's daughter looked through a window, and saw king David leaping and
dancing before the LORD; and she despised him in her heart. And they
brought in the ark of the LORD, and set it in his place, in the midst of the
tabernacle that David had pitched for it: and David offered burnt offerings
and peace offerings before the LORD. . . .

   Then David returned to bless his household. And Michal the daughter of
Saul came out to meet David, and said, How glorious was the king of Israel
today, who uncovered himself today in the eyes of the handmaids of his
servants, as one of the vain fellows shamelessly uncovereth himself!

King David Dances ﹏ JOHN BERRYMAN

Aware to the dry throat of the wide hell in the world,
O trampling empires, and mine one of them,
and mine one gross desire against His sight,
slaughter devising there,
some good behind, ambiguous ahead,
revolted sons, a pierced son, bound to hear,
mid hypocrites amongst idolaters,
mocked in abysm by one shallow wife,
with the ponder both of priesthood & of State
heavy upon me, yea,
all the black same I dance my blue head off!

11:2   And it came to pass in an eveningtide, that David arose from off
his bed, and walked upon the roof of the king's house: and from the roof
he saw a woman washing herself; and the woman was very beautiful to
look upon.

from *Love of King David and Fair Bethsabe* ﹏
GEORGE PEELE

Hot sun, cool fire, tempered with sweet air,
Black shade, fair nurse, shadow my white hair.
Shine, sun; burn, fire; breathe, air, and ease me;
Shadow, my sweet nurse, keep me from burning,
Make not my glad cause cause of mourning.

Let not my beauty's fire
Inflame unstaid desire,
Nor pierce any bright eye
That wandereth lightly.

11:3–12:7   And David sent and enquired after the woman. And one said, Is not this Bathsheba, the daughter of Eliam, the wife of Uriah the Hittite? And David sent messengers, and took her; and she came in unto him, and he lay with her. . . .

And the LORD sent Nathan unto David. And he came unto him, and said unto him, There were two men in one city; the one rich, and the other poor. The rich man had exceeding many flocks and herds: But the poor man had nothing, save one little ewe lamb, which he had bought and nourished up: and it grew up together with him, and with his children; it did eat of his own meat, and drank of his own cup, and lay in his bosom, and was unto him as a daughter. And there came a traveller unto the rich man, and he spared to take of his own flock and of his own herd, to dress for the wayfaring man that was come unto him; but took the poor man's lamb, and dressed it for the man that was come to him.

And David's anger was greatly kindled against the man; and he said to Nathan, As the LORD liveth, the man that hath done this thing shall surely die: And he shall restore the lamb fourfold, because he did this thing, and because he had no pity.

And Nathan said to David, Thou art the man. . . .

from *Penitential Psalms*   ✣   SIR THOMAS WYATT
Prologue

Love to give law unto his subject hearts
Stood in the eyes of Barsabe the bright,
And in a look anon himself converts
Cruelly pleasant before King David's sight;
First dazed his eyes, and further forth he starts
With venomed breath, as softly as he might
Touched his senses, and overruns his bones
With creeping fire, sparpled for the nonce.

And when he saw that kindled was the flame,
The moist poison in his heart he lanced,

So that the soul did tremble with the same.
And in this brawl as he stood and tranced,
Yielding unto the figure and the frame
That those fair eyes had in his presence glanced,
The form that Love had printed in his breast
He honoreth as thing of things the best.

So that forgot the wisdom and forecast
(Which woes to realms when that these kings doth lack),
Forgetting eke God's majesty as fast,
Yea, and his own, forthwith he doth to make
Uriah to go into the field in haste,
Uriah I say, that was his idols make,
Under pretence of certain victory
For enemies' swords a ready prey to die.

Whereby he may enjoy her out of doubt
Whom more than God or himself he mindeth.
And after he had brought this thing about
And of that lust possessed himself, he findeth
That hath and doth reverse and clean turn out
Kings from kingdoms, and cities undermineth:
He blinded thinks this train so bold and close
To blind all thing that nought may it disclose.

But Nathan hath spied out this treachery,
With rueful cheer and sets afore his face
The offence, outrage and injury
That he hath done to God, as in this case
By murder for to cloak adultery.
He showeth him eke from heaven the threats alas
So sternly sore, this prophet, this Nathan,
That all amazed this aged woeful man.

Like him that meets with horror and with fear
The heat doth straight forsake the limbs cold;
The color eke droopeth down from his cheer,
So doth he feel his fire manifold;
His heat, his lust and pleasure all in fear
Consume and waste, and straight his crown of gold,
His purple pall, his sceptre he lets fall,
And to the ground he throwth himself withal.

The pompous pride of state and dignity
Forthwith rebates repentant humbleness;
Thinner vile cloth than clotheth poverty
Doth scantly hide and clad his nakedness;
His fair hoar beard of reverent gravity
With ruffled hair, knowing his wickedness,
More like was he the selfsame repentance
Than stately prince of worldly governance.

His harp he taketh in hand to be his guide,
Wherewith he offereth his plaints his soul to save
That from his heart distills on every side,
Withdrawing him into a dark cave
Within the ground, wherein he might him hide,
Fleeing the light, as in prison or grave:
In which as soon as David entered had
The dark horror did make his soul adrad.

But he without prolonging or delay
Of that that might his Lord his God appease
Fallth on his knees, and with his harp I say
Afore his breast, fraughted with disease
Of stormy sighs, his cheer coloured like clay,
Dressed upright, seeking to counterpese
His song with sighs and touching of the strings
With tender heart, . . . to God he sings.

12:7–12:13   Thus saith the LORD God of Israel, I anointed thee king over Israel, and I delivered thee out of the hand of Saul; And I gave thee thy master's house, and thy master's wives into thy bosom, and gave thee the house of Israel and of Judah; and if that had been too little, I would moreover have given unto thee such and such things. Wherefore hast thou despised the commandment of the LORD, to do evil in his sight? thou hast killed Uriah the Hittite with the sword, and hast taken his wife to be thy wife, and hast slain him with the sword of the children of Ammon. Now therefore the sword shall never depart from thine house; because thou hast despised me, and hast taken the wife of Uriah the Hittite to be thy wife. Thus saith the LORD, Behold, I will raise up evil against thee out of thine own house, and I will take thy wives before thine eyes, and give them unto thy neighbour, and

he shall lie with thy wives in the sight of this sun. For thou didst it secretly:
but I will do this thing before all Israel, and before the sun.

And David said unto Nathan, I have sinned against the LORD. . . .

David's *Peccavi* ₰ ROBERT SOUTHWELL

In eaves sole sparrow sits not more alone,
   Nor mourning pelican in desert wild,
Than seely I, that solitary moan,
   From highest hopes to hardest hap exiled:
Sometime, O blissful time! was virtue's mead.
Aim to my thoughts, guide to my word and deed.

But fears are now my feres, grief my delight,
   My tears my drink, my famished thoughts my bread;
Day full of dumps, nurse of unrest the night,
   My garments gyves, a bloody field my bed;
My sleep is rather death than death's ally,
Yet killed with murdering pangs I cannot die.

This is the change of my ill changed choice,
   Ruth for my rest, for comforts cares I find:
To pleasing tunes succeeds a plaining voice,
   The doleful echo of my wailing mind;
Which, taught to know the worth of virtue's joys,
Doth hate itself, for loving fancy's toys.

If wiles of wit had overwrought my will,
   Or subtle trains mislead my steps awry,
My foil had found excuse in want of skill,
   Ill deed I might, though not ill doom, deny.
But wit and will must now confess with shame,
Both deed and doom to have deserved blame.

I fancy deemed fit guide to lead my way,
   And as I deemed I did pursue her track,
Wit lost his aim and will was fancy's prey;
   The rebel won, the ruler went to wrack.
But now since fancy did with folly end,
Wit bought with loss, will taught by wit, will mend.

14:14   For we must needs die, and are as water spilt on the ground, which
cannot be gathered up again; neither doth God respect any person: yet doth
he devise means, that his banished be not expelled from him.

The Rabbi's Song   ❧   RUDYARD KIPLING

If thought can reach to Heaven,
    On Heaven let it dwell,
For fear thy Thought be given
    Like power to reach Hell.
For fear the desolation
    And darkness of thy mind
Perplex an habitation
    Which thou hast left behind.

Let nothing linger after—
    No whimpering ghost remain,
In wall, or beam, or rafter,
    Of any hate or pain.
Cleanse and call home thy spirit,
    Deny her leave to cast,
On aught thy heirs inherit,
    The shadow of her past.

For think, in all thy sadness,
    What road our griefs may take;
Whose brain reflect our madness,
    Or whom our terrors shake:
For think, lest any languish
    By cause of thy distress—
The arrows of our anguish
    Fly farther than we guess.

Our lives, our tears, as water,
    Are spilled upon the ground;
God giveth no man quarter,
    Yet God a means hath found,
Though Faith and Hope have vanished,
    And even Love grows dim—
A means whereby His banished
    Be not expelled from Him!

23:8–23:17   These be the names of the mighty men whom David had: . . .
And three of the thirty chief went down, and came to David in the harvest
time unto the cave of Adullam: and the troop of the Philistines pitched in
the valley of Rephaim. And David was then in an hold, and the garrison of
the Philistines was then in Bethlehem. And David longed, and said, Oh that
one would give me drink of the water of the well of Bethlehem, which is by
the gate! And the three mighty men brake through the host of the
Philistines, and drew water out of the well of Bethlehem, that was by the
gate, and took it, and brought it to David: nevertheless he would not drink
thereof, but poured it out unto the LORD. And he said, Be it far from me, O
LORD, that I should do this: is not this the blood of the men that went in
jeopardy of their lives? therefore he would not drink it. These things did
these three mighty men.

David in the Cave of Adullam   ✍   CHARLES LAMB

David and his three captains bold
Kept ambush once within a hold.
It was in Adullam's cave,
Nigh which no water they could have,
Nor spring, nor running brook was near
To quench the thirst that parched them there.
Then David, king of Israel,
Straight bethought him of a well,
Which stood beside the city gate,
At Bethlem; where, before his state
Of kingly dignity, he had
Oft drunk his fill, a shepherd lad;
But now his fierce Philistine foe
Encamped before it he does know.
Yet ne'er the less, with heat oppressed,
Those three bold captains he addressed;
And wished that one to him would bring
Some water from his native spring.
His valiant captains instantly
To execute his will did fly.
The mighty Three the ranks broke through
Of armed foes, and water drew
For David, their beloved king,
At his own sweet native spring.

Back through their armed foes they haste,
With the hard-earned treasure graced.
But when the good king David found
What they had done, he on the ground
The water poured. "Because," said he,
"That it was at the jeopardy
Of your three lives this thing ye did,
That I should drink it, God forbid."

FIRST KINGS
combined with
FIRST and SECOND CHRONICLES

FIRST KINGS 1:1–1:4   Now king David was old and stricken in years; and they covered him with clothes, but he gat no heat. Wherefore his servants said unto him, Let there be sought for my lord the king a young virgin: and let her stand before the king, and let her cherish him, and let her lie in thy bosom, that my lord the king may get heat. So they sought for a fair damsel throughout all the coasts of Israel, and found Abishag a Shunammite, and brought her to the king. And the damsel was very fair, and cherished the king, and ministered to him: but the king knew her not.

Provide, Provide ✌ ROBERT FROST

The witch that came (the withered hag)
To wash the steps with pail and rag
Was once the beauty Abishag,

The picture pride of Hollywood.
Too many fall from great and good
For you to doubt the likelihood.

Die early and avoid the fate
Or if predestined to die late
Make up your mind to die in state.

Make the whole stock exchange your own!
If need be, occupy a throne,
Where nobody can call *you* crone.

Some have relied on what they knew,
Others on simply being true.
What worked for them might work for you.

No memory of having starred
Atones for later disregard
Or keeps the end from being hard.

Better to go down dignified
With boughten friendship at your side
Than none at all. Provide, provide!

FIRST KINGS 2:1–2:11   Now the days of David drew nigh that he should die; and he charged Solomon his son, saying, I go the way of all the earth: be thou strong therefore, and shew thyself a man; And keep the charge of the LORD thy God, to walk in his ways, to keep his statutes, and his commandments, and his judgments, and his testimonies, as it is written in the law of Moses, that thou mayest prosper in all that thou doest, and whithersoever thou turnest thyself: That the LORD may continue his word which he spake concerning me, saying, If thy children take heed to their way, to walk before me in truth with all their heart and with all their soul, there shall not fail thee (said he) a man on the throne of Israel. . . .

So David slept with his fathers, and was buried in the city of David. And the days that David reigned over Israel were forty years: seven years reigned he in Hebron, and thirty and three years reigned he in Jerusalem

In Salem Dwelt a Glorious King ᴄᴈ THOMAS TRAHERNE

In Salem dwelt a glorious king,
    Raised from a shepherd's lowly state,
That did his praises like an angel sing
        Who did the world create.
    By many great and bloody wars,
    He was advanced unto thrones:
    But more delighted in the stars,
Than in the splendor of his precious stones.
Nor gold nor silver did his eye regard:
The works of God were his sublime reward.

A warlike champion he had been,
And many feats of chivalry
Had done: in kingly courts his eye had seen
A vast variety
Of earthly joys: Yet he despised
Those fading honors and false pleasures
Which are by mortals so much prized;
And placed his happiness in other treasures.
No state of life which in this world we find
Could yield contentment to his greater mind.

His fingers touched his trembling lyre,
And every quavering string did yield
A sound that filled all the Jewish choir,
And echoed in the field.
No pleasure was so great to him
As in a silent night to see
The moon and stars: a cherubim
Above them even here he seemed to be.
Enflamed with love, it was his great desire
To sing, contemplate, ponder, and admire.

He was a prophet, and foresaw
Things extant in the world to come:
He was a judge, and ruled by a law
That than the honey comb
Was sweeter far: He was a sage,
And all his people could advise;
An oracle, whose every page
Contained in verse the greatest mysteries
But most he then enjoyed himself when he
Did as a poet praise the Deity.

A shepherd, soldier, and divine,
A judge, a courtier, and a king,
Priest, angel, prophet, oracle, did shine
At once; when he did sing.
Philosopher and poet too
Did in his melody appear;
All these in him did please the view

Of those that did his heavenly music hear,
And every drop that from his flowing quill
Came down, did all the world with nectar fill.

    He had a deep and perfect sense
    Of all the glories and the pleasures
That in God's works are hid, the excellence
        Of such transcendent treasures
    Made him on Earth an heavenly king,
    And filled his solitudes with joy;
    He never did more sweetly sing
Than when alone, though that doth mirth destroy:
Sense did his soul with heavenly life inspire
And made him seem in God's celestial choir.

    Rich, sacred, deep, and precious things
    Did here on Earth the man surround:
With all the glory of the King of Kings
        He was most strangely crowned.
    His clear soul and open sight
    Among the sons of God did see
    Things filling angels with delight
His ear did hear their heavenly melody
And when he was alone he all became
That bliss implied, or did increase his fame.

    All arts he then did exercise
    And as his God he did adore,
By secret ravishments above the skies
        He carried was, before
    He died. His soul did see and feel
    What others know not; and became
    While he before his God did kneel,
A constant heavenly pure seraphic flame.
O that I might unto his throne aspire;
And all his joys above the stars admire!

The Harp the Monarch Minstrel Swept ౨ఎ

GEORGE NOEL GORDON, LORD BYRON

The harp the monarch minstrel swept,
    The king of men, the loved of Heaven,
Which music hallowed while she wept
    O'er tones her heart of hearts had given,
    Redoubled be her tears, its chords are riven!
It softened men of iron mould,
    It gave them virtues not their own;
No ear so dull, no soul so cold,
    That felt not, fired not to the tone,
    Till David's lyre grew mightier than his throne!

It told the triumphs of our king,
    It wafted glory to our God;
It made our gladdened valleys ring,
    The cedars bow, the mountains nod;
    Its sound aspired to heaven and there abode!
Since then, though heard on earth no more,
    Devotion and her daughter Love
Still bid the bursting spirit soar
    To sounds that seem as from above,
    In dreams that day's broad light can not remove.

SECOND CHRONICLES 1:1   And Solomon the son of David was strength-
ened in his kingdom, and the LORD his God was with him, and magnified
him exceedingly.

FIRST KINGS 3:5–4:34   In Gibeon the LORD appeared to Solomon in a
dream by night: and God said, Ask what I shall give thee.
    And Solomon said, . . . O LORD my God, thou hast made thy servant
king instead of David my father: and I am but a little child: I know not how
to go out or come in. . . . Give therefore thy servant an understanding heart
to judge thy people, that I may discern between good and bad: for who is
able to judge this thy so great a people?
    . . . And God gave Solomon wisdom and understanding exceeding
much, and largeness of heart, even as the sand that is on the sea shore.
And Solomon's wisdom excelled the wisdom of all the children of the east
country, and all the wisdom of Egypt. . . . And he spake three thousand

proverbs: and his songs were a thousand and five. And he spake of trees, from the cedar tree that is in Lebanon even unto the hyssop that springeth out of the wall: he spake also of beasts, and of fowl, and of creeping things, and of fishes. And there came of all people to hear the wisdom of Solomon, from all kings of the earth, which had heard of his wisdom.

O to be a Dragon ↭ MARIANNE MOORE

If I, like Solomon,. . .
could have my wish—

my wish . . . O to be a dragon,
a symbol of the power of Heaven—of silkworm
size or immense; at times invisible.
  Felicitous phenomenon!

FIRST KINGS 6:14–7:51   So Solomon built the house, and finished it. And he built the walls of the house within with boards of cedar, . . . and he covered them on the inside with wood, and covered the floor of the house with planks of fir. . . . And the cedar of the house within was carved with knops and open flowers: all was cedar; there was no stone seen. And the oracle he prepared in the house within, to set there the ark of the covenant of the LORD. . . .

So Solomon overlaid the house within with pure gold: and he made a partition by the chains of gold before the oracle; and he overlaid it with gold. And the whole house he overlaid with gold, until he had finished all the house: also the whole altar that was by the oracle he overlaid with gold. . . . And he carved all the walls of the house round about with carved figures of cherubims and palm trees and open flowers, within and without. And the floor of the house he overlaid with gold, within and without. . . . And Solomon made all the vessels that pertained unto the house of the LORD: the altar of gold, and the table of gold, whereupon the shewbread was, And the candlesticks of pure gold, five on the right side, and five on the left, before the oracle, with the flowers, and the lamps, and the tongs of gold, And the bowls, and the snuffers, and the basons, and the spoons, and the censers of pure gold; and the hinges of gold, both for the doors of the inner house, the most holy place. . . .

So was ended all the work that king Solomon made for the house of the LORD. And Solomon brought in the things which David his father had dedicated; even the silver, and the gold, and the vessels, did he put among the treasures of the house of the LORD.

Sion ♄ GEORGE HERBERT

Lord, with what glory wast thou served of old,
When Solomon's temple stood and flourished!
   Where most things were of purest gold;
   The wood was all embellished
With flowers and carvings, mystical and rare:
All showed the builders, craved the seers care.

Yet all this glory, all this pomp and state
Did not affect thee much, was not thy aim;
   Something there was, that sowed debate:
   Wherefore thou quitt'st thy ancient claim
And now thy architecture meets with sin;
For all thy frame and fabric is within.

There thou art struggling with a peevish heart,
Which sometimes crosseth thee, thou sometimes it:
   The fight is hard on either part.
   Great God doth fight, he doth submit.
All Solomon's sea of brass and world of stone
Is not so dear to thee as one good groan.

And truly brass and stones are heavy things,
Tombs for the dead, not temples fit for thee:
   But groans are quick, and full of wings,
   And all their motions upward be;
And ever as they mount, like larks they sing;
The note is sad, yet music for a king.

FIRST KINGS 10:1–10:9   And when the queen of Sheba heard of the fame of Solomon concerning the name of the LORD, she came to prove him with hard questions. And she came to Jerusalem with a very great train, with camels that bare spices, and very much gold, and precious stones: and when she was come to Solomon, she communed with him of all that was in her heart. And Solomon told her all her questions: there was not any thing hid from the king, which he told her not. And when the queen of Sheba had seen all Solomon's wisdom, and the house that he had built, And the meat of his table, and the sitting of his servants, and the attendance of his ministers, and their apparel, and his cupbearers, and his ascent by which he went up unto the house of the LORD; there was no more spirit in her. And she said to the king, It was a true report that I heard in mine own land of thy acts and of thy wisdom. Howbeit I believed not the words, until I came, and mine eyes had seen it: and, behold, the half was not told me: thy wisdom and prosperity exceedeth the fame which I heard. Happy are thy men, happy are these thy servants, which stand continually before thee, and that hear thy wisdom. Blessed be the LORD thy God, which delighted in thee, to set thee on the throne of Israel: because the LORD loved Israel for ever, therefore made he thee king, to do judgment and justice.

King Solomon and the Ants ✺
JOHN GREENLEAF WHITTIER

Out from Jerusalem
    The King rode with his great
    War chiefs and lords of state,
And Sheba's queen with them;

Comely, but black withal,
    To whom, perchance, belongs
    That wondrous Song of songs,
Sensuous and mystical,

Whereto devout souls turn
    In fond, ecstatic dream,
    And through its earth-born theme
The Love of loves discern.

Proud in the Syrian sun,
    In gold and purple sheen,
    The dusky Ethiop queen
Smiled on King Solomon.

Wisest of men, he knew
    The languages of all
    The creatures great or small
That trod the earth or flew.

Across an ant-hill led
      The king's path, and he heard
      Its small folk, and their word
He thus interpreted:

"Here comes the king men greet
      As wise and good and just,
      To crush us in the dust
Under his heedless feet."

The great king bowed his head,
      And saw the wide surprise
      Of the Queen of Sheba's eyes
As he told her what they said.

"O king!" she whispered sweet,
      "Too happy fate have they
      Who perish in thy way
Beneath thy gracious feet!

"Thou of the God-lent crown,
      Shall these vile creatures dare
      Murmur against thee where
The knees of kings kneel down?"

"Nay," Solomon replied,
      "The wise and strong should seek
      The welfare of the weak,"
And turned his horse aside.

His train, with quick alarm
      Curved with their leader round
      The ant-hill's peopled mound
And left it free from harm.

The jewelled head bent low;
      "O king!" she said, "henceforth
      The secret of thy worth
And wisdom I well know.

"Happy must be the state
  Whose ruler heedeth more
  The murmurs of the poor
Than the flatteries of the great."

FIRST KINGS 19:1–19:13   . . . And he said, Go forth, and stand upon the mount before the LORD. And, behold, the LORD passed by, and a great and strong wind rent the mountains, and brake in pieces the rocks before the LORD; but the LORD was not in the wind: and after the wind an earthquake; but the LORD was not in the earthquake: And after the earthquake a fire; but the LORD was not in the fire: and after the fire a still small voice.

And it was so, when Elijah heard it, that he wrapped his face in his mantle, and went out, and stood in the entering in of the cave. And, behold, there came a voice unto him, and said, What doest thou here, Elijah?

A Successful Summer ᛉ DAVID SCHUBERT

The still small voice unto
My still small voice, I listen.
Hardly awake, I breathe, vulnerably,
As in summer trees, the messages
Of telegraphed errands buzz along
July's contour of green.

SECOND KINGS
combined with
FIRST and SECOND CHRONICLES

SECOND KINGS 2:1–2:11   . . . And it came to pass, when they were gone over, that Elijah said unto Elisha, Ask what I shall do for thee, before I be taken away from thee. And Elisha said, I pray thee, let a double portion of thy spirit be upon me. And he said, Thou hast asked a hard thing: nevertheless, if thou see me when I am taken from thee, it shall be so unto thee; but if not, it shall not be so. And it came to pass, as they still went on, and talked, that, behold, there appeared a chariot of fire, and horses of fire, and parted them both asunder; and Elijah went up by a whirlwind into heaven.

And did those feet ✍ WILLIAM BLAKE

And did those feet in ancient time
Walk upon England's mountains green?
And was the holy Lamb of God
On England's pleasant pastures seen?

And did the Countenance Divine
Shine forth upon our clouded hills?
And was Jerusalem builded here
Among these dark Satanic Mills?

Bring me my bow of burning gold:
Bring me my Arrows of desire:
Bring me my Spear: O clouds unfold!
Bring me my Chariot of fire.

I will not cease from Mental Fight,
Nor shall my Sword sleep in my hand[8]
Till we have built Jerusalem
In England's green and pleasant Land.

"Would to God that all the Lord's people were Prophets."

SECOND KINGS 2:12–2:14   And Elisha saw it, and he cried, My father, my father, the chariot of Israel, and the horsemen thereof. And he saw him no more: and he took hold of his own clothes, and rent them in two pieces. He took up also the mantle of Elijah that fell from him, and went back and stood by the bank of Jordan; And he took the mantle of Elijah that fell from him, and smote the waters, and said, Where is the LORD God of Elijah? and when he also had smitten the waters, they parted hither and thither: and Elisha went over.

Elijah's Wagon knew no thill ✍ EMILY DICKINSON

Elijah's Wagon knew no thill
Was innocent of Wheel
Elijah's horses as unique
As was his vehicle –

8 Numbers, xi. ch., 29 v.

Elijah's journey to portray
Expire with him the skill
Who justified Elijah
In feats inscrutable –

SECOND KINGS 5:9–6:14   So Naaman came with his horses and with his chariot, and stood at the door of the house of Elisha. And Elisha sent a messenger unto him, saying, Go and wash in Jordan seven times, and thy flesh shall come again to thee, and thou shalt be clean. But Naaman was wroth, and went away, and said, Behold, I thought, He will surely come out to me, and stand, and call on the name of the LORD his God, and strike his hand over the place, and recover the leper. Are not Abana and Pharpar, rivers of Damascus, better than all the waters of Israel? may I not wash in them, and be clean? So he turned and went away in a rage. And his servants came near, and spake unto him, and said, My father, if the prophet had bid thee do some great thing, wouldest thou not have done it? how much rather then, when he saith to thee, Wash, and be clean? Then went he down, and dipped himself seven times in Jordan, according to the saying of the man of God: and his flesh came again like unto the flesh of a little child, and he was clean.

Naaman's Song   ↗   RUDYARD KIPLING

"Go wash thyself in Jordan—go, wash thee and be clean!"
Nay, not for any Prophet will I plunge a toe therein!
For the banks of curious Jordan are parcelled into sites,
Commanded and embellished and patrolled by Israelites.

There rise her timeless capitals of Empires daily born,
Whose plinths are laid at midnight, and whose streets are packed
        at morn;
And here come hired youths and maids that feign to love or sin
In tones like rusty razor-blades to tunes like smitten tin.

And here be merry murtherings, and steeds with fiery hooves;
And furious hordes with guns and swords, and clamberings
        over rooves;
And horrid tumblings down from Heaven, and flights with
        wheels and wings;
And always one weak virgin who is chased through all these things.

And here is mock of faith and truth, for children to behold;
And every door of ancient dirt reopened to the old;
With every word that taints the speech, and show that weakens
    thought;
And Israel watcheth over each, and—doth not watch for nought. . . .

But Pharpar—but Abana—which Hermon launcheth down—
They perish fighting desert sands beyond Damascus-town.
But yet their pulse is of the snows—their strength is from on high—
And, if they cannot cure my woes, a leper will I die!

SECOND KINGS 9:29–9:37   And in the eleventh year of Joram the son of
Ahab began Ahaziah to reign over Judah. And when Jehu was come to
Jezreel, Jezebel heard of it; and she painted her face, and tired her head,
and looked out at a window. And as Jehu entered in at the gate, she said,
Had Zimri peace, who slew his master? And he lifted up his face to the
window, and said, Who is on my side? who? And there looked out to him
two or three eunuchs. And he said, Throw her down. So they threw her
down: and some of her blood was sprinkled on the wall, and on the horses:
and he trode her under foot. And when he was come in, he did eat and
drink, and said, Go, see now this cursed woman, and bury her: for she is a
king's daughter. And they went to bury her: but they found no more of her
than the skull, and the feet, and the palms of her hands. Wherefore they
came again, and told him. And he said, This is the word of the LORD,
which he spake by his servant Elijah the Tishbite, saying, In the portion of
Jezreel shall dogs eat the flesh of Jezebel: And the carcase of Jezebel shall
be as dung upon the face of the field in the portion of Jezreel; so that they
shall not say, This is Jezebel.

Song for the Clatter-bones   ᦓ   F. R. HIGGINS

God rest that Jewy woman,
Queen Jezebel, the bitch
Who peeled the clothes from her shoulder-bones
Down to her spent teats
As she stretched out of the window
Among the geraniums, where
She chaffed and laughed like one half daft
Titivating her painted hair—

King Jehu he drove to her,
She tipped him a fancy beck;
But he from his knacky side-car spoke,
"Who will break that dewlapped neck?"
And so she was thrown from the window;
Like Lucifer she fell
Beneath the feet of the horses and they beat
The light out of Jezebel.

That corpse wasn't planted in clover;
Ah, nothing of her was found
Save those grey bones that Hare-foot Mike
Gave me for their lovely sound;
And as once her dancing body
Made star-lit princes sweat,
So I'll just clack: though her ghost lacks a back
There's music in the old bones yet.

SECOND CHRONICLES 32:1–32:8   After these things, and the establishment thereof, Sennacherib king of Assyria came, and entered into Judah, and encamped against the fenced cities, and thought to win them for himself. And when Hezekiah saw that Sennacherib was come, and that he was purposed to fight against Jerusalem,. . .

SECOND KINGS 19:15–19:20   Hezekiah prayed before the LORD. . . . Then Isaiah the son of Amoz sent to Hezekiah, saying, Thus saith the LORD God of Israel, That which thou hast prayed to me against Sennacherib king of Assyria I have heard.

SECOND KINGS 19:31–19:37   For out of Jerusalem shall go forth a remnant, and they that escape out of mount Zion: the zeal of the LORD of hosts shall do this. Therefore thus saith the LORD concerning the king of Assyria, He shall not come into this city, nor shoot an arrow there, nor come before it with shield, nor cast a bank against it. By the way that he came, by the same shall he return, and shall not come into this city, saith the LORD. For I will defend this city, to save it, for mine own sake, and for my servant David's sake.

And it came to pass that night, that the angel of the LORD went out, and smote in the camp of the Assyrians an hundred fourscore and five thousand: and when they arose early in the morning, behold, they were all dead corpses.

So Sennacherib king of Assyria departed, and went and returned, and
dwelt at Nineveh. And it came to pass, as he was worshipping in the house
of Nisroch his god, that Adrammelech and Sharezer his sons smote him
with the sword: and they escaped into the land of Armenia. And
Esarhaddon his son reigned in his stead.

The Destruction of Sennacherib ᠊ᢣ
GEORGE NOEL GORDON, LORD BYRON

The Assyrian came down like the wolf on the fold,
And his cohorts were gleaming in purple and gold;
And the sheen of their spears was like stars on the sea,
When the blue wave rolls nightly on deep Galilee.

Like the leaves of the forest when summer is green,
That host with their banners at sunset were seen:
Like the leaves of the forest when autumn hath blown,
That host on the morrow lay withered and strown.

For the Angel of Death spread his wings on the blast,
And breathed in the face of the foe as he passed;
And the eyes of the sleepers waxed deadly and chill,
And their hearts but once heaved—and for ever grew still!

And there lay the steed with his nostril all wide,
But through it there rolled not the breath of his pride;
And the foam of his gasping lay white on the turf,
And cold as the spray of the rock-beating surf.

And there lay the rider distorted and pale,
With the dew on his brow, and the rust on his mail;
And the tents were all silent, the banners alone,
The lances unlifted, the trumpet unblown.

And the widows of Ashur are loud in their wail,
And the idols are broke in the temples of Baal;
And the might of the Gentile, unsmote by the sword,
Hath melted like snow in the glance of the Lord!

SECOND KINGS 25:1–25:7   And it came to pass in the ninth year of his reign, in the tenth month, in the tenth day of the month, that Nebuchadnezzar king of Babylon came, he, and all his host, against Jerusalem, and pitched against it; and they built forts against it round about. And the city was besieged unto the eleventh year of king Zedekiah. And on the ninth day of the fourth month the famine prevailed in the city, and there was no bread for the people of the land. And the city was broken up, and all the men of war fled by night by the way of the gate between two walls, which is by the king's garden: (now the Chaldees were against the city round about:) and the king went the way toward the plain. And the army of the Chaldees pursued after the king, and overtook him in the plains of Jericho: and all his army were scattered from him. So they took the king, and brought him up to the king of Babylon to Riblah; and they gave judgment upon him. And they slew the sons of Zedekiah before his eyes, and put out the eyes of Zedekiah, and bound him with fetters of brass, and carried him to Babylon.

SECOND CHRONICLES 36:17–36:20   . . . young man or maiden, old man, or him that stooped for age: he gave them all into his hand. And all the vessels of the house of God, great and small, and the treasures of the house of the LORD, and the treasures of the king, and of his princes; all these he brought to Babylon. And they burnt the house of God, and brake down the wall of Jerusalem, and burnt all the palaces thereof with fire, and destroyed all the goodly vessels thereof. And them that had escaped from the sword carried he away to Babylon; where they were servants to him and his sons until the reign of the kingdom of Persia: To fulfil the word of the LORD by the mouth of Jeremiah,[9] until the land had enjoyed her sabbaths: for as long as she lay desolate she kept sabbath, to fulfil threescore and ten years.[10]

Sion Lies Waste   ❧   FULKE GREVILLE

Sion lies waste, and thy Jerusalem
O Lord, is fallen to utter desolation.
Against thy prophets and thy holy men
The sin hath wrought a fatal combination:
    Profaned thy name, thy worship overthrown,
    And made thee, living Lord, a God unknown.

9 see JER 21:1 –10
10 see JER 25:11 –12 and JER 52:1 –15

Thy powerful laws, thy wonders of creation,
Thy word incarnate, glorious heaven, dark hell,
Lie shadowed under man's degeneration,
Thy Christ still crucified for doing well.
   Impiety, O Lord, sits on thy throne,
   Which makes thee, living light, a God unknown.

Man's superstition hath thy truths entombed,
His atheism again her pomps defaceth;
That sensual unsatiable vast womb
Of thy seen church thy unseen church disgraceth.
   There lives no truth with them that seem thine own,
   Which makes thee, living Lord, a God unknown.

Yet unto thee, Lord, mirror of transgression,
We who for earthly idols have forsaken
Thy heavenly image, sinless, pure impression,
And so in nets of vanity lie taken
   All desolate implore that to thine own,
   Lord, thou no longer live a God unknown.

Yet, Lord, let Israel's plagues not be eternal,
Nor sin forever cloud thy sacred mountains,
Nor with false flames, spiritual but infernal,
Dry up thy mercy's ever springing fountains.
   Rather, sweet Jesus, fill up time and come
   To yield the sin her everlasting doom.

NEHEMIAH

8:13–9:7   And on the second day were gathered together the chief of the
fathers of all the people, the priests, and the Levites, unto Ezra the scribe,
even to understand the words of the law. And they found written in the law
which the LORD had commanded by Moses, . . .
   Now in the twenty and fourth day of this month the children of Israel
were assembled with fasting, and with sackclothes, and earth upon them.
And the seed of Israel separated themselves from all strangers, and stood
and confessed their sins, and the iniquities of their fathers. And they stood
up in their place, and read in the book of the law of the LORD their God

one fourth part of the day; and another fourth part they confessed, and wor-
shipped the LORD their God. . . .

   Then the Levites, Jeshua, and Kadmiel, Bani, Hashabniah, Sherebiah,
Hodijah, Shebaniah, and Pethahiah, said, Stand up and bless the LORD
your God for ever and ever: and blessed be thy glorious name, which is
exalted above all blessing and praise. Thou, even thou, art LORD alone;
thou hast made heaven, the heaven of heavens, with all their host, the
earth, and all things that are therein, the seas, and all that is therein, and
thou preservest them all; and the host of heaven worshippeth thee. Thou
art the LORD the God, who didst choose Abram, and broughtest him forth
out of Ur of the Chaldees, and gavest him the name of Abraham;

Services ✌ CARL RAKOSI

There was a man in the land of Ur.

Who's that at my coattails?
A pale cocksman.

Hush!
The rabbi walks in thought
                as in an ordained measure
to the Ark
        and slowly opens its great doors.
The congregation rises
                and faces the six torahs
and the covenant
                and all beyond.
The Ark glows.
        Hear, O Israel!

The rabbi stands before the light
inside, alone, and prays.
It is a modest prayer
for the responsibilities of his office.
The congregation is silent.

I too pray:
Let Leah my wife be recompensed for her sweet smile
and our many years of companionship

and not stick me when she cuts my hair.
And let her stay at my side at large gatherings.
And let my son George and his wife Leanna
and my daughter Barbara be close,
and let their children, Jennifer, Julie and Joanna
be my sheep
        and I their old shepherd.
Let them remain as they are.

And let not my white hair frighten me.

The tiger leaps,
the baboon cries,
Pity, pity.
The rabbi prays.

I, son of Leopold and Flora,
also pray:
I pray for meaning.
I pray for the physical,
for my soul needs no suppliant.
I pray for man.

And may a special providence look out
for those who feel deeply.

ESTHER

7:1–7:6 So the king and Haman came to banquet with Esther the queen.
And the king said again unto Esther on the second day at the banquet of
wine, What is thy petition, queen Esther? and it shall be granted thee: and
what is thy request? and it shall be performed, even to the half of the
kingdom.

    Then Esther the queen answered and said, If I have found favour in thy
sight, O king, and if it please the king, let my life be given me at my peti-
tion, and my people at my request: For we are sold, I and my people, to be
destroyed, to be slain, and to perish. But if we had been sold for bondmen
and bondwomen, I had held my tongue, although the enemy could not
countervail the king's damage.

Then the king Ahasuerus answered and said unto Esther the queen, Who is he, and where is he, that durst presume in his heart to do so?

And Esther said, The adversary and enemy is this wicked Haman. . . .

From Life to Love ↜ COUNTEE CULLEN

Four winds and seven seas have called me friend,
And countless roads have known my restless feet;
Deep crystal springs and pollened buds were sweet
For sustenance their princely fare to lend,
While nameless birds from grove and blossomed bend
Deluged my soul with song; if it were meet
To love Life so, then Love will but complete
My joy, for Life with Love can never end.
Love, I have heard the sweet of your voice, have seen
You pass the dawn-flushed singing hills between;
Now suppliant I kneel and pray you show
The mercied sceptre favored Esther saw;
The dawn in me has broke, and well I know
That Love is king and creed and Persian law.

JOB

1:1–1:7 There was a man in the land of Uz, whose name was Job; and that man was perfect and upright, and one that feared God, and eschewed evil. And there were born unto him seven sons and three daughters. His substance also was seven thousand sheep, and three thousand camels, and five hundred yoke of oxen, and five hundred she asses, and a very great household; so that this man was the greatest of all the men of the east. And his sons went and feasted in their houses, every one his day; and sent and called for their three sisters to eat and to drink with them. And it was so, when the days of their feasting were gone about, that Job sent and sanctified them, and rose up early in the morning, and offered burnt offerings according to the number of them all: for Job said, It may be that my sons have sinned, and cursed God in their hearts. Thus did Job continually.

Now there was a day when the sons of God came to present themselves before the LORD, and Satan came also among them. And the LORD said unto Satan, Whence comest thou? Then Satan answered the LORD, and said, From going to and fro in the earth, and from walking up and down in it.

To Brooklyn Bridge ॐ HART CRANE

*From going to and fro in the earth,
and from walking up and down in it.*

How many dawns, chill from his rippling rest
The seagull's wings shall dip and pivot him,
Shedding white rings of tumult, building high
Over the chained bay waters Liberty—

Then with inviolate curve, forsake our eyes
As apparitional as sails that cross
Some page of figures to be filed away;
—Till elevators drop us from our day. . .

I think of cinemas, panoramic sleights
With multitudes bent toward some flashing scene
Never disclosed, but hastened to again,
Foretold to other eyes on the same screen;

And Thee, across the harbor, silver-paced
As though the sun took step of thee, yet left
Some motion ever unspent in thy stride,—
Implicitly thy freedom staying thee!

Out of some subway scuttle, cell or loft
A bedlamite speeds to thy parapets,
Tilting there momently, shrill shirt ballooning,
A jest falls from the speechless caravan.

Down Wall, from girder into street noon leaks,
A rip-tooth of the sky's acetylene;
All afternoon the cloud-flown derricks turn. . .
Thy cables breathe the North Atlantic still.

And obscure as that heaven of the Jews,
Thy guerdon . . . Accolade thou dost bestow
Of anonymity time cannot raise:
Vibrant reprieve and pardon thou dost show.

O harp and altar, of the fury fused,
(How could mere toil align thy choiring strings!)
Terrific threshold of the prophet's pledge,
Prayer of pariah, and the lover's cry,—

Again the traffic lights that skim thy swift
Unfractioned idiom, immaculate sigh of stars,
Beading thy path—condense eternity:
And we have seen night lifted in thine arms.

Under thy shadow by the piers I waited;
Only in darkness is thy shadow clear.
The City's fiery parcels all undone,
Already snow submerges an iron year. . .

O Sleepless as the river under thee,
Vaulting the sea, the prairies' dreaming sod,
Unto us lowliest sometime sweep, descend
And of the curveship lend a myth to God.

1:8–1:21   And the LORD said unto Satan, Hast thou considered my servant
Job, that there is none like him in the earth, a perfect and an upright man,
one that feareth God, and escheweth evil?

   Then Satan answered the LORD, and said, Doth Job fear God for
nought? Hast not thou made an hedge about him, and about his house,
and about all that he hath on every side? thou hast blessed the work of his
hands, and his substance is increased in the land. But put forth thine hand
now, and touch all that he hath, and he will curse thee to thy face.

   And the LORD said unto Satan, Behold, all that he hath is in thy power;
only upon himself put not forth thine hand. So Satan went forth from the
presence of the LORD.

   And there was a day when his sons and his daughters were eating and
drinking wine in their eldest brother's house: And there came a messenger
unto Job, and said, The oxen were plowing, and the asses feeding beside
them: And the Sabeans fell upon them, and took them away; yea, they have
slain the servants with the edge of the sword; and I only am escaped alone
to tell thee. While he was yet speaking, there came also another, and said,
The fire of God is fallen from heaven, and hath burned up the sheep, and
the servants, and consumed them; and I only am escaped alone to tell thee.
While he was yet speaking, there came also another, and said, The

Chaldeans made out three bands, and fell upon the camels, and have carried
them away, yea, and slain the servants with the edge of the sword; and I only
am escaped alone to tell thee. While he was yet speaking, there came also
another, and said, Thy sons and thy daughters were eating and drinking wine
in their eldest brother's house: And, behold, there came a great wind from
the wilderness, and smote the four corners of the house, and it fell upon the
young men, and they are dead; and I only am escaped alone to tell thee.

Then Job arose, and rent his mantle, and shaved his head, and fell down
upon the ground, and worshipped, And said, Naked came I out of my
mother's womb, and naked shall I return thither: the LORD gave, and the
LORD hath taken away; blessed be the name of the LORD.

Job I ↝ JOHN HALL

Out of my mother's womb
All naked came I lo:
And naked shall I turn again,
To earth that I came fro.

The Lord gave at the first,
As his good pleasure was,
And at his will did take again,
As it is come to pass.

The Lord his holy name
Be praised now therefore,
As it hath been, as it is now,
And shall be evermore.

1:22–2:12   In all this Job sinned not, nor charged God foolishly.

Again there was a day when the sons of God came to present them-
selves before the LORD, and Satan came also among them to present him-
self before the LORD. And the LORD said unto Satan, From whence comest
thou? And Satan answered the LORD, and said, From going to and fro in
the earth, and from walking up and down in it. And the LORD said unto
Satan, Hast thou considered my servant Job, that there is none like him in
the earth, a perfect and an upright man, one that feareth God, and
escheweth evil? and still he holdeth fast his integrity, although thou
movedst me against him, to destroy him without cause. And Satan

answered the LORD, and said, Skin for skin, yea, all that a man hath will he give for his life. But put forth thine hand now, and touch his bone and his flesh, and he will curse thee to thy face. And the LORD said unto Satan, Behold, he is in thine hand; but save his life.

So went Satan forth from the presence of the LORD, and smote Job with sore boils from the sole of his foot unto his crown. And he took him a potsherd to scrape himself withal; and he sat down among the ashes.

Then said his wife unto him, Dost thou still retain thine integrity? curse God, and die. But he said unto her, Thou speakest as one of the foolish women speaketh. What? shall we receive good at the hand of God, and shall we not receive evil? In all this did not Job sin with his lips.

Now when Job's three friends heard of all this evil that was come upon him, they came every one from his own place; Eliphaz the Temanite, and Bildad the Shuhite, and Zophar the Naamathite: for they had made an appointment together to come to mourn with him and to comfort him. And when they lifted up their eyes afar off, and knew him not, they lifted up their voice, and wept; and they rent every one his mantle, and sprinkled dust upon their heads toward heaven.

Job ⚯ ELIZABETH SEWELL

They did not know this face
Where the chin rested on the sunken breastbone,
So changed it was, emptied, rinsed out and dried,
And for some future purpose put aside.
Expecting torment, they were much perplexed.

His world had gone
And he sat isolated, foul and flyblown,
Without a world, with nothing but a mind
Staggered to silence since it could not find
Language to utter its amazing text.

For where was Job?
In some strange state, unknown and yet well-known,
A mask that stared hollowly in God's breath,
Mind that perceived the irrelevance of death,
And the astonished heart unmoved, unvexed.

They did not see his soul
Perched like a bird upon the broken hearthstone,
    Piping incessantly above the ashes
What next what next what next what next what next

2:13   So they sat down with him upon the ground seven days and seven
nights, and none spake a word unto him: for they saw that his grief was
very great.

Cæsura ↗ JOHN ASHBERY

Job sat in a corner of the dump eating asparagus
With one hand and scratching his unsightly eruptions
With the other. Pshaw, it'd blow over. In the office
They'd like discussing it. His thoughts

Were with the office now: how protected it was,
Though still a place to work. Sit up straight, the
Monitor inside said. It worked for a second
But didn't improve the posture of his days, taken

As a cross section of the times. Correction: of our time.
And it was (it was again): "Have you made your list up?
I have one ambulance three nuns two (black-
And-white list) cops dressed as Keystone Kops lists, a red light

At leafy intersection list." Then it goes blank, pulp-color.
Until at the end where they give out the list
Of awardees. The darkness and light have returned. It was still
The weather of the soul, vandalized, out-at-elbow. A blight. Spared,
        though.

4:12–21   Now a thing was secretly brought to me, and mine ear received a
little thereof. In thoughts from the visions of the night, when deep sleep fal-
leth on men, Fear came upon me, and trembling, which made all my bones
to shake. Then a spirit passed before my face; the hair of my flesh stood up:
It stood still, but I could not discern the form thereof: an image was before
mine eyes, there was silence, and I heard a voice, saying, Shall mortal man

be more just than God? shall a man be more pure than his maker? Behold,
he put no trust in his servants; and his angels he charged with folly: How
much less in them that dwell in houses of clay, whose foundation is in the
dust, which are crushed before the moth? They are destroyed from morning
to evening: they perish for ever without any regarding it. Doth not their
excellency which is in them go away? they die, even without wisdom.

A Spirit Passed Before Me ↵
GEORGE NOEL GORDON, LORD BYRON

A spirit passed before me: I beheld
The face of immortality unveiled—
Deep sleep came down on every eye save mine—
And there it stood,—all formless—but divine;
Along my bones the creeping flesh did quake;
And as my damp hair stiffened, thus it spake:

'Is man more just than God? Is man more pure
Than he who deems even seraphs insecure?
Creatures of clay—vain dwellers in the dust!
The moth survives you, and are ye more just?
Things of a day! you wither ere the night,
Heedless and blind to wisdom's wasted light!'

7:17–10:22   What is man, that thou shouldest magnify him? and that thou
shouldest set thine heart upon him? And that thou shouldest visit him every
morning, and try him every moment? How long wilt thou not depart from
me, nor let me alone till I swallow down my spittle? I have sinned; what
shall I do unto thee, O thou preserver of men? why hast thou set me as a
mark against thee, so that I am a burden to myself? And why dost thou not
pardon my transgression, and take away my iniquity? for now shall I sleep
in the dust; and thou shalt seek me in the morning, but I shall not be. . . .
     Wherefore then hast thou brought me forth out of the womb? Oh that I
had given up the ghost, and no eye had seen me! I should have been as
though I had not been; I should have been carried from the womb to the
grave. Are not my days few? cease then, and let me alone, that I may take
comfort a little, Before I go whence I shall not return, even to the land of dark-
ness and the shadow of death; A land of darkness, as darkness itself; and of
the shadow of death, without any order, and where the light is as darkness.

Death   HENRY VAUGHAN
A *Dialogue*

Soul
'Tis a sad Land, that in one day
Hath dulled thee thus, when death shall freeze
Thy blood to ice, and thou must stay
Tenant for years, and centuries,
How wilt thou brook't? —

Body
I cannot tell, —
But if all sense wings not with thee,
And something still be left the dead,
I'll wish my curtains off to free
Me from so dark, and sad a bed;

A nest of nights, a gloomy sphere,
Where shadows thicken, and the cloud
Sits on the sun's brow all the year,
And nothing moves without a shroud;

Soul
'Tis so: But as thou sawest that night
We travelled in, our first attempts
Were dull, and blind, but custom straight
Our fears, and falls brought to contempt,

Then, when the ghastly *twelve* was past
We breathed still for a blushing *East*,
And bad the lazy sun make haste,
And on sure hopes, though long, did feast;

But when we saw the clouds to crack
And in those crannies light appeared,
We thought the day then was not slack,
And pleased our selves with what we feared;

Just so it is in death. But thou
Shalt in thy mother's bosom sleep
Whilst I each minute groan to know
How near Redemption creeps.

Then shall we meet to mix again, and met,
'Tis last good-night, our sun shall never set.

13:14–13:18   Wherefore do I take my flesh in my teeth, and put my life in
mine hand? Though he slay me, yet will I trust in him: but I will maintain
mine own ways before him. He also shall be my salvation: for an hypocrite
shall not come before him. Hear diligently my speech, and my declaration
with your ears.
  Behold now, I have ordered my cause; I know that I shall be justified.

The Enthusiast   ↝   HERMAN MELVILLE

Shall hearts that beat no base retreat
    In youth's magnanimous years—
Ignoble hold it, if discreet
    When interest tames to fears;
Shall spirits that worship light
    Perfidious deem its sacred glow,
    Recant, and trudge where worldlings go,
Conform and own them right?

Shall time with creeping influence cold
    Unnerve and cow? the heart
Pine for the heartless ones enrolled
    With palterers of the mart?
Shall faith abjure her skies,
    Or pale probation blench her down
    To shrink from truth so still, so lone
Mid loud gregarious lies?

Each burning boat in Caesar's rear,
    Flames—No return through me!
So put the torch to ties though dear,
    If ties but tempters be.
Nor cringe if come the night:
    Walk through the cloud to meet the pall,
    Though light forsake thee, never fall
From fealty to light.

14:1–14:10 Man that is born of a woman is of few days, and full of trouble. He cometh forth like a flower, and is cut down: he fleeth also as a shadow, and continueth not. And dost thou open thine eyes upon such an one, and bringest me into judgment with thee? Who can bring a clean thing out of an unclean? not one. Seeing his days are determined, the number of his months are with thee, thou hast appointed his bounds that he cannot pass; Turn from him, that he may rest, till he shall accomplish, as an hireling, his day. For there is hope of a tree, if it be cut down, that it will sprout again, and that the tender branch thereof will not cease. Though the root thereof wax old in the earth, and the stock thereof die in the ground; Yet through the scent of water it will bud, and bring forth boughs like a plant. But man dieth, and wasteth away: yea, man giveth up the ghost, and where is he?

Grace ॐ GEORGE HERBERT

My stock lies dead, and no increase
Doth my dull husbandry improve:
O let thy graces without cease
    Drop from above!

If still the sun should hide his face,
Thy house would but a dungeon prove,
Thy works nights captives: O let grace
    Drop from above!

The dew doth every morning fall;
And shall the dew out-strip thy dove?
The dew, for which grass cannot call,
    Drop from above.

Death is still working like a mole,
And digs my grave at each remove:
Let grace work too, and on my soul
    Drop from above.

Sin is still hammering my heart
Unto a hardness, void of love:
Let suppling grace, to cross his art,
    Drop from above.

O come! for thou dost know the way.
Or if to me thou wilt not move,
Remove me, where I need not say,
                    Drop from above.

38:1–38:30   Then the LORD answered Job out of the whirlwind, and said,
Who is this that darkeneth counsel by words without knowledge? Gird up
now thy loins like a man; for I will demand of thee, and answer thou me.
Where wast thou when I laid the foundations of the earth? declare, if thou
hast understanding. . . . Who hath divided a watercourse for the overflowing
of waters, or a way for the lightning of thunder; To cause it to rain on the
earth, where no man is; on the wilderness, wherein there is no man; To sat-
isfy the desolate and waste ground; and to cause the bud of the tender herb
to spring forth? Hath the rain a father? or who hath begotten the drops of
dew? Out of whose womb came the ice? and the hoary frost of heaven, who
hath gendered it? The waters are hid as with a stone, and the face of the
deep is frozen.

Hath the Rain a Father?   ᕱ   JONES VERY

We say, "It rains." An unbelieving age!
Its very words its unbelief doth show;
Forgot the lessons of the sacred page,
Spoken by men of faith so long ago!
No farther than they see men's faith extends;
The mighty changes of the earth and sky
To them are causeless all, where Science ends;
An Unseen Cause they know not or deny.
They hear not in the whirlwind, or the storm,
The mighty Voice which spake to man of old;
They see not in the clouds of heaven His form,
Nor in His ceaseless works his power behold;
Who maketh small the countless drops of rain,
And sendeth showers upon the springing grain.

42:10–42:16   And the LORD turned the captivity of Job, when he prayed
for his friends: also the LORD gave Job twice as much as he had before.
Then came there unto him all his brethren, and all his sisters, and all they

that had been of his acquaintance before, and did eat bread with him in his house: and they bemoaned him, and comforted him over all the evil that the LORD had brought upon him: every man also gave him a piece of money, and every one an earring of gold.

So the LORD blessed the latter end of Job more than his beginning: for he had fourteen thousand sheep, and six thousand camels, and a thousand yoke of oxen, and a thousand she asses. He had also seven sons and three daughters. And he called the name of the first, Jemima; and the name of the second, Kezia; and the name of the third, Kerenhappuch. And in all the land were no women found so fair as the daughters of Job: and their father gave them inheritance among their brethren.

After this lived Job an hundred and forty years, and saw his sons, and his sons' sons, even four generations.

The Beauty of Job's Daughters ✄ JAY MACPHERSON

The old, the mad, the blind have fairest daughters.
Take Job: the beasts the accuser sends at evening
Shoulder his house and shake it; he's not there,
Attained in age to inwardness of daughters,
In all the land no women found so fair.

Angels and sons of God are nearest neighbours,
And even the accuser may repair
To walk with Job in pleasures of his daughters:
Wide shining rooms more warmly lit at evening,
Gardens beyond whose secrets scent the air.

Not wiles of men nor envy of the neighbours,
Riches of earth, nor what heaven holds more rare,
Can take from Job the beauty of his daughters,
The gardens in the rock, music at evening,
And cup so full that all who come must share.

Perhaps we passed them? it was late, or evening,
And surely those were desert stumps, not daughters,
In fact we doubt that they were ever there.
The old, the mad, the blind have fairest daughters.
In all the land no women found so fair.

PSALMS

Stanzas on the Psalms ᴦ THOMAS WARTON THE ELDER

Not the songs that nobly tell,
How Troy was sacked, and Rome began,
Not the numbers that reveal
The wars of Heaven to falling man;

Can boast that true celestial fire,
That equal strength and ease,
Or with such various charms conspire,
To move, to teach, to please.

Those complaints how sadly sweet,
Which weeping seraphim repeat;
Those prayers how happily preferred,
Which God himself inspired and heard.

Ye partial wits no longer boast
Of Pindar's fire in David's lost!
Who to the Hebrew harp must yield,
As Jove by great Jehovah is excelled.

12:1–12:8   Help, LORD; for the godly man ceaseth;
    for the faithful fail from among the children of men.
They speak vanity every one with his neighbour:
    with flattering lips and with a double heart do they speak.
The LORD shall cut off all flattering lips,
    and the tongue that speaketh proud things:
Who have said, With our tongue will we prevail; our lips are our own:
    who is lord over us?
For the oppression of the poor, for the sighing of the needy, now will I arise,
    saith the LORD; I will set him in safety from him that puffeth at him.
The words of the LORD are pure words:
    as silver tried in a furnace of earth, purified seven times.
Thou shalt keep them, O LORD, thou shalt preserve them
    from this generation for ever.
The wicked walk on every side, when the vilest men are exalted.

Rochester *Extempore* ♪

JOHN WILMOT, EARL OF ROCHESTER

And after singing Psalm the Twelfth,
He laid his book upon the shelf
And looked much simply like himself;
With eyes turned up, as white as ghost,
He cried, "Ah, Lard! ah, Lard of Hosts!
I am a rascal, that thou knowst!"

23:1–23:6   The LORD is my shepherd; I shall not want.
He maketh me to lie down in green pastures:
    he leadeth me beside the still waters.
He restoreth my soul:
    he leadeth me in the paths of righteousness for his name's sake.
Yea, though I walk through the valley of the shadow of death, I will fear no evil:
    for thou art with me; thy rod and thy staff they comfort me.
Thou preparest a table before me in the presence of mine enemies:
    thou anointest my head with oil; my cup runneth over.
Surely goodness and mercy shall follow me all the days of my life:
    and I will dwell in the house of the LORD for ever.

Psalm 23   ♪   RICHARD CRASHAW

Happy me! o happy sheep!
Whom my God vouchsafes to keep;
Even my God, even he it is,
That points me to these ways of bliss;
On whose pastures cheerful spring,
All the year doth sit and sing,
And rejoicing smiles to see
Their green backs were his livery:
Pleasure sings my soul to rest,
Plenty wears me at her breast,
Whose sweet temper teaches me
Nor wanton, nor in want to be.
At my feet the blubbering mountain
Weeping, melts into a fountain,
Whose soft silver-sweating streams

Make high noon forget his beams:
When my wayward breath is flying,
He calls home my soul from dying,
Strokes and tames my rabid grief,
And does woo me into life:
When my simple weakness strays,
(Tangled in forbidden ways)
He (my Shepherd) is my guide,
He's before me, on my side,
And behind me, he beguiles
Craft in all her knotty wiles;
He expounds the giddy wonder
Of my weary steps, and under
Spreads a path clear as the day,
Where no churlish rub says nay
To my joy-conducted feet,
Whilst they gladly go to meet
Grace and peace, to meet new lays
Tuned to my great Shepherd's praise.
Come now all ye terrors, sally
Muster forth into the valley,
Where triumphant darkness hovers
With a sable wing, that covers
Brooding horror. Come thou Death,
Let the damps of thy dull breath
Overshadow even the shade,
And make darkness self afraid;
There my feet, even there shall find
Way for a resolved mind.
Still my Shepherd, still my God,
Thou art with me, still thy rod,
And thy staff, whose influence
Gives direction, gives defence.
At the whisper of thy Word
Crowned abundance spreads my board:
While I feast, my foes do feed
Their rank malice not their need,
So that with the self-same bread
They are starved, and I am fed.
How my head in ointment swims!
How my cup o'erlooks her brims!

So, even so still may I move
By the line of thy dear love;
Still may thy sweet mercy spread
A shady arm above my head,
About my paths, so shall I find
The fair center of my mind
Thy temple, and those lovely walls
Bright ever with a beam that falls
Fresh from the pure glance of thine eye,
Lighting to Eternity.
There I'll dwell forever, there
Will I find a purer air
To feed my life with, there I'll sup
Balm and nectar in my cup,
And thence my ripe soul will I breath
Warm into the arms of Death.

27:1   The LORD is my light and my salvation; whom shall I fear?
the LORD is the strength of my life; of whom shall I be afraid?

Psalm III   ᵔ   ALLEN GINSBERG

To God: to illuminate all men. Beginning with Skid Road.
Let Occidental and Washington be transformed into a higher place,
        the plaza of eternity,
Illuminate the welders in shipyards with the brilliance of their torches.
Let the crane operator lift up his arm for joy.
Let elevators creak and speak, ascending and descending in awe.
Let the mercy of the flower's direction beckon in the eye.
Let the straight flower bespeak its purpose in straightness—to seek
        the light.
Let the crooked flower bespeak its purpose in crookedness—to seek
        the light.
Let the crookedness and straightness bespeak the light.
Let Puget Sound be a blast of light.
I feed on your Name like a cockroach on a crumb—this cockroach is
        holy.

                                                    Seattle 1956

34:8   O taste and see that the LORD is good:
blessed is the man that trusteth in him.

O Taste and See ᕹ DENISE LEVERTOV

The world is
not with us enough.
O taste and see

the subway Bible poster said,
meaning The Lord, meaning
if anything all that lives
to the imagination's tongue,

grief, mercy, language,
tangerine, weather, to
breathe them, bite
savor, chew, swallow, transform

into our flesh our
deaths, crossing the street, plum, quince,
living in the orchard and being

hungry, and plucking
the fruit.

38:19–38:22   But mine enemies are lively, and they are strong:
and they that hate me wrongfully are multiplied.
They also that render evil for good are mine adversaries;
because I follow the thing that good is.
Forsake me not, O LORD: O my God, be not far from me.
Make haste to help me, O Lord my salvation.

Complaining ᕹ GEORGE HERBERT

Do not beguile my heart,
        Because thou art
My power and wisdom. Put me not to shame,

              Because I am
         Thy clay that weeps, thy dust that calls.

         Thou art the Lord of glory:
                   The deed and story
         Are both thy due: but I a silly fly
                   That live or die
         According as the weather falls.

         Art thou all justice, Lord?
                   Shows not thy word
         More attributes? Am I all throat or eye,
                   To weep or cry?
         Have I no parts but those of grief ?

         Let not thy wrathful power
                   Afflict my hour,
         My inch of life: or let thy gracious power
                   Contract my hour,
         That I may climb and find relief.

39:1–39:5   I said, I will take heed to my ways, that I sin not with my tongue:
     I will keep my mouth with a bridle, while the wicked is before me.
I was dumb with silence, I held my peace, even from good;
     and my sorrow was stirred.
My heart was hot within me, while I was musing the fire burned:
     then spake I with my tongue,
LORD, make me to know mine end, and the measure of my days, what it is:
     that I may know how frail I am.
Behold, thou hast made my days as an handbreadth;
     and mine age is as nothing before thee:
     verily every man at his best state is altogether vanity. Selah.

Awake, awake, thou heavy sprite ⤳ THOMAS CAMPION

         Awake, awake, thou heavy sprite,
         That sleepst the deadly sleep of sin;
              Rise now, and walk the ways of light:
         'Tis not too late yet to begin.

Seek heaven early, seek it late,
True faith still finds an open gate.

Get up, get up, thou leaden man:
Thy tracks to endless joy or pain
Yields but the model of a span;
Yet burns out thy life's lamp in vain.
One minute bounds thy bane, or bliss,
Then watch, and labor while time is.

40:1–40:6 I waited patiently for the LORD; and he inclined unto me,
and heard my cry.
He brought me up also out of an horrible pit, out of the miry clay,
and set my feet upon a rock, and established my goings.
And he hath put a new song in my mouth, even praise unto our God:
many shall see it, and fear, and shall trust in the LORD.
Blessed is that man that maketh the LORD his trust,
and respecteth not the proud, nor such as turn aside to lies.
Many, O LORD my God, are thy wonderful works which thou hast done,
and thy thoughts which are to us-ward:
they cannot be reckoned up in order unto thee:
if I would declare and speak of them,
they are more than can be numbered.
Sacrifice and offering thou didst not desire; mine ears hast thou opened:
burnt offering and sin offering hast thou not required.

When Israel, of the Lord Beloved — SIR WALTER SCOTT

When Israel, of the Lord beloved,
Out from the land of bondage came,
Her fathers' God before her moved,
An awful guide in smoke and flame.
By day, along the astonished lands
The cloudy pillar glided slow;
By night, Arabia's crimsoned sands
Returned the fiery column's glow.

There rose the choral hymn of praise,
    And trump and timbrel answered keen,
And Zion's daughters poured their lays,
    With priest's and warrior's voice between.
No portents now our foes amaze,
    Forsaken Israel wanders lone;
Our fathers would not know Thy ways,
    And Thou hast left them to their own.

But present still, though now unseen!
    When brightly shines the prosperous day,
Be thoughts of Thee a cloudy screen
    To temper the deceitful ray.
And oh, when stoops on Judah's path
    In shade and storm the frequent night,
Be Thou, long-suffering, slow to wrath,
    A burning and a shining light!

Our harps we left by Babel's streams,[11]
    The tyrant's jest, the Gentile's scorn;
No censer round our altar beams,
    And mute are timbrel, harp, and horn.
But Thou hast said, The blood of goat,
    The flesh of rams I will not prize;
A contrite heart, a humble thought,
    Are mine accepted sacrifice.

45:1–45:2   My heart is inditing a good matter:
    I speak of the things which I have made touching the king:
    my tongue is the pen of a ready writer.
Thou art fairer than the children of men: grace is poured into thy lips:
    therefore God hath blessed thee for ever.

Meditation Seven ᧒ EDWARD TAYLOR

Thy human frame, my glorious Lord, I spy.
    A golden still with heavenly choice drugs filled:

---

11 PSA 137:1 –2

Thy holy love, the glowing heat whereby
    The spirit of grace is graciously distilled.
    Thy mouth the neck through which these spirits still;
    My soul thy vial make, and therewith fill.

Thy speech the liquour in thy vessel stands,
    Well tinged with grace, a blessed tincture, lo,
Thy words distilled grace in thy lips poured, and
    Give graces tincture in them where they go.
    Thy words in graces tincture stilled, Lord, may
    The tincture of thy grace in me convey.

That golden mint of words thy mouth divine
    Doth tip these words, which by my fall were spoiled:
And dub with gold dug out of graces mine,
    That they thine image might have in them foiled.
    Grace in thy lips poured out's as liquid gold:
    Thy bottle make my soul, Lord, it to hold.

79:1–79:8   O God, the heathen are come into thine inheritance;
    thy holy temple have they defiled; they have laid Jerusalem on heaps.
The dead bodies of thy servants have they given to be meat
    unto the fowls of the heaven,
    the flesh of thy saints unto the beasts of the earth.
Their blood have they shed like water round about Jerusalem;
    and there was none to bury them.
We are become a reproach to our neighbours,
    a scorn and derision to them
    that are round about us.
How long, LORD? wilt thou be angry for ever? shall thy jealousy burn like fire?
Pour out thy wrath upon the heathen that have not known thee,
    and upon the kingdoms that have not called upon thy name.
For they have devoured Jacob, and laid waste his dwelling place.
O remember not against us former iniquities:
    let thy tender mercies speedily prevent us:
    for we are brought very low.

On Jordan's Banks ꙮ

GEORGE NOEL GORDON, LORD BYRON

On Jordan's banks the Arab's camels stray,
On Sion's hill the False One's votaries pray,
The Baal-adorer bows on Sinai's steep—
Yet there—even there—Oh God! thy thunders sleep:

There—where thy finger scorched the tablet stone!
There—where thy shadow to thy people shone!
Thy glory shrouded in its garb of fire:
Thyself—none living see and not expire!

Oh! in the lightning let thy glance appear;
Sweep from his shivered hand the oppressor's spear!
How long by tyrants shall thy land be trod?
How long thy temples worshipless, Oh God?

98:1   O sing unto the LORD a new song; for he hath done marvellous things:
his right hand, and his holy arm, hath gotten him the victory.

Te Deum ꙮ   CHARLES REZNIKOFF

Not because of victories
I sing,
having none,
but for the common sunshine,
the breeze,
the largess of the spring.

Not for victory
but for the day's work done
as well as I was able;
not for a seat upon the dais
but at the common table.

102:1–102:17   Hear my prayer, O LORD, and let my cry come unto thee.
Hide not thy face from me in the day when I am in trouble;
incline thine ear unto me:

in the day when I call answer me speedily.
For my days are consumed like smoke, and my bones are burned as an hearth.
My heart is smitten, and withered like grass; so that I forget to eat my bread.
By reason of the voice of my groaning my bones cleave to my skin.
I am like a pelican of the wilderness: I am like an owl of the desert.
I watch, and am as a sparrow alone upon the house top.
Mine enemies reproach me all the day;
    and they that are mad against me are sworn against me.
For I have eaten ashes like bread, and mingled my drink with weeping.
Because of thine indignation and thy wrath: for thou hast lifted me up,
    and cast me down.
My days are like a shadow that declineth; and I am withered like grass.
But thou, O LORD, shall endure for ever;
    and thy remembrance unto all generations.
Thou shalt arise, and have mercy upon Zion:
    for the time to favour her, yea, the set time, is come.
For thy servants take pleasure in her stones, and favour the dust thereof.
So the heathen shall fear the name of the LORD,
    and all the kings of the earth thy glory.
When the LORD shall build up Zion, he shall appear in his glory.
He will regard the prayer of the destitute, and not despise their prayer.

Lord, Hear My Prayer   JOHN CLARE

Lord, hear my prayer when trouble glooms,
Let sorrow find a way,
And when the day of trouble comes,
Turn not thy face away:
My bones like hearthstones burn away,
My life like vapoury smoke decays.

My heart is smitten like the grass,
That withered lies and dead,
And I, so lost to what I was
Forget to eat my bread.
My voice is groaning all the day,
My bones prick through this skin of clay.

The wilderness's pelican,
The desert's lonely owl—

I am their like, a desert man
In ways as lone and foul.
As sparrows on the cottage top
I wait till I with fainting drop.

I hear my enemies reproach,
All silently I mourn;
They on my private peace encroach,
Against me they are sworn.
Ashes as bread my trouble shares,
And mix my food with weeping cares.

Yet not for them is sorrow's toil,
I fear no mortal's frowns—
But thou hast held me up awhile
And thou has cast me down.
My days like shadows waste from view,
I mourn like withered grass in dew.

But thou, Lord, shalt endure for ever,
All generations through;
Thou shalt to Zion be the giver
Of joy and mercy too.
Her very stones are in thy trust,
Thy servants reverence her dust.

Heathens shall hear and fear thy name,
All kings of earth thy glory know
When thou shalt build up Zion's fame
And live in glory there below.
He'll not despise their prayers, though mute,
But still regard the destitute.

121:1   I will lift up mine eyes unto the hills, from whence cometh my help.

The Hills   ↜   D. H. LAWRENCE

I lift up mine eyes unto the hills
and there they are, but no strength comes from them to me.

Only from darkness
and ceasing to see
strength comes.

127:1–127:2   Except the LORD build the house, they labour in vain that build it:
   except the LORD keep the city, the watchman waketh but in vain.
It is vain for you to rise up early, to sit up late, to eat the bread of sorrows:
   for so he giveth his beloved sleep.

The Sleep   ELIZABETH BARRETT BROWNING

Of all the thoughts of God that are
Borne inward unto souls afar,
Along the Psalmist's music deep,
Now tell me if that any is,
For gift or grace, surpassing this:
"He giveth his beloved—sleep?"

What would we give to our beloved?
The hero's heart to be unmoved,
The poet's star-tuned harp to sweep,
The patriot's voice to teach and rouse,
The monarch's crown to light the brows?
He giveth his beloved—sleep.

What do we give to our beloved?
A little faith all undisproved,
A little dust to overweep,
And bitter memories to make
The whole earth blasted for our sake:
He giveth his beloved—sleep.

"Sleep soft, beloved!" we sometimes say,
Who have no tune to charm away
Sad dreams that through the eyelids creep:
But never doleful dream again
Shall break the happy slumber when
He giveth his beloved—sleep.

O earth, so full of dreary noises!
O men, with wailing in your voices!
O delved gold, the wailers heap!
O strife, O curse, that o'er it fall!
God strikes a silence through you all,
And giveth his beloved—sleep.

His dews drop mutely on the hill,
His cloud above it saileth still,
Though on its slope men sow and reap:
More softly than the dew is shed,
Or cloud is floated overhead,
He giveth his beloved—sleep.

Aye, men may wonder while they scan
A living, thinking, feeling man
Confirmed in such a rest to keep;
But angels say,—and through the word
I think their happy smile is heard—
"He giveth his beloved—sleep."

For me, my heart that erst did go
Most like a tired child at a show,
That sees through tears the mummers leap,
Would now its wearied vision close,
Would childlike on his love repose
Who giveth his beloved—sleep.

And friends, dear friends, when it shall be
That this low breath is gone from me,
And round my bier ye come to weep,
Let One, most loving of you all,
Say "Not a tear must o'er her fall!
He giveth his beloved—sleep."

130:1–130:8   Out of the depths have I cried unto thee, O LORD.
Lord, hear my voice: let thine ears be attentive to the voice of my supplications.
If thou, LORD, shouldest mark iniquities, O Lord, who shall stand?
But there is forgiveness with thee, that thou mayest be feared.
I wait for the LORD, my soul doth wait, and in his word do I hope.

My soul waiteth for the Lord more than they that watch for the morning:
> I say, more than they that watch for the morning.

Let Israel hope in the LORD:
> for with the LORD there is mercy, and with him is plenteous redemption.

And he shall redeem Israel from all his iniquities.

Introduction to the Psalm of *De profundis*   ᴈ
GEORGE GASCOIGNE

The skies gan scowl, o'ercast with misty clouds,
When (as I rode alone by London way,
Cloakless, unclad) thus did I sing and say:
Behold, quoth I, bright Titan how he shrouds
His head aback, and yields the rain his reach,
'Til in his wrath, Dan Jove have soused the soil,
And washed me, wretch, which in his travail toil.
But holla (here) doth rudeness me appeach,
Since Jove is Lord and king of mighty power,
Which can command the sun to show his face,
And (when him list) to give the rain his place.
Why do not I my weary muses frame,
(Although I be well soused in this shower,)
To write some verse in honor of his name?

Gascoigne's *De profundis*

From depth of dole wherein my soul doth dwell,
From heavy heart which harbors in my breast,
From troubled sprite which seldom taketh rest,
From hope of heaven, from dread of darksome hell,
O gracious God, to thee I cry and yell.
My God, my Lord, my lovely Lord alone,
To thee I call, to thee I make my moan.
And thou (good God) vouchsafe in gree to take,
> This woeful plaint,
> Wherein I faint.

Oh hear me then for thy great mercy's sake.

Oh bend thine ears attentively to hear,
Oh turn thine eyes, behold me how I wail,

Oh hearken Lord, give ear for mine avail,
Oh mark in mind the burdens that I bear:
See how I sink in sorrows everywhere.
Behold and see what dolors I endure,
Give ear and hark what plaints I put in ure.
Bend willing ear: and pity therewithall,
    My wailing voice,
    Which hath no choice.
But evermore upon thy name to call.

 If thou good Lord shouldst take thy rod in hand,
If thou regard what sins are daily done,
If thou take hold where we our works begun,
If thou decree in judgement for to stand,
And be extreme to see our scuses scanned,
If thou take note of every thing amiss,
And write in roles how frail our nature is,
O glorious God, O King, O Prince of power,
    What mortal wight,
    May then have light,
To feel thy frown, if thou have list to lower?

 But thou art good, and hast of mercy store,
Thou not delightst to see a sinner fall,
Thou heark'nest first, before we come to call.
Thine ears are set wide open evermore,
Before we knock thou comest to the door.
Thou art more pressed to hear a sinner cry,
Than he is quick to climb to thee on high.
Thy mighty name be praised then alway,
    Let faith and fear,
    True witness bear.
How fast they stand which on thy mercy stay.

 I look for thee (my lovely Lord) therefore.
For thee I wait, for thee I tarry still,
Mine eyes do long to gaze on thee my fill.
For thee I watch, for thee I pry and pore.
My soul for thee attendeth evermore.
My soul doth thirst to take of thee a taste,
My soul desires with thee for to be placed.

And to thy word (which can no man deceive)
    Mine only trust,
    My love and lust
In confidence continually shall cleave.

 Before the break or dawning of the day,
Before the light be seen in lofty skies,
Before the sun appear in pleasant wise,
Before the watch (before the watch I say)
Before the ward that waits therefore alway:
My soul, my sense, my secret thought, my sprite,
My will, my wish, my joy, and my delight:
Unto the Lord that sits in heaven on high,
    With hasty wing,
    From me doth fling,
And striveth still, unto the Lord to fly.

 O Israel, O household of the Lord,
O Abraham's Brats, O brood of blessed seed,
O chosen sheep that love the Lord in deed:
O hungry hearts, feed still upon his word,
And put your trust in him with one accord.
For he hath mercy evermore at hand,
His fountains flow, his springs do never stand.
And plenteously he loveth to redeem,
    Such sinners all,
    As on him call,
And faithfully his mercies most esteem.

 He will redeem our deadly drooping state,
He will bring home the sheep that go astray,
He will help them that hope in him alway:
He will appease our discord and debate,
He will soon save, though we repent us late.
He will be ours if we continue his,
He will bring bale to joy and perfect bliss.
He will redeem the flock of his elect,
    From all that is,
    Or was amiss.
Since Abraham's heirs did first his Laws reject.

    Ever or never.

139:1–139:18   O LORD, thou hast searched me, and known me.
Thou knowest my downsitting and mine uprising,
> thou understandest my thought afar off.
Thou compassest my path and my lying down,
> and art acquainted with all my ways.
For there is not a word in my tongue, but, lo, O LORD,
> thou knowest it altogether.
Thou hast beset me behind and before, and laid thine hand upon me.
Such knowledge is too wonderful for me; it is high, I cannot attain unto it.
Whither shall I go from thy spirit? or whither shall I flee from thy presence?
If I ascend up into heaven, thou art there:
> if I make my bed in hell, behold, thou art there.
If I take the wings of the morning, and dwell in the uttermost parts of the sea;
Even there shall thy hand lead me, and thy right hand shall hold me.
If I say, Surely the darkness shall cover me;
> even the night shall be light about me.
Yea, the darkness hideth not from thee; but the night shineth as the day:
> the darkness and the light are both alike to thee.
For thou hast possessed my reins:
> thou hast covered me in my mother's womb.
I will praise thee; for I am fearfully and wonderfully made:
> marvellous are thy works; and that my soul knoweth right well.
My substance was not hid from thee, when I was made in secret,
> and curiously wrought in the lowest parts of the earth.
Thine eyes did see my substance, yet being unperfect;
> and in thy book all my members were written,
> which in continuance were fashioned, when as yet there was none of them.
How precious also are thy thoughts unto me, O God!
> how great is the sum of them!
If I should count them, they are more in number than the sand:
> when I awake, I am still with thee.

A Paraphrase upon Part of the CXXXIX Psalm

THOMAS STANLEY

Great Monarch, whose feared hands the thunder fling,
And whose quick eyes, all darkness vanquishing,
Pierce in a moment earth's remotest parts,
The night of futures, and abyss of hearts;
My breast, the closest thoughts which there reside,

From thy all-seeing knowledge cannot hide;
The number of my steps before thee lies,
And my intents (ere mine) before thy eyes.
Thou knowest me, when my self I cannot know,
And without error seest what is not so.

Speech, that light garment, which our thoughts attires,
The image of our wishes and desires,
Daughter of air, from soul to soul which flies,
And in her mother's bosom melting dies:
By higher flight appears before thee, long
Before she birth receiveth from my tongue,
Before she from my lips had learnt to frame
Those accents, which my heart did first enflame,
And this invisible body flying hence,
Assumes, by which she is betrayed to sense.

The past and future still with thee abide,
The present, which from us like streams doth slide,
With a firm constant foot before thee stays,
To thee nought young is, nought oppressed with days;
Man (as if that bright fire thine eye reflects,
Consumed of mortal objects the defects,
And changed the changing laws of his frail breath)
A heap of scattered dust, a mass of earth,
A work almost below mortality,
Immortal in thy knowledge is like thee.

But if thy anger's dreadful storm break forth,
The Orient, or the West, the South, or North,
Can no profound abyss or exile lend,
Whose depth may hide, or strength my life defend;
Though swifter than the morning I could fly,
Thy thunder, which that speed doth far outvie,
Outstripping me, my flight would soon restrain:
Though I could dive into th'unsounded main,
Which nightly quencheth the bright light o'th'skies,
I should lie open to thy brighter eyes.

Yet I not wonder, if unveiled thou find
The darkest secrets of my naked mind;

As a learned artist thou mayst well foresee
The motions of that work is framed by thee:
Thou first into this dust a soul didst send,
Thy hand my skin did o'er my bones extend,
Which greater masterpiece, whilst I admire,
I fall down lost, in seeking to rise higher:
And finding 'bove my self, my self to be,
Turn to that nothing, from whence raised by thee.

141:1–141:10   LORD, I cry unto thee: make haste unto me;
    give ear unto my voice, when I cry unto thee.
Let my prayer be set forth before thee as incense;
    and the lifting up of my hands as the evening sacrifice.
Set a watch, O LORD, before my mouth; keep the door of my lips.
Incline not my heart to any evil thing, to practice wicked works
    with men that work iniquity: and let me not eat of their dainties.
Let the righteous smite me; it shall be a kindness: and let him reprove me;
    it shall be an excellent oil, which shall not break my head:
    for yet my prayer also shall be in their calamities.
When their judges are overthrown in stony places, they shall hear my words;
    for they are sweet.
Our bones are scattered at the grave's mouth,
    as when one cutteth and cleaveth wood upon the earth.
But mine eyes are unto thee, O GOD the Lord: in thee is my trust;
    leave not my soul destitute.
Keep me from the snares which they have laid for me,
    and the gins of the workers of iniquity.
Let the wicked fall into their own nets, whilst that I withal escape.

142:1–142:4   I cried unto the LORD with my voice;
    with my voice unto the LORD did I make my supplication.
I poured out my complaint before him; I shewed before him my trouble.
When my spirit was overwhelmed within me, then thou knewest my path.
    In the way wherein I walked have they privily laid a snare for me.
I looked on my right hand, and beheld,
    but there was no man that would know me:
    refuge failed me; no man cared for my soul.

In Tenebris ᴔ THOMAS HARDY

When the clouds' swoln bosoms echo back the shouts of the many
     and strong
That things are all as they best may be, save a few to be right ere long,
And my eyes have not the vision in them to discern what to these is
     so clear,
The blot seems straightway in me alone; one better he were not here.

The stout upstanders say, All's well with us: ruers have nought to rue!
And what the potent say so oft, can it fail to be somewhat true?
Breezily go they, breezily come; their dust smokes around their career,
Till I think I am one born out of due time, who has no calling here.

Their dawns bring lusty joys, it seems; their evenings all that is sweet;
Our times are blessed times, they cry: Life shapes it as is most meet,
And nothing is much the matter; there are many smiles to a tear;
Then what is the matter is I, I say. Why should such an one be here?. . .

Let him in whose ears the low-voiced Best is killed by the clash of
     the First,
Who holds that if way to the Better there be, it exacts a full look at
     the Worst,
Who feels that delight is a delicate growth cramped by crookedness,
     custom, and fear,
Get him up and be gone as one shaped awry; he disturbs the order here.

PROVERBS

6:6–6:8   Go to the ant, thou sluggard; consider her ways, and be wise:
Which having no guide, overseer, or ruler, Provideth her meat in the
summer, and gathereth her food in the harvest.

Proverbs 6:6 ᴔ DAVID CURZON

Go to the ant, you sluggard,

and watch it lug an object
forward single file

with no short breaks for
coffee, gossip, a croissant,

and no stopping to apostrophize
blossom, by-passed because
pollen is not its job,
no pause for trampled companions:

consider her ways—and be content.

6:9–6:11   How long wilt thou sleep, O sluggard? when wilt thou arise out
of thy sleep? Yet a little sleep, a little slumber, a little folding of the hands to
sleep: So shall thy poverty come as one that travelleth, and thy want as an
armed man.

Paraphrase ༈ SAMUEL JOHNSON

Turn on the prudent ant thy heedless eyes,
Observe her labours, sluggard, and be wise;
No stern command, no monitory voice,
Prescribes her duties, or directs her choice;
Yet, timely provident, she hastes away
To snatch the blessings of a plenteous day;
When fruitful summer loads the teeming plain,
She crops the harvest and she stores the grain.
How long shall sloth usurp thy useless hours,
Unnerve thy vigor, and enchain thy powers?
While artful shades thy downy couch enclose,
And soft solicitation courts repose,
Amidst the drowsy charms of dull delight,
Year chases year with unremitted flight,
Till want now following, fraudulent and slow,
Shall spring to seize thee, like an ambushed foe.

25:24   It is better to dwell in the corner of the house top, than with a
brawling woman and in a wide house.

For a Mouthy Woman   ᔐ   COUNTEE CULLEN

God and the devil still are wrangling
    Which should have her, which repel;
God wants no discord in his heaven;
    Satan has enough in hell.

27:17–27:19   Iron sharpeneth iron; so a man sharpeneth the countenance
of his friend. Whoso keepeth the fig tree shall eat the fruit thereof: so he
that waiteth on his master shall be honoured. As in water face answereth to
face, so the heart of man to man.

Do the Others Speak of Me Mockingly, Maliciously?   ᔐ
DELMORE SCHWARTZ

Do they whisper behind my back? Do they speak
Of my clumsiness? Do they laugh at me,
Mimicking my gestures, retailing my shame?
I'll whirl about, denounce them, saying
That they are shameless, they are treacherous,
No more my friends, nor will I once again
Never, amid a thousand meetings in the street,
Recognize their faces, take their hands,
Not for our common love or old times' sake:
They whispered behind my back, they mimicked me.

I know the reason why, I too have done this,
Cruel for wit's sake, behind my dear friend's back,
And to amuse betrayed his private love,
His nervous shame, her habit, and their weaknesses;
I have mimicked them, I have been treacherous,
For wit's sake, to amuse, because their being weighed
Too grossly for a time, to be superior,
To flatter the listeners by this, the intimate,
Betraying the intimate, but for the intimate,
To free myself of friendship's necessity,
Fearing from time to time that they would hear,
Denounce me and reject me, say once for all

That they would never meet me, take my hands,
Speaking for old times' sake and our common love.

What an unheard-of thing it is, in fine,
To love another and equally be loved!
What sadness and what joy! How cruel it is
That pride and wit distort the heart of man,
How vain, how sad, what cruelty, what need,
For this is true and sad, that I need them
And they need me. What can we do? We need
Each other's clumsiness, each other's wit,
Each other's company and our own pride. I need
My face unshamed, I need my wit, I cannot
Turn away. We know our clumsiness,
Our weakness, our necessities, we cannot
Forget our pride, our faces, our common love.

30:21–30:23   For three things the earth is disquieted, and for four which it
cannot bear: For a servant when he reigneth; and a fool when he is filled
with meat; For an odious woman when she is married; and an handmaid
that is heir to her mistress.

'A Servant when He Reigneth' ✺ RUDYARD KIPLING

Three things make earth unquiet
And four she cannot brook
The godly Agur counted them
And put them in a book—
Those Four Tremendous Curses
With which mankind is cursed;
But a Servant when He Reigneth
Old Agur entered first.

An Handmaid that is Mistress
We need not call upon.
A Fool when he is full of Meat
Will fall asleep anon.

An Odious Woman Married
May bear a babe and mend;
But a Servant when He Reigneth
Is Confusion to the end.

His feet are swift to tumult,
His hands are slow to toil,
His ears are deaf to reason,
His lips are loud in broil.
He knows no use for power
Except to show his might.
He gives no heed to judgment
Unless it prove him right.

Because he served a master
Before his Kingship came,
And hid in all disaster
Behind his master's name,
So, when his Folly opens
The unnecessary hells,
A Servant when He Reigneth
Throws the blame on some one else.

His vows are lightly spoken,
His faith is hard to bind,
His trust is easy broken,
He fears his fellow-kind.
The nearest mob will move him
To break the pledge he gave—
Oh, a Servant when He Reigneth
Is more than ever slave!

31:6–31:7 Give strong drink unto him that is ready to perish, and wine unto those that be of heavy hearts. Let him drink, and forget his poverty, and remember his misery no more.

Scotch Drink ✌ ROBERT BURNS

Gie him strong Drink until he wink,
That's sinking in despair;
An' liquor guid, to fire his bluid,
That's prest wi' grief an' care:
There let him bowse an' deep carouse,
Wi' bumpers flowing o'er,
Till he forgets his loves or debts,
An' minds his griefs no more.
    Solomon's Proverbs, Ch. 31st V. 6, 7.

Let other Poets raise a fracas
'Bout vines, an' wines, an' druken Bacchus,
An' crabbed names an' stories wrack us,
                    An' grate our lug,
I sing the juice Scotch bear can mak us,
                    In glass or jug.

O thou, my MUSE! guid, auld SCOTCH DRINK!
Whether thro' wimplin worms thou jink,
Or, richly brown, ream owre the brink,
                    In glorious faem,
Inspire me, till I lisp an' wink,
                    To sing thy name!

Let husky Wheat the haughs adorn,
And Aits set up their awnie horn,
An' Pease an' Beans, at een or morn,
                    Perfumes the plain,
Leeze me on thee John Barleycorn,
                    Thou king o' grain!

On the thee aft Scotland chows her cood,
In souple scones, the wale o' food!
Or tumbling in the boiling flood
                    Wi' kail an' beef;
But when thou pours thy strong heart's blood,
                    There thou shines chief.

Food fills the wame, an' keeps us livin:
Tho' life's a gift no worth receivin,
When heavy-dragg'd wi' pine an' grievin;
        But oil'd by thee,
The wheels o' life gae down-hill, scrievin,
        Wi' rattlin glee.

Thou clears the head o' doited Lear;
Thou chears the heart o' drooping Care;
Thou strings the nerves o' Labor-sair,
        At 's weary toil;
Thou ev'n brightens dark Despair,
        Wi' gloomy smile.

Aft, clad in massy, siller weed,
Wi' Gentles thou erects thy head;
Yet, humbly kind, in time o' need,
        The poorman's wine,
His wee drap pirratch, or his bread,
        Thou kitchens fine.

Thou art the life o' public haunts;
But thee, what were our fairs an' rants?
Ev'n goodly meetings o' the saunts,
        By thee inspir'd,
When gaping they besiege the tents,
        Are doubly fir'd.

That merry night we get the corn in
O sweetly, then, thou reams the horn in!
Or reekan on a New-year-mornin
        In cog or bicker,
An' just a wee drap sp'ritual burn in,
        An' gusty sucker!

When Vulcan gies his bellys breath,
An' Ploughmen gather wi' their graith,
O rare! to see thee fiz an' fraeth
        I' the lugget caup!
Then Burnewin comes on like Death,
        At ev'ry chap.

Nae mercy, then, for airn or steel;
The brawnie, banie, Ploughman-chiel
Brings hard owrehip, wi' sturdy wheel,
                    The strong forehammer,
Till block an' studdie ring an' reel
                    Wi' dinsome clamour.

When skirlin weanies see the light,
Thou maks the gossips clatter bright,
How fumbling coofs their dearies slight,
                    Wae worth the name!
Nae Howdie gets a social night,
                    Or plack frae them.

When neebors anger at a plea,
An' just as wud as wud can be,
How easy can the barley-bree
                    Cement the quarrel!
It's ay the cheapest Lawyer's fee
                    To taste the barrel.

Alake! that e'er my Muse has reason
To wyte her countrymen wi' treason!
But mony daily weet their weason
                    Wi' liquors nice,
An' hardly, in a winter season,
                    E'er spier her price.

Wae worth that Brandy, burnan trash!
Fell source o' monie a pain an' brash!
Twins mony a poor, doylt, druken hash
                    O' half his days;
An' sends, beside, auld Scotland's cash
                    To her warst faes.

Ye Scots wha wish auld Scotland well,
Ye chief, to you my tale I tell,
Poor, plackless devils like mysel,
                    It sets you ill,
Wi' bitter, dearthfu' wines to mell
                    Or foreign gill.

May Gravels round his blather wrench,
An' Gouts torment him, inch by inch,
Wha twists his gruntle wi' a glunch
          O' sour disdain,
Out owre a glass o' Whisky-punch
            Wi' honest men!

O Whisky! soul o' plays an' pranks!
Accept a Bardie's gratefu' thanks!
When wanting thee, what tuneless cranks
          Are my poor Verses!
Thou comes—they rattle i' their ranks
            At ither's arses!

Thee, Ferintosh! O sadly lost!
Scotland lament frae coast to coast!
Now colic-grips, an' barkin hoast,
          May kill us a';
For loyal Forbes' Charter'd boast
            Is taen awa!

Thae curst horse-leeches o' th' Excise,
Wha mak the Whisky stills their prize!
Haud up thy han' Deil! ance, twice, thrice!
          There, sieze the blinkers!
An' bake them up in brunstane pies
            For poor damn'd Drinkers.

Fortune, if thou'll but gie me still
Hale breeks, a scone, an' Whisky gill,
An' rowth o' rhyme to rave at will,
          Tak a' the rest,
An' deal 't about as thy blind skill
            Directs thee best.

31:10–31:31 Who can find a virtuous woman? for her price is far above
rubies. The heart of her husband doth safely trust in her, so that he shall
have no need of spoil. . . . Give her of the fruit of her hands; and let her own
works praise her in the gates.

On Woman ~ WILLIAM BUTLER YEATS

May God be praised for woman
That gives up all her mind,
A man may find in no man
A friendship of her kind
That covers all he has brought
As with her flesh and bone,
Nor quarrels with a thought
Because it is not her own.

Though pedantry denies,
It's plain the Bible means
That Solomon grew wise
While talking with his queens,
Yet never could, although
They say he counted grass,
Count all the praises due
When Sheba was his lass,
When she the iron wrought, or
When from the smithy fire
It shuddered in the water:
Harshness of their desire
That made them stretch and yawn,
Pleasure that comes with sleep,
Shudder that made them one.
What else He give or keep
God grant me—no, not here,
For I am not so bold
To hope a thing so dear
Now I am growing old,
But when, if the tale's true,
The Pestle of the moon
That pounds up all anew
Brings me to birth again—
To find what once I had
And know what once I have known,
Until I am driven mad,
Sleep driven from my bed,
By tenderness and care,
Pity, an aching head,

Gnashing of teeth, despair;
And all because of some one
Perverse creature of chance,
And live like Solomon
That Sheba led a dance.

ECCLESIASTES

1:5–1:11   The sun also ariseth, and the sun goeth down, and hasteth to his
place where he arose. The wind goeth toward the south, and turneth about
unto the north; it whirleth about continually, and the wind returneth again
according to his circuits. All the rivers run into the sea; yet the sea is not full;
unto the place from whence the rivers come, thither they return again.

All things are full of labour; man cannot utter it: the eye is not satisfied
with seeing, nor the ear filled with hearing. The thing that hath been, it is
that which shall be; and that which is done is that which shall be done: and
there is no new thing under the sun. Is there any thing whereof it may be
said, See, this is new? it hath been already of old time, which was before us.
There is no remembrance of former things; neither shall there be any
remembrance of things that are to come with those that shall come after.

The Vanity of All Worldly Things   ∿   ANNE BRADSTREET

As he said vanity, so vain say I,
Oh! vanity, O vain all under sky;
Where is the man can say, "Lo, I have found
On brittle earth a consolation sound"?
What is't in honor to be set on high?
No, they like beasts and sons of men shall die,
And whilst they live, how oft doth turn their fate;
He's now a captive that was king of late.
What is't in wealth great treasures to obtain?
No, that's but labor, anxious care, and pain.
He heaps up riches, and he heaps up sorrow,
It's his today, but who's his heir tomorrow?
What then? Content in pleasures canst thou find?
More vain than all, that's but to grasp the wind.
The sensual senses for a time they please,

Meanwhile the conscience rage, who shall appease?
What is't in beauty? No that's but a snare,
They're foul enough today, that once were fair.
What is't in flowering youth, or manly age?
The first is prone to vice, the last to rage.
Where is it then, in wisdom, learning, arts?
Sure if on earth, it must be in those parts;
Yet these the wisest man of men did find
But vanity, vexation of mind.
And he that knows the most doth still bemoan
He knows not all that here is to be known.
What is it then? to do as stoics tell,
Nor laugh, nor weep, let things go ill or well?
Such stoics are but stocks, such teaching vain,
While man is man, he shall have ease or pain.
If not in honor, beauty, age, nor treasure,
Nor yet in learning, wisdom, youth, nor pleasure,
Where shall I climb, sound, seek, search, or find
That *summum bonum* which may stay my mind?
There is a path no vulture's eye hath seen
Where lion fierce, nor lion's whelps have been,
Which leads unto that living crystal fount,
Who drinks thereof, the world doth nought account.
The depth and sea have said "'Tis not in me,"
With pearl and gold it shall not valued be.
For sapphire, onyx, topaz who would change;
It's hid from eyes of men, they count it strange.
Death and destruction the fame hath heard,
But where and what it is from heaven's declared;
It brings to honor which shall ne'er decay,
It stores with wealth which time can't wear away.
It yieldeth pleasures far beyond conceit,
And truly beautifies without deceit.
Nor strength, nor wisdom, nor fresh youth shall fade,
Nor death shall see, but are immortal made.
This pearl of price, this tree of life, this spring,
Who is possessed of shall reign a king.
Nor change of state nor cares shall ever see,
But wear his crown unto eternity.
This satiates the soul, this stays the mind,
And all the rest, but vanity we find.

1:12–1:14   I the Preacher was king over Israel in Jerusalem. And I gave my heart to seek and search out by wisdom concerning all things that are done under heaven: this sore travail hath God given to the sons of man to be exercised therewith. I have seen all the works that are done under the sun; and, behold, all is vanity and vexation of spirit.

Ecclesiastes ❧ DEREK MAHON

God, you could grow to love it, God-fearing, God-
    chosen purist little puritan that,
for all your wiles and smiles, you are (the
    dank churches, the empty streets,
the shipyard silence, the tied-up swings) and
    shelter your cold heart from the heat
of the world, from woman-inquisition, from the
    bright eyes of children. Yes, you could
wear black, drink water, nourish a fierce zeal
    with locusts and wild honey, and not
feel called upon to understand and forgive
    but only to speak with a bleak
afflatus, and love the January rains when they
    darken the dark doors and sink hard
into the Antrim hills, the bog meadows, the heaped
    graves of your fathers. Bury that red
bandana and stick, that banjo. This is your
    country, close one eye and be king.
Your people await you, their heavy washing
    flaps for you in the housing estates—
a credulous people. God, you could do it, God
    help you, stand on a corner stiff
with rhetoric, promising nothing under the sun.

2:15–2:16   Then said I in my heart, As it happeneth to the fool, so it happeneth even to me; and why was I then more wise? Then I said in my heart, that this also is vanity. For there is no remembrance of the wise more than of the fool for ever; seeing that which now is in the days to come shall all be forgotten. And how dieth the wise man? as the fool.

A Spirit Appeared to Me ᴐ   HERMAN MELVILLE

A spirit appeared to me, and said
'Where now would you choose to dwell?
In the Paradise of the Fool,
Or in wise Solomon's hell?'

Never he asked me twice:
'Give me the Fool's Paradise.'

3:1–3:8   To every thing there is a season, and a time to every purpose
under the heaven: A time to be born, and a time to die; a time to plant, and
a time to pluck up that which is planted; A time to kill, and a time to heal; a
time to break down, and a time to build up; A time to weep, and a time to
laugh; a time to mourn, and a time to dance; A time to cast away stones,
and a time to gather stones together; a time to embrace, and a time to
refrain from embracing; A time to get, and a time to lose; a time to keep,
and a time to cast away; A time to rend, and a time to sew; a time to keep
silence, and a time to speak; A time to love, and a time to hate; a time of
war, and a time of peace.

Times go by Turns ᴐ   ROBERT SOUTHWELL

The lopped tree in time may grow again;
Most naked plants renew both fruit and flower;
The sorriest wight may find release of pain,
The driest soil suck in some moistening shower;
Times go by turns and chances change by course,
From foul to fair, from better hap to worse.

The sea of fortune doth not ever flow,
She draws her favors to the lowest ebb;
Her tide hath equal times to come and go,
Her loom doth weave the fine and coarsest web;
No joy so great but runneth to an end,
No hap so hard but may in time amend.

Not always fall of leaf nor ever spring,
No endless night yet not eternal day;

The saddest birds a season find to sing,
The roughest storm a calm may soon allay;
Thus with succeeding turns God tempereth all,
That man may hope to rise yet fear to fall.

A chance may win that by mischance was lost;
The net that holds no great, takes little fish;
In some things all, in all things none are crossed,
Few all they need, but none have all they wish;
Unmeddled joys here to no man befall,
Who least hath some, who most hath never all.

7:24　That which is far off, and exceeding deep, who can find it out?

In Ecclesiastes I Read ·ᔆ· J. P. WHITE

In Ecclesiastes I read,
"That which is far off and exceeding deep,
Who can find it out?"
Who can tell the earth's tale of wearing down,
building up, erosion, creation,
a swirl of embers breathing amethyst and tourmaline,
a suffering bounded by the four baleful rivers of Hell
and a sun that will one day collapse,
engulfing it in one long dragon breath of dying out?
The ancients said earth was immovable —
that every daffodil and sequoia
was fixed in its own sky-blue mirror.
Now we know this planet is like others,
restless, driven, continually torn apart
and reassembled by a shifting of plates
grinding beneath the surface like nervous molars.
The globe itself a work in progress
with its iced poles wandering
and its fires bubbling below the seas.
Even its path through space
is an egg-shaped, elliptical orbit, hardly circular.
It is here on what used to be called solid ground
that we live—fragile, torn by our need

for love, food and mercy
Most of us worried there will be too little time
to light the lamps of our fingers
and walk the narrow path in the rain.
But what of the earth? Who can find it out—
embrace its drifting continents,
who can love it as it is—unfinished,
smudged with the dust of rare constellations,
flickering on and off like a rain-drenched fire in the woods?

9:11–9:12   I returned, and saw under the sun, that the race is not to the swift, nor the battle to the strong, neither yet bread to the wise, nor yet riches to men of understanding, nor yet favour to men of skill; but time and chance happeneth to them all. For man also knoweth not his time: as the fishes that are taken in an evil net, and as the birds that are caught in the snare; so are the sons of men snared in an evil time, when it falleth suddenly upon them.

Race and Battle   ↗   D. H. LAWRENCE

The race is not to the swift
but to those that can sit still
and let the waves go over them.

The battle is not to the strong
but to the frail, who know best
how to efface themselves
to save the streaked pansy of the heart from being trampled to mud.

12:1–12:2   Remember now thy Creator in the days of thy youth, while the evil days come not, nor the years draw nigh, when thou shalt say, I have no pleasure in them; While the sun, or the light, or the moon, or the stars, be not darkened, nor the clouds return after the rain:

Past Thinking of Solomon ᔭ FRANCIS THOMPSON

Wise-Unto-Hell Ecclesiast,
Who sievedst life to the gritted last!

This thy sting, thy darkness, Mage—
Cloud upon sun, upon youth age?

Now is come a darker thing,
And is come a colder sting,

Unto us, who find the womb
Opes on the courtyard of the tomb.

Now in this fuliginous
City of flesh our sires for us

Darkly built, the sun at prime
Is hidden, and betwixt the time

Of day and night is variance none,
Who know not altern moon and sun;

Whose deposed heaven through dungeon-bars
Looks down blinded of its stars.

Yea, in the days of youth, God wot,
Now we say: They please me not.

12:8   Vanity of vanities, saith the preacher; all is vanity.

'All is Vanity, Saith the Preacher' ᔭ
GEORGE NOEL GORDON, LORD BYRON

Fame, wisdom, love, and power were mine,
    And health and youth possessed me;
My goblets blushed from every vine,
    And lovely forms caressed me;

I sunned my heart in beauty's eyes,
    And felt my soul grow tender;
All earth can give, or mortal prize,
    Was mine of regal splendour.

I strive to number o'er what days
    Remembrance can discover,
Which all that life or earth displays
    Would lure me to live over.
There rose no day, there rolled no hour
    Of pleasure unembittered;
And not a trapping decked my power
    That galled not while it glittered.

The serpent of the field, by art
    And spells, is won from harming;
But that which coils around the heart,
    Oh! who hath power of charming?
It will not list to wisdom's lore,
    Nor music's voice can lure it;
But there it stings for evermore
    The soul that must endure it.

12:13–12:14   Let us hear the conclusion of the whole matter: Fear God, and keep his commandments: for this is the whole duty of man. For God shall bring every work into judgment, with every secret thing, whether it be good, or whether it be evil.

The Conclusion of the Matter ᕰ CHRISTOPHER SMART

Fear God—obey his just decrees,
And do it hand, and heart, and knees;
For after all our utmost care
There's nought like penitence and prayer.

Then weigh the balance in your mind,
Look forward, not one glance behind;
Let no foul fiend retard your pace,
Hosanna! Thou hast won the race.

SONG OF SOLOMON

1:1–1:3   The song of songs, which is Solomon's.
Let him kiss me with the kisses of his mouth: for thy love is better than wine.
Because of the savour of thy good ointments
   thy name is as ointment poured forth, therefore do the virgins love thee.

Let Him with Kisses of His Mouth   ᘏ   ANONYMOUS

Let him with kisses of his mouth
Be pleased me to kiss.
Because much better than the wine
Thy loving kindness is.
Thy name as poured forth ointment is,
Because of the sweet smell
Of thy good ointments, therefore do
The virgins love thee well.

4:10–4:15   How fair is thy love, my sister, my spouse!
   how much better is thy love than wine!
   and the smell of thine ointments than all spices!
Thy lips, O my spouse, drop as the honeycomb:
   honey and milk are under thy tongue;
   and the smell of thy garments is like the smell of Lebanon.
A garden inclosed is my sister, my spouse;
   a spring shut up, a fountain sealed.
Thy plants are an orchard of pomegranates, with pleasant fruits;
   camphire, with spikenard,
Spikenard and saffron; calamus and cinnamon, with all trees of frankincense;
   myrrh and aloes, with all the chief spices:
A fountain of gardens, a well of living waters, and streams from Lebanon.

Sandalwood comes to my mind   ᘏ   CARL RAKOSI

Sandalwood comes to my mind
when I think of you
and the triumph of your shoulders.
Greek chorus girls came to me

in the course of the day
and from a distance
Celtic vestals too,
but you bring me the Holy Land
and the sound of deep themes
in the inner chamber.

I give you praise
in the language
of wells and vineyards.

Your hand recalls
the salty heat of barbarism.
Your mouth is a pouch
for the accents of queens.
Your eyes flow over
with a gentle psalm
like the fawn eyes
of the woodland.

Your black hair
plucks my strings.

In the foggy wilderness
is not your heart
a hermit thrush?

You are timeless
as the mirrors,
Jewess of the palm country,
isolate as the frost
on the queen of swans.

Now that I have seen
the royal stones and fountains
and the tetrarch's lovely swans,
I am satisfied that you are
a mindful of white birds
in the folly of an old Jew.

Because of the coral
of your two breasts
are the prophets angry
but I have my lips upon them
and the song shall go on.

4:16   Awake, O north wind; and come, thou south;
   blow upon my garden, that the spices thereof may flow out.
Let my beloved come into his garden, and eat his pleasant fruits.

Regeneration ∽   HENRY VAUGHAN

A ward, and still in bonds, one day
                          I stole abroad,
It was high-spring, and all the way
                          Primrosed, and hung with shade;
                          Yet, was it frost within,
                                    And surly winds
Blasted my infant buds, and sin
                          Like clouds eclipsed my mind.

Stormed thus; I straight perceived my spring
                          Mere stage, and show,
My walk a monstrous, mountained thing
                          Rough-cast with rocks, and snow;
                          And as a pilgrim's eye
                                    Far from relief,
Measures the melancholy sky
                          Then drops, and rains for grief,

So sighed I upwards still, at last
                          'Twixt steps, and falls
I reached the pinnacle, where placed
                          I found a pair of scales
                          I took them up and laid
                                    In th'one late pains,
The other smoke, and pleasures weighed
                          But proved the heavier grains;

With that, some cried, Away; straight I
                                    Obeyed, and led
Full East, a fair, fresh field could spy
                              Some called it, *Jacob's Bed*;
                              A virgin-soil, which no
                                    Rude feet e'er trod,
Where (since he stepped there,) only go
                              Prophets, and friends of God.

Here, I reposed; but scarce well set,
                                    A grove descried
Of stately height, whose branches met
                              And mixed on every side;
                              I entered, and once in
                                    (Amazed to see't,)
Found all was changed, and a new spring
                              Did all my senses greet;

The unthrift sun shot vital gold
                                    A thousand pieces,
And heaven its azure did unfold
                              Checkered with snowy fleeces,
                              The air was all in spice
                                    And every bush
A garland wore; thus fed my eyes
                              But all the ear lay hush.

Only a little fountain lent
                                    Some use for ears,
And on the dumb shades language spent
                              The music of her tears;
                              I drew her near, and found
                                    The cistern full
Of diverse stones, some bright, and round
                              Others ill-shaped, and dull.

The first (pray mark,) as quick as light
                                    Danced through the flood,
But, th'last more heavy than the night
                              Nailed to the center stood;
                              I wondered much, but tired

At last with thought,
My restless eye that still desired
As strange an object brought;

It was a bank of flowers, where I descried
(Though 'twas mid-day,)
Some fast asleep, others broad-eyed
And taking in the ray,
Here musing long, I heard
A rushing wind
Which still increased, but whence it stirred
No where I could not find;

I turned me round, and to each shade
Dispatched an eye,
To see, if any leaf had made
Least motion, or reply,
But while I listening sought
My mind to ease
By knowing, where 'twas, or where not,
It whispered; Where I please.

Lord, then said I, *On me one breath*
And let me die before my death!

5:2 I sleep, but my heart waketh:
it is the voice of my beloved that knocketh, saying,
Open to me, my sister, my love, my dove, my undefiled:
for my head is filled with dew, and my locks with the drops of the night.

My dove, my beautiful one ☙ JAMES JOYCE

My dove, my beautiful one,
Arise, arise!
The night-dew lies
Upon my lips and eyes.

The odorous winds are weaving
A music of sighs:

Arise, arise,
My dove, my beautiful one!

I wait by the cedar tree,
    My sister, my love.
    White breast of the dove,
My breast shall be your bed.

The pale dew lies
    Like a veil on my head.
    My fair one, my fair dove,
Arise, arise!

8:7–8:10   Many waters cannot quench love, neither can the floods drown it:
        if a man would give all the substance of his house for love,
        it would utterly be contemned.
We have a little sister, and she hath no breasts:
        what shall we do for our sister in the day when she shall be spoken for?
If she be a wall, we will build upon her a palace of silver:
        and if she be a door, we will inclose her with boards of cedar.
I am a wall, and my breasts like towers:
        then was I in his eyes as one that found favour.

The Book of Wisdom   ❧   ROBERT LOWELL

Can I go on loving anyone at fifty,
still cool to the brief and five-times wounded lives
of those we loathed with wild idealism young?
Though the gods only toss me twenty cards,
twenty, thirty, or fifty years of work,
I shiver up vertical like a baby pigeon,
palate-sprung for the worm, senility—
to strap the gross artillery to my back,
lash on destroying what I lurch against,
not with anger, but unwieldy feet,
ballooning like the spotted, warty, blow-rib toad,
King Solomon croaking, "This too is vanity;
her lips are a scarlet thread, her breasts are towers,"
hymns of the terrible organ in decay.

ISAIAH

1:16–1:18   Wash you, make you clean; put away the evil of your doings
from before mine eyes; cease to do evil; Learn to do well; seek judgment,
relieve the oppressed, judge the fatherless, plead for the widow. Come
now, and let us reason together, saith the LORD: though your sins be as
scarlet, they shall be as white as snow; though they be red like crimson,
they shall be as wool.

Beyond Knowledge ✑ ALICE MEYNELL

Into the rescued world newcomer,
   The newly-dead stepped up, and cried,
"O what is that, sweeter than summer
   Was to my heart before I died?
Sir (to an angel), what is yonder
   More bright than the remembered skies,
A lovelier sight, a softer splendour
   Than when the moon was wont to rise?
Surely no sinner wears such seeming
   Even the Rescued World within?"

"O the success of His redeeming!
   O child, it is a rescued sin!"

14:12–14:18   How art thou fallen from heaven, O Lucifer, son of the morn-
ing! how art thou cut down to the ground, which didst weaken the nations!
For thou hast said in thine heart, I will ascend into heaven, I will exalt my
throne above the stars of God: I will sit also upon the mount of the congre-
gation, in the sides of the north: I will ascend above the heights of the
clouds; I will be like the most High. Yet thou shalt be brought down to hell,
to the sides of the pit. They that see thee shall narrowly look upon thee, and
consider thee, saying, Is this the man that made the earth to tremble, that
did shake kingdoms; That made the world as a wilderness, and destroyed
the cities thereof; that opened not the house of his prisoners? All the kings
of the nations, even all of them, lie in glory, every one in his own house.

Lucifer in Starlight ~ GEORGE MEREDITH

On a starred night Prince Lucifer uprose.
Tired of his dark dominion swung the fiend
Above the rolling ball in cloud part screened,
Where sinners hugged their spectre of repose
Poor prey to his hot fit of pride were those.
And now upon his western wing he leaned,
Now his huge bulk o'er Afric's sands careened,
Now the black planet shadowed arctic snows.
Soaring through wider zones that pricked his scars
With memory of the old revolt from awe,
He reached a middle height, and at the stars,
Which are the brain of heaven, he looked, and sank.
Around the ancient track marched, rank on rank,
The army of unalterable law.

29:11–29:14   And the vision of all is become unto you as the words of a
book that is sealed, which men deliver to one that is learned, saying, Read
this, I pray thee: and he saith, I cannot; for it is sealed: And the book is
delivered to him that is not learned, saying, Read this, I pray thee: and he
saith, I am not learned. Wherefore the Lord said, Forasmuch as this people
draw near me with their mouth, and with their lips do honour me, but have
removed their heart far from me, and their fear toward me is taught by the
precept of men: Therefore, behold, I will proceed to do a marvellous work
among this people, even a marvellous work and a wonder: for the wisdom
of their wise men shall perish, and the understanding of their prudent men
shall be hid.

Isaiah by Kerosene Lantern Light ~ ROBERT HARRIS

This voice an older friend has kept
to patronise the single name he swears by
saying aha, aha to me.

The heresy hunter, sifting these lines
another shrieks through serepax and heroin
that we have a 'culture'.

These are the very same who shall wait
for plainer faces after they've glutted on beauty,
a mild people back from the dead

shall speak the doors down
to the last hullo reaching the last crooked hutch
in forest or forest-like deeps of the town.

These who teach with the fingers and answer
with laughter, with anger, shall be in derision
and the waiting long, and the blue and white days

like a grave in a senseless universe.
I believe this wick and this open book
in the light's oval, and I disbelieve

everything this generation has told me.

40:6–40:8   The voice said, Cry. And he said, What shall I cry? All flesh is
grass, and all the goodliness thereof is as the flower of the field: The grass
withereth, the flower fadeth: because the spirit of the LORD bloweth upon
it: surely the people is grass. The grass withereth, the flower fadeth: but the
word of our God shall stand for ever.

The Steed Bit his Master   ろ   ANONYMOUS

The steed bit his master:
How came this to pass?
He heard the good pastor
Cry, "All flesh is grass."

47:1   Come down, and sit in the dust, O virgin daughter of Babylon, sit on
the ground: there is no throne, O daughter of the Chaldeans: for thou shalt
no more be called tender and delicate.

Babylon ·ᵔ· ALFRED, LORD TENNYSON

Bow, daughter of Babylon, bow thee to dust!
Thine heart shall be quelled, and thy pride shall be crushed:
Weep, Babylon, weep! for thy splendour is past;
And they come like the storm in the day of the blast.

Howl, desolate Babylon, lost one and lone!
And bind thee in sackcloth—for where is thy throne?
Like a winepress in wrath will I trample thee down,
And rend from thy temples the pride of thy crown.

Though thy streets be a hundred, thy gates be all brass,
Yet thy proud ones of war shall be withered like grass;
Thy gates shall be broken, thy strength be laid low,
And thy streets shall resound to the shouts of the foe!

Though thy chariots of power on thy battlements bound,
And the grandeur of waters encompass thee round;
Yet thy walls shall be shaken, thy waters shall fail,
Thy matrons shall shriek, and thy king shall be pale.

The terrible day of thy fall is at hand,
When my rage shall descend on the face of thy land;
The lances are pointed, the keen sword is bared,
The shields are anointed,[12] the helmets prepared.

I call upon Cyrus! He comes from afar,
And the armies of nations are gathered to war;
With the blood of thy children his path shall be red,
And the bright sun of conquest shall blaze o'er his head.

Thou glory of kingdoms! thy princes are drunk,[13]
But their loins shall be loosed, and their hearts shall be sunk;
They shall crouch to the dust, and be counted as slaves,
At the roll of his wheels, like the rushing of waves!

12 ISA 21:5
13 JER 51:57

For I am the Lord, who have mightily spanned
The breadth of the heavens, and the sea and the land;
And the mountains shall flow at my presence,[14] and earth
Shall reel to and fro in the glance of my wrath!

Your proud domes of cedar on earth shall be thrown
And the rank grass shall wave o'er the lonely hearthstone;
And your sons and your sires and your daughters shall bleed
By the barbarous hands of the murdering Mede!

I will sweep ye away in destruction and death,
As the whirlwind that scatters the chaff with its breath;
And the fanes of your gods shall be sprinkled with gore,
And the course of your streams shall be heard of no more![15]

There the wandering Arab shall ne'er pitch his tent,
But the beasts of the desert shall wail and lament;
In their desolate houses the dragons shall lie,
And the satyrs shall dance, and the bitterns shall cry![16]

55:1–55:2   Ho, every one that thirsteth, come ye to the waters, and he
that hath no money; come ye, buy, and eat; yea, come, buy wine and milk
without money and without price. Wherefore do ye spend money for that
which is not bread? and your labour for that which satisfieth not? hearken
diligently unto me, and eat ye that which is good, and let your soul delight
itself in fatness.

The Invitation   ჯ   GEORGE HERBERT

Come ye hither all, whose taste
                    Is our waste;
Save your cost, and mend your fare.
God is here prepared and dressed,
                    And the feast,
God, in whom all dainties are.

14 ISA 64:1
15 JER 50:38
16 ISA 13:20 –22

Come ye hither all, whom wine
                    Doth define,
Naming you not to your good:
Weep what ye have drunk amiss,
                    And drink this.
Which before ye drink is blood.

Come ye hither all, whom pain
                    Doth arraign.
Bringing all your sins to sight:
Taste and fear not: God is here
                    In this cheer,
And on sin doth cast the fright.

Come ye hither all, whom joy
                    Doth destroy,
While ye graze without your bounds:
Here is joy that drowneth quite
                    Your delight,
As a flood the lower grounds.

Come ye hither all, whose love
                    Is your dove,
And exalts you to the sky:
Here is love, which having breath
                    Ev'n in death,
After death can never die.

Lord I have invited all,
                    And I shall
Still invite, still call to thee:
For it seems but just and right
                    In my sight,
Where is all, there all should be.

Ho, everyone that thirsteth ⌇ A. E. HOUSMAN

Ho, everyone that thirsteth
    And hath the price to give,
Come to the stolen waters,
    Drink and your soul shall live.

Come to the stolen waters,
   And leap the guarded pale,
And pull the flower in season
   Before desire shall fail.

It shall not last for ever,
   No more than earth and skies;
But he that drinks in season
   Shall live before he dies.

June suns, you cannot store them
   To warm the winter's cold,
The lad that hopes for heaven
   Shall fill his mouth with mould.

60:15–60:20   Whereas thou hast been forsaken and hated, so that no man went through thee, I will make thee an eternal excellency, a joy of many generations. Thou shalt also suck the milk of the Gentiles, and shalt suck the breast of kings: and thou shalt know that I the LORD am thy Saviour and thy Redeemer, the mighty One of Jacob. For brass I will bring gold, and for iron I will bring silver, and for wood brass, and for stones iron: I will also make thy officers peace, and thine exactors righteousness. Violence shall no more be heard in thy land, wasting nor destruction within thy borders; but thou shalt call thy walls Salvation, and thy gates Praise. The sun shall be no more thy light by day; neither for brightness shall the moon give light unto thee: but the LORD shall be unto thee an everlasting light, and thy God thy glory. Thy sun shall no more go down; neither shall thy moon withdraw itself: for the LORD shall be thine everlasting light, and the days of thy mourning shall be ended.

Hymn 10   WILLIAM COWPER

Hear what God the Lord hath spoken,
O my people, weak and few;
Comfortless, afflicted, broken,
Fair abodes I build for you:
Thorns of heart-felt tribulation
Shall no more perplex your ways;
You shall name your walls, Salvation,
And your gates shall all be praise.

Then, like streams that feed the garden,
Pleasures, without end, shall flow;
For the Lord, your faith rewarding,
All his bounty shall bestow:
Still in undisturbed possession,
Peace and righteousness shall reign;
Never shall you feel oppression,
Hear the voice of war again.

You no more your suns descending,
Waning moons no more shall see;
But your griefs, for ever ending,
Find eternal noon in me;
God shall rise, and shining o'er you,
Change to day the gloom of night;
He, the Lord, shall be your glory,
God your everlasting light.

63:1–63:6   Who is this that cometh from Edom, with dyed garments from Bozrah? this that is glorious in his apparel, travelling in the greatness of his strength? I that speak in righteousness, mighty to save. Wherefore art thou red in thine apparel, and thy garments like him that treadeth in the winefat? I have trodden the winepress alone; and of the people there was none with me: for I will tread them in mine anger, and trample them in my fury; and their blood shall be sprinkled upon my garments, and I will stain all my raiment. For the day of vengeance is in mine heart, and the year of my redeemed is come. And I looked, and there was none to help; and I wondered that there was none to uphold: therefore mine own arm brought salvation unto me; and my fury, it upheld me. And I will tread down the people in mine anger, and make them drunk in my fury, and I will bring down their strength to the earth.

What is he, this lordling   ⁓   FRIAR WILLIAM HEREBERT

What is he, this lordling, that cometh from the fight
With blood-red weed so grisliche y-dight,
So fair y-cointisëd, so seemly in sight,
So stiflichë gangeth, so doughty a knight?

'I it am, I it am, that ne speak butë right,
Champion to healen mankind in fight.'

'Why then is thy shroud red, with blood all y-ment,
As treaderës in wring with must all besprent?'

'The wring I have y-trodden all myself one,
And of all mankind ne was none other wone.
I them have y-trodden in wrath and in grame
And all my weed is besprent with their blood y-same,
And all my robe y-foulëd to their greatë shame.
The day of th'ilkë wrechë liveth in my thought;
The year of meedës yielding ne forget I nought.

I looked all aboutë some helping man;
I sought all the routë, but help n'as there none.
It was mine ownë strengthë that this botë wrought,
Myn ownë doughtinessë that help there me brought.'

'On Godës milsfulness I will bethinkë me,
And herien him in allë thing that he yieldeth me.'

'I have y-trodden the folk in wrath and in grame,
Adreint all with shenness, y-drawn down with shame.'

65:25   The wolf and the lamb shall feed together, and the lion shall eat
straw like the bullock: and dust shall be the serpent's meat. They shall not
hurt nor destroy in all my holy mountain, saith the LORD.

On Falling Asleep by Firelight   ✸   WILLIAM MEREDITH

Around the fireplace, pointing at the fire,
As in the prophet's dream of the last truce,
The animals lie down; they doze or stare,
Their hoofs and paws in comical disuse;
A few still run in dreams. None seems aware
Of the laws of prey that lie asleep here, too,
The dreamer unafraid who keeps the zoo.

Some winter nights impel us to take in
Whatever lopes outside, beastly or kind;
Nothing that gibbers in or out of mind
But the hearth bestows a sleepy sense of kin.
Promiscuous hosts, we bid the causeless slime
Come in; its casualness remains a crime,
But metaphysics bites less sharp than wind.

Now, too, a ghostly, gradually erect
Company lies down, weary of the walk—
Parents with whom we would, but cannot, talk,
Beside them on the floor their artifacts:
Weapons we gave them, which they now bring back.
If they see our privilege, they do not object,
And we are not ashamed to be their stock.

All we had thought unkind were all the while
Alike, the firelight says, and strikes us dumb;
We dream there is no ravening or guile
And take it kindly of the beasts to come
And suffer hospitality, the heat
Turns softly on the hearth into that dust
Isaiah said would be the serpent's meat.

66:1–66:2 Thus saith the LORD, The heaven is my throne, and the earth is my footstool: where is the house that ye build unto me? and where is the place of my rest? For all those things hath mine hand made, and all those things have been, saith the LORD: but to this man will I look, even to him that is poor and of a contrite spirit, and trembleth at my word.

Lightworks: Chapter 66 — DAVID ROSENBERG

The Lord speaks
this way
the sky

and all ways behind it
is a royal seat for me
space

                    is where I rest
            and the earth my footrest
                    in time

        where could you build a house
                    for me
                where a place

            especially for me to rest
            as if I would sleep or abide
                there   or there

            when I made all this
        all of it comes from my hand
        all that is came into being

                    from me
                    my Lord
                    is speaking

        but I look at man especially
            for the man or woman
                poor and powerless

            when he knows he is
            broken in spirit and
            filled with humility

            his body trembling
            open to the others
                to my words.

66:6–66:13   A voice of noise from the city, a voice from the temple, a voice
of the LORD that rendereth recompence to his enemies. Before she travailed,
she brought forth; before her pain came, she was delivered of a man child.
   Who hath heard such a thing? who hath seen such things? Shall the
earth be made to bring forth in one day? or shall a nation be born at once?
for as soon as Zion travailed, she brought forth her children. Shall I bring to
the birth, and not cause to bring forth? saith the LORD: shall I cause to
bring forth, and shut the womb? saith thy God.

Rejoice ye with Jerusalem, and be glad with her, all ye that love her: rejoice for joy with her, all ye that mourn for her: That ye may suck, and be satisfied with the breasts of her consolations; that ye may milk out, and be delighted with the abundance of her glory. For thus saith the LORD, Behold, I will extend peace to her like a river, and the glory of the Gentiles like a flowing stream: then shall ye suck, ye shall be borne upon her sides, and be dandled upon her knees. As one whom his mother comforteth, so will I comfort you; and ye shall be comforted in Jerusalem.

Isaiah 66:11 ✌ FRANCIS QUARLES

What, never filled? Be thy lips screwed so fast
    To th' earth's full breast? For shame, for shame unseize thee:
Thou tak'st a surfeit where thou shouldst but taste,
        And mak'st too much not half enough to please thee.
            Ah fool, forbear; Thou swallowst at one breath
Both food and poison down; thou drawst both milk and death.

The uberous breasts, when fairly drawn, repast
    The thriving infant with their milky flood,
But being overstrained, return at last
        Unwholesome gulps composed of wind and blood.
            A moderate use does both repast and please;
Who strains beyond a mean draws in and gulps disease.

But, O that mean whose good the least abuse
    Makes bad, is too too hard to be directed:
Can thorns bring grapes, or crabs a pleasing juice?
        There's nothing wholesome, where the whole's infected.
            Unseize thy lips: Earth's milk's a ripened core
That drops from her disease, that matters from her sore.

Thinkst thou that paunch that burlies out thy coat,
    Is thriving fat; or flesh, that seems so brawny?
Thy paunch is dropsied and thy cheeks are bloat;
        Thy lips are white and thy complexion tawny;
            Thy skin's a bladder blown with watery tumors;
Thy flesh a trembling bog, a quagmire full of humors.

And thou whose thriveless hands are ever straining
    Earth's fluent breasts into an empty sieve,
That always hast, yet always art complaining,
    And whin'st for more than earth has power to give;
        Whose treasure flows and flees away as fast;
That ever hast, and hast, yet hast not what thou hast:

Go choose a substance, fool, that will remain
    Within the limits of thy leaking measure;
Or else go seek an urn that will retain
    The liquid body of thy slippery treasure:
        Alas, how poorly are thy labors crowned?
Thy liquour's neither sweet, nor yet thy vessel sound.

What less than fool is Man, to prog and plot,
    And lavish out the cream of all his care,
To gain poor seeming goods, which, being got,
    Make firm possession but a thoroughfare:
        Or if they stay, they furrow thoughts the deeper,
And being kept with care, they lose their careful keeper.

JEREMIAH

3:6   The LORD said also unto me in the days of Josiah the king, Hast thou seen that which backsliding Israel hath done? she is gone up upon every high mountain and under every green tree, and there hath played the harlot.

Israel   ෨   CARL RAKOSI

I hear the voice
          of David and Bathsheba
and the judgment
          on the continual
backslidings
          of the Kings of Israel

I have stumbled
          on the ancient voice

of honesty

            and tremble

at the voice

            of my people.

12:1 Righteous art thou, O Lord, when I plead with thee: yet let me talk with thee of thy judgments:[17] Wherefore doth the way of the wicked prosper? wherefore are all they happy that deal very treacherously?

Thou art Indeed Just, Lord ✌ GERARD MANLEY HOPKINS

Thou art indeed just, Lord, if I contend
With thee; but, sir, so what I plead is just.
Why do sinners' ways prosper? and why must
Disappointment all I endeavour end?
    Wert thou mine enemy, O thou my friend,
How wouldst thou worse, I wonder, than thou dost
Defeat, thwart me? Oh, the sots and thralls of lust
Do in spare hours more thrive than I that spend,
Sir, life upon thy cause. See, banks and brakes
Now, leavèd how thick! lacèd they are again
With fretty chervil, look, and fresh wind shakes
Them; birds build—but not I build; no, but strain,
Time's eunuch, and not breed one work that wakes.
Mine, O thou lord of life, send my roots rain.

51:20–51:23 Thou art my battle ax and weapons of war: for with thee will I break in pieces the nations, and with thee will I destroy kingdoms; And with thee will I break in pieces the horse and his rider; and with thee will I break in pieces the chariot and his rider; With thee also will I break in pieces man and woman; and with thee will I break in pieces old and young; and with thee will I break in pieces the young man and the maid; I will also break in pieces with thee the shepherd and his flock; and with thee will I break in pieces the husbandman and his yoke of oxen; and with thee will I break in pieces captains and rulers.

17 In the Douay Vulgate: Thou indeed, O Lord, art just, if I plead with thee, but yet I will speak
    what is just to thee:

In Time of 'The Breaking of Nations' ⋙
THOMAS HARDY

Only a man harrowing clods
    In a slow silent walk
With an old horse that stumbles and nods
    Half asleep as they stalk.

Only thin smoke without flame
    From the heaps of couch-grass;
Yet this will go onward the same
    Though Dynasties pass.

Yonder a maid and her wight
    Come whispering by:
War's annals will cloud into night
    Ere their story die.

LAMENTATIONS

1:1   How doth the city sit solitary, that was full of people! how is she become as a widow! she that was great among the nations, and princess among the provinces, how is she become tributary!

Wednesday of Holy Week, 1940 ⋙   KENNETH REXROTH

Out of the east window a storm
Blooms spasmodically across the moonrise;
In the west, in the haze, the planets
Pulsate like standing meteors.
We listen in the darkness to the service of Tenebrae,
Music older than the Resurrection,
The voice of the ruinous, disorderly Levant:
"Why doth the city sit solitary
That was full of people?"
The voices of the Benedictines are massive, impersonal;
They neither fear this agony nor are ashamed of it.
Think . . . six hours ago in Europe,

Thousands were singing these words,
Putting out the candles psalm by psalm. . .
Albi like a fort in the cold dark,
Aachen, the voices fluttering in the ancient vaulting,
The light of the last candle
In Munich on the gnarled carving.
"Jerusalem, Jerusalem,
Return ye unto the Lord thy God."
Thousands kneeling in the dark,
Saying, "Have mercy upon me O God."
We listen appreciatively, smoking, talking quietly,
The voices are coming from three thousand miles.
On the white garden wall the shadows
Of the date palm thresh wildly;
The full moon of the spring is up,
And a gale with it.

EZEKIEL

1:15–1:21   Now as I beheld the living creatures, behold one wheel upon
the earth by the living creatures, with his four faces. The appearance of the
wheels and their work was like unto the colour of a beryl: and they four had
one likeness: and their appearance and their work was as it were a wheel in
the middle of a wheel. When they went, they went upon their four sides: and
they turned not when they went. As for their rings, they were so high that
they were dreadful; and their rings were full of eyes round about them four.
And when the living creatures went, the wheels went by them: and when the
living creatures were lifted up from the earth, the wheels were lifted up.
Whithersoever the spirit was to go, they went, thither was their spirit to go;
and the wheels were lifted up over against them: for the spirit of the living
creature was in the wheels. When those went, these went; and when those
stood, these stood; and when those were lifted up from the earth, the
wheels were lifted up over against them: for the spirit of the living creature
was in the wheels.

LIVE, EVIL VEIL ᔕ JOHN WHEELWRIGHT
for Dorothy Day

The Church of Heaven's triumphal Car
by Justice and by Mercy veiled
(Car of wing'd, wheel'd Eyes
Wisdom's pulvery cornbin
winevat, bespattering, of Love)
steeled with mirroring moon and moon
whose spherical rims fall
desiring to climb, and rise
returning to their prime
(each eye-rimmed wheel, a wing'd eyeball)
clangs over empounded flame
with here a saw, and there a hoe
and shadows of smoke like flame.

Thin Wings wire the Crucified's umbra;
other Wings gyre,—His own;
the Pallium sails amid intactile fire;
the Shibboleth[18] hovers over shadows
with here a sickle, and there a scythe
and here and there a hammer.

Shadows, returned to cover
three-fold, double-folded veils,
separately converge
into trine Countenance's radiances;
but starry Messengers behold:
their fires, to these fires, are
as yellow haze to gold,
their joyous innocence
to this lean anger, cold:—
with here a scythe, and there a hammer
and here a saw, and there a saw
and here and there a hoe.

The Eyes swoon while the Wings moan:
"Wake us from our repeating dream

18 JUDGES 12:4–6

within this clanging bell.
Search the unpaved cage
we pace confined. Cruel Eyes gleam
in sable moon and silver moon;
wake us from our repeating dream
of Hell."
With here a hoe, and there a hoe
and there and there a scythe.

Talons rage to claw the image
of the mirrored, iron Face's
clinging, clanging tongues.
Lion Jaws, to devour the other
(which is a mirrored brother)
call on crispate light to melt
prismatic wires, about them, of Mercy:
(with Justice, below, blackly reflected)
"Wake us from dreams repeated."
(They remain undefeated
recurring days; they will not die.)
"Wake us to fact; dreams lie;
wake us to Grace."
(These snakes, frozen on the waters,
were Wings.
These embers among dark cinders
are blind.)
With here a hammer, and there a sickle
and here a scythe, and there a saw
and here and there a hoe.

Loud, abundant strength of clang
—colorless, colorful, colorless—
(yet similar in righteousness)
shakes horny hearing
which once caused its song;
until, at length
the Wings revive. The Eyes awake.
The haze divides; the frozen Lake
of fire melts to spiral Space
where Justice (that doubles Satan's Face)
clung and clangs

as the hammer strikes, and the sickle swings;
and (as Watchers dreamt) it clings
to the Car's veiled Cross
in whose dead embrace
dead
Man hangs.

23:1–23:49   . . . Therefore, O Aholibah, thus saith the Lord GOD; Behold,
I will raise up thy lovers against thee, from whom thy mind is alienated,
and I will bring them against thee on every side; The Babylonians, and all
the Chaldeans, Pekod, and Shoa, and Koa, and all the Assyrians with them:
all of them desirable young men, captains and rulers, great lords and
renowned, all of them riding upon horses. And they shall come against
thee with chariots, wagons, and wheels, and with an assembly of people,
which shall set against thee buckler and shield and helmet round about:
and I will set judgment before them, and they shall judge thee according to
their judgments. And I will set my jealousy against thee, and they shall
deal furiously with thee: they shall take away thy nose and thine ears; and
thy remnant shall fall by the sword: they shall take thy sons and thy daugh-
ters; and thy residue shall be devoured by the fire. They shall also strip
thee out of thy clothes, and take away thy fair jewels. Thus will I make thy
lewdness to cease from thee, and thy whoredom brought from the land of
Egypt: so that thou shalt not lift up thine eyes unto them, nor remember
Egypt any more. . . .

Aholibah ✍ ALGERNON CHARLES SWINBURNE

In the beginning God made thee
    A woman well to look upon,
Thy tender body as a tree
    Whereon cool wind hath always blown
    Till the clean branches be well grown.

There was none like thee in the land;
    The girls that were thy bondwomen
Did bind thee with a purple band
    Upon thy forehead, that all men
    Should know thee for God's handmaiden.

Strange raiment clad thee like a bride,
    With silk to wear on hands and feet
And plates of gold on either side:
        Wine made thee glad, and thou didst eat
        Honey, and choice of pleasant meat.

And fishers in the middle sea
    Did get thee sea-fish and sea-weeds
In colour like the robes on thee;
        And curious work of plaited reeds,
        And wools wherein live purple bleeds.

And round the edges of thy cup
    Men wrought thee marvels out of gold,
Strong snakes with lean throats lifted up,
        Large eyes whereon the brows had hold,
        And scaly things their slime kept cold.

For thee they blew soft wind in flutes
    And ground sweet roots for cunning scent;
Made slow because of many lutes,
        The wind among thy chambers went
        Wherein no light was violent.

God called thy name Aholibah,
    His tabernacle being in thee,
A witness through waste Asia;
        Thou wert a tent sewn cunningly
        With gold and colours of the sea.

God gave thee gracious ministers
    And all their work who plait and weave:
The cunning of embroiderers
        That sew the pillow to the sleeve,
        And likeness of all things that live.

Thy garments upon thee were fair
    With scarlet and with yellow thread;
Also the weaving of thine hair
        Was as fine gold upon thy head,
        And thy silk shoes were sewn with red.

All sweet things he bade sift, and ground
 As a man grindeth wheat in mills
With strong wheels alway going round;
 He gave thee corn, and grass that fills
 The cattle on a thousand hills.

The wine of many seasons fed
 Thy mouth, and made it fair and clean;
Sweet oil was poured out on thy head
 And ran down like cool rain between
 The strait close locks it melted in.

The strong men and the captains knew
 Thy chambers wrought and fashioned
With gold and covering of blue,
 And the blue raiment of thine head
 Who satest on a stately bed.

All these had on their garments wrought
 The shape of beasts and creeping things
The body that availeth not,
 Flat backs of worms and veined wings,
 And the lewd bulk that sleeps and stings.

Also the chosen of the years,
 The multitude being at ease,
With sackbuts and with dulcimers
 And noise of shawms and psalteries
 Made mirth within the ears of these.

But as a common woman doth,
 Thou didst think evil and devise;
The sweet smell of thy breast and mouth
 Thou madest as the harlot's wise,
 And there was painting on thine eyes.

Yea, in the woven guest-chamber
 And by the painted passages
Where the strange gracious paintings were,
 State upon state of companies,
 There came on thee the lust of these.

Because of shapes on either wall
    Sea-coloured from some rare blue shell
At many a Tyrian interval,
    Horsemen on horses, girdled well,
    Delicate and desirable,

Thou saidest: I am sick of love:
    Stay me with flagons, comfort me
With apples for my pain thereof
    Till my hands gather in his tree
    That fruit wherein my lips would be.

Yea, saidest thou, I will go up
    When there is no more shade than one
May cover with a hollow cup,
    And make my bed against the sun
    Till my blood's violence be done.

Thy mouth was leant upon the wall
    Against the painted mouth, thy chin
Touched the hair's painted curve and fall;
    Thy deep throat, fallen lax and thin,
    Worked as the blood's beat worked therein.

Therefore, O thou Aholibah,
    God is not glad because of thee;
And thy fine gold shall pass away
    Like those fair coins of ore that be
    Washed over by the middle sea.

Then will one make thy body bare
    To strip it of all gracious things,
And pluck the cover from thine hair,
    And break the gift of many kings,
    Thy wrist-rings and thine ankle-rings.

Likewise the man whose body joins
    To thy smooth body, as was said,
Who hath a girdle on his loins
    And dyed attire upon his head—
    The same who, seeing, worshipped,

Because thy face was like the face
   Of a clean maiden that smells sweet,
Because thy gait was as the pace
   Of one that opens not her feet
   And is not heard within the street—

Even he, O thou Aholibah,
   Made separate from thy desire,
Shall cut thy nose and ears away
And bruise thee for thy body's hire
   And burn the residue with fire.

Then shall the heathen people say,
   The multitude being at ease;
Lo, this is that Aholibah
   Whose name was blown among strange seas,
   Grown old with soft adulteries.

Also her bed was made of green,
   Her windows beautiful for glass
That she had made her bed between:
   Yea, for pure lust her body was
   Made like white summer-coloured grass.

Her raiment was a strongman's spoil;
   Upon a table by a bed
She set mine incense and mine oil
   To be the beauty of her head
   In chambers walled about with red.

Also between the walls she had
   Fair faces of strong men portrayed;
All girded round the loins, and clad
   With several cloths of woven braid
   And garments marvellously made.

Therefore the wrath of God shall be
   Set as a watch upon her way;
And whoso findeth by the sea
   Blown dust of bones will hardly say
   If this were that Aholibah.

37:1–37:6   The hand of the LORD was upon me, and carried me out in the
spirit of the LORD, and set me down in the midst of the valley which was
full of bones, And caused me to pass by them round about: and, behold,
there were very many in the open valley; and, lo, they were very dry. And he
said unto me, Son of man, can these bones live? And I answered, O Lord
GOD, thou knowest. Again he said unto me, Prophesy upon these bones,
and say unto them, O ye dry bones, hear the word of the LORD. Thus saith
the Lord GOD unto these bones; Behold, I will cause breath to enter into
you, and ye shall live: And I will lay sinews upon you, and will bring up flesh
upon you, and cover you with skin, and put breath in you, and ye shall live;
and ye shall know that I am the LORD.

The End   ᔊ   WILFRED OWEN

After the blast of lightning from the east,
The flourish of loud clouds, the Chariot Throne;
After the drums of time have rolled and ceased,
And by the bronze west long retreat is blown,

Shall Life renew these bodies? Of a truth
All death will he annul, all tears assuage? —
Or fill these void veins full again with youth,
And wash, with an immortal water, Age?

When I do ask white Age he saith not so:
"My head hangs heavy weighed with snow."
And when I hearken to the Earth, she saith:
"My fiery heart shrinks, aching. It is death.
Mine ancient scars shall not be glorified,
Nor my titanic tears, the seas, be dried."

DANIEL

2:1–2:3   And in the second year of the reign of Nebuchadnezzar,
Nebuchadnezzar dreamed dreams, wherewith his spirit was troubled, and
his sleep brake from him. Then the king commanded to call the magicians,
and the astrologers, and the sorcerers, and the Chaldeans, for to shew the

king his dreams. So they came and stood before the king. And the king said
unto them, I have dreamed a dream, and my spirit was troubled to know
the dream.

Nebuchadnezzar   ELINOR WYLIE

My body is weary to death of my mischievous brain;
I am weary forever and ever of being brave;
Therefore I crouch on my knees while the cool white rain
Curves the clover over my head like a wave.

The stem and the frosty seed of the grass are ripe;
I have devoured their strength; I have drunk them deep;
And the dandelion is gall in a thin green pipe;
But the clover is honey and sun and the smell of sleep.

2:31–2:33   Thou, O king, sawest, and behold a great image. This great
image, whose brightness was excellent, stood before thee; and the form
thereof was terrible. This image's head was of fine gold, his breast and his
arms of silver, his belly and his thighs of brass, His legs of iron, his feet part
of iron and part of clay.

Nebuchadnezzar's Dream   JOHN KEATS

Before he went to feed with owls and bats
   Nebuchadnezzar had an ugly dream,
   Worse than an Hus'if's when she thinks her cream
Made a Naumachia for mice and rats.
      So scared, he sent for that 'Good King of Cats'
Young Daniel, who soon did pluck the beam
   From out his eye, and said 'I do not deem
      Your sceptre worth a straw—your Cushions old door-mats'.
A horrid nightmare similar somewhat
   Of late has haunted a most valiant crew
      Of loggerheads and Chapmen—we are told
That any Daniel though he be a sot
   Can make their lying lips turn pale of hue
      By drawling out 'ye are that head of Gold.'

5:24–5:30   Then was the part of the hand sent from him; and this writing was written. And this is the writing that was written, MENE, MENE, TEKEL, UPHARSIN.

This is the interpretation of the thing: MENE; God hath numbered thy kingdom, and finished it. TEKEL; Thou art weighed in the balances, and art found wanting. PERES; Thy kingdom is divided, and given to the Medes and Persians.

Then commanded Belshazzar, and they clothed Daniel with scarlet, and put a chain of gold about his neck, and made a proclamation concerning him, that he should be the third ruler in the kingdom.

In that night was Belshazzar the king of the Chaldeans slain.

Belshazzar had a Letter –   ⟿ EMILY DICKINSON

Belshazzar had a Letter –
He never had but one –
Belshazzar's Correspondent
Concluded and begun
In that immortal Copy
The Conscience of us all
Can read without its Glasses
On Revelation's Wall –

6:19–6:24   Then the king arose very early in the morning, and went in haste unto the den of lions. And when he came to the den, he cried with a lamentable voice unto Daniel: and the king spake and said to Daniel, O Daniel, servant of the living God, is thy God, whom thou servest continually, able to deliver thee from the lions? Then said Daniel unto the king, O king, live for ever. My God hath sent his angel, and hath shut the lions' mouths, that they have not hurt me: forasmuch as before him innocency was found in me; and also before thee, O king, have I done no hurt. Then was the king exceeding glad for him, and commanded that they should take Daniel up out of the den. So Daniel was taken up out of the den, and no manner of hurt was found upon him, because he believed in his God. And the king commanded, and they brought those men which had accused Daniel, and they cast them into the den of lions, them, their children, and their wives; and the lions had the mastery of them, and brake all their bones in pieces or ever they came at the bottom of the den.

Nebuchadnezzar's Kingdom-Come ᭡

DAVID ROWBOTHAM

Daniel in the lion's den
Confounded those who cast him in,
The priests and kings of Babylon
So like the beasts he prayed among.

The god of the land they stole him from
In Nebuchadnezzar's kingdom-come
Gave him mercy and release,
And undefiled he found his peace.

Now in the dens of Babylons
That lure or steal believing ones,
With tawny thoroughness the beasts
Spring as the prides of kings and priests.

For in the present kingdoms-come
The ancient gods are rendered dumb;
To be devoured is Daniel's doom,
And mauled angels stumble home.

Now prayer provokes the savagery
Which priests and kings in beasts set free
On captured innocence in the den,
Confounding deities, not men.

MINOR PROPHETS

HOSEA 4:1–4:7   Hear the word of the LORD, ye children of Israel: for the
LORD hath a controversy with the inhabitants of the land, because there is
no truth, nor mercy, nor knowledge of God in the land. By swearing, and
lying, and killing, and stealing, and committing adultery, they break out, and
blood toucheth blood. Therefore shall the land mourn, and every one that
dwelleth therein shall languish, with the beasts of the field, and with the
fowls of heaven; yea, the fishes of the sea also shall be taken away. Yet let
no man strive, nor reprove another: for thy people are as they that strive
with the priest. Therefore shalt thou fall in the day, and the prophet also

shall fall with thee in the night, and I will destroy thy mother. My people are destroyed for lack of knowledge: because thou hast rejected knowledge, I will also reject thee, that thou shalt be no priest to me: seeing thou hast forgotten the law of thy God, I will also forget thy children. As they were increased, so they sinned against me: therefore will I change their glory into shame.

My People are Destroyed for Lack of Knowledge ᴗ

JONES VERY

For lack of knowledge do my people die!
No fell diseases in our land abound,
No pestilential vapors fill the sky,
No drought or barrenness has cursed the ground;
The harvest-fields are white on every side,
For God has given to all with liberal hand;
To none His sun and rain has He denied,
But with abundance blessed our fruitful land.
But Him who gives to all, they have not known!
His truth, His mercy, and unfailing love;
Who sends not on one favored race alone
His gifts and mercies from the heavens above; —
Therefore the land doth mourn; and, day by day,
War wastes our fields and doth the people slay!

JONAH 1:17–2:10   Now the LORD had prepared a great fish to swallow up Jonah. And Jonah was in the belly of the fish three days and three nights.

Then Jonah prayed unto the LORD his God out of the fish's belly, And said, I cried by reason of mine affliction unto the LORD, and he heard me; out of the belly of hell cried I, and thou heardest my voice. . . . But I will sacrifice unto thee with the voice of thanksgiving; I will pay that that I have vowed. Salvation is of the LORD.

And the LORD spake unto the fish, and it vomited out Jonah upon the dry land.

The Ribs and Terrors. . .   ☞   HERMAN MELVILLE

The ribs and terrors in the whale,
   Arched over me a dismal gloom,
While all God's sun-lit waves rolled by,
   And lift me to a deeper doom.

I saw the opening maw of hell,
   With endless pains and sorrows there;
Which none but they that feel can tell—
   Oh, I was plunging to despair.

In black distress, I called my God,
   When I could scarce believe Him mine,
He bowed His ear to my complaints—
   No more the whale did me confine.

With speed He flew to my relief,
   As on a radiant dolphin borne;
Awful, yet bright, as lightning shone
   The face of my Deliverer God.

My song for ever shall record
   That terrible, that joyful hour;
I give the glory to my God,
   His all the mercy and the power.

JONAH 3:1–4:4   And the word of the LORD came unto Jonah the second time, saying, Arise, go unto Nineveh, that great city, and preach unto it the preaching that I bid thee. So Jonah arose, and went unto Nineveh, according to the word of the LORD. Now Nineveh was an exceeding great city of three days' journey. And Jonah began to enter into the city a day's journey, and he cried, and said, Yet forty days, and Nineveh shall be overthrown.

So the people of Nineveh believed God, and proclaimed a fast, and put on sackcloth, from the greatest of them even to the least of them. For word came unto the king of Nineveh, and he arose from his throne, and he laid his robe from him, and covered him with sackcloth, and sat in ashes. And he caused it to be proclaimed and published through Nineveh by the decree of the king and his nobles, saying, Let neither man nor beast, herd nor flock, taste any thing: let them not feed, nor drink water: But let man and beast be covered with sackcloth, and cry mightily unto God: yea, let them turn every one from his evil way, and from the violence that is in their hands. Who can tell if God will turn and repent, and turn away from his fierce anger, that we perish not? And God saw their works, that they turned from their evil way; and God repented of the evil, that he had said that he would do unto them; and he did it not.

But it displeased Jonah exceedingly, and he was very angry. And he prayed unto the LORD, and said, I pray thee, O LORD, was not this my saying, when I was yet in my country? Therefore I fled before unto Tarshish: for I knew that thou art a gracious God, and merciful, slow to anger, and of great kindness, and repentest thee of the evil. Therefore now, O LORD, take, I beseech thee, my life from me; for it is better for me to die than to live.

Then said the LORD, Doest thou well to be angry?

Jonah ✧ RANDALL JARRELL

As I lie here in the sun
And gaze out, a day's journey, over Nineveh,
The sailors in the dark hold cry to me:
"What meanest thou, O sleeper? Arise and call upon
Thy God; pray with us, that we perish not."

All thy billows and thy waves passed over me.
The waters compassed me, the weeds were wrapped about my head;
The earth with her bars was about me forever.
A naked worm, a man no longer,
I writhed beneath the dead:

But thou art merciful.
When my soul was dead within me I remembered thee,
From the depths I cried to thee. For thou art merciful:
Thou hast brought my life up from corruption,
O Lord my God. . . . When the king said, "Who can tell

But God may yet repent, and turn away
From his fierce anger, that we perish not?"
My heart fell; for I knew thy grace of old—
In my own country, Lord, did I not say
That thou art merciful?

Now take, Lord, I beseech thee,
My life from me; it is better that I die. . .
But I hear, "Doest thou well, then, to be angry?"
And I say nothing, and look bitterly
Across the city; a young gourd grows over me

And shades me—and I slumber, clean of grief.
I was glad of the gourd. But God prepared
A worm that gnawed the gourd; but God prepared
The east wind, the sun beat upon my head
Till I cried, "Let me die!" And God said, "Doest thou well

To be angry for the gourd?"
And I said in my anger, "I do well
To be angry, even unto death." But the Lord God
Said to me, "Thou hast had pity on the gourd"—
And I wept, to hear its dead leaves rattle—

"Which came up in a night, and perished in a night.
And should I not spare Nineveh, that city
Wherein are more than six-score thousand persons
Who cannot tell their left hand from their right;
And also much cattle?"

In a Blind Garden   ꝸ   DAVID SHAPIRO

The whale
is a room
A light blue room
a blind garden
The skulls make room too
And what is the whale
behind you
It's a complex note
When the whale strains
The little fish die
must die like a school
of lances trained on
our friend of two openings
a blowhole a slippery

prey pointed like a joint
in a design of teeth
Can you guess
which whale
Imagine you are a
whale: what a waste
of captured energy
Jonah sulking
like light in a pyramid

and the summer eats
through you like an
island or like
an island whale
with a huge watery tongue
pushing Jonah to that
elusive depth
where the jaw's
sounds pierce him
ear to ear: it is
fear, fear of the bottom
fear of the crashing filter
of these open mouths
skinning us, squeezing
us and gulping our happy eyes
Jonah stands naked in the
room with no solutions
throwing lots like a blanket

and the whale also drowns
like he/she slightly singing
The first part to break
is the hole tightly closed
Next the subject
Next the streamlined shape
As we are young
we have reached the zero surface
Mother's nipple our first meal
nurses for two years
the richest of all animals
Jonah, grow on this

rich milk
in the unique ribs
collapsing under pressure
like Nineveh of grime
The airplane learns
the song is almost continuous
and the prophet's perfume
is then engraved with a picture
The scratches are filled with soot

In a blind garden
think of the whale
as helping Jonah
a joke in poor taste
in relation to a lack
of consciousness of nonsense
Now think of Nineveh
of madness and associated cities
Dear whale of my youth
you are alive and I am swallowed
Now think of a rotting palm
of a rotting royal palm
under which you dream
of a curse like sperm or teeth
of a continuing city's fine song
that can never be heard
by idiotic ears

the prophet's a skeleton now
what about a coral skull
or a coral penis
or coral without the body
We must blind one another
like pollen in the bright
sun's dust Mercifully
mercy concludes the story
Your dreams are those
of a young architect
You don't want to be seen, but to inspect
the curious architecture
of the island bird's throat

as you grow aware of the
increasing dark green ground
of the truncated future

MICAH 3:1–3:7   And I said, Hear, I pray you, O heads of Jacob, and ye
princes of the house of Israel; Is it not for you to know judgment? Who hate
the good, and love the evil; who pluck off their skin from off them, and their
flesh from off their bones; Who also eat the flesh of my people, and flay
their skin from off them; and they break their bones, and chop them in
pieces, as for the pot, and as flesh within the caldron. Then shall they cry
unto the LORD, but he will not hear them: he will even hide his face from
them at that time, as they have behaved themselves ill in their doings. Thus
saith the LORD concerning the prophets that make my people err, that bite
with their teeth, and cry, Peace; and he that putteth not into their mouths,
they even prepare war against him. Therefore night shall be unto you, that
ye shall not have a vision; and it shall be dark unto you, that ye shall not
divine; and the sun shall go down over the prophets, and the day shall be
dark over them. Then shall the seers be ashamed, and the diviners con-
founded: yea, they shall all cover their lips; for there is no answer of God.

A Dream Question   ↢   THOMAS HARDY

I asked the Lord: 'Sire, is this true
Which hosts of theologians hold,
That when we creatures censure you
For shaping griefs and ails untold
(Deeming them punishments undue)
You rage, as Moses wrote of old?

When we exclaim: "Beneficent
He is not, for he orders pain,
Or, if so, not omnipotent:
To a mere child the thing is plain!"
Those who profess to represent
You, cry out: "Impious and profane!" '

He: 'Save me from my friends, who deem
That I care what my creatures say!
Mouth as you list: sneer, rail, blaspheme,

O manikin, the livelong day,
Not one grief-groan or pleasure-gleam
Will you increase or take away.

'Why things are thus, whoso derides,
May well remain my secret still. . . .
A fourth dimension, say the guides,
To matter is conceivable.
Think some such mystery resides
Within the ethic of my will.'

ZEPHANIAH 1:14–1:18   The great day of the LORD is near, it is near, and
hasteth greatly, even the voice of the day of the LORD: the mighty man shall
cry there bitterly. That day is a day of wrath, a day of trouble and distress, a
day of wasteness and desolation, a day of darkness and gloominess, a day
of clouds and thick darkness, A day of the trumpet and alarm against the
fenced cities, and against the high towers. And I will bring distress upon
men, that they shall walk like blind men, because they have sinned against
the LORD: and their blood shall be poured out as dust, and their flesh as
the dung. Neither their silver nor their gold shall be able to deliver them in
the day of the LORD'S wrath; but the whole land shall be devoured by the
fire of his jealousy: for he shall make even a speedy riddance of all them
that dwell in the land.

The Day of Judgement   ᴊᴏɴᴀᴛʜᴀɴ SWIFT

With a whirl of thought oppressed
I sink from revery to rest.
An horrid vision seized my head,
I saw the graves give up their dead.
Jove, armed with terrors, burst the skies,
And thunder roars, and lightning flies!
Amazed, confused, its fate unknown,
The World stands trembling at his throne.
While each pale sinner hangs his head,
Jove, nodding, shook the heavens, and said,
"Offending race of human kind,
By nature, reason, learning, blind;
You who through frailty stepped aside,

And you who never fell—through pride;
You who in different sects have shammed,
And come to see each other damned;
(So some folks told you, but they knew
No more of Jove's designs than you)
The World's mad business now is o'er,
And I resent these pranks no more.
I to such blockheads set my wit!
I damn such fools! Go, go, you're bit."

ZECHARIAH 1:7–1:11   Upon the four and twentieth day of the eleventh
month, which is the month Sebat, in the second year of Darius, came the
word of the LORD unto Zechariah, the son of Berechiah, the son of Iddo
the prophet, saying, I saw by night, and behold a man riding upon a red
horse, and he stood among the myrtle trees that were in the bottom; and
behind him were there red horses, speckled, and white. Then said I, O my
lord, what are these? And the angel that talked with me said unto me, I will
shew thee what these be. And the man that stood among the myrtle trees
answered and said, These are they whom the LORD hath sent to walk to
and fro through the earth. And they answered the angel of the LORD that
stood among the myrtle trees, and said, We have walked to and fro through
the earth, and, behold, all the earth sitteth still, and is at rest.

In a Myrtle Shade   ঙ   WILLIAM BLAKE

O, how sick and weary I
Underneath my myrtle lie,
Like to dung upon the ground
Underneath my myrtle bound.

Why should I be bound to thee,
O my lovely myrtle tree?
Love, free love, cannot be bound
To any tree that grows on ground.

Oft my myrtle sighed in vain
To behold my heavy chain.
Oft my father saw us sigh,
And laughed at our simplicity.

So I smote him and his gore
Stained the roots my myrtle bore.
But the time of youth is fled,
And grey hairs are on my head.

ZECHARIAH 1:18–1:21   Then lifted I up mine eyes, and saw, and behold
four horns. And I said unto the angel that talked with me, What be these?
And he answered me, These are the horns which have scattered Judah,
Israel, and Jerusalem. And the LORD shewed me four carpenters. Then said
I, What come these to do? And he spake, saying, These are the horns which
have scattered Judah, so that no man did lift up his head: but these are
come to fray them, to cast out the horns of the Gentiles, which lifted up
their horn over the land of Judah to scatter it.

from *Jubilate Agno*   ∽   CHRISTOPHER SMART

For I prophesy that we shall have our horns again.
For in the day of David Man as yet had a glorious horn upon
    his forehead.
For this horn was a bright substance in colour & consistence as the
    nail of the hand.
For it was broad, thick and strong so as to serve for defence as well
    as ornament.
For it brightened to the Glory of God, which came upon the human
    face at morning prayer.
For it was largest and brightest in the best men.
For it was taken away all at once from all of them.
For this was done in the divine contempt of a general pusillanimity.
For this happened in a season after their return from the Babylonish
    captivity.
For their spirits were broke and their manhood impaired by foreign
    vices for exaction.
For I prophesy that the English will recover their horns the first.
For I prophesy that all the nations in the world will do the like in turn.
For I prophesy that all Englishmen will wear their beards again.
For a beard is a good step to a horn.
For when men get their horns again, they will delight to go
    uncovered.

For it is not good to wear any thing upon the head.

For a man should put no obstacle between his head and the blessing
of Almighty God.

For a hat was an abomination of the heathen. Lord have mercy upon
the Quakers.

For the ceiling of the house is an obstacle and therefore we pray on
the house-top.

For the head will be liable to less disorders on the recovery of
its horn.

For the horn on the forehead is a tower upon an arch.

For it is a strong munition against the adversary, who is sickness
and death.

For it is instrumental in subjecting the woman.

For the insolence of the woman has increased ever since man has
been crest-fallen.

For they have turned the horn into scoff and derision without ceasing.

For we are amerced of God, who has his horn.

For we are amerced of the blessed angels, who have their horns.

For when they get their horns again they will put them upon the altar.

For they give great occasion for mirth and music.

For our Blessed Saviour had not his horn upon the face of the earth.

For this was in meekness and condescension to the infirmities of
human nature at that time.

For at his second coming his horn will be exalted in glory.

For his horn is the horn of Salvation.

For Christ Jesus has exalted my voice to his own glory.

For he has answered me in the air as with a horn from Heaven to the
ears of many people.

For the horn is of plenty.

For this has been the sense of all ages.

For Man and Earth suffer together.

For when Man was amerced of his horn, earth lost part of her fertility.

For the art of Agriculture is improving.

For this is evident in flowers.

For it is more especially manifest in double flowers.

For earth will get it up again by the blessing of God on the industry
of man.

For the horn is of plenty because of milk and honey.

For I pray God be gracious to the Bees and the Beeves this day.

ZECHARIAH 9:9–9:11   Rejoice greatly, O daughter of Zion; shout, O daughter of Jerusalem: behold, thy King cometh unto thee: he is just, and having salvation; lowly, and riding upon an ass, and upon a colt the foal of an ass. And I will cut off the chariot from Ephraim, and the horse from Jerusalem, and the battle bow shall be cut off: and he shall speak peace unto the heathen: and his dominion shall be from sea even to sea, and from the river even to the ends of the earth. As for thee also, by the blood of thy covenant I have sent forth thy prisoners out of the pit wherein is no water.

Meditation Seventy-Seven ﹏ EDWARD TAYLOR
Second Series

A state, a state, oh! dungeon state indeed.
    In which me headlong, long ago sin pitched:
As dark as pitch; where nastiness doth breed:
    And filth defiles: and I am with it ditched.
    A sinfull state: This pit no water's in't.
    A bugbear state: as black as any ink.

I once sat singing on the summit high
    'Mong the celestial choir in music sweet:
On highest bough of paradisal joy;
    Glory and innocence did in me meet.
    I as a gold-finched nighting gale, tuned o'er
    Melodious songs 'fore glory's palace door.

But on this bough I tuning perched not long:
    Th'infernal foe shot out a shaft from Hell;
A fiery dart piled with sins poison strong:
    That struck my heart, and down I headlong fell:
    And from the highest pinnacle of light
    Into this lowest pit more dark than night.

A pit indeed of sin: No water's here:
    Whose bottom's furthest off from Heaven bright.
And is next door to Hell gate: to it near:
    And here I dwell in sad and solemn night.
    My gold-finched angel feathers dappled in
    Hells scarlet dye fat, blood red grown with sin.

I in this pit all destitute of light
    Crammed full of horrid darkness, here do crawl
Up over head, and ears, in nauseous plight:
    And swinelike wallow in this mire and gall:
    No heavenly dews nor holy waters drill:
    Nor sweet air breeze, nor comfort here distil.

Here for companions, are fears, heart-aches, grief,
    Frogs, toads, newts, bats, horrid hob-goblins, ghosts,
Ill spirits haunt this pit: and no relief:
    Nor cord can fetch me hence in creatures coasts.
    I who once lodged at Heaven's palace gate
    With full fledged angels, now possess this fate.

But yet, my Lord, thy golden chain of grace
    Thou canst let down, and draw me up into
Thy holy air, and glory's happy place,
    Out from these hellish damps and pit so low.
    And if thy grace shall do't, My harp I'll raise,
    Whose strings touched by this grace, will twang thy praise.

MALACHI 4:2   But unto you that fear my name shall the Sun of righteous-
ness arise with healing in his wings; and ye shall go forth, and grow up as
calves of the stall.

Easter Wings ✌ GEORGE HERBERT

Lord, who createdst man in wealth and store,
Though foolishly he lost the same,
Decaying more and more,
Till he became
Most poor:
With thee
O let me rise
As larks, harmoniously
And sing this day thy victories:
Then shall the fall further the flight in me.

My tender age in sorrow did begin:
And still with sicknesses and shame
Thou didst so punish sin,
That I became
Most thin.
With thee
Let me combine,
And feel this day thy victory:
For, if I imp my wing on thine,
Affliction shall advance the flight in me.

PART TWO

GOSPELS THROUGH REVELATION

Matthew, Mark, Luke, and John,
Bless the bed that I lie on:

Four corners to my bed,
Four angels round my head;
One to watch and one to pray
And two to bear my soul away

TRADITIONAL NURSERY RHYME
The White Paternoster
(17th Century)

EXTRACTS

To the Christians   FRANCIS LAUDERDALE ADAMS

Take, then, your paltry Christ,
    Your gentleman God.
We want the carpenter's son,
    With his saw and hod.

We want the man who loved
    The poor and oppressed,
Who hated the rich man and king
    And the scribe and the priest.

We want the Galilean
    Who knew cross and rod.
It's your 'good taste' that prefers
    A bastard God!

The Carpenter's Son   JOHN BERRYMAN

The child stood in the shed. The child went mad,
later, & saned the wisemen. People gathered
as he conjoined the Jordan joint
ánd he spoke with them until he got smothered
amongst their passion for   mysterious healing had.
They could not take his point:

—Repent, & love, he told them frightened throngs,
and it is so he did. Díd some of them?
Which now comes hard to say.
The date's in any event a matter of wrongs
later upon him, lest we would not know him,
medieval, on Christmas Day.

Pass me a cookie. O one absolutely did
lest we not know him. Fasten to your fire
the blessing of the living God.
It's far to seek if it will do as good

whether in our womanly or in our manlihood,
this great man sought his retire.

from *Milton, a Poem in 2 Books* ᔌ WILLIAM BLAKE
Preface

The Stolen and Perverted Writings of Homer and Ovid, of Plato and
Cicero, which all Men ought to contemn, are set up by artifice
against the Sublime of the Bible; but when the New Age is at leisure
to Pronounce, all will be set right, and those Grand Works of the
more ancient and consciously and professedly Inspired Men will hold
their proper rank, and the Daughters of Memory shall become the
Daughters of Inspiration. Shakespeare and Milton were both curbed
by the general malady and infection from the silly Greek and Latin
slaves of the Sword.

Rouze up, O Young Men of the New Age! For we have Hirelings
in the Camp, the Court and the University, who would, if they could,
for ever depress Mental and prolong Corporeal War. Painters! on you
I call. Sculptors! Architects! Suffer not the fashionable Fools to
depress your powers by the prices they pretend to give for con-
temptible works, or the expensive advertizing boasts that they make of
such works; believe Christ and his Apostles that there is a Class of
Men whose whole delight is in Destroying. We do not want either
Greek or Roman Models if we are but just and true to our own
Imaginations, those Worlds of Eternity in which we shall live forever
in Jesus our Lord.

The Respectable Burgher ᔌ THOMAS HARDY
On 'The Higher Criticism'

Since Reverend Doctors now declare
That clerks and people must prepare
To doubt if Adam ever were;
To hold the flood a local scare;
To argue, through the stolid stare,
That everything had happened ere
The prophets to its happening sware;

That David was no giant-slayer,
Nor one to call a God-obeyer
In certain details we could spare,
But rather was a debonair
Shrewd bandit, skilled as a banjo-player:
That Solomon sang the fleshly Fair,
And gave the Church no thought whate'er,
That Esther, with her royal wear,
And Mordecai, the son of Jair,
And Joshua's triumphs, Job's despair,
And Balaam's ass's bitter blare;
Nebuchadnezzar's furnace-flare,
And Daniel and the den affair,
And other stories rich and rare,
Were writ to make old doctrine wear
Something of a romantic air:
That the Nain widow's only heir,
And Lazarus with cadaverous glare
(As done in oils by Piombo's care)
Did not return from Sheol's lair:
That Jael set a fiendish snare,
That Pontius Pilate acted square,
That never a sword cut Malchus' ear;
And (but for shame I must forbear)
That —— —— did not reappear! . . .
– Since thus they hint, nor turn a hair,
All churchgoing I will forswear,
And sit on Sundays in my chair,
And read that moderate man Voltaire.

H. Scriptures ✍ HENRY VAUGHAN

Welcome dear book, soul's joy, and food! The feast
   Of spirits, Heaven extracted lies in thee;
   Thou art life's charter, the dove's spotless nest
Where souls are hatched unto Eternity.

In thee the hidden stone, the manna lies,
   Thou art the great elixir, rare, and choice;
   The key that opens to all mysteries,
The Word in characters, God in the voice.

O that I had deep cut in my hard heart
   Each line in thee! Then would I plead in groans
   Of my Lord's penning, and by sweetest art
Return upon himself the Law, and stones.
   Read here, my faults are thine. This book, and I
   Will tell thee so; *Sweet Savior thou didst die!*

To Him that was Crucified ᴗ WALT WHITMAN

My spirit to yours dear brother,
Do not mind because many sounding your name do not
      understand you,
I do not sound your name, but I understand you,
I specify you with joy O my comrade to salute you, and to salute
      those who are with you, before and since, and those to
      come also,
That we all labor together transmitting the same charge and
      succession,
We few equals indifferent of lands, indifferent of times,
We, enclosers of all continents, all castes, allowers of all theologies,
Compassionaters, perceivers, rapport of men,
We walk silent among disputes and assertions, but reject not the
      disputers nor any thing that is asserted,
We hear the bawling and din, we are reached at by divisions,
      jealousies, recriminations on every side,
They close peremptorily upon us to surround us, my comrade,
Yet we walk unheld, free, the whole earth over, journeying up and
      down till we make our ineffaceable mark upon time and the
      diverse eras,
Till we saturate time and eras, that the men and women of races,
      ages to come, may prove brethren and lovers as we are.

A Christmas Hymn ✌ RICHARD WILBUR

A stable-lamp is lighted
Whose glow shall wake the sky;
The stars shall bend their voices,
And every stone shall cry.
And every stone shall cry,
And straw like gold shall shine;
A barn shall harbor heaven,
A stall become a shrine.

This child through David's city
Shall ride in triumph by;
The palm shall strew its branches,
And every stone shall cry.
And every stone shall cry,
Though heavy, dull, and dumb,
And lie within the roadway
To pave his kingdom come.

Yet he shall be forsaken,
And yielded up to die;
The sky shall groan and darken,
And every stone shall cry.
And every stone shall cry
For stony hearts of men:
God's blood upon the spearhead,
God's love refused again.

But now, as at the ending,
The low is lifted high;
The stars shall bend their voices,
And every stone shall cry.
And every stone shall cry
In praises of the child
By whose descent among us
The worlds are reconciled.

MATTHEW, MARK, LUKE, and JOHN, HARMONIZED

Prologue

JOHN 1:1–1:5   In the beginning was the Word, and the Word was with God, and the Word was God. The same was in the beginning with God. All things were made by him; and without him was not any thing made that was made. In him was life; and the life was the light of men. And the light shineth in darkness; and the darkness comprehended it not.

In the Beginning   ﹏   DYLAN THOMAS

In the beginning was the three-pointed star,
One smile of light across the empty face;
One bough of bone across the rooting air,
The substance forked that marrowed the first sun;
And, burning ciphers on the round of space,
Heaven and hell mixed as they spun.

In the beginning was the pale signature,
Three-syllabled and starry as the smile;
And after came the imprints on the water,
Stamp of the minted face upon the moon;
The blood that touched the crosstree and the grail
Touched the first cloud and left a sign.

In the beginning was the mounting fire
That set alight the weathers from a spark,
A three-eyed, red-eyed spark, blunt as a flower;
Life rose and spouted from the rolling seas,
Burst in the roots, pumped from the earth and rock
The secret oils that drive the grass.

In the beginning was the word, the word
That from the solid bases of the light
Abstracted all the letters of the void;
And from the cloudy bases of the breath
The word flowed up, translating to the heart
First characters of birth and death.

In the beginning was the secret brain.
The brain was celled and soldered in the thought
Before the pitch was forking to a sun;
Before the veins were shaking in their sieve,
Blood shot and scattered to the winds of light
The ribbed original of love.

JOHN 1:14 And the Word was made flesh, and dwelt among us,

A Word made Flesh is seldom — EMILY DICKINSON

A Word made Flesh is seldom
And tremblingly partook
Nor then perhaps reported
But have I not mistook
Each one of us has tasted
With ecstasies of stealth
The very food debated
To our specific strength –

A Word that breathes distinctly
Has not the power to die
Cohesive as the Spirit
It may expire if He –
"Made Flesh and dwelt among us"
Could condescension be
Like this consent of Language
This loved Philology.

The Body of God — D. H. LAWRENCE

God is the great urge that has not yet found a body
but urges towards incarnation with the great creative urge.
And becomes at last a clove carnation: lo! that is god!
and becomes at last Helen, or Ninon: any lovely and generous
woman
at her best and her most beautiful, being god, made manifest,
any clear and fearless man being god, very god.

There is no god
apart from poppies and the flying fish,
men singing songs, and women brushing their hair in the sun.
The lovely things are god that has come to pass, like Jesus came.
The rest, the undiscoverable, is the demiurge.

JOHN 1:14   (and we beheld his glory, the glory as of the only begotten of
the Father,) full of grace and truth.

from *The Everlasting Gospel*   ✍   WILLIAM BLAKE

The Vision of Christ that thou dost see
Is my Vision's Greatest Enemy:
Thine has a great hook nose like thine,
Mine has a snub nose like to mine:
Thine is the friend of All Mankind.
Mine speaks in parables to the Blind:
Thine loves the same world that mine hates,
Thy Heaven doors are my Hell Gates.
Socrates taught what Meletus
Loathed as a Nation's bitterest Curse.
And Caiphas was in his own Mind
A benefactor to Mankind:
Both read the Bible day and night,
But thou readst black where I read white.

The Birth

LUKE 1:26–1:27   And in the sixth month the angel Gabriel was sent from
God unto a city of Galilee, named Nazareth, To a virgin espoused to a
man whose name was Joseph, of the house of David; and the virgin's
name was Mary.

The Virgin ✑ LAURA (RIDING) JACKSON

My flesh is at a distance from me.
Yet approach and touch it:
It is as near as anyone can come.

This vestiary stuff
Is a true relic,
Though I have never worn it,
Though I shall never be dead.

And the possession?
The violence will be over,
A forgotten passion,
Before I learn of it.

LUKE 1:28 And the angel came in unto her, and said, Hail, thou that art
highly favoured, the Lord is with thee: blessed art thou among women.

Ave Maria Gratia Plena ✑ OSCAR WILDE

Was this His coming! I had hoped to see
A scene of wondrous glory, as was told
Of some great God who in a rain of gold
Broke open bars and fell on Danaë:
Or a dread vision as when Semele,
Sickening for love and unappeased desire,
Prayed to see God's clear body, and the fire
Caught her brown limbs and slew her utterly.
With such glad dreams I sought this holy place,
And now with wondering eyes and heart I stand
Before this supreme mystery of Love:
Some kneeling girl with passionless pale face,
An angel with a lily in his hand,
And over both the white wings of a Dove.

LUKE 1:29 And when she saw him, she was troubled at his saying, and
cast in her mind what manner of salutation this should be.

The Annunciation   ∽   EDWIN MUIR

The angel and the girl are met.
Earth was the only meeting place.
For the embodied never yet
Travelled beyond the shore of space.
The eternal spirits in freedom go.

See, they have come together, see,
While the destroying minutes flow,
Each reflects the other's face
Till heaven in hers and earth in his
Shine steady there. He's come to her
From far beyond the farthest star,
Feathered through time. Immediacy
Of strangest strangeness is the bliss
That from their limbs all movement takes.
Yet the increasing rapture brings
So great a wonder that it makes
Each feather tremble on his wings.

Outside the window footsteps fall
Into the ordinary day
And with the sun along the wall
Pursue their unreturning way.
Sound's perpetual roundabout
Rolls its numbered octaves out
And hoarsely grinds its battered tune.

But through the endless afternoon
These neither speak nor movement make,
But stare into their deepening trance
As if their gaze would never break.

LUKE 1:30–1:35   And the angel said unto her, Fear not, Mary: for thou hast
found favour with God. And, behold, thou shalt conceive in thy womb, and
bring forth a son, and shalt call his name JESUS. He shall be great, and
shall be called the Son of the Highest: and the Lord God shall give unto him
the throne of his father David: And he shall reign over the house of Jacob
for ever; and of his kingdom there shall be no end.

Then said Mary unto the angel, How shall this be, seeing I know not a man?

And the angel answered and said unto her, The Holy Ghost shall come upon thee, and the power of the Highest shall overshadow thee: therefore also that holy thing which shall be born of thee shall be called the Son of God.

Annunciation ~ JOHN DONNE

Salvation to all that will is nigh;
That All, which always is All every where,
Which cannot sin, and yet all sins must bear,
Which cannot die, yet cannot choose but die,
Lo, faithful Virgin, yields himself to lie
In prison, in thy womb; and though he there
Can take no sin, nor thou give, yet he will wear
Taken from thence, flesh, which death's force may try.
Ere by the spheres time was created, thou
Wast in his mind, who is thy Son, and Brother;
Whom thou conceiv'st, conceived; yea thou art now
Thy Maker's maker, and thy Father's mother;
Thou hast light in dark; and shut'st in little room,
Immensity cloistered in thy dear womb.

LUKE 1:38   And Mary said, Behold the handmaid of the Lord; be it unto me according to thy word. And the angel departed from her.

Mary and Gabriel ~ RUPERT BROOKE

Young Mary, loitering once her garden way,
Felt a warm splendour grow in the April day,
As wine that blushes water through. And soon,
Out of the gold air of the afternoon,
One knelt before her: hair he had, or fire,
Bound back above his ears with golden wire,
Baring the eager marble of his face.
Not man's or woman's was the immortal grace
Rounding the limbs beneath that robe of white,

And lighting the proud eyes with changeless light,
Incurious. Calm as his wings, and fair,
That presence filled the garden.
                              She stood there,
Saying, "What would you, Sir?"
                              He told his word,
"Blessed art thou of women!" Half she heard,
Hands folded and face bowed, half long had known,
The message of that clear and holy tone,
That fluttered hot sweet sobs about her heart;
Such serene tidings moved such human smart.
Her breath came quick as little flakes of snow.
Her hands crept up her breast. She did but know
It was not hers. She felt a trembling stir
Within her body, a will too strong for her
That held and filled and mastered all. With eyes
Closed, and a thousand soft short broken sighs,
She gave submission; fearful, meek, and glad. . . .

    She wished to speak. Under her breasts she had
Such multitudinous burnings, to and fro,
And throbs not understood; she did not know
If they were hurt or joy for her; but only
That she was grown strange to herself, half lonely,
All wonderful, filled full of pains to come
And thoughts she dare not think, swift thoughts and dumb,
Human, and quaint, her own, yet very far,
Divine, dear, terrible, familiar. . .
Her heart was faint for telling; to relate
Her limbs' sweet treachery, her strange high estate,
Over and over, whispering, half revealing,
Weeping; and so find kindness to her healing.
'Twixt tears and laughter, panic hurrying her,
She raised her eyes to that fair messenger.
He knelt unmoved, immortal; with his eyes
Gazing beyond her, calm to the calm skies;
Radiant, untroubled in his wisdom, kind.
His sheaf of lilies stirred not in the wind.
How should she, pitiful with mortality,
Try the wide peace of that felicity
With ripples of her perplexed shaken heart,

And hints of human ecstasy, human smart,
And whispers of the lonely weight she bore,
And how her womb within was hers no more
And at length hers?
                    Being tired, she bowed her head;
And said, "So be it!"
                    The great wings were spread
Showering glory on the fields, and fire.
The whole air, singing, bore him up, and higher,
Unswerving, unreluctant. Soon he shone
A gold speck in the gold skies; then was gone.

The air was colder, and grey. She stood alone.

MATTHEW 1:18   Now the birth of Jesus Christ was on this wise: When as his mother Mary was espoused to Joseph, before they came together, she was found with child of the Holy Ghost.

I Sing of a Maiden   ᷧ   ANONYMOUS (15TH CENTURY)

I sing of a maiden
   That is makeless:
King of all kings
   To her son she ches.

He came also still
   Where his mother was
As dew in April
   That falleth on the grass.

He came also still
   To his mother's bower
As dew in April
   That falleth on the flower.

He came also still
   Where his mother lay
As dew in April
   That falleth on the spray.

Mother and maiden
   Was never none but she—
Well may such a lady
   God's mother be.

MATTHEW 1:24   Then Joseph being raised from sleep did as the angel of
the Lord had bidden him, and took unto him his wife:

Joseph   ↜   G. K. CHESTERTON

If the stars fell; night's nameless dreams
   Of bliss and blasphemy came true,
If skies were green and snow were gold,
   And you loved me as I love you;

O long light hands and curled brown hair,
   And eyes where sits a naked soul;
Dare I even then draw near and burn
   My fingers in the aureole?

Yes, in the one wise foolish hour
   God gives this strange strength to a man.
He can demand, though not deserve,
   Where ask he cannot, seize he can.

But once the blood's wild wedding o'er,
   Were not dread his, half dark desire,
To see the Christ-child in the cot,
   The Virgin Mary by the fire?

MATTHEW 1:25   And knew her not till she had brought forth her
firstborn son: . . .

A Stick of Incense   ↜   WILLIAM BUTLER YEATS

Whence did all that fury come?
From empty tomb or Virgin womb?

Saint Joseph thought the world would melt
But liked the way his fingers smelt.

LUKE 2:1–2:3   And it came to pass in those days, that there went out a
decree from Caesar Augustus that all the world should be taxed. (And this
taxing was first made when Cyrenius was governor of Syria.) And all went to
be taxed, every one into his own city.

Christmas Day. The Family Sitting   ᧕
JOHN MEADE FALKNER

In the days of Caesar Augustus
   There went forth this decree:
Si quis rectus et justus
   Liveth in Galilee,
Let him go up to Jerusalem
   And pay his scot to me.

There are passed one after the other
   Christmases fifty-three,
Since I sat here with my mother
   And heard the great decree:
How they went up to Jerusalem
   Out of Galilee.

They have passed one after the other
   Father and mother died,
Brother and sister and brother
   Taken and sanctified.
I am left alone in the sitting,
   With none to sit beside.

On the fly-leaves of these old prayer-books
   The childish writings fade,
Which show that once they were their books
   In the days when prayer was made
For other kings and princesses,
   William and Adelaide.

The pillars are twisted with holly,
    And the font is wreathed with yew.
Christ forgive me for folly,
    Youth's lapses—not a few,
For the hardness of my middle life,
    For age's fretful view.

Cotton-wool letters on scarlet,
    All the ancient lore,
Tell how the chieftains starlit
    To Bethlehem came to adore;
To hail Him King in the manger,
    Wonderful, Counsellor.

The bells ring out in the steeple
    The gladness of erstwhile,
And the children of other people
    Are walking up the aisle;
They brush my elbow in passing,
    Some turn to give me a smile.

Is the almond-blossom bitter?
    Is the grasshopper heavy to bear?
Christ make me happier, fitter
    To go to my own over there:
Jerusalem the Golden,
    What bliss beyond compare!

My Lord, where I have offended
    Do Thou forgive it me.
That so when, all being ended,
    I hear Thy last decree,
I may go up to Jerusalem
    Out of Galilee.

LUKE 2:4–2:7   And Joseph also went up from Galilee, out of the city of Nazareth, into Judaea, unto the city of David, which is called Bethlehem; (because he was of the house and lineage of David:) To be taxed with Mary his espoused wife, being great with child. And so it was, that, while they were there, the days were accomplished that she should be delivered. And she brought forth her firstborn son, and wrapped him in swaddling clothes, and laid him in a manger; because there was no room for them in the inn.

Nativity ✌ JOHN DONNE

Immensity cloistered in thy dear womb,
Now leaves his well-beloved imprisonment,
There he hath made himself to his intent
Weak enough, now into our world to come;
But Oh, for thee, for him, hath th' Inn no room?
Yet lay him in this stall, and from the Orient,
Stars, and wisemen will travel to prevent
Th' effect of Herod's jealous general doom.
Seest thou, my Soul, with thy faith's eyes, how he
Which fills all place, yet none holds him, doth lie?
Was not his pity towards thee wondrous high,
That would have need to be pitied by thee?
Kiss him, and with him into Egypt go,
With his kind mother, who partakes thy woe.

Upon Christ his Birth ✌ SIR JOHN SUCKLING

Strange news! a city full? will none give way
To lodge a guest that comes not every day?
No inn, nor tavern void? yet I descry
One empty place alone, where we may lie:
In too much fullness is some want: but where?
Men's empty hearts: let's ask for lodging there.
But if they not admit us, then we'll say
Their hearts, as well as inns, are made of clay.

Salus Mundi ✌ MARY COLERIDGE

I saw a stable, low and very bare,
    A little child in a manger.
The oxen knew Him, had Him in their care,
    To men He was a stranger.
The safety of the world was lying there,
    And the world's danger.

The Nativity ⁓ C. S. LEWIS

Among the oxen (like an ox I'm slow)
I see a glory in the stable grow
Which, with an ox's dullness might at length
Give me an ox's strength.

Among the asses (stubborn I as they)
I see my Saviour where I looked for hay;
So may my beastlike folly learn at least
The patience of a beast.

Among the sheep (I like a sheep have strayed)
I watch the manger where my Lord is laid;
Oh that my baa-ing nature would win thence
Some woolly innocence!

LUKE 2:8–2:12 And there were in the same country shepherds abiding in the field, keeping watch over their flock by night. And, lo, the angel of the Lord came upon them, and the glory of the Lord shone round about them: and they were sore afraid. And the angel said unto them, Fear not: for, behold, I bring you good tidings of great joy, which shall be to all people. For unto you is born this day in the city of David a Saviour, which is Christ the Lord. And this shall be a sign unto you; Ye shall find the babe wrapped in swaddling clothes, lying in a manger.

The Shepherds ⁓ HENRY VAUGHAN

Sweet, harmless lives! (on whose holy leisure
Waits innocence and pleasure,)
Whose leaders to those pastures, and clear springs,
Were patriarchs, saints, and kings,
How happened it that in the dead of night
You only saw true light,
While Palestine was fast asleep, and lay
Without one thought of day?
Was it because those first and blesséd swains
Were pilgrims on those plains

When they received the promise, for which now
    'Twas there first shown to you?
'Tis true, he loves that dust whereon they go
    That serve him here below,
And therefore might for memory of those
    His love there first disclose;
But wretched Salem once his love, must now
    No voice, nor vision know,
Her stately piles with all their height and pride
    Now languished and died,
And Beth'lem's humble cots above them stepped
    While all her seers slept;
Her cedar, fir, hewed stones and gold were all
    Polluted through their fall,
And those once sacred mansions were now
    Mere emptiness and show,
This made the Angel call at reeds and thatch,
    Yet where the shepherds watch,
And God's own lodging (though he could not lack,)
    To be a common rack;
No costly pride, no soft-clothed luxury
    In those thin cells could lie,
Each stirring wind and storm blew through their cots
    Which never harbored plots,
Only content, and love, and humble joys
    Lived there without all noise,
Perhaps some harmless cares for the next day
    Did in their bosoms play,
As where to lead their sheep, what silent nook,
    What springs or shades to look,
But that was all; And now with gladsome care
    They for the town prepare,
They leave their flock, and in a busy talk
    All towards Beth'lem walk
To see their souls' great shepherd, who was come
    To bring all stragglers home,
Where now they find him out, and taught before
    That Lamb of God adore,
That Lamb whose days great kings and prophets wished
    And longed to see, but missed.

The first light they beheld was bright and gay
    And turned their night to day,
But to this later light they saw in him,
    Their day was dark, and dim.

LUKE 2:13–2:16   And suddenly there was with the angel a multitude of the
heavenly host praising God, and saying, Glory to God in the highest, and on
earth peace, good will toward men. And it came to pass, as the angels were
gone away from them into heaven, the shepherds said one to another, Let
us now go even unto Bethlehem, and see this thing which is come to pass,
which the Lord hath made known unto us. And they came with haste, and
found Mary, and Joseph, and the babe lying in a manger.

A Hymn on the Nativity of My Savior   ᔗ   BEN JONSON

I sing the birth, was born tonight,
The author both of life, and light;
    The angels so did sound it,
And like the ravished shepherds said,
Who saw the light, and were afraid,
    Yet searched, and true they found it.

The Son of God, th' Eternal King,
That did us all salvation bring,
    And freed the soul from danger;
He whom the whole world could not take,
The Word, which heaven, and earth did make,
    Was now laid in a manger.

The Father's wisdom willed it so,
The Son's obedience knew no No,
    Both wills were in one stature,
And as that wisdom had decreed,
The Word was now made Flesh indeed,
    And took on him our nature.

What comfort by him do we win?
Who made himself the prince of sin,

To make us heirs of glory?[19]
To see this babe, all innocence;
A martyr born in our defence;
    Can man forget this story?

Christus Natus Est ॐ COUNTEE CULLEN

In Bethlehem
On Christmas morn,
The lowly gem
Of love was born.
Hosannah! *Christu natus est.*

Bright in her crown
Of fiery star,
Judea's town
Shone from afar:
Hosannah! *Christu natus est.*

While beasts in stall,
On bended knee,
Did carol all
Most joyously:
Hosannah! *Christu natus est.*

For bird and beast
He did not come,
But for the least
Of mortal scum.
Hosannah! *Christu natus est.*

Who lies in ditch?
Who begs his bread?
Who has no stitch
For back or head?
Hosannah! *Christu natus est.*

19 ROM 8:16 and also JAS 2:5

Who wakes to weep,
Lies down to mourn?
Who in his sleep
Withdraws from scorn?
Hosannah! *Christu natus est.*

Ye outraged dust,
On field and plain,
To feed the lust
Of madmen slain:
Hosannah! *Christu natus est.*

The manger still
Outshines the throne;
Christ must and will
Come to his own.
Hosannah! *Christu natus est.*

LUKE 2:18–2:19   And all they that heard it wondered at those things which were told them by the shepherds. But Mary kept all these things, and pondered them in her heart.

The Mother of God   ᧰   WILLIAM BUTLER YEATS

The threefold terror of love; a fallen flare
Through the hollow of an ear;
Wings beating about the room;
The terror of all terrors that I bore
The Heavens in my womb.

Had I not found content among the shows
Every common woman knows,
Chimney corner, garden walk,
Or rocky cistern where we tread the clothes
And gather all the talk ?

What is this flesh I purchased with my pains,
This fallen star my milk sustains,
This love that makes my heart's blood stop

Or strikes a sudden chill into my bones
And bids my hair stand up?

LUKE 2:20 –2:21   And the shepherds returned, glorifying and praising God
for all the things that they had heard and seen, as it was told unto them.
And when eight days were accomplished for the circumcising of the child,
his name was called JESUS, which was so named of the angel before he was
conceived in the womb.

To his Savior. The New Years Gift ๛ ROBERT HERRICK

That little pretty bleeding part
    Of foreskin send to me:
And I'll return a bleeding heart,
    For New-year's gift to thee.

Rich is the gem that thou didst send,
    Mine's faulty too, and small:
But yet this gift Thou wilt commend,
    Because I send Thee *all*.

Upon the Circumcision ๛ JOHN MILTON

Ye flaming powers, and winged warriors bright,
That erst with music and triumphant song
First heard by happy watchful shepherds' ear,
So sweetly sung your joy the clouds along
Through the soft silence of the listening night,
Now mourn, and, if sad share with us to bear
Your fiery essence can distill no tear,
Burn in your sighs, and borrow
Seas wept from our deep sorrow:
He, who with all Heaven's heraldry whilere
Entered the world, now bleeds to give us ease;
Alas, how soon our sin
    Sore doth begin
        His Infancy to seize!
O more exceeding love or law more just?

Just law indeed, but more exceeding love!
For we by rightful doom remediless
Were lost in death, till he that dwelt above
High-throned in secret bliss, for us frail dust
Emptied his glory, even to nakedness;
And that great Covenant which we still transgress
Entirely satisfied,
And the full wrath beside
Of vengeful Justice bore for our excess,
And seals obedience first with wounding smart
This day; but Oh! ere long
Huge pangs and strong
    Will pierce more near his heart.

LUKE 2:25–2:35   And, behold, there was a man in Jerusalem, whose name was Simeon; and the same man was just and devout, waiting for the consolation of Israel: and the Holy Ghost was upon him. And it was revealed unto him by the Holy Ghost, that he should not see death, before he had seen the Lord's Christ. And he came by the Spirit into the temple: and when the parents brought in the child Jesus, to do for him after the custom of the law, Then took he him up in his arms, and blessed God, and said, Lord, now lettest thou thy servant depart in peace, according to thy word: For mine eyes have seen thy salvation, Which thou hast prepared before the face of all people; A light to lighten the Gentiles, and the glory of thy people Israel. And Joseph and his mother marvelled at those things which were spoken of him. And Simeon blessed them, and said unto Mary his mother, Behold, this child is set for the fall and rising again of many in Israel; and for a sign which shall be spoken against; (Yea, a sword shall pierce through thy own soul also,) that the thoughts of many hearts may be revealed.

A Song for Simeon   ↝   T. S. ELIOT

Lord, the Roman hyacinths are blooming in bowls and
The winter sun creeps by the snow hills;
The stubborn season has made stand.
My life is light, waiting for the death wind,
Like a feather on the back of my hand.
Dust in sunlight and memory in corners
Wait for the wind that chills towards the dead land.

Grant us thy peace.
I have walked many years in this city,
Kept faith and fast, provided for the poor,
Have given and taken honour and ease.
There went never any rejected from my door.
Who shall remember my house, where shall live my children's
        children
When the time of sorrow is come?
They will take to the goat's path, and the fox's home,
Fleeing from the foreign faces and the foreign swords.

Before the time of cords and scourges and lamentation
Grant us thy peace.
Before the stations of the mountain of desolation,
Before the certain hour of maternal sorrow,
Now at this birth season of decease,
Let the Infant, the still unspeaking and unspoken Word,
Grant Israel's consolation
To one who has eighty years and no to-morrow.

According to thy word.
They shall praise Thee and suffer in every generation
With glory and derision,
Light upon light, mounting the saints' stair.
Not for me the martyrdom, the ecstasy of thought and prayer,
Not for me the ultimate vision.
Grant me thy peace.
(And a sword shall pierce thy heart,
Thine also).
I am tired with my own life and the lives of those after me,
I am dying in my own death and the deaths of those after me.
Let thy servant depart,
Having seen thy salvation.

MATTHEW 2:7–2:9   Then Herod, when he had privily called the wise men,
enquired of them diligently what time the star appeared. And he sent them
to Bethlehem, and said, Go and search diligently for the young child; and
when ye have found him, bring me word again, that I may come and wor-
ship him also. When they had heard the king, they departed; and, lo, the
star, which they saw in the east, went before them, till it came and stood
over where the young child was.

The Magi ᴧ WILLIAM BUTLER YEATS

Now as at all times I can see in the mind's eye,
In their stiff, painted clothes, the pale unsatisfied ones
Appear and disappear in the blue depth of the sky
With all their ancient faces like rain-beaten stones,
And all their helms of silver hovering side by side,
And all their eyes still fixed, hoping to find once more,
Being by Calvary's turbulence unsatisfied,
The uncontrollable mystery on the bestial floor.

MATTHEW 2:10–2:11   When they saw the star, they rejoiced with exceeding great joy. And when they were come into the house, they saw the young child with Mary his mother, and fell down, and worshipped him: and when they had opened their treasures, they presented unto him gifts; gold, and frankincense, and myrrh.

To his Savior, a Child; a Present, by a Child ᴧ
ROBERT HERRICK

Go pretty child, and bear this flower
Unto thy little Savior;
And tell him, by that bud now blown,
He is the Rose of Sharon known:
When thou hast said so, stick it there
Upon his bib or stomacher:
And tell him, (for good handsell too)
That thou hast brought a whistle new,
Made of a clean strait oaten reed,
To charm his cries, (at time of need:)
Tell him, for coral, thou hast none;
But if thou hadst, he should have one;
But poor thou art, and known to be
Even as moneyless, as he.
Lastly, if thou canst win a kiss
From those mellifluous lips of his;
Then never take a second on,
To spoil the first impression.

The Gift   ↝   WILLIAM CARLOS WILLIAMS

As the wise men of old brought gifts
        guided by a star
                to the humble birthplace

of the god of love,
        the devils
                as an old print shows
retreated in confusion.

        What could a baby know
                of gold ornaments
or frankincense and myrrh,
        of priestly robes
                and devout genuflections?

But the imagination
        knows all stories
                before they are told
and knows the truth of this one
        past all defection

The rich gifts
        so unsuitable for a child
                though devoutly proffered,
stood for all that love can bring.
        The men were old
                how could they know

of a mother's needs
        or a child's
                appetite?

But as they kneeled
        the child was fed.
                They saw it
and gave praise!
                A miracle

had taken place,
    hard gold to love,
a mother's milk!
    before
        their wondering eyes.

The ass brayed
    the cattle lowed.
        It was their nature.

All men by their nature give praise.
    It is all
        they can do.

The very devils
    by their flight give praise.
        What is death,
beside this?
    Nothing. The wise men
        came with gifts

and bowed down
    to worship
        this perfection.

MATTHEW 2:12   And being warned of God in a dream that they should not return to Herod, they departed into their own country another way.

The Three Kings   HENRY WADSWORTH LONGFELLOW

Three Kings came riding from far away,
    Melchior and Gaspar and Baltasar;
Three Wise Men out of the East were they.
And they travelled by night and they slept by day
    For their guide was a beautiful, wonderful star.

The star was so beautiful, large, and clear,
    That all the other stars of the sky
Became a white mist in the atmosphere.

And by this they knew that the coming was near
    Of the Prince foretold in prophecy.

Three caskets they bore on their saddlebows,
    Three caskets of gold with golden keys;
Their robes were of crimson silk with rows
Of bells and pomegranates and furbelows,
    Their turbans like blossoming almond-trees.

And so the Three Kings rode into the West,
    Through the dusk of night, over hill and dell,
And sometimes they nodded with beard on breast,
And sometimes talked, as they paused to rest,
    With the people they met at some wayside well.

"Of the child that is born," said Baltasar.
    "Good people, I pray you, tell us the news;
For we in the East have seen his star,
And have ridden fast, and have ridden far,
    To find and worship the King of the Jews."

And the people answered, "You ask in vain;
    We know of no king but Herod the Great!"
They thought the Wise Men were men insane,
As they spurred their horses across the plain,
    Like riders in haste, and who cannot wait.

And when they came to Jerusalem,
    Herod the Great, who had heard this thing,
Sent for the Wise Men and questioned them;
And said, "Go down unto Bethlehem,
    And bring me tidings of this new king."

So they rode away; and the star stood still,
    The only one in the gray of morn;
Yes, it stopped,—it stood still of its own free will,
Right over Bethlehem on the hill,
    The city of David, where Christ was born.

And the Three Kings rode through the gate and the guard,
    Through the silent street, till their horses turned

And neighed as they entered the great inn yard;
But the windows were closed and the doors were barred,
   And only a light in the stable burned.

And cradled there in the scented hay,
   In the air made sweet by the breath of kine,
The little child in the manger lay,
The child that would be king one day
   Of a kingdom not human but divine.

His mother Mary of Nazareth
   Sat watching beside his place of rest,
Watching the even flow of his breath,
For the joy of life and the terror of death
   Were mingled together in her breast.

They laid their offerings at his feet:
   The gold was their tribute to a King,
The frankincense, with its odor sweet,
Was for the Priest, the Paraclete,
   The myrrh for the body's burying.

And the mother wondered and bowed her head,
   And sat as still as a statue of stone;
Her heart was troubled yet comforted,
Remembering what the Angel had said
   Of an endless reign and of David's throne.

Then the Kings rode out of the city gate,
   With a clatter of hoofs in proud array;
But they went not back to Herod the Great,
For they knew his malice and feared his hate,
   And returned to their homes by another way.

MATTHEW 2:13–2:15   And when they were departed, behold, the angel of
the Lord appeareth to Joseph in a dream, saying, Arise, and take the young
child and his mother, and flee into Egypt, and be thou there until I bring
thee word: for Herod will seek the young child to destroy him. When he
arose, he took the young child and his mother by night, and departed into

Egypt: And was there until the death of Herod: that it might be fulfilled which was spoken of the Lord by the prophet, saying, Out of Egypt have I called my son.

The Flight in the Desert ⨪ WILLIAM EVERSON

The last settlement scraggled out with a barbed wire fence
And fell from sight. They crossed coyote country:
Mesquite, sage, the bunchgrass knotted in patches;
And there the prairie dog yapped in the valley;
And on the high plateau the short-armed badger
Delved his clay. But beyond that the desert,
Raw, unslakable, its perjured dominion wholly contained
In the sun's remorseless mandate, where the dim trail
Died ahead in the watery horizon: God knows where.

And there the failures: skull of the ox,
Where the animal terror trembled on in the hollowed eyes;
The catastrophic wheel, split, sandbedded;
And the sad jawbone of a horse. These the denials
Of the retributive tribes, fiercer than pestilence,
Whose scrupulous realm this was.

Only the burro took no notice: the forefoot
Placed with the nice particularity of one
To whom the evil of the day is wholly sufficient.
Even the jocular ears marked time.
But they, the man and the anxious woman,
Who stared pinch-eyed into the settling sun,
They went forward into its denseness
All apprehensive, and would many a time have turned
But for what they carried. That brought them on.
In the gritty blanket they bore the world's great risk,
And knew it; and kept it covered, near to the blind heart,
That hugs in a bad hour its sweetest need,
Possessed against the drawn night
That comes now, over the dead arroyos,
Cold and acrid and black.

This was the first of his goings forth into the wilderness of the world.
There was much to follow: much of portent, much of dread.
But what was so meek then and so mere, so slight and strengthless,
(Too tender, almost, to be touched)—what they nervously guarded
Guarded them. As we, each day, from the lifted chalice,
That strengthless Bread the mildest tongue subsumes,
To be taken out in the blatant kingdom
Where Herod sweats, and his deft henchmen
Riffle the tabloids—that keeps us.

Over the campfire the desert moon
Slivers the west, too chaste and cleanly
To mean hard luck. The man rattles the skillet
To take the raw edge off the silence;
The woman lifts up her heart; the Infant
Knuckles the generous breast, and feeds.

MATTHEW 2:16   Then Herod, when he saw that he was mocked of the wise
men, was exceeding wroth, and sent forth, and slew all the children that
were in Bethlehem, and in all the coasts thereof, from two years old and
under, according to the time which he had diligently enquired of the wise
men.

Lulla, my Sweet Little Baby   ∿   WILLIAM BYRD

Lulla, la lulla, lulla lullaby.
My sweet little baby, what meanest thou to cry?
Be still, my blessed babe, though cause thou hast to mourn,
Whose blood most innocent to shed the cruel king hath sworn.
And lo, alas, behold what slaughter he doth make,
Shedding the blood of infants all, sweet Savior, for thy sake
A King is born, they say, which King this king would kill.
Oh woe, and woeful heavy day, when wretches have their will!

Lulla, la lulla, lulla lullaby.
My sweet little baby, what meanest thou to cry?
Three kings this King of kings to see are come from far,
To each unknown, with offerings great, by guiding of a star.
And shepherds heard the song which angels bright did sing,

Giving all glory unto God for coming of this King,
Which must be made away, King Herod would him kill.
Oh woe, and woeful heavy day, when wretches have their will!

    Lulla, la lulla, lulla lullaby.
  My sweet little baby, what meanest thou to cry?
Lo, my little babe, be still, lament no more;
From fury thou shalt step aside, help have we still in store.
We heavenly warning have some other soil to seek,
From death must fly the Lord of life, as lamb both mild and meek.
Thus must my babe obey the king that would him kill.
Oh woe, and woeful heavy day, when wretches have their will!

    Lulla, la lulla, lulla lullaby.
  My sweet little baby, what meanest thou to cry?
But thou shalt live and reign as Sibyls have foresaid,
As all the prophets prophesy, whose mother, yet a maid
And perfect virgin pure, with her breasts shall upbreed
Both God and man, that all hath made, the Son of heavenly seed,
Whom caitiffs none can 'tray, whom tyrants none can kill.
Oh joy, and joyful happy day, when wretches want their will!

MATTHEW 2:17–2:18   Then was fulfilled that which was spoken by Jeremy the prophet, saying, In Rama was there a voice heard, lamentation, and weeping, and great mourning, Rachel weeping for her children, and would not be comforted, because they are not.

To the Infant Martyrs ↣ RICHARD CRASHAW

Go smiling souls, your new built cages break,
In Heaven you'll learn to sing ere here to speak,
Nor let the milky fonts that bathe your thirst,
    Be your delay;
The place that calls you hence, is at the worst
    Milk all the way.

A Curse on Herod ~ AMY WITTING

May you live forever. In that eternity
may birdcries from the playground ring in your ear
incessantly. When you plan your forays, may
on your terrible blueprints starfish prints appear.

May short fierce arms be locked about your knees
wherever you turn, and small fists drag at your hem
while voices whine of weewee and icecream. These
are your children. You have made them. Care for them.

May you have no rest. May you wake at night with a cry
chilled by a nightmare that you can't dispel.
May the bogeyman be thirty inches high
and immortal. These are your children. Guard them well.

May they weary you till death appears to be
brighter than the walking doll or the tin drum,
the loveliest present on the Christmas tree—
but to the bad children, Christmas does not come.

LUKE 2:40–2:50   And the child grew, and waxed strong in spirit, filled with
wisdom: and the grace of God was upon him.
   Now his parents went to Jerusalem every year at the feast of the
passover. And when he was twelve years old, they went up to Jerusalem
after the custom of the feast. . . .
   And it came to pass, that after three days they found him in the temple,
sitting in the midst of the doctors, both hearing them, and asking them
questions. And all that heard him were astonished at his understanding and
answers. And when they saw him, they were amazed: and his mother said
unto him, Son, why hast thou thus dealt with us? behold, thy father and I
have sought thee sorrowing. And he said unto them, How is it that ye
sought me? wist ye not that I must be about my Father's business? And
they understood not the saying which he spake unto them.

Temple ✌ JOHN DONNE

With his kind mother who partakes thy woe,
Joseph turn back; see where your child doth sit,
Blowing, yea blowing out those sparks of wit,
Which himself on the Doctors did bestow;
The Word but lately could not speak, and lo,
It suddenly speaks wonders, whence comes it,
That all which was, and all which should be writ,
A shallow seeming child, should deeply know?
His godhead was not soul to his manhood,
Nor had time mellowed him to this ripeness,
But as for one which hath a long task, 'tis good,
With the sun to begin his business,
He in his age's morning thus began
By miracles exceeding power of man.

from *The Everlasting Gospel* ✌ WILLIAM BLAKE

Was Jesus Humble? or did he
Give any Proofs of Humility?
Boast of high Things with Humble tone
And give with Charity a Stone?
When but a Child he ran away
And left his Parents in dismay.
When they had wandered three days long
These were the words upon his tongue:
"No Earthly Parents I confess:
"I am doing my Father's business."
When the rich learned Pharisee
Came to consult him secretly,
Upon his heart with Iron pen
He wrote, "Ye must be born again."
He was too proud to take a bribe;
He spoke with authority, not like a Scribe.
He says with most consummate Art,
"Follow me, I am meek and lowly of heart,"
As that is the only way to escape
The Miser's net and the Glutton's trap.
What can be done with such desperate Fools
Who follow after the Heathen Schools?

I was standing by when Jesus died;
What I called Humility, they called Pride.
He who loves his Enemies betrays his Friends;
This surely is not what Jesus intends,
But the sneaking Pride of Heroic Schools,
And the Scribes' and Pharisees' Virtuous Rules;
For he acts with honest, triumphant Pride,
And this is the cause that Jesus died.
He did not die with Christian ease,
Asking pardon of his Enemies:
If he had, Caiaphas would forgive;
Sneaking submission can always live.
He had only to say that God was the devil,
And the devil was God, like a Christian Civil:
Mild Christian regrets to the devil confess
For affronting him thrice in the Wilderness;
Like dr. Priestly and Bacon and Newton—
Poor Spiritual Knowledge is not worth a button!
He had soon been bloody Caesar's Elf;
And at last he would have been Caesar himself.
For thus the Gospel Sir Isaac confutes:
"God can only be known by his Attributes;
"And as for the Indwelling of the Holy Ghost
"Or of Christ and his Father, it's all a boast
"And Pride and Vanity of the imagination,
"That disdains to follow this World's Fashion."
To teach doubt and Experiment
Certainly was not what Christ meant.
What was he doing all that time,
From twelve years old to manly prime?
Was he then Idle, or the Less
About his Father's business?
Or was his wisdom held in scorn
Before his wrath began to burn
In Miracles throughout the Land,
That quite unnerved Caiaphas' hand?
If he had been Antichrist, Creeping Jesus,
He'd have done any thing to please us—
Gone sneaking into Synagogues
And not used the Elders and Priests like dogs,
But Humble as a Lamb or Ass
Obeyed himself to Caiaphas.

God wants not Man to Humble himself:
This is the trick of the ancient Elf.
This is the Race that Jesus ran:
Humble to God, Haughty to Man,
Cursing the Rulers before the People
Even to the temple's highest Steeple
And when he Humbled himself to God,
Then descended the Cruel Rod.
"If thou humblest thyself, thou humblest me;
"Thou also dwellst in Eternity.
"Thou art a Man, God is no more,
"Thy own humanity learn to adore,
"For that is my Spirit of Life.
"Awake, arise to Spiritual Strife
"And thy Revenge abroad display
"In terrors at the Last Judgment day.
"God's Mercy and Long Suffering
"Is but the Sinner to Judgment to bring.
"Thou on the Cross for them shalt pray
"And take Revenge at the Last Day."
Jesus replied and thunders hurled:
"I never will Pray for the World.
"Once I did so when I prayed in the Garden;
"I wished to take with me a Bodily Pardon."
Can that which was of woman born
In the absence of the Morn,
When the Soul fell into Sleep
And Archangels round it weep,
Shooting out against the Light
Fibres of a deadly night,
Reasoning upon its own dark fiction,
In doubt which is Self Contradiction?
Humility is only doubt,
And does the Sun and Moon blot out,
Rooting over with thorns and stems
The buried Soul and all its Gems.
This Life's dim Window of the Soul
Distorts the Heavens from Pole to Pole
And leads you to Believe a Lie
When you see with, not through, the Eye
That was born in a night to perish in a night,
When the Soul slept in the beams of Light.

The Call

MARK 1:2–1:6   . . .Behold, I send my messenger before thy face, which shall prepare thy way before thee. The voice of one crying in the wilderness, Prepare ye the way of the Lord, make his paths straight. John did baptize in the wilderness, and preach the baptism of repentance for the remission of sins. And there went out unto him all the land of Judaea, and they of Jerusalem, and were all baptized of him in the river of Jordan, confessing their sins. And John was clothed with camel's hair, and with a girdle of a skin about his loins; and he did eat locusts and wild honey;

For the Baptist ᴈ
WILLIAM DRUMMOND OF HAWTHORNDEN

The last and greatest herald of Heaven's King,
Girt with rough skins, hies to the deserts wild,
Among that savage brood the woods forth bring,
Which he than man more harmless found and mild:
His food was blossoms, and what young doth spring,
With honey that from virgin hives distilled;
Parched body, hollow eyes, some uncouth thing
Made him appear, long since from Earth exiled.
There burst he forth; All ye, whose hopes rely
On God, with me amidst these deserts mourn,
Repent, repent, and from old errors turn.
Who listened to his voice, obeyed his cry?
    Only the echoes which he made relent,
    Rung from their marble caves, repent, repent.

MATTHEW 3:11–3:12   I indeed baptize you with water unto repentance: but he that cometh after me is mightier than I, whose shoes I am not worthy to bear: he shall baptize you with the Holy Ghost, and with fire: Whose fan is in his hand, and he will throughly purge his floor, and gather his wheat into the garner; but he will burn up the chaff with unquenchable fire.

Midnight ᔛ HENRY VAUGHAN

When to my eyes
(Whilst deep sleep others catches,)
Thine host of spies
The stars shine in their watches,
I do survey
Each busy ray,
And how they work, and wind,
And wish each beam
My soul doth stream,
With the like ardor shined;
What emanations,
Quick vibrations
And bright stars are there?
What thin ejections,
Cold affections,
And slow motions here?

Thy heavens (some say,)
Are a fiery-liquid light,
Which mingling aye
Streams, and flames thus to the sight.
Come then, my God!
Shine on this blood,
And water in one beam,
And thou shalt see
Kindled by thee
Both liquors burn, and stream.
O what bright quickness,
Active brightness,
And celestial flows
Will follow after
On that water,
Which thy spirit blows!

LUKE 4:1 And Jesus being full of the Holy Ghost returned from Jordan, and
was led by the Spirit into the wilderness, MATTHEW 4:2 And when he had
fasted forty days and forty nights, he was afterward an hungred.

In the Wilderness ஃ ROBERT GRAVES

Christ of His gentleness
Thirsting and hungering,
Walked in the wilderness;
Soft words of grace He spoke
Unto lost desert-folk
That listened wondering.
He heard the bitterns call
From ruined palace-wall,
Answered them brotherly.
He held communion
With the she-pelican
Of lonely piety.
Basilisk, cockatrice,
Flocked to His homilies,
With mail of dread device,
With monstrous barbed slings,
With eager dragon-eyes;
Great bats on leathern wings
And poor blind broken things
Foul in their miseries.
And ever with Him went,
Of all His wanderings
Comrade, with ragged coat,
Gaunt ribs—poor innocent—
Bleeding foot, burning throat,
The guileless old scapegoat;
For forty nights and days
Followed in Jesus' ways,
Sure guard behind Him kept,
Tears like a lover wept.

MATTHEW 4:3–4:8   And when the tempter came to him, he said, If thou be the Son of God, command that these stones be made bread. But he answered and said, It is written, Man shall not live by bread alone, but by every word that proceedeth out of the mouth of God.

Then the devil taketh him up into the holy city, and setteth him on a pin- nacle of the temple, And saith unto him, If thou be the Son of God, cast thyself down: for it is written, He shall give his angels charge concerning thee: and in their hands they shall bear thee up, lest at any time thou dash thy foot against a stone. Jesus said unto him, It is written again, Thou shalt not tempt the Lord thy God. Again, the devil taketh him up into an exceeding high mountain, and sheweth him all the kingdoms of the world, and the glory of them; *LUKE 4:6* And the devil said unto him, All this power will I give thee, and the glory of them: for that is delivered unto me; and to whomsoever I will I give it. *MATTHEW 4:9* . . . if thou wilt fall down and worship me. *LUKE 4:8* And Jesus answered and said unto him, Get thee behind me, Satan: for it is written, Thou shalt worship the Lord thy God, and him only shalt thou serve.

from *Paradise Regained, Bk IV* ∿ JOHN MILTON
ll. 155–232; 285–352

To whom the Tempter impudent replied.
I see all offers made by me how slight
Thou valu'st, because offered, and reject'st:
Nothing will please the difficult and nice,
Or nothing more than still to contradict:
On th' other side know also thou, that I
On what I offer set as high esteem,
Nor what I part with mean to give for naught;
All these which in a moment thou beholdst,
The kingdoms of the world to thee I give;
For given to me, I give to whom I please,
No trifle; yet with this reserve, not else,
On this condition, if thou wilt fall down,
And worship me as thy superior Lord,
Easily done, and hold them all of me;
For what can less so great a gift deserve?
Whom thus our Savior answered with disdain.
I never liked thy talk, thy offers less,
Now both abhor, since thou hast dared to utter
Th' abominable terms, impious condition;
But I endure the time, till which expired,
Thou hast permission on me. It is written
The first of all Commandments, Thou shalt worship
The Lord thy God, and only him shalt serve;
And dar'st thou to the Son of God propound
To worship thee accursed, now more accursed

For this attempt bolder than that on Eve,
And more blasphemous? which expect to rue.
The kingdoms of the world to thee were given,
Permitted rather, and by thee usurped,
Other donation none thou canst produce:
If given, by whom but by the King of Kings,
God over all supreme? If given to thee,
By thee how fairly is the giver now
Repaid? But gratitude in thee is lost
Long since. Wert thou so void of fear or shame,
As offer them to me the Son of God,
To me my own, on such abhorred pact,
That I fall down and worship thee as God?
Get thee behind me; plain thou now appearst
That Evil one, Satan for ever damned.
    To whom the Fiend with fear abashed replied.
Be not so sore offended, Son of God,
Though Sons of God both angels are and men;
If I to try whether in higher sort
Than these thou bearst that title, have proposed
What both from men and angels I receive,
Tetrarchs of fire, air, flood, and on the earth
Nations besides from all the quartered winds,
God of this world invoked and world beneath;
Who then thou art, whose coming is foretold
To me so fatal, me it most concerns.
The trial hath endamaged thee no way,
Rather more honor left and more esteem;
Me naught advantaged, missing what I aimed.
Therefore let pass, as they are transitory,
The kingdoms of this world; I shall no more
Advise thee, gain them as thou canst, or not.
And thou thyself seemst otherwise inclined
Than to a worldly crown, addicted more
To contemplation and profound dispute,
As by that early action may be judged,
When slipping from thy mother's eye thou wentst
Alone into the temple; there wast found
Among the gravest Rabbis disputant
On points and questions fitting Moses' Chair,
Teaching not taught; the childhood shows the man,

As morning shows the day. Be famous then
By wisdom; as thy empire must extend,
So let extend thy mind o'er all the world,
In knowledge, all things in it comprehend.
All knowledge is not couched in Moses' Law,
The *Pentateuch* or what the Prophets wrote;
The Gentiles also know, and write, and teach
To admiration, led by nature's light
And with the Gentiles much thou must converse,
Ruling them by persuasion as thou meanst,
Without their learning how wilt thou with them,
Or they with thee hold conversation meet?. . .

    To whom our Savior sagely thus replied.
Think not but that I know these things; or think
I know them not; not therefore am I short
Of knowing what I ought: he who receives
Light from above, from the fountain of light,
No other doctrine needs, though granted true;
But these are false, or little else but dreams,
Conjectures, fancies, built on nothing firm.
The first and wisest of them all professed
To know this only, that he nothing knew;
The next to fabling fell and smooth conceits;
A third sort doubted all things, though plain sense;
Others in virtue placed felicity,
But virtue joined with riches and long life;
In corporal pleasure he, and careless ease;
The Stoic last in philosophic pride,
By him called virtue; and his virtuous man,
Wise, perfect in himself, and all possessing
Equal to God, oft shames not to prefer,
As fearing God nor man, contemning all
Wealth, pleasure, pain or torment, death and life,
Which when he lists, he leaves, or boasts he can,
For all his tedious talk is but vain boast,
Or subtle shifts conviction to evade.
Alas! what can they teach, and not mislead;
Ignorant of themselves, of God much more,
And how the world began, and how man fell
Degraded by himself, on grace depending?

Much of the Soul they talk, but all awry,
And in themselves seek virtue, and to themselves
All glory arrogate, to God give none,
Rather accuse him under usual names,
Fortune and Fate, as one regardless quite
Of mortal things. Who therefore seeks in these
True Wisdom, finds her not, or by delusion
Far worse, her false resemblance only meets,
An empty cloud. However, many books
Wise men have said are wearisome; who reads
Incessantly, and to his reading brings not
A spirit and judgment equal or superior
(And what he brings, what needs he elsewhere seek)
Uncertain and unsettled still remains,
Deep versed in books and shallow in himself,
Crude or intoxicate, collecting toys,
And trifles for choice matters, worth a sponge;
As children gathering pebbles on the shore.
Or if I would delight my private hours
With music or with poem, where so soon
As in our native language can I find
That solace? All our law and story strewed
With hymns, our psalms with artful terms inscribed
Our hebrew songs and harps in Babylon,
That pleased so well our victors' ear, declare
That rather Greece from us these arts derived;
Ill imitated, while they loudest sing
The vices of their deities, and their own
In fable, hymn, or song, so personating
Their gods ridiculous, and themselves past shame.
Remove their swelling epithets thick laid
As varnish on a harlot's cheek, the rest,
Thin sown with aught of profit or delight,
Will far be found unworthy to compare
With Sion's songs, to all true tastes excelling,
Where God is praised aright, and godlike men,
The Holiest of Holies, and his Saints;
Such are from God inspired, not such from thee;
Unless where moral virtue is expressed
By light of nature, not in all quite lost.

JOHN 1:29   The next day John seeth Jesus coming unto him, and saith, Behold the Lamb of God, which taketh away the sin of the world.

The Lamb ✥ WILLIAM BLAKE

Little Lamb, who made thee?
Dost thou know who made thee?
Gave thee life, and bid thee feed
By the stream and o'er the mead;
Gave thee clothing of delight,
Softest clothing, wooly, bright;
Gave thee such a tender voice,
Making all the vales rejoice?
Little Lamb, who made thee?
Dost thou know who made thee?

Little Lamb, I'll tell thee
Little Lamb, I'll tell thee:
He is called by thy name,
For he calls himself a Lamb.
He is meek, and he is mild;
He became a little child.
I a child, and thou a lamb,
We are called by his name.
Little Lamb, God bless thee!
Little Lamb, God bless thee!

JOHN 2:1–2:10   And the third day there was a marriage in Cana of Galilee; and the mother of Jesus was there: And both Jesus was called, and his disciples, to the marriage. And when they wanted wine, the mother of Jesus saith unto him, They have no wine. Jesus saith unto her, Woman, what have I to do with thee? mine hour is not yet come. His mother saith unto the servants, Whatsoever he saith unto you, do it. And there were set there six waterpots of stone, after the manner of the purifying of the Jews, containing two or three firkins apiece. Jesus saith unto them, Fill the waterpots with water. And they filled them up to the brim. And he saith unto them, Draw out now, and bear unto the governor of the feast. And they bare it. When the ruler of the feast had tasted the water that was made wine, and knew not whence it was: (but the servants which drew the water knew;) the gover-

nor of the feast called the bridegroom, And saith unto him, Every man at
the beginning doth set forth good wine; and when men have well drunk,
then that which is worse: but thou hast kept the good wine until now.

The Wedding Feast ⁊ EDGAR LEE MASTERS

Said the chief of the marriage feast to the groom,
    Whence is this blood of the vine?
Men serve at first the best, he said,
    And at the last, poor wine.

Said the chief of the marriage feast to the groom,
    When the guests have drunk their fill
They drink whatever wine you serve,
    Nor know the good from the ill.

How have you kept the good till now
    When our hearts nor care nor see?
Said the chief of the marriage feast to the groom,
    Whence may this good wine be?

Said the chief of the marriage feast, this wine
    Is the best of all by far.
Said the groom, there stand six jars without
    And the wine fills up each jar.

Said the chief of the marriage feast, we lacked
    Wine for the wedding feast.
How comes it now one jar of wine
    To six jars is increased?

Who makes our cup to overflow?
    And who has the wedding blessed?
Said the groom to the chief of the feast, a stranger
    Is here as a wedding guest.

Said the groom to the chief of the wedding feast,
    Moses by power divine
Smote water at Meribah from the rock,
    But this man makes us wine.

Said the groom to the chief of the wedding feast,
    Elisha by power divine
Made oil for the widow to sell for bread,
    But this man, wedding wine.

He changed the use of the jars, he said,
    From an outward rite and sign:
Where water stood for the washing of feet,
    For heart's delight there's wine.

So then 'tis he, said the chief of the feast,
    Who the wedding feast has blessed?
Said the groom to the chief of the feast, the stranger
    Is the merriest wedding guest.

He laughs and jests with the wedding guests,
    He drinks with the happy bride.
Said the chief of the wedding feast to the groom
    Go bring him to my side.

Jesus of Nazareth came up,
    And his body was fair and slim.
Jesus of Nazareth came up,
    And his mother came with him.

Jesus of Nazareth stands with the dancers
    And his mother by him stands.
The bride kneels down to Jesus of Nazareth
    And kisses his rosy hands.

The bridegroom kneels to Jesus of Nazareth
    And Jesus blesses the twain.
I go a way, said Jesus of Nazareth,
    Of darkness, sorrow and pain.

After the wedding feast is labor,
    Suffering, sickness, death,
And so I make you wine for the wedding,
    Said Jesus of Nazareth.

My heart is with you, said Jesus of Nazareth,
    As the grape is one with the vine.
Your bliss is mine, said Jesus of Nazareth,
    And so I make you wine.

Youth and love I bless, said Jesus,
    Song and the cup that cheers.
The rosy hands of Jesus of Nazareth
    Are wet with the young bride's tears.

Love one another, said Jesus of Nazareth,
    Ere cometh the evil of years.
The rosy hands of Jesus of Nazareth
    Are wet with the bridegroom's tears.

Jesus of Nazareth goes with his mother,
    The dancers are dancing again.
There's a woman who pauses without to listen,
    'Tis Mary Magdalen.

Forth to the street a Scribe from the wedding
    Goes with a Sadducee.
Said the Scribe, this shows how loose a fellow
    Can come out of Galilee!

The Signs

JOHN 3:1–3:2   There was a man of the Pharisees, named Nicodemus, a
ruler of the Jews: The same came to Jesus by night, and said unto him,
Rabbi, we know that thou art a teacher come from God: for no man can do
these miracles that thou doest, except God be with him.

The Night   ↷   HENRY VAUGHAN

        Through that pure Virgin-shrine,
That sacred veil drawn o'er thy glorious noon
That men might look and live as glow-worms shine,
            And face the moon:

Wise Nicodemus saw such light
As made him know his God by night.

Most blessed believer he!
Who in that land of darkness and blind eyes
Thy long expected healing wings could see,
When thou didst rise,
And what more can be done,
Did at midnight speak with the sun!

O who will tell me, where
He found thee at that dead and silent hour!
What hallowed solitary ground did bear
So rare a flower
Within whose sacred leafs did lie
The fulness of the Deity.

No mercy-seat of gold,
No dead and dusty cherub, nor carved stone,
But his own living works did my Lord hold
And lodge alone;
Where trees and herbs did watch and peep
And wonder, while the Jews did sleep.

Dear night! this world's defeat;
The stop to busy fools; care's check and curb;
The day of spirits; my soul's calm retreat
Which none disturb!
Christ's[20] progress, and his prayer time;
The hours to which high Heaven doth chime.

God's silent, searching flight:
When my Lord's head is filled with dew, and all
His locks are wet with the clear drops of night;[21]
His still, soft call;
His knocking time; The souls dumb watch,
When spirits their fair kindred catch.

20 *Mark, chap.* 1. 35. S. *Luke, chap.* 21. 37. [Vaughan's note]
21 SONG OF SOL 5:2

Were all my loud, evil days
Calm and unhaunted as is thy dark tent,
Whose peace but by some angel's wing or voice
        Is seldom rent;
   Then I in Heaven all the long year
   Would keep, and never wander here.

But living where the sun
Doth all things wake, and where all mix and tire
Themselves and others, I consent and run
        To every mire,
   And by this world's ill-guiding light,
   Err more than I can do by night.

There is in God (some say)
A deep, but dazzling darkness; As men here
Say it is late and dusky, because they
        See not all clear;
   O for that night! where I in him
   Might live invisible and dim.

JOHN 3:8   The wind bloweth where it listeth, and thou hearest the sound thereof, but canst not tell whence it cometh, and whither it goeth: so is every one that is born of the Spirit.

The Wind ᘓ   CHRISTINA GEORGINA ROSSETTI

Who has seen the wind?
   Neither I nor you.
But when the leaves hang trembling,
   The wind is passing through.
Who has seen the wind?
   Neither you nor I.
But when the trees bow their heads,
   The wind is passing by.

JOHN 3:16–3:19   For God so loved the world, that he gave his only begotten Son, that whosoever believeth in him should not perish, but have everlasting life. For God sent not his Son into the world to condemn the world; but that the world through him might be saved. He that believeth on him is not condemned: but he that believeth not is condemned already, because he hath not believed in the name of the only begotten Son of God. And this is the condemnation, that light is come into the world, and men loved darkness rather than light, because their deeds were evil.

But Men Loved Darkness Rather than Light ↝
RICHARD CRASHAW

The world's light shines; shine as it will,
The world will love its darkness still:
I doubt though when the world's in Hell,
It will not love its darkness half so well.

The Master

JOHN 5:1–5:9   After this there was a feast of the Jews; and Jesus went up to Jerusalem. Now there is at Jerusalem by the sheep market a pool, which is called in the Hebrew tongue Bethesda, having five porches. In these lay a great multitude of impotent folk, of blind, halt, withered, waiting for the moving of the water. For an angel went down at a certain season into the pool, and troubled the water: whosoever then first after the troubling of the water stepped in was made whole of whatsoever disease he had. . .

Nocturne at Bethesda ↝ ARNA BONTEMPS

I thought I saw an angel flying low,
I thought I saw the flicker of a wing
Above the mulberry trees; but not again.
Bethesda sleeps. This ancient pool that healed
A host of bearded Jews does not awake.
This pool that once the angels troubled does not move.
No angel stirs it now, no Saviour comes
With healing in His hands to raise the sick
And bid the lame man leap upon the ground.

The golden days are gone. Why do we wait
So long upon the marble steps, blood
Falling from our open wounds? and why
Do our black faces search the empty sky?
Is there something we have forgotten? some precious thing
We have lost, wandering in strange lands?

There was a day, I remember now,
I beat my breast and cried, "Wash me God,
Wash me with a wave of wind upon
The barley; O quiet One, draw near, draw near!
Walk upon the hills with lovely feet
And in the waterfall stand and speak.

"Dip white hands in the lily pool and mourn
Upon the harps still hanging in the trees
Near Babylon along the river's edge,
But oh, remember me, I pray, before
The summer goes and rose leaves lose their red."

The old terror takes my heart, the fear
Of quiet waters and of faint twilights.
There will be better days when I am gone
And healing pools where I cannot be healed.
Fragrant stars will gleam forever and ever
Above the place where I lie desolate.

Yet I hope, still I long to live.
And if there can be returning after death
I shall come back. But it will not be here;
If you want me you must search for me
Beneath the palms of Africa. Or if
I am not there then you may call to me
Across the shining dunes, perhaps I shall
Be following a desert caravan.

I may pass through centuries of death
With quiet eyes, but I'll remember still
A jungle tree with burning scarlet birds.
There is something I have forgotten, some precious thing.
I shall be seeking ornaments of ivory,
I shall be dying for a jungle fruit.

You do not hear, Bethesda.
O still green water in a stagnant pool!
Love abandoned you and me alike.
There was a day you held a rich full moon
Upon your heart and listened to the words
Of men now dead and saw the angels fly.
There is a simple story on your face;
Years have wrinkled you. I know, Bethesda!
You are sad. It is the same with me.

MATTHEW 4:17–4:22   From that time Jesus began to preach, and to say,
Repent: for the kingdom of heaven is at hand.

And Jesus, walking by the sea of Galilee, saw two brethren, Simon
called Peter, and Andrew his brother, casting a net into the sea: for they
were fishers. And he saith unto them, Follow me, and I will make you fish-
ers of men. And they straightway left their nets, and followed him. And
going on from thence, he saw other two brethren, James the son of
Zebedee, and John his brother, in a ship with Zebedee their father, mend-
ing their nets; and he called them. And they immediately left the ship and
their father, and followed him.

from *Jubilate Agno*   ঌ   CHRISTOPHER SMART

Let Peter rejoice with the Moonfish who keeps up the life in the
    waters by night.
Let Andrew rejoice with the Whale, who is arrayed in beauteous blue
    and is a combination of bulk and activity.
Let James rejoice with the Skuttle-Fish, who foils his foe by the effu-
    sion of his ink.
Let John rejoice with Nautilus who spreads his sail and plies his oar,
    and the Lord is his pilot.
Let Philip rejoice with Boca, which is a fish that can speak.
Let Bartholemew rejoice with the Eel, who is pure in proportion to
    where he is found and how he is used.
Let Thomas rejoice with the Sword-Fish, whose aim is perpetual and
    strength insuperable.
Let Matthew rejoice with Uranoscopus, whose eyes are lifted up to
    God.

Let James the less, rejoice with the Haddock, who brought the piece
    of money for the Lord and Peter.
Let Jude bless with the Bream, who is of melancholy from his depth
    and serenity.
Let Simon rejoice with the Sprat, who is pure and innumerable.
Let Matthias rejoice with the Flying-Fish, who has a part with the
    birds, and is sublimity in his conceit.
Let Stephen rejoice with Remora – The Lord remove all obstacles to
    his glory.
Let Paul rejoice with the Seal, who is pleasant and faithful, like God's
    good Englishman.
Let Agrippa, which is Agricola, rejoice with Elops, who is a choice
    fish.
Let Joseph rejoice with the Turbut, whose capture makes the poor
    fisher-man sing.
Let Mary rejoice with the Maid – blessed be the name of the
    Immaculate Conception.
Let John, the Baptist, rejoice with the Salmon – blessed be the name
    of the Lord Jesus for infant Baptism.
Let Mark rejoice with the Mullet, who is John Dore, God be gracious
    to him and his family.
Let Barnabas rejoice with the Herring – God be gracious to the Lord's
    fishery.
Let Cleopas rejoice with the Mackerel, who cometh in a shoal after a
    leader.

LUKE 6:12–6:16   And it came to pass in those days, that he went out into a
mountain to pray, and continued all night in prayer to God. And when it was
day, he called unto him his disciples: and of them he chose twelve, whom
also he named apostles; Simon, (whom he also named Peter,) and Andrew
his brother, James and John, Philip and Bartholomew, Matthew and
Thomas, James the son of Alphaeus, and Simon called Zelotes, And Judas
the brother of James, and Judas Iscariot, which also was the traitor.

MATTHEW 10:1   And when he had called unto him his twelve disciples, he
gave them power against unclean spirits, to cast them out, and to heal all
manner of sickness and all manner of disease.

Starlight Like Intuition Pierced the Twelve ❧
DELMORE SCHWARTZ

The starlight's intuitions pierced the twelve,
The brittle night sky sparkled like a tune
Tinkled and tapped out on the xylophone.
Empty and vain, a glittering dune, the moon
Arose too big, and, in the mood which ruled,
Seemed like a useless beauty in a pit;
And then one said, after he carefully spat:
"No matter what we do, he looks at it!

"I cannot see a child or find a girl
Beyond his smile which glows like that spring moon."
"—Nothing no more the same," the second said,
"Though all may be forgiven, never quite healed
The wound I bear as witness, standing by;
No ceremony surely appropriate,
Nor secret love, escape or sleep because
No matter what I do, he looks at it——"

"Now," said the third, "no thing will be the same:
I am as one who never shuts his eyes,
The sea and sky no more are marvellous,
And I no longer understand surprise!"
"Now," said the fourth, "nothing will be enough
—I heard his voice accomplishing all wit:
No word can be unsaid, no deed withdrawn
—No matter what is said, he measures it!"

"Vision, imagination, hope or dream,
Believed, denied, the scene we wished to see?
It does not matter in the least: for what
Is altered, if it is not true? That we
Saw goodness, as it is—this is the awe
And the abyss which we will not forget,
His story now the sky which holds all thought:
No matter what I think, I think of it!"

"And I will never be what once I was,"
Said one for long as narrow as a knife,
"And we will never be what once we were;
We have died once; this is a second life."
"My mind is spilled in moral chaos," one
Righteous as Job exclaimed, "now infinite
Suspicion of my heart stems what I will
—No matter what I choose, he stares at it!"

"I am as one native in summer places
—Ten weeks' excitement paid for by the rich;
Debauched by that and then all winter bored,"
The sixth declared. "His peak left us a ditch!"
"He came to make this life more difficult,"
The seventh said, "No one will ever fit
His measure's heights, all is inadequate:
No matter what I do, what good is it?"

"He gave forgiveness to us: what a gift!"
The eighth chimed in. "But now we know how much
Must be forgiven. But if forgiven, what?
The crime which was will be; and the least touch
Revives the memory: what is forgiveness worth?"
The ninth spoke thus: "Who now will ever sit
At ease in Zion at the Easter feast?
No matter what the place, he touches it!"

"And I will always stammer, since he spoke,"
One, who had been most eloquent, said, stammering.
"I looked too long at the sun; like too much light,
So too much goodness is a boomerang,"
Laughed the eleventh of the troop. "I must
Try what he tried: I saw the infinite
Who walked the lake and raised the hopeless dead:
No matter what the feat, he first accomplished it!"

So spoke the twelfth; and then the twelve in chorus:
"Unspeakable unnatural goodness is
Risen and shines, and never will ignore us;
He glows forever in all consciousness;
Forgiveness, love, and hope possess the pit,

And bring our endless guilt, like shadow's bars:
No matter what we do, he stares at it!
What pity then deny? what debt defer?
We know he looks at us like all the stars,
And we shall never be as once we were,
This life will never be what once it was!"

MATTHEW 10:5–10:10   These twelve Jesus sent forth, and commanded
them, saying, Go not into the way of the Gentiles, and into any city of the
Samaritans enter ye not: But go rather to the lost sheep of the house of
Israel. And as ye go, preach, saying, The kingdom of heaven is at hand.
Heal the sick, cleanse the lepers, raise the dead, cast out devils: freely ye
have received, freely give. Provide neither gold, nor silver, nor brass in your
purses, Nor scrip for your journey, neither two coats, neither shoes, nor
yet staves: . . .

The Passionate Man's Pilgrimage ♏

SIR WALTER RALEIGH

Supposed to be written by one at the point of death

Give me my scallop shell of quiet,
My staff of faith to walk upon,
My scrip of joy, immortal diet,
My bottle of salvation:
My gown of glory, hope's true gage,
And thus I'll take my pilgrimage.

Blood must be my body's balmer,
No other balm will there be given
Whilst my soul like a white palmer
Travels to the land of heaven,
Over the silver mountains,
Where spring the nectar fountains:
And there I'll kiss
The bowl of bliss,
And drink my eternal fill
On every milken hill.
My soul will be a-dry before,
But after, it will ne'er thirst more.

And by the happy blissful way
More peaceful pilgrims I shall see,
That have shook off their gowns of clay,
And go apparelled fresh like me.
I'll bring them first
To slake their thirst,
And then to taste those nectar suckets
At the clear wells
Where sweetness dwells,
Drawn up by saints in crystal buckets.

And when our bottles and all we,
Are filled with immortality:
Then the holy paths we'll travel
Strewed with rubies thick as gravel,
Ceilings of diamonds, sapphire floors,
High walls of coral and pearl bowers.

From thence to heaven's bribeless hall
Where no corrupted voices brawl,
No conscience molten into gold,
Nor forged accusers bought and sold,
No cause deferred, nor vain spent journey,
For there Christ is the King's Attorney:
Who pleads for all without degrees,
And he hath angels, but no fees.

When the grand twelve million jury,
Of our sins and sinful fury,
Gainst our souls black verdicts give,
Christ pleads his death, and then we live,
Be thou my speaker taintless pleader,
Unblotted lawyer, true proceeder,
Thou movest salvation even for alms:
Not with a bribed lawyer's palms.

And this is my eternal plea,
To him that made Heaven, Earth and Sea,
Seeing my flesh must die so soon,
And want a head to dine next noon,
Just at the stroke when my veins start and spread

Set on my soul an everlasting head.
Then am I ready like a palmer fit,
To tread those blessed paths which before I writ.

MATTHEW 5:13–5:16   Ye are the salt of the earth: but if the salt have lost his savour, wherewith shall it be salted? it is thenceforth good for nothing, but to be cast out, and to be trodden under foot of men. Ye are the light of the world. A city that is set on an hill cannot be hid. Neither do men light a candle, and put it under a bushel, but on a candlestick; and it giveth light unto all that are in the house. Let your light so shine before men, that they may see your good works, and glorify your Father which is in heaven.

The Candle Indoors   ✁   GERARD MANLEY HOPKINS

Some candle clear burns somewhere I come by.
I muse at how its being puts blissful back
With yellowy moisture mild night's blear-all black,
Or to-fro tender trambeams truckle at the eye.
By that window what task what fingers ply,
I plod wondering, a-wanting, just for lack
Of answer the eagerer a-wanting Jessy or Jack
There   God to aggrándise, God to glorify.—

Come you indoors, come home; your fading fire
Mend first and vital candle in close heart's vault:
You there are master, do your own desire;
What hinders? Are you beam-blind, yet to a fault
In a neighbour deft-handed? are you that liar
And, cast by conscience out, spendsavour salt?

MATTHEW 5:17–5:20   Think not that I am come to destroy the law, or the prophets: I am not come to destroy, but to fulfil. For verily I say unto you, Till heaven and earth pass, one jot or one tittle shall in no wise pass from the law, till all be fulfilled. Whosoever therefore shall break one of these least commandments, and shall teach men so, he shall be called the least in the kingdom of heaven: but whosoever shall do and teach them, the same shall be called great in the kingdom of heaven. For I say unto you, That except your righteousness shall exceed the righteousness of the scribes and Pharisees, ye shall in no case enter into the kingdom of heaven.

Progress ❧ MATTHEW ARNOLD

The Master stood upon the mount, and taught.
He saw a fire in his disciples' eyes;
'The old law', they said, 'is wholly come to naught!
    Behold the new world rise!'

'Was it', the Lord then said, 'with scorn ye saw
The old law observed by Scribes and Pharisees?
I say unto you, see *ye* keep that law
    More faithfully than these!

'Too hasty heads for ordering worlds, alas!
Think not that I to annul the law have willed;
No jot, no tittle from the law shall pass,
    Till all hath been fulfilled.'

So Christ said eighteen hundred years ago.
And what then shall be said to those to-day,
Who cry aloud to lay the old world low
    To clear the new world's way?

'Religious fervours! ardour misapplied!
Hence, hence,' they cry, 'ye do but keep man blind!
But keep him self-immersed, preoccupied,
    And lame the active mind!'

Ah! from the old world let some one answer give:
'Scorn ye this world, their tears, their inward cares?
I say unto you, see that *your* souls live
    A deeper life than theirs!

'Say ye: The spirit of man has found new roads,
And we must leave the old faiths, and walk therein? —
Leave then the Cross as ye have left carved gods,
    But guard the fire within!

'Bright, else, and fast the stream of life may roll,
And no man may the other's hurt behold;
Yet each will have one anguish — his own soul
    Which perishes of cold.'

Here let that voice make end; then let a strain,
From a far lonelier distance, like the wind
Be heard, floating through heaven, and fill again
    These men's profoundest mind:

'Children of men! the unseen Power, whose eye
For ever doth accompany mankind,
Hath looked on no religion scornfully
    That men did ever find.

'Which has not taught weak wills how much they can?
Which has not fallen on the dry heart like rain?
Which has not cried to sunk, self-weary man:
    Thou must be born again!

'Children of men! not that your age excel
In pride of life the ages of your sires,
But that you think clear, feel deep, bear fruit well,
    The Friend of man desires.'

MATTHEW 6:25–6:28   Therefore I say unto you, Take no thought for your life, what ye shall eat, or what ye shall drink; nor yet for your body, what ye shall put on. Is not the life more than meat, and the body than raiment? Behold the fowls of the air: for they sow not, neither do they reap, nor gather into barns; yet your heavenly Father feedeth them. Are ye not much better than they? Which of you by taking thought can add one cubit unto his stature? And why take ye thought for raiment? Consider the lilies of the field, how they grow; they toil not, neither do they spin:

The Habit of Perfection   ॐ   GERARD MANLEY HOPKINS

Elected Silence, sing to me
And beat upon my whorlèd ear,
Pipe me to measures still and be
The music that I care to hear.

Shape nothing, lips; be lovely-dumb:
It is the shut, the curfew sent

From there where all surrenders come
Which only makes you eloquent.

Be shellèd, eyes, with double dark
And find the uncreated light:
This ruck and reel which you remark
Coils, keeps, and teases simple sight.

Palate, the hutch of tasty lust,
Desire not to be rinsed with wine:
The can must be so sweet, the crust
So fresh that come in fasts divine!

Nostrils, your careless breath that spend
Upon the stir and keep of pride,
What relish shall the censers send
Along the sanctuary side!

O feel-of-primrose hands, O feet
That want the yield of plushy sward,
But you shall walk the golden street
And you unhouse and house the Lord.

And, Poverty, be thou the bride
And now the marriage feast begun,
And lily-coloured clothes provide
Your spouse not laboured-at nor spun.

MATTHEW 6:29   And yet I say unto you, That even Solomon in all his glory
was not arrayed like one of these.

For Daughters of Magdalen ⁓ COUNTEE CULLEN

Ours is the ancient story:
    Delicate flowers of sin,
Lilies, arrayed in glory,
    That would not toil or spin.

MATTHEW 7:2   For with what judgment ye judge, ye shall be judged: and with what measure ye mete, it shall be measured to you again.

Judge Not ✿ THEODORE ROETHKE

Faces greying faster than loam-crumbs on a harrow;
Children, their bellies swollen like blown-up paper bags,
Their eyes rich as plums, staring from newsprint, —
These images haunted me noon and midnight.
I imagined the unborn, starving in wombs, curling;
I asked: May the blessings of life, O Lord, descend on the living.

Yet when I heard the drunkards howling,
Smelled the carrion at entrances,
Saw women, their eyelids like little rags,
I said: On all these, Death, with gentleness, come down.

MATTHEW 7:13–7:14   Enter ye in at the strait gate: for wide is the gate, and broad is the way, that leadeth to destruction, and many there be which go in thereat: Because strait is the gate, and narrow is the way, which leadeth unto life, and few there be that find it.

H. Baptism (II) ✿ GEORGE HERBERT

Since, Lord, to thee
A narrow way and little gate
Is all the passage, on my infancy
Thou didst lay hold, and antedate
My faith in me.

O let me still
Write thee great God, and me a child:
Let me be soft and supple to thy will,
Small to my self, to others mild,
Be hither ill.

Although by stealth
My flesh get on; yet let her sister

My soul bid nothing, but preserve her wealth:
   The growth of flesh is but a blister;
      Childhood is health.

LUKE 7:18–7:24 And the disciples of John shewed him of all these things. And John calling unto him two of his disciples sent them to Jesus, saying, Art thou he that should come? or look we for another? When the men were come unto him, they said, John Baptist hath sent us unto thee, saying, Art thou he that should come? or look we for another? And in that same hour he cured many of their infirmities and plagues, and of evil spirits; and unto many that were blind he gave sight. Then Jesus answering said unto them, Go your way, and tell John what things ye have seen and heard; how that the blind see, the lame walk, the lepers are cleansed, the deaf hear, the dead are raised, to the poor the gospel is preached. And blessed is he, whosoever shall not be offended in me. And when the messengers of John were departed, he began to speak unto the people concerning John, What went ye out into the wilderness for to see? A reed shaken with the wind?

John ~ JONES VERY

What went ye out to see? a shaken reed?
In him whose voice proclaims "prepare the way;"
Behold the oak that stormy centuries feed!
Though but the buried acorn of My day;
What went ye out to see? a kingly man?
In the soft garments clothed that ye have worn;
Behold a servant whom the hot suns tan,
His raiment from the rough-haired camel torn;
Ye seek ye know not what; blind children all,
Who each his idle fancy will demand;
Nor heed my true-sent prophet's warning call,
That you may learn of me the new command,
And see the Light that cometh down from heaven,
Repent! and see, while yet its light is given.

LUKE 7:36–7:38 And one of the Pharisees desired him that he would eat with him. And he went into the Pharisee's house, and sat down to meat. And, behold, a woman in the city, which was a sinner, when she knew that

Jesus sat at meat in the Pharisee's house, brought an alabaster box of oint-
ment, And stood at his feet behind him weeping, and began to wash his
feet with tears, and did wipe them with the hairs of her head, and kissed his
feet, and anointed them with the ointment.

Saint Mary Magdalene or The Weeper
RICHARD CRASHAW

Lo where a wounded heart with bleeding eyes conspire.
Is she a flaming fountain, or a weeping fire?

> Hail sister springs,
> Parents of silver-forded rills!
> Ever bubbling things!
> Thawing crystal! snowy hills!
> Still spending, never spent; I mean
> Thy fair eyes sweet Magdalene.

> Heavens thy fair eyes be,
> Heavens of ever-falling stars,
> Tis seed-time still with thee
> And stars thou sow'st, whose harvest dares
> Promise the earth to countershine
> What ever makes Heaven's fore-head fine.

> But we are deceived all,
> Stars they are indeed too true,
> For they but seem to fall
> As Heaven's other spangles do:
> It is not for our Earth and us,
> To shine in things so precious.

> Upwards thou dost weep.
> Heaven's bosom drinks the gentle stream.
> Where th' milky rivers meet,
> Thine crawls above and is the cream.
> Heaven, of such fair floods as this,
> Heaven the Crystal Ocean is.

Every morn from hence,
A brisk Cherub something sips
Whose soft influence
Adds sweetness to his sweetest lips.
Then to his Music, and his song
Tastes of this breakfast all day long.

When some new bright guest
Takes up among the stars a room,
And Heaven will make a feast,
Angels with their bottles come;
And draw from these full eyes of thine,
Their master's water, their own wine.

The dew no more will weep,
The primroses pale cheek to deck,
The dew no more will sleep,
Nuzzled in the lilies' neck.
Much rather would it tremble here,
And leave them both to be thy tear.

Not the soft gold which
Steals from the amber-weeping tree,
Makes sorrow half so rich.
As the drops distilled from thee.
Sorrow's best jewels lie in these
Caskets, of which Heaven keeps the keys.

When Sorrow would be seen
In her brightest majesty,
(For she is a Queen)
Then is she dressed by none but thee.
Then, and only then she wears
Her richest pearls, I mean thy tears.

Not in the evening's eyes
When they red with weeping are,
For the sun that dies,
Sits sorrow with a face so fair.
Nowhere but here did ever meet
Sweetness so sad, sadness so sweet.

Sadness all the while
She sits in such a throne as this,
     Can do nought but smile,
Nor believes she sadness is.
Gladness itself would be more glad
To be made so sweetly sad.

There is no need at all
That the balsam-sweating bough
     So coyly should let fall,
His medicinable tears; for now
Nature hath learned t'extract a dew,
More sovereign and sweet from you.

Yet the poor drops weep,
Weeping is the ease of woe,
     Softly let them creep
Sad that they are vanquished so,
They, though to others no relief
May balsam be for their own grief.

Golden though he be,
Golden Tagus murmurs though,
     Might he flow from thee
Content and quiet would he go,
Richer far does he esteem
Thy silver, than his golden stream.

Well does the May that lies
Smiling in thy cheeks, confess,
     The April in thine eyes,
Mutual sweetness they express.
No April e'er lent softer showers,
Nor May returned fairer flowers.

Thus dost thou melt the year
Into a weeping motion,
     Each minute waiteth here;
Takes his tear and gets him gone;
By thine eyes tinct ennobled thus
Time lays him up: he's precious.

Time as by thee he passes,
Makes thy ever-watery eyes
His hour-glasses.
By them his steps he rectifies.
The sands he used no longer please,
For his own sands he'll use thy seas.

Does thy song lull the air?
Thy tears' just cadence still keeps time.
Does thy sweet breathed Prayer
Up in clouds of incense climb?
Still at each sigh, that is each stop:
A bead, that is a tear doth drop.

Does the Night arise?
Still thy tears do fall, and fall.
Does night loose her eyes?
Still the fountain weeps for all.
Let night or day do what they will
Thou hast thy task, thou weepest still.

Not, so long she lived,
Will thy tomb report of thee
But *so long she grieved*,
Thus must we date thy memory.
Others by days, by months, by years
Measure their ages, thou by tears.

Say watery Brothers
Ye simpering sons of those fair eyes,
Your fertile Mothers.
What hath our world that can entice
You to be born? what is't can borrow
You from her eyes swoll'n wombs of sorrow.

Whither away so fast?
O whither? for the sluttish Earth
Your sweetness cannot taste
Nor does the dust deserve your birth.
Whither hast ye then? o say
Why ye trip so fast away?

We go not to seek
The darlings of Aurora's bed,
        The rose's modest cheek
Nor the violet's humble head.
No such thing; we go to meet
A worthier object, Our Lord's feet.

LUKE 7:44   And he turned to the woman, and said unto Simon, Seest thou this woman? I entered into thine house, thou gavest me no water for my feet: but she hath washed my feet with tears, and wiped them with the hairs of her head.

For the Magdalene ৵
WILLIAM DRUMMOND OF HAWTHORNDEN

These eyes (dear Lord) once brandons of desire,
Frail scouts betraying what they had to keep,
Which their own heart, then others set on fire,
Their traitorous black before thee here out-weep:
These locks, of blushing deeds the fair attire,
Smooth-frizzled waves, sad shelfs which shadow deep,
Soul-stinging serpents in gilt curls which creep,
To touch thy sacred feet do now aspire.
In seas of care behold a sinking bark,
By winds of sharp remorse unto thee driven,
O let me not exposed be ruin's mark,
My faults confessed (Lord) say they are forgiven.
    Thus sighed to Jesus the Bethanian fair,
    His tear-wet feet still drying with her hair.

MATTHEW 12:27–12:32   And if I by Beelzebub cast out devils, by whom do your children cast them out? therefore they shall be your judges. But if I cast out devils by the Spirit of God, then the kingdom of God is come unto you. Or else how can one enter into a strong man's house, and spoil his goods, except he first bind the strong man? and then he will spoil his house. He that is not with me is against me; and he that gathereth not with me scattereth abroad. Wherefore I say unto you, All manner of sin and blasphemy shall be forgiven unto men: but the blasphemy against the Holy

Ghost shall not be forgiven unto men. And whosoever speaketh a word against the Son of man, it shall be forgiven him: but whosoever speaketh against the Holy Ghost, it shall not be forgiven him, neither in this world, neither in the world to come.

The Unpardonable Sin ॐ VACHEL LINDSAY

This is the sin against the Holy Ghost:—
To speak of bloody power as right divine,
And call on God to guard each vile chief's house, ·
And for such chiefs, turn men to wolves and swine:—

To go forth killing in White Mercy's name,
Making the trenches stink with spattered brains,
Tearing the nerves and arteries apart,
Sowing with flesh the unreaped golden plains,—

In any Church's name to sack fair towns,
And turn each home into a screaming sty,
To make the little children fugitive,
And have their mothers for a quick death cry,—

This is the sin against the Holy Ghost:
This is the sin no purging can atone:—
To send forth rapine in the name of Christ:—
To set the face and make the heart a stone.

MATTHEW 13:10–13:13   And the disciples came, and said unto him, Why speakest thou unto them in parables? He answered and said unto them, Because it is given unto you to know the mysteries of the kingdom of heaven, but to them it is not given. For whosoever hath, to him shall be given, and he shall have more abundance: but whosoever hath not, from him shall be taken away even that he hath. Therefore speak I to them in parables: because they seeing see not; and hearing they hear not, neither do they understand.

On the Holy Scriptures   ♺   FRANCIS QUARLES

Why did our blessed Savior please to break
His sacred thoughts in parables; and speak
In dark enigmas? Whosoe'er thou be
That findst them so, they were not spoke to thee:
In what a case is he, that haps to run
Against a post, and cries, *How dark's the sun?*
Or he, in summer, that complains of frost?
The Gospel's hid to none, but who are lost:
The Scripture is a ford, wherein, 'tis said,
An elephant shall swim; a lamb may wade.

MATTHEW 13:45–13:46   Again, the kingdom of heaven is like unto a merchant man, seeking goodly pearls: Who, when he had found one pearl of great price, went and sold all that he had, and bought it.

The Pearl   ♺   GEORGE HERBERT

I know the ways of learning; both the head
And pipes that feed the press, and make it run;
What reason hath from nature borrowed,
Or of it self, a good housewife, spun
In laws and policy; what the stars conspire,
What willing nature speaks, what forced by fire;
Both th' old discoveries, and the new-found seas,
The stock and surplus, cause and history:
All these stand open, or I have the keys:
         Yet I love thee.

I know the ways of honor, what maintains
The quick returns of courtesy and wit:
In vies of favors whether party gains,
When glory swells the heart, and moldeth it
To all expressions both of hand and eye,
Which on the world a true-love-knot may tie,
And bear the bundle, wheresoe'er it goes:
How many drams of spirit there must be
To sell my life unto my friends or foes:
         Yet I love thee.

I know the ways of pleasure, the sweet strains,
The lullings and the relishes of it;
The propositions of hot blood and brains;
What mirth and music mean; what love and wit
Have done these twenty hundred years, and more;
I know the projects of unbridled store:
My stuff is flesh, not brass; my senses live,
And grumble oft, that they have more in me
Than he that curbs them being but one to five:
                        Yet I love thee.

I know all these, and have them in my hand:
Therefore not sealed, but with open eyes
I fly to thee, and fully understand
Both the main gale, and the commodities;
And at what rate and price I have thy love;
With all the circumstances that may move:
Yet through the labyrinths, not my groveling wit,
But thy silk twist let down from heaven to me,
Did both conduct and teach me, how by it
                        To climb to thee.

MATTHEW 14:1–14:7   At that time Herod the tetrarch heard of the fame of Jesus, And said unto his servants, This is John the Baptist; he is risen from the dead; and therefore mighty works do show forth themselves in him. For Herod had laid hold on John, and bound him, and put him in prison for Herodias' sake, his brother Philip's wife. For John said unto him, It is not lawful for thee to have her. And when he would have put him to death, he feared the multitude, because they counted him as a prophet. But when Herod's birthday was kept, the daughter of Herodias danced before them, and pleased Herod. Whereupon he promised with an oath to give her whatsoever she would ask.

The Daughter of Herodias ᧒ HENRY VAUGHAN

Vain, sinful Art! who first did fit
Thy lewd loathed motions unto sounds,
And made grave music like wild wit
Err in loose airs beyond her bounds?

What fires hath he heaped on his head?
Since to his sins (as needs it must,)
His art adds still (though he be dead,)
New fresh accounts of blood and lust.

Leave then[22] young Sorceress; the ice
Will those coy spirits cast asleep,
Which teach thee now to please[23] his eyes
Who doth thy loathsome mother keep.

But thou hast pleased so well, he swears,
And gratifies thy sin with vows:
His shameless lust in public wears,
And to thy soft arts strongly bows.

Skillful Enchantress and true bred!
Who out of evil can bring forth good?
Thy mother's nets in thee were spread,
She tempts to incest, thou to blood.

Portrait (II) ✎ E. E. CUMMINGS

Babylon slim
-ness of
evenslicing
eyes are chisels

scarlet Goes
with her
whitehot
face,gashed

by hair's blue cold

jolts of
lovecrazed abrupt

---

22 Her name was Salome; in passing over a frozen river, the ice broke under her, and chopped off
   her head. [Vaughan's note]
23 Herod Antipas. [Vaughan's note]

flesh split "Pretty
Baby"
to
numb rhythm before christ

MATTHEW 14:8–14:11   And she, being before instructed of her mother,
said, Give me here John Baptist's head in a charger. And the king was sorry:
nevertheless for the oath's sake, and them which sat with him at meat, he
commanded it to be given her. And he sent, and beheaded John in the
prison. And his head was brought in a charger, and given to the damsel:
and she brought it to her mother.

On S. John the Baptist ﹖ THOMAS STANLEY

As the youthful morning's light,
Chasing the dark shades of night,
By its blushes doth betray,
The approaching of the day:
So this Star that doth forerun
The day of our salvation;
Dyed in's purple blood, doth rise,
And the sun appearing, dies.

MATTHEW 14:15–14:21   And when it was evening, his disciples came to him,
saying, This is a desert place, and the time is now past; send the multitude
away, that they may go into the villages, and buy themselves victuals. But
Jesus said unto them, They need not depart; give ye them to eat. And they
say unto him, We have here but five loaves, and two fishes. He said, Bring
them hither to me. And he commanded the multitude to sit down on the
grass, and took the five loaves, and the two fishes, and looking up to heav-
en, he blessed, and brake, and gave the loaves to his disciples, and the dis-
ciples to the multitude. And they did all eat, and were filled: and they took
up of the fragments that remained twelve baskets full. And they that had
eaten were about five thousand men, beside women and children.

Business Reverses ↴ EDGAR LEE MASTERS

Everything! Counter and scales—
    I'll take whatever you give.
I'm through and off to Athens, .
    Where a man like me can live.

And Hipparch, the baker, is going;
    My chum, who came with me
To follow the crowds who follow
    The prophet of Galilee.

We two were there at Damascus
    Dealing in figs and wine.
Nice little business! Some one
    Said: "Here, I'll give you a line!

"Buy fish, and set up a booth,
    Get a tent and make your bread.
There are thousands come to listen,
    They are hungry, and must be fed."

And so we went. Believe me,
    There were crowds, and hungry, too.
Five thousand stood in the desert
    And listened the whole day through.

Famished? Well, yes. The disciples
    Were saying to send them away
To buy their bread in the village,
    But the prophet went on to say:

"Feed them yourselves, O you
    Of little faith." But they said:
"We have just two little fishes
    And five little loaves of bread."

We heard it, me and Hipparch,
    And rubbed our hands. You see
We were there to make some money
    In the land of Galilee.

We had stock in plenty. We waited.
    I wiped the scales, and my chum
Restacked the loaves. We bellowed,
    But no one seemed to come.

"Fresh fish!" I bawled my lungs out:
    "Nice bread!" poor Hipparch cried,
But what did they do? Sat down there
    In fifties, side by side,

In ranks, the whole five thousand.
    Then—well, the prophet spoke,
And broke the two little fishes,
    And the five little loaves he broke,

And fed the whole five thousand.
    Why, yes! So gorged they slept.
And we stood beaten and bankrupt.
    Poor Hipparch swore and wept.

They gathered up twelve baskets
    Full from the loaves of bread;
Two fishes made twelve baskets
    Of fragments after they fed.

And we—what was there to do
    But dump our stock on the sand?
That's what we got for our labor
    And thrift, in such a land.

We met a man near Damascus
    Who had joined the mystagogues.
He said: "I was wicked as you men
    Until I lost my hogs."

Now Hipparch and I are going
    To Athens, beautiful, free.
No more adventures for us two
    In the land of Galilee.

MATTHEW 14:22–14:25   And straightway Jesus constrained his disciples to get into a ship, and to go before him unto the other side, while he sent the multitudes away. And when he had sent the multitudes away, he went up into a mountain apart to pray: and when the evening was come, he was there alone. But the ship was now in the midst of the sea, tossed with waves: for the wind was contrary. And in the fourth watch of the night Jesus went unto them, walking on the sea.

In the Twentieth Century ༄ JAMES MCAULEY

Christ, you walked on the sea,
But cannot walk in a poem,
Not in our century.

There's something deeply wrong
Either with us or with you.
Our bright loud world is strong

And better in some ways
Than the old haunting kingdoms:
I don't reject our days.

But in you I taste bread,
Freshness, the honey of being,
And rising from the dead:

Like yolk in a warm shell—
Simplicities of power,
And water from a well.

We live like diagrams
Moving on a screen.
Somewhere a door slams

Shut, and emptiness spreads.
Our loves are processes
Upon foam-rubber beds.

Our speech is chemical waste;
The words have a plastic feel,
An antibiotic taste.

And yet we dream of song
Like parables of joy.
There's something deeply wrong.

Like shades we must drink blood
To find the living voice
That flesh once understood.

MATTHEW 14:26   And when the disciples saw him walking on the sea, they
were troubled, saying, It is a spirit; and they cried out for fear.

Walking on Water   ✍   JAMES DICKEY

Feeling it with me
On it, barely float, the narrow plank on the water,
I stepped from the clam-shell beach,
Breaking in nearly down through the sun
Where it lay on the sea,
And poled off, gliding upright
Onto the shining topsoil of the bay.

Later, it came to be said
That I was seen walking on water,
Not moving my legs
Except for the wrong step of sliding:
A child who leaned on a staff,
A curious pilgrim hiking
Between two open blue worlds,

My motion a miracle,
Leaving behind me no footprint,
But only the shimmering place
Of an infinite step upon water,
In which sat still and were shining
Many marsh-birds and pelicans.
Alongside my feet, the shark

Lay buried and followed,
His eyes on my childish heels.

Thus, taking all morning to stalk
From one littered beach to another
I came out on land, and dismounted
Making marks in the sand with my toes
Which truly had walked there, on water,

With the pelicans beating their shadows
Through the mirror carpet
Down, and the shark pursuing
The boy on the burning deck
Of a bare single ship-wrecked board.
Shoving the plank out to sea, I walked
Inland, on numb sparkling feet,

With the sun on the sea unbroken,
Nor the long quiet step of the miracle
Doing anything behind me but blazing,
With the birds in it nodding their heads
That must ponder that footstep forever
Rocking, or until I return
In my ghost, which shall have become, then,

A boy with a staff,
To loose them, beak and feather, from the spell
Laid down by a balancing child,
Unstable, tight-lipped, and amazed,
And, under their place of enthrallment,
A huge, hammer-headed spirit
Shall pass, as if led by the nose into Heaven.

MARK 6:50   For they all saw him, and were troubled. And immediately he
talked with them, and saith unto them, Be of good cheer: it is I; be not afraid.

Galilee Shore ∽ ALLEN GINSBERG

With the blue-dark dome old-starred at night, green boat-lights
        purring over water,
a faraway necklace of cliff-top Syrian electrics,
bells ashore, music from a juke-box trumpeted,

shadow of death against my left breast prest
—cigarette, match-flare, skull wetting its lips—

Fisherman-nets over wood walls, light wind in dead willow branch
on a grassy bank—the saxophone relaxed and brutal, silver horns
          echo—
Was there a man named Solomon? Peter walked here? Christ on this
          sweet water?
Blessings on thee Peacemaker!
                              English spoken
on the street bearded Jews' sandals & Arab white head cloth—
the silence between Hebrew and Arabic—
the thrill of the first Hashish in a holy land—
Over hill down the valley in a blue bus, past Cana no weddings—
I have no name I wander in a nameless countryside—
young boys all at the movies seeing a great Western—
art gallery closed, pipe razor & tobacco on the floor.

To touch the beard of Martin Buber
to watch a skull faced Gershom Scholem lace his shoes
to pronounce Capernaum's name & see stone doors of a tomb
to be meek, alone, beside a big dark lake at night—
to pass thru Nazareth dusty afternoon, and smell the urine down near
          Mary's well
to watch the orange moon peep over Syria, weird promise—
to wait beside Galilee—night with Orion, lightning, negro voices,
          Burger's Disease, a glass of lemon tea—feel my left hand on my
          shaved chin—
all you have to do is suffer the metaphysical pain of dying.
Art is just a shadow, like cows or tea—
keep the future open, make no dates it's all here
with moonrise and soft music on phonograph memory—
Just think how amazing! someone getting up and walking on
          the water.

MATTHEW 14:28–14:32   And Peter answered him and said, Lord, if it be
thou, bid me come unto thee on the water. And he said, Come. And when
Peter was come down out of the ship, he walked on the water, to go to
Jesus. But when he saw the wind boisterous, he was afraid; and beginning
to sink, he cried, saying, Lord, save me. And immediately Jesus stretched

forth his hand, and caught him, and said unto him, O thou of little faith, wherefore didst thou doubt? And when they were come into the ship, the wind ceased.

E Tenebris ↝ OSCAR WILDE

Come down, O Christ, and help me! reach thy hand,
    For I am drowning in a stormier sea
    Than Simon on thy lake of Galilee:
The wine of life is spilt upon the sand,
My heart is in some famine-murdered land
    Whence all good things have perished utterly,
    And well I know my soul in Hell must lie
If I this night before God's throne should stand.
"He sleeps perchance, or rideth to the chase,
    Like Baal, when his prophets howled that name
    From morn to noon on Carmel's smitten height."
Nay, peace, I shall behold, before the night,
    The feet of brass, the robe more white than flame,
The wounded hands, the weary human face.

The Beloved

JOHN 6:47–6:51   Verily, verily, I say unto you, He that believeth on me hath everlasting life. I am that bread of life. Your fathers did eat manna in the wilderness, and are dead. This is the bread which cometh down from heaven, that a man may eat thereof, and not die. I am the living bread which came down from heaven: if any man eat of this bread, he shall live for ever: and the bread that I will give is my flesh, which I will give for the life of the world.

Meditation Eight ↝ EDWARD TAYLOR

I kenning through astronomy divine
    The world's bright battlement, wherein I spy
A golden path my pencil cannot line
    From that bright throne unto my threshold lie.

And while my puzzled thoughts about it pore,
I find the Bread of Life in't at my door.

When that this Bird of Paradise put in
    This wicker cage (my corpse) to tweedle praise
Had pecked the fruit forbid: and so did fling
    Away its food, and lost its golden days,
    It fell into celestial famine sore,
    And never could attain a morsel more.

Alas! alas! poor bird, what wilt thou do?
    This creatures' field no food for souls e'er gave:
And if thou knock at angels' doors, they show
    An empty barrel: they no soul bread have.
    Alas! poor bird, the world's white loaf is done,
    And cannot yield thee here the smallest crumb.

In this sad state, God's tender bowels run
    Out streams of grace: And he to end all strife,
The purest wheat in Heaven, his dear-dear Son
    Grinds, and kneads up into this Bread of Life:
    Which Bread of Life from Heaven down came and stands
    Dished in thy table up by angels' hands.

Did God mold up this bread in Heaven, and bake,
    Which from his table came, and to thine goeth?
Doth he bespeak thee thus: This soul bread take;
    Come, eat thy fill of this, thy God's white loaf?
    It's food too fine for angels; yet come, take
    And eat thy fill! It's Heaven's sugar cake.

What grace is this knead in this loaf? This thing
    Souls are but petty things it to admire.
Ye Angels, help: This fill would to the brim
    Heaven's whelmed-down crystal meal Bowl, yea and higher.
    This Bread of Life dropped in thy mouth doth cry:
    Eat, eat me, Soul, and thou shalt never die.

The Given Flesh Returns Nothing but Bread ॐ
AILEEN KELLY

The given flesh returns nothing but bread.
Quick breath is clothed in words, fold upon fold,
And after all, what's said is barely said.

Articulate skeleton fleshed in song and wed
To fire and flight; portioned, appraised and sold
The given flesh returns nothing but bread.

Starved night's afoot before the day's abed.
Love milled between two skins strikes hot or cold
And, after all, what's said is barely said.

Ploughed to blank earth the urgent, generous dead
Surge through green shoots to freight the season's gold:
The given flesh returns, nothing but bread.

Pent love and flight and song—stunned heart, hard head
Forbidding—break out lightwards unparoled;
And after all, what's said is barely said.

Word upon breakers cast, unheard, half-read,
Rises a silent harvest ocean-fold:
The given flesh returns nothing but bread.

And after all what's said is barely said.

MATTHEW 16:18–16:23   And I say also unto thee, That thou art Peter, and
upon this rock I will build my church; and the gates of hell shall not prevail
against it. And I will give unto thee the keys of the kingdom of heaven: and
whatsoever thou shalt bind on earth shall be bound in heaven: and whatso-
ever thou shalt loose on earth shall be loosed in heaven. . . . Then Peter
took him, and began to rebuke him, saying, Be it far from thee, Lord: this
shall not be unto thee. But he turned, and said unto Peter, Get thee behind
me, Satan: thou art an offence unto me: for thou savourest not the things
that be of God, but those that be of men.

'Retro Me, Sathana' ᔋ DANTE GABRIEL ROSSETTI

Get thee behind me. Even as heavy-curled,
    Stooping against the wind a charioteer
    Is snatched from out his chariot by the hair,
So shall Time be; and as the void car, hurled
Abroad by reinless steeds, even so the world:
    Yea, even as chariot-dust upon the air,
    It shall be sought and not found anywhere.

Get thee behind me, Satan. Oft unfurled,
Thy perilous wings can beat and break like lath
    Much mightiness of men to win thee praise.
    Leave these weak feet to tread in narrow ways.
Thou still, upon the broad vine-sheltered path,
Mayst wait the turning of the phials of wrath
    For certain years, for certain months and days.[24]

MATTHEW 16:27–16:28   For the Son of man shall come in the glory of his Father with his angels; and then he shall reward every man according to his works. Verily I say unto you, There be some standing here, which shall not taste of death, till they see the Son of man coming in his kingdom.

Do People moulder equally ᔋ EMILY DICKINSON

Do People moulder equally,
They bury, in the Grave?
I do believe a Species
As positively live

As I, who testify it
Deny that I – am dead –
And fill my Lungs, for Witness –
From Tanks – above my Head –

I say to you, said Jesus –
That there be standing here –

24 See REV 16

A Sort, that shall not taste of Death –
If Jesus was sincere –

I need no further Argue –
That statement of the Lord
Is not a controvertible –
He told me, Death was dead –

MATTHEW 18:2–18:3   And Jesus called a little child unto him, and set him
in the midst of them, And said, Verily I say unto you, Except ye be converted,
and become as little children, ye shall not enter into the kingdom of heaven.

Innocence   ⟋   THOMAS TRAHERNE

But that which most I wonder at, which most
I did esteem my bliss, which most I boast
And ever shall enjoy, is that within
    I felt no stain, nor spot of sin.

    No darkness then did overshade,
    But all within was pure and bright,
    No guilt did crush nor fear invade,
    But all my soul was full of light.

    A joyful sense and purity
        Is all I can remember.
    The very night to me was bright,
    'Twas Summer in December.

A serious meditation did employ
My soul within, which, taken up with joy,
Did seem no outward thing to note, but fly
    All objects that do feed the eye.

    While it those very objects did
    Admire, and prize, and praise, and love,
    Which in their glory most are hid,
    Which presence only doth remove.

Their constant daily presence I
    Rejoicing at, did see;
And that which takes them from the eye
Of others, offered them to me.

No inward inclination did I feel
To avarice or pride: my soul did kneel
In admiration all the day. No lust, nor strife,
    Polluted then my infant life.

    No fraud nor anger in me moved,
    No malice, jealousy or spite;
    All that I saw I truly loved.
    Contentment only and delight

    Were in my soul. O Heaven! what bliss
        Did I enjoy and feel!
    What powerful delight did this
    Inspire! for this I daily kneel.

Whether it be that nature is so pure,
And custom only vicious, or that sure
God did by miracle the guilt remove,
    And make my soul to feel his love,

    So early; Or that 'twas one day
    Where in this happiness I found,
    Whose strength and brightness so do ray,
    That still it seems me to surround:

    What e'er it is, it is a light
        So endless unto me
    That I a world of true delight
    Did then and to this day do see.

That prospect was the Gate of Heaven, that day
The ancient Light of Eden did convey
Into my soul: I was an Adam there,
    A little Adam in a sphere

Of joys! O there my ravished sense
Was entertained in paradise,
And had a sight of innocence,
Which was beyond all bound and price.

An antepast of Heaven sure!
    I on the Earth did reign.
Within, without me, all was pure.
I must become a Child again.

MATTHEW 18:9   And if thine eye offend thee, pluck it out, and cast it from thee: it is better for thee to enter into life with one eye, rather than having two eyes to be cast into hell fire.

Poem 45 of *A Shropshire Lad* ✣ A. E. HOUSMAN

If it chance your eye offend you,
    Pluck it out, lad, and be sound:
'Twill hurt, but here are salves to friend you,
    And many a balsam grows on ground.

And if your hand or foot offend you,
    Cut it off, lad, and be whole;
But play the man, stand up and end you,
    When your sickness is your soul.

JOHN 7:1–8:11   . . . Jesus went unto the mount of Olives. And early in the morning he came again into the temple, and all the people came unto him; and he sat down, and taught them. And the scribes and Pharisees brought unto him a woman taken in adultery; and when they had set her in the midst, They say unto him, Master, this woman was taken in adultery, in the very act. Now Moses in the law commanded us, that such should be stoned: but what sayest thou? This they said, tempting him, that they might have to accuse him. But Jesus stooped down, and with his finger wrote on the ground, as though he heard them not. So when they continued asking him, he lifted up himself, and said unto them, He that is without sin among you, let him first cast a stone at her. And again he stooped down, and wrote on the ground. And they which heard it, being convicted by their own con-

science, went out one by one, beginning at the eldest, even unto the last:
and Jesus was left alone, and the woman standing in the midst. When Jesus
had lifted up himself, and saw none but the woman, he said unto her,
Woman, where are those thine accusers? hath no man condemned thee?
She said, No man, Lord. And Jesus said unto her, Neither do I condemn
thee: go, and sin no more.

from *The Everlasting Gospel*   ✀   WILLIAM BLAKE

Was Jesus Chaste? or did he
Give any Lessons of Chastity?
The morning blushed fiery red:
Mary was found in Adulterous bed;
Earth groaned beneath, and Heaven above
Trembled at discovery of Love.
Jesus was sitting in Moses' Chair,
They brought the trembling Woman There.
Moses commands she be stoned to death,
What was the sound of Jesus' breath?
He laid His hand on Moses' Law:
The Ancient Heavens, in Silent Awe
Writ with Curses from Pole to Pole,
All away began to roll:
The Earth trembling and Naked lay
In secret bed of Mortal Clay,
On Sinai felt the hand divine
Putting back the bloody shrine,
And she heard the breath of God
As she heard by Eden's flood:
"Good and Evil are no more!
"Sinai's trumpets, cease to roar!
"Cease, finger of God, to write!
"The Heavens are not clean in thy Sight.
"Thou art Good, and thou Alone;
"Nor may the sinner cast one stone.
"To be Good only, is to be
"A God or else a Pharisee.
"Thou Angel of the Presence Divine
"That didst create this Body of Mine,

"Wherefore has thou writ these Laws
"And Created Hell's dark jaws?
"My Presence I will take from thee:
"A Cold Leper thou shalt be.
"Though thou wast so pure and bright
"That Heaven was Impure in thy Sight,
"Though thy Oath turned Heaven Pale,
"Though thy Covenant built Hell's Jail,
"Though thou didst all to Chaos roll
"With the Serpent for its soul,
"Still the breath Divine does move
"And the breath Divine is Love.
"Mary, Fear Not! Let me see
"The Seven Devils that torment thee:
"Hide not from my Sight thy Sin,
"That forgiveness thou maist win.
"Has no Man Condemned thee?"
"No Man, Lord." "Then what is he
"Who shall Accuse thee? Come Ye forth,
"Fallen fiends of Heavenly birth
"That have forgot your ancient love
"And driven away my trembling Dove.
"You shall bow before her feet;
"You shall lick the dust for Meat;
"And though you cannot Love, but Hate,
"Shall be beggars at Love's Gate.
"What was thy love? Let me see it;
"Was it love or Dark Deceit?"
"Love too long from Me has fled;
" 'twas dark deceit, to Earn my bread;
" 'twas Covet, or 'twas Custom, or
"Some trifle not worth caring for;
"That they may call a shame and Sin
"Love's temple that God dwelleth in,
"And hide in secret hidden Shrine
"The Naked Human form divine,
"And render that a Lawless thing
"On which the Soul Expands its wing.
"But this, O Lord, this was my Sin
"When first I let these Devils in

"In dark pretence to Chastity:
"Blaspheming Love, blaspheming thee.
"Thence Rose Secret Adulteries,
"And thence did Covet also rise.
"My sin thou hast forgiven me,
"Canst thou forgive my Blasphemy?
"Canst thou return to this dark Hell,
"And in my burning bosom dwell?
"And canst thou die that I may live?
"And canst thou Pity and forgive?"
Then Rolled the shadowy Man away
From the Limbs of Jesus, to make them his prey,
An Ever devouring appetite
Glittering with festering Venoms bright,
Crying, "Crucify this cause of distress,
"Who don't keep the secrets of Holiness!
"All Mental Powers by Diseases we bind,
"But he heals the deaf and the Dumb and the Blind.
"Whom God has afflicted for Secret Ends,
"He comforts and Heals and calls them Friends."
But, when Jesus was Crucified,
Then was perfected his glittering pride:
In three Nights he devoured his prey,
And still he devours the Body of Clay;
For dust and Clay is the Serpent's meat,
Which never was made for Man to Eat.

LUKE 10:30–10:34   And Jesus answering said, A certain man went down from Jerusalem to Jericho, and fell among thieves, which stripped him of his raiment, and wounded him, and departed, leaving him half dead. And by chance there came down a certain priest that way: and when he saw him, he passed by on the other side. And likewise a Levite, when he was at the place, came and looked on him, and passed by on the other side. But a certain Samaritan, as he journeyed, came where he was: and when he saw him, he had compassion on him, And went to him, and bound up his wounds, pouring in oil and wine, and set him on his own beast, and brought him to an inn, and took care of him.

a man who had fallen among thieves ॐ
E. E. CUMMINGS

a man who had fallen among thieves
lay by the roadside on his back
dressed in fifteenthrate ideas
wearing a round jeer for a hat

fate per a somewhat more than less
emancipated evening
had in return for consciousness
endowed him with a changeless grin

whereon a dozen staunch and leal
citizens did graze at pause
then fired by hypercivic zeal
sought newer pastures or because

swaddled with a frozen brook
of pinkest vomit out of eyes
which noticed nobody he looked
as if he did not care to rise

one hand did nothing on the vest
its wideflung friend clenched weakly dirt
while the mute trouserfly confessed
a button solemnly inert.

Brushing from whom the stiffened puke
i put him all into my arms
and staggered banged with terror through
a million billion trillion stars

LUKE 11:27   And it came to pass, as he spake these things, a certain
woman of the company lifted up her voice, and said unto him, Blessed is
the womb that bare thee, and the paps which thou hast sucked.

Blessed Be the Paps ✤ RICHARD CRASHAW

Suppose he had been tabled at thy teats,
    Thy hunger feels not what he eats:
He'll have his teat ere long (a bloody one)
    The Mother then must suck the Son.

LUKE 12:37   Blessed are those servants, whom the lord when he cometh
shall find watching: verily I say unto you, that he shall gird himself, and
make them to sit down to meat, and will come forth and serve them.

Love (III) ✤ GEORGE HERBERT

Love bade me welcome: yet my soul drew back,
    Guilty of dust and sin.
But quick-eyed Love, observing me grow slack
    From my first entrance in,
Drew nearer to me, sweetly questioning,
    If I lacked any thing.

A guest, I answered, worthy to be here:
    Love said, You shall be he.
I the unkind, ungrateful? Ah my dear,
    I cannot look on thee.
Love took my hand, and smiling did reply,
    Who made the eyes but I?

Truth Lord, but I have marred them: let my shame
    Go where it doth deserve.
And know you not, says Love, who bore the blame?
    My dear, then I will serve.
You must sit down, says Love, and taste my meat:
    So I did sit and eat.

LUKE 14:12–14:14   Then said he also to him that bade him, When thou
makest a dinner or a supper, call not thy friends, nor thy brethren, neither
thy kinsmen, nor thy rich neighbours; lest they also bid thee again, and a
recompence be made thee. But when thou makest a feast, call the poor,

the maimed, the lame, the blind: And thou shalt be blessed; for they cannot recompense thee: for thou shalt be recompensed at the resurrection of the just.

His Metrical Prayer

JAMES GRAHAM, MARQUIS OF MONTROSE

(On the eve of his own execution)

Let them bestow on ev'ry airth a limb;
Open all my veins, that I may swim
To Thee my Savior, in that crimson lake;
Then place my par-boiled head upon a stake;
Scatter my ashes, throw them in the air:
Lord (since Thou knowst where all these atoms are)
I'm hopeful, once Thou'lt recollect my dust,
And confident Thou'lt raise me with the just.

LUKE 14:34–15:15 . . . And he said, A certain man had two sons: And the younger of them said to his father, Father, give me the portion of goods that falleth to me. And he divided unto them his living. And not many days after the younger son gathered all together, and took his journey into a far country, and there wasted his substance with riotous living. And when he had spent all, there arose a mighty famine in that land; and he began to be in want. And he went and joined himself to a citizen of that country; and he sent him into his fields to feed swine.

The Prodigal Son

ROBERT BLY

The Prodigal Son is kneeling in the husks.
He remembers the man about to die
who cried, "Don't let me die, Doctor!"
The swine go on feeding in the sunlight.

When he folds his hands, his knees on corncobs,
he sees the smoke of ships
floating off the isles of Tyre and Sidon,
and father beyond father beyond father.

An old man once, being dragged across the floor
by his shouting son, cried:
"Don't drag me any farther than that crack on the floor—
I only dragged my father that far!"

My father is seventy five years old.
How difficult it is,
bending the head, looking into the water.
Under the water there's a door the pigs have gone through.

LUKE 16:19–16:26   There was a certain rich man, which was clothed in
purple and fine linen, and fared sumptuously every day: And there was a
certain beggar named Lazarus, which was laid at his gate, full of sores, And
desiring to be fed with the crumbs which fell from the rich man's table:
moreover the dogs came and licked his sores. And it came to pass, that the
beggar died, and was carried by the angels into Abraham's bosom: the rich
man also died, and was buried; And in hell he lift up his eyes, being in tor-
ments, and seeth Abraham afar off, and Lazarus in his bosom. And he cried
and said, Father Abraham, have mercy on me, and send Lazarus, that he
may dip the tip of his finger in water, and cool my tongue; for I am torment-
ed in this flame. But Abraham said, Son, remember that thou in thy lifetime
receivedst thy good things, and likewise Lazarus evil things: but now he is
comforted, and thou art tormented. And beside all this, between us and you
there is a great gulf fixed: so that they which would pass from hence to you
cannot; neither can they pass to us, that would come from thence.

To Dives   ↝   HILAIRE BELLOC

Dives, when you and I go down to Hell
Where scribblers end and millionaires as well,
We shall be carrying on our separate backs
Two very large but very different packs;
And as you stagger under yours, my friend,
Down the dull shore where all our journeys end
And go before me (as your rank demands)
Toward the infinite flat underlands,
And that dear river of forgetfulness—
Charon, a man of exquisite address

(For as your wife's progenitors could tell,
They're very strict on etiquette in Hell),
Will, since you are a lord, observe, "My lord,
We cannot take these weighty things aboard!"
Then down they go, my wretched Dives, down—
The fifteen sorts of boots you kept for town,
The hat to meet the Devil in; the plain
But costly ties; the cases of champagne;
The solid watch, and seal, and chain, and charm;
The working model of a Burning Farm
(To give the little Belials); all the three
Biscuits for Cerberus; the guarantee
From Lambeth that the rich can never burn,
And even promising a safe return;
The admirable overcoat, designed
To cross Cocytus—very warmly lined;
Sweet Dives, you will leave them all behind
And enter Hell as tattered and as bare
As was your father when he took the air
Behind a barrow-load in Leicester Square.
Then turned to me, and noting one that brings
With careless step a mist of shadowy things;
Laughter and memories, and a few regrets,
Some honor, and a quantity of debts,
A doubt or two of sorts, a trust in God,
And (what will seem to you extremely odd)
His father's granfer's father's father's name,
Unspoilt, untitled, even spelt the same;
Charon, who twenty thousand times before
Has ferried Poets to the ulterior shore,
Will estimate the weight I bear and cry—
"Comrade!" (He has himself been known to try
His hand at Latin and Italian verse
Much in the style of Vergil—only worse)
"We let such vain imaginaries pass!"
Then tell me, Dives, which will look the ass—
You, or myself? Or Charon? Who can tell?
They order things so damnably in Hell.

JOHN 11:30–11:44   Now Jesus was not yet come into the town, but was in that place where Martha met him. The Jews then which were with her in the house, and comforted her, when they saw Mary, that she rose up hastily and went out, followed her, saying, She goeth unto the grave to weep there.
Then when Mary was come where Jesus was, and saw him, she fell down at his feet, saying unto him, Lord, if thou hadst been here, my brother had not died. When Jesus therefore saw her weeping, and the Jews also weeping which came with her, he groaned in the spirit, and was troubled. And said, Where have ye laid him? They said unto him, Lord, come and see.
Jesus wept. . . .
And when he thus had spoken, he cried with a loud voice, Lazarus, come forth. And he that was dead came forth, bound hand and foot with grave-clothes: and his face was bound about with a napkin. Jesus saith unto them, Loose him, and let him go.

On Lazarus Raised from Death ⤳ HENRY COLMAN

Where am I, or how came I here, hath death
      Bereaved me of my breath,
         Or do I dream?
   Nor can that be, for sure I am
These are no ensigns of a living man,
        Beside, the stream
        Of life did fly
From hence, and my blessed soul did soar on high;
       And well remember I,
     My friends on either hand
        Did weeping stand
        To see me die;
Most certain then it is my soul was fled
Forth of my clay, and I am buried.

These linens plainly show this cave did keep
      My flesh in its dead sleep,
        And yet a noise
   Me-thought I heard, of such strange force
As would have raised to life the dullest corse,
        So sweet a voice
        As spite of death
Distilled through every vein a living breath,

And sure I heard it charge
Me by my name, even thus
O Lazarus
Come forth at large,
And so nought hinders, I will straightway then
Appear, (though thus dressed) ere it call again.

Was't my Redeemer called, no marvel then
Though dead, I live again,
His word alone
Can raise a soul, though dead in sin,
Ready the grave of hell to tumble in
High as the Throne;
In all things he
Is the true powerful Eternity:
Since thou hast pleased to raise
My body then, let my spirit
Heaven inherit
And thee praise.
And let thy miracle upon my clay
Prepare, and fit me 'gainst the reckoning day.

An Epistle Containing the Strange Medical Experience of Karshish, the Arab Physician ☞

ROBERT BROWNING

Karshish, the picker-up of learning's crumbs,
The not-incurious in God's handiwork
(This man's-flesh he hath admirable made,
Blown like a bubble, kneaded like a paste,
To coop up and keep down on earth a space
That puff of vapour from his mouth, man's soul)
– To Abib, all-sagacious in our art,
Breeder in me of what poor skill I boast,
Like me inquisitive how pricks and cracks
Befall the flesh through too much stress and strain,
Whereby the wily vapour fain would slip
Back and rejoin its source before the term,
And aptest in contrivance (under God)
To baffle it by deftly stopping such: –

The vagrant Scholar to his Sage at home
Sends greeting (health and knowledge, fame with peace)
Three samples of true snakestone – rarer still,
One of the other sort, the melon-shaped,
(But fitter, pounded fine, for charms than drugs)
And writeth now the twenty-second time.

    My journeyings were brought to Jericho:
Thus I resume. Who studious in our art
Shall count a little labour unrepaid?
I have shed sweat enough, left flesh and bone
On many a flinty furlong of this land.
Also, the country-side is all on fire
With rumours of a marching hitherward:
Some say Vespasian cometh, some, his son.
A black lynx snarled and pricked a tufted ear;
Lust of my blood inflamed his yellow balls:
I cried and threw my staff and he was gone.
Twice have the robbers stripped and beaten me,
And once a town declared me for a spy;
But at the end, I reach Jerusalem,
Since this poor covert where I pass the night,
This Bethany, lies scarce the distance thence
A man with plague-sores at the third degree
Runs till he drops down dead. Thou laughest here!
'Sooth, it elates me, thus reposed and safe,
To void the stuffing of my travel-scrip
And share with thee whatever Jewry yields.
A viscid choler is observable
In tertians, I was nearly bold to say;
And falling-sickness hath a happier cure
Than our school wots of: there's a spider here
Weaves no web, watches on the ledge of tombs,
Sprinkled with mottles on an ash-grey back;
Take five and drop them. . . but who knows his mind,
The Syrian runagate I trust this to?
His service payeth me a sublimate
Blown up his nose to help the ailing eye.
Best wait: I reach Jerusalem at morn,
There set in order my experiences,
Gather what most deserves, and give thee all –

Or I might add, Judea's gum-tragacanth
Scales off in purer flakes, shines clearer-grained,
Cracks 'twixt the pestle and the porphyry,
In fine exceeds our produce. Scalp-disease
Confounds me, crossing so with leprosy –
Thou hadst admired one sort I gained at Zoar –
But zeal outruns discretion. Here I end.

   Yet stay: my Syrian blinketh gratefully,
Protesteth his devotion is my price –
Suppose I write what harms not, though he steal?
I half resolve to tell thee, yet I blush,
What set me off a-writing first of all.
An itch I had, a sting to write, a tang!
For, be it this town's barrenness – or else
The Man had something in the look of him –
His case has struck me far more than 'tis worth.
So, pardon if – (lest presently I lose
In the great press of novelty at hand
The care and pain this somehow stole from me)
I bid thee take the thing while fresh in mind,
Almost in sight – for, wilt thou have the truth?
The very man is gone from me but now,
Whose ailment is the subject of discourse.
Thus then, and let thy better wit help all!

   'Tis but a case of mania – subinduced
By epilepsy, at the turning-point
Of trance prolonged unduly some three days:
When, by the exhibition of some drug
Or spell, exorcization, stroke of art
Unknown to me and which 'twere well to know,
The evil thing out-breaking all at once
Left the man whole and sound of body indeed, –
But, flinging (so to speak) life's gates too wide,
Making a clear house of it too suddenly,
The first conceit that entered might inscribe
Whatever it was minded on the wall
So plainly at that vantage, as it were,
(First come, first served) that nothing subsequent
Attaineth to erase those fancy-scrawls

The just-returned and new-established soul
Hath gotten now so thoroughly by heart
That henceforth she will read or these or none.
And first – the man's own firm conviction rests
That he was dead (in fact they buried him)
– That he was dead and then restored to life
By a Nazarene physician of his tribe:
– 'Sayeth, the same bade 'Rise,' and he did rise.
'Such cases are diurnal,' thou wilt cry.
Not so this figment! – not, that such a fume,
Instead of giving way to time and health,
Should eat itself into the life of life,
As saffron tingeth flesh, blood, bones and all!
For see, how he takes up the after-life.
The man – it is one Lazarus, a Jew,
Sanguine, proportioned, fifty years of age,
The body's habit wholly laudable,
As much, indeed, beyond the common health
As he were made and put aside to show.
Think, could we penetrate by any drug
And bathe the wearied soul and worried flesh,
And bring it clear and fair, by three days' sleep!
When has the man the balm that brightens all?
This grown man eyes the world now like a child.
Some elders of his tribe, I should premise,
Led in their friend, obedient as a sheep,
To bear my inquisition. While they spoke,
Now sharply, now with sorrow, – told the case, –
He listened not except I spoke to him,
But folded his two hands and let them talk,
Watching the flies that buzzed: and yet no fool.
And that's a sample how his years must go.
Look, if a beggar, in fixed middle-life,
Should find a treasure, – can he use the same
With straitened habits and with tastes starved small,
And take at once to his impoverished brain
The sudden element that changes things,
That sets the undreamed-of rapture at his hand
And puts the cheap old joy in the scorned dust?
Is he not such an one as moves to mirth –
Warily parsimonious, when no need,

Wasteful as drunkenness at undue times?
All prudent counsel as to what befits
The golden mean, is lost on such an one:
The man's fantastic will is the man's law.
So here – we call the treasure knowledge, say,
Increased beyond the fleshly faculty –
Heaven opened to a soul while yet on earth,
Earth forced on a soul's use while seeing heaven:
The man is witless of the size, the sum,
The value in proportion of all things,
Or whether it be little or be much.
Discourse to him of prodigious armaments
Assembled to besiege his city now,
And of the passing of a mule with gourds –
'Tis one! Then take it on the other side,
Speak of some trifling fact, – he will gaze rapt
With stupor at its very littleness,
(Far as I see) as if in that indeed
He caught prodigious import, whole results;
And so will turn to us the bystanders
In ever the same stupor (note this point)
That we too see not with his opened eyes.
Wonder and doubt come wrongly into play,
Preposterously, at cross-purposes.
Should his child sicken unto death, – why, look
For scarce abatement of his cheerfulness,
Or pretermission of the daily craft!
While a word, gesture, glance from that same child
At play or in the school or laid asleep,
Will startle him to an agony of fear,
Exasperation, just as like. Demand
The reason why – ''tis but a word,' object –
'A gesture' – he regards thee as our lord
Who lived there in the pyramid alone,
Looked at us (dost thou mind?) when, being young,
We both would unadvisedly recite
Some charm's beginning, from that book of his,
Able to bid the sun throb wide and burst
All into stars, as stars grown old are wont.
Thou and the child have each a veil alike
Thrown o'er your heads, from under which ye both

340

Stretch your blind hands and trifle with a match
Over a mine of Greek fire, did ye know!
He holds on firmly to some thread of life –
(It is the life to lead perforcedly)
Which runs across some vast distracting orb
Of glory on either side that meagre thread,
Which, conscious of, he must not enter yet –
The spiritual life around the earthly life:
The law of that is known to him as this,
His heart and brain move there, his feet stay here.
So is the man perplexed with impulses
Sudden to start off crosswise, not straight on,
Proclaiming what is right and wrong across,
And not along, this black thread through the blaze –
'It should be' balked by 'here it cannot be.'
And oft the man's soul springs into his face
As if he saw again and heard again
His sage that bade him 'Rise' and he did rise.
Something, a word, a tick o' the blood within
Admonishes: then back he sinks at once
To ashes, who was very fire before,
In sedulous recurrence to his trade
Whereby he earneth him the daily bread;
And studiously the humbler for that pride,
Professedly the faultier he knows
God's secret, while he holds the thread of life.
Indeed the especial marking of the man
Is prone submission to the heavenly will –
Seeing it, what it is, and why it is.
'Sayeth, he will wait patient to the last
For that same death which must restore his being
To equilibrium, body loosening soul
Divorced even now by premature full growth:
He will live, nay, it pleaseth him to live
So long as God please, and just how God please.
He even seeketh not to please God more
(Which meaneth, otherwise) than as God please.
Hence, I perceive not he affects to preach
The doctrine of his sect whate'er it be,
Make proselytes as madmen thirst to do:
How can he give his neighbour the real ground,

His own conviction? Ardent as he is –
Call his great truth a lie, why, still the old
'Be it as God please' reassureth him.
I probed the sore as thy disciple should:
'How, beast,' said I, 'this stolid carelessness
Sufficeth thee, when Rome is on her march
To stamp out like a little spark thy town,
Thy tribe, thy crazy tale and thee at once?'
He merely looked with his large eyes on me.
The man is apathetic, you deduce?
Contrariwise, he loves both old and young,
Able and weak, affects the very brutes
And birds – how say I? flowers of the field –
As a wise workman recognizes tools
In a master's workshop, loving what they make.
Thus is the man, as harmless as a lamb:
Only impatient, let him do his best,
At ignorance and carelessness and sin –
An indignation which is promptly curbed:
As when in certain travels I have feigned
To be an ignoramus in our art
According to some preconceived design,
And happed to hear the land's practitioners
Steeped in conceit sublimed by ignorance,
Prattle fantastically on disease,
Its cause and cure – and I must hold my peace!

Thou wilt object – Why have I not ere this
Sought out the sage himself, the Nazarene
Who wrought this cure, inquiring at the source,
Conferring with the frankness that befits?
Alas! it grieveth me, the learned leech
Perished in a tumult many years ago,
Accused, – our learning's fate, – of wizardry,
Rebellion, to the setting up a rule
And creed prodigious as described to me.
His death, which happened when the earthquake fell
(Prefiguring, as soon appeared, the loss
To occult learning in our lord the sage
Who lived there in the pyramid alone)
Was wrought by the mad people – that's their wont!

On vain recourse, as I conjecture it,
To his tried virtue, for miraculous help –
How could he stop the earthquake? That's their way!
The other imputations must be lies:
But take one, though I loathe to give it thee,
In mere respect for any good man's fame.
(And after all, our patient Lazarus
Is stark mad; should we count on what he says?
Perhaps not: though in writing to a leech
'Tis well to keep back nothing of a case.)
This man so cured regards the curer, then,
As – God forgive me! who but God himself,
Creator and sustainer of the world,
That came and dwelt in flesh on it awhile!
– 'Sayeth that such an one was born and lived,
Taught, healed the sick, broke bread at his own house,
Then died, with Lazarus, for aught I know,
And yet was . . . what I said nor choose repeat,
And must have so avouched himself, in fact,
In hearing of this very Lazarus
Who saith – but why all this of what he saith?
Why write of trivial matters, things of price
Calling at every moment for remark?
I noticed on the margin of a pool
Blue-flowering borage, the Aleppo sort,
Aboundeth, very nitrous. It is strange!

Thy pardon for this long and tedious case,
Which, now that I review it, needs must seem
Unduly dwelt on, prolixly set forth!
Nor I myself discern in what is writ
Good cause for the peculiar interest
And awe indeed this man has touched me with.
Perhaps the journey's end, the weariness
Had wrought upon me first. I met him thus:
I crossed a ridge of short sharp broken hills
Like an old lion's cheek teeth. Out there came
A moon made like a face with certain spots
Multiform, manifold and menacing:
Then a wind rose behind me. So we met
In this old sleepy town at unaware,

The man and I. I send thee what is writ.
Regard it as a chance, a matter risked
To this ambiguous Syrian – he may lose,
Or steal, or give it thee with equal good.
Jerusalem's repose shall make amends
For time this letter wastes, thy time and mine;
Till when, once more thy pardon and farewell!

    The very God! think, Abib; dost thou think?
So, the All-Great, were the All-Loving too –
So, through the thunder comes a human voice
Saying, 'O heart I made, a heart beats here!
Face, my hands fashioned, see it in myself!
Thou hast no power nor mayst conceive of mine,
But love I gave thee, with myself to love,
And thou must love me who have died for thee!'
The madman saith He said so: it is strange.

LUKE 18:9–14   . . . And he spake this parable unto certain which trusted in themselves that they were righteous, and despised others: Two men went up into the temple to pray; the one a Pharisee, and the other a publican. The Pharisee stood and prayed thus with himself, God, I thank thee, that I am not as other men are, extortioners, unjust, adulterers, or even as this publican. I fast twice in the week, I give tithes of all that I possess. And the publican, standing afar off, would not lift up so much as his eyes unto heaven, but smote upon his breast, saying, God be merciful to me a sinner. I tell you, this man went down to his house justified rather than the other: for every one that exalteth himself shall be abased; and he that humbleth himself shall be exalted.

Two Went Up into the Temple to Pray   ◞
RICHARD CRASHAW

Two went to pray? o rather say
One went to brag, th'other to pray:

One stands up close and treads on high,
Where th'other dares not send his eye.

One nearer to God's altar trod,
The other to the altar's God.

LUKE 13:23–13:24   Then said one unto him, Lord, are there few that be
saved? And he said unto them, Strive to enter in at the strait gate: for many,
I say unto you, will seek to enter in, and shall not be able.

To Heaven ᘒ ROBERT HERRICK

   Open thy gates
To him, who weeping waits
   And might come in,
But that held back by sin.
   Let mercy be
So kind, to set me free,
   And I will strait
Come in, or force the gate.

MARK 10:46   And they came to Jericho: and as he went out of Jericho with
his disciples and a great number of people, blind Bartimæus, the son of
Timæus, sat by the highway side begging.

Blind Bartimæus ᘒ HENRY WADSWORTH LONGFELLOW

Blind Bartimæus at the gates
Of Jericho in darkness waits;
He hears the crowd—he hears a breath
Say, "It is Christ of Nazareth!"
And calls, in tones of agony,
"Jesus, have mercy now on me!"

The thronging multitudes increase;
Blind Bartimæus, hold thy peace!
But still, above the noisy crowd,
The beggar's cry is shrill and loud;
Until they say, "He calleth thee!"
"Fear not, arise, He calleth thee!"

Then saith the Christ, as silent stands
The crowd, "What wilt thou at my hands?"
And he replies, "O give me light!
Rabbi, restore the blind man's sight!"
And Jesus answers, "Go in peace,
Thy faith from blindness gives release!"

Ye that have eyes, yet cannot see,
In darkness and in misery,
Recall those mighty Voices Three,
"Jesus, have mercy now on me!
Fear not, arise, and go in peace!
Thy faith from blindness gives release!"

The Crucified

LUKE 19:32–19:35   And they that were sent went their way, and found even as he had said unto them. And as they were loosing the colt, the owners thereof said unto them, Why loose ye the colt? And they said, The Lord hath need of him. And they brought him to Jesus: and they cast their garments upon the colt, and they set Jesus thereon.

A Gloze upon this Text, *Dominus iis opus habet* ᧤
GEORGE GASCOIGNE

My reckless race is run, green youth and pride be past,
My riper mellowed years begin to follow on as fast.
My glancing looks are gone, which wonted were to pry,
In every gorgeous garish glass, that glistered in mine eye.
My sight is now so dim, it can behold none such,
No mirror but the merry mean, can please my fancy much.
And in that noble glass, I take delight to view,
The fashions of the wonted world, compared by the new.
For mark who list to look, each man is for himself.
And beats his brain to hoard and heap, this trash and worldly pelf.
Our hands are closed up, great gifts go not abroad,
Few men will lend a lock of hay, but for to gain a load.
Give Gave is a good man, what need we lash it out,
The world is wondrous fearful now, for danger bids men doubt.

And ask how chanceth this? or what means all this meed?
Forsooth the common answer is, because *the Lord hath need*.
A noble jest by guess, I find it in my glass,
The same freehold our savior Christ, conveyed to his ass.
A text to try the truth, and for this time full fit,
For where should we our lessons learn, but out of holy writ?
First mark our only God, which ruleth all the roost,
He sets aside all pomp and pride, wherein fond worldlings boast.
His train is not so great, as filthy Satan's band,
A smaller herd may serve to feed, at our great master's hand.
Next mark the heathens' gods, and by them shall we see,
They be not now so good fellows, as they were wont to be.
Jove, Mars, and Mercury, Dame Venus and the rest,
They banquet not as they were wont, they know it were not best.
So kings and princes both, have left their halls at large,
Their privy chambers cost enough, they cut off every charge.
And when an office falls, as chance sometimes may be,
First keep it close a year or twain, then geld it by the fee.
And give it out at last, but yet with this proviso,
(A bridle for a brainsick jade) *durante bene placito.*[25]
Some think these ladders low, to climb aloft with speed:
Well let them creep at leisure then, for sure *the Lord hath need*.
Dukes, earls, and barons bold, have learned like lesson now,
They break up house and come to court, they live not by the plow.
Percase their rooms be scant, not like their stately bower,
A field bed in a corner couched, a pallet on the floor.
But what for that? no force, they make thereof no boast,
They feed them selves with delicates, and at the prince's cost.
And as for all their men, their pages and their swains,
They choke them up with chines of beef, to multiply their gains.
Themselves lie near to look, when any leaf doth fall,
Such crumbs were wont to feed poor grooms, but now ye Lords
      lick all.
And why? oh sir, because, both dukes and lords have need,
I mock not I, my text is true, believe it as your creed.
Our prelates and our priests, can tell this text with me,
They can hold fast their fattest farms, and let no lease go free.
They have both wife and child, which may not be forgot,
The scriptures say *the Lord hath need*, and therefore blame them not.

---

25 It continues at my pleasure.

Then come a little lower, unto the country knight,
The squire and the gentleman, they leave the country quite,
Their halls were all too large, their tables were too long,
The clouted shoes came in so fast, they kept too great a throng,
And at the porter's lodge, where lubbers wont to feed,
The porter learns to answer now, hence hence *the Lord hath need*.
His guests came in too thick, their diet was too great,
Their horses eat up all the hay, which should have fed his neat:
Their teeth were far too fine, to feed on pork and souse,
Five flocks of sheep could scarce maintain good mutton for
      his house.
And when this count was cast, it was no biding here,
Unto the good town is he gone, to make his friends good cheer.
And welcome there that will, but shall I tell you how:
At his own dish he feedeth them, that is the fashion now,
Side boards be laid aside, the tables end is gone,
His cook shall make you noble cheer, but hostler hath he none.
The chargers now be changed, wherein he wont to eat,
An old fruit dish is big enough to hold a joint of meat.
A salad or a sauce, to taste your cates with all,
Some strange device to feed men's eyes, men's stomachs now
      be small.
And when the tenants come to pay their quarter's rent,
They bring some fowl at Midsummer, a dish of fish in Lent,
At Christmas a capon, at Michelmas a goose:
And somewhat else at Newyear's tide, for fear their lease fly loose.
Good reason by my troth, when gentlemen lack groats,
Let plowmen pinch it out for pence, and patch their russet coats:
For better farmers fast, than manor houses fall,
The Lord hath need, then says the text, bring old Ass colt and all.
Well lowest now at last, let see the country lout,
And mark how he doth swink and sweat, to bring this gear about:
His feastings be but few, cast whipstocks clout his shoon,
The wheaten loaf is locked up as soon as dinner's done:
And where he wont to keep a lubber, two or three,
Now hath he learned to keep no more, but Sim his son and he,
His wife and Maude his maid, a boy to pitch the cart,
And turn him up at Hollontide, to feel the winter smart:
Dame Alyson his wife doth know the price of meal,
Her bride cakes be not half so big as she was wont to steal:
She wears no silver hooks, she is content with worse,

Her pendants and her silver pins she putteth in her purse.
Thus learn I by my glass, that merry mean is best,
And he most wise that finds the mean, to keep himself at rest.
Perchance some open mouth will mutter now and then,
And at the market tell his mate, our landlords a zore man:
He racketh up our rents, and keeps the best in hand,
He makes a wondrous deal of good out of his own mesne land:
Yea let such pelters prate, saint *Needam* be their speed,
We need no text to answer them, but this, *the Lord hath need.*
                    Ever or never

JOHN 12:12–12:13   On the next day much people that were come to the feast, when they heard that Jesus was coming to Jerusalem, Took branches of palm trees, and went forth to meet him, . . .

The Donkey   ᘓ   G. K. CHESTERTON

When fishes flew and forests walked
    And figs grew upon thorn,
Some moment when the moon was blood,
    Then surely I was born;

With monstrous head and sickening cry
    And ears like errant wings,
The devil's walking parody
    On all four-footed things.

The tattered outlaw of the earth,
    Of ancient crooked will;
Starve, scourge, deride me: I am dumb,
    I keep my secret still.

Fools! For I also had my hour;
    One far fierce hour and sweet:
There was a shout about my ears,
    And palms before my feet!

MARK 11:19–11:21   And when even was come, he went out of the city. And in the morning, as they passed by, they saw the fig tree dried up from the roots. And Peter calling to remembrance saith unto him, Master, behold, the fig tree which thou cursedst is withered away.

A Small Fig Tree   ᘒ   DONALD HALL

I am dead, to be sure,
for thwarting Christ's pleasure,
Jesus Christ called Saviour.

I was a small fig tree.
Unjust it seems to me
that I should withered be.

If justice sits with God,
Christ is cruel Herod
and I by magic dead.

If there is no justice
where great Jehovah is,
I will the devil kiss.

MARK 12:29–12:31   And Jesus answered him, The first of all the commandments is, Hear, O Israel; The Lord our God is one Lord: And thou shalt love the Lord thy God with all thy heart, and with all thy soul, and with all thy mind, and with all thy strength: this is the first commandment. And the second is like, namely this, Thou shalt love thy neighbour as thyself. There is none other commandment greater than these.

Love thy Neighbour   ᘒ   D. H. LAWRENCE

I love my neighbour
but
are these things my neighbours?
these two-legged things that walk and talk
and eat and cachinnate, and even seem to smile
seem to smile, ye gods!

Am I told that these things are my neighbours?

All I can say then is Nay! nay! nay! nay! nay!

MATTHEW 23:27–23:33   Woe unto you, scribes and Pharisees, hypocrites!
for ye are like unto whited sepulchres, which indeed appear beautiful outward,
but are within full of dead men's bones, and of all uncleanness. Even so
ye also outwardly appear righteous unto men, but within ye are full of
hypocrisy and iniquity. Woe unto you, scribes and Pharisees, hypocrites!
because ye build the tombs of the prophets, and garnish the sepulchres of
the righteous, And say, If we had been in the days of our fathers, we would
not have been partakers with them in the blood of the prophets. Wherefore
ye be witnesses unto yourselves, that ye are the children of them which
killed the prophets. Fill ye up then the measure of your fathers. Ye serpents,
ye generation of vipers, how can ye escape the damnation of hell?

The Place of the Damned ᴈ JONATHAN SWIFT

All folks who pretend to religion and grace,
Allow there's a Hell, but dispute of the place;
But if Hell may by logical rules be defined,
The place of the Damned,—I will tell you my mind.
    Wherever the Damned do chiefly abound,
Most certainly there is Hell to be found,
Damned Poets, Damned Critics, Damned Block-Heads, Damned
        Knaves,
Damned Senators bribed, Damned prostitute Slaves;
Damned Lawyers and Judges, Damned Lords and Damned Squires,
Damned Spies and Informers, Damned Friends and Damned Liars;
Damned Villains, corrupted in every station,
Damned Time-Serving Priests all over the nation;
And into the bargain, I'll readily give ye,
Damned Ignorant Prelates, and Councillors Privy.
Then let us no longer by parsons be flammed,
For we know by these marks, the place of the Damned;
And Hell to be sure is at Paris or Rome,
How happy for us, that it is not at home.

MARK 13:1–13:33   And as he went out of the temple, one of his disciples saith unto him, Master, see what manner of stones and what buildings are here! And Jesus answering said unto him, Seest thou these great buildings? there shall not be left one stone upon another, that shall not be thrown down. . . . Take ye heed, watch and pray: for ye know not when the time is.

Take Ye Heed, Watch and Pray ↷ JONES VERY

Come suddenly, O Lord, or slowly come,
  I wait Thy will, Thy servant ready is;
Thou hast prepared Thy follower a home,
  The heaven in which Thou dwellest, too, is his.

Come in the morn, at noon, or midnight deep,
  Come, for Thy servant still doth watch and pray
E'en when the world around is sunk in sleep,
  I wake, and long to see Thy glorious day.

I would not fix the time, the day, nor hour,
  When Thou with all Thine angels shalt appear;
When in Thy kingdom Thou shalt come with power,
  E'en now, perhaps, the promised day is near!

For though, in slumber deep, the world may lie,
  And e'en Thy church forget Thy great command;
Still year by year Thy coming draweth nigh,
  And in its power Thy kingdom is at hand.

Not in some future world alone 't will be,
  Beyond the grave, beyond the bounds of Time;
But on the earth Thy glory we shall see,
  And share Thy triumph, peaceful, pure, sublime.

Lord! help me that I faint not, weary grow,
  Nor at Thy coming slumber too, and sleep;
For Thou hast promised, and full well I know,
  Thou wilt to us Thy word of promise keep.

MARK 13:34–13:37   For the Son of Man is as a man taking a far journey, who left his house, and gave authority to his servants, and to every man his work, and commanded the porter to watch. Watch ye therefore: for ye know not when the master of the house cometh, at even, or at midnight, or at the cockcrowing, or in the morning: Lest coming suddenly he find you sleeping. And what I say unto you I say unto all, Watch.

The Lamp ✣ HENRY VAUGHAN

'Tis dead night round about: Horror doth creep
And move on with the shades; stars nod, and sleep,
And through the dark air spin a fiery thread
Such as doth gild the lazy glow-worm's bed.
    Yet, burnst thou here, a full day; while I spend
My rest in cares, and to the dark world lend
These flames, as thou dost thine to me, I watch
That hour, which must thy life, and mine dispatch;
But still thou dost out-go me, I can see
Met in thy flames, all acts of piety;
Thy light, is charity; thy heat, is zeal;
And thy aspiring, active fires reveal
Devotion still on wing; Then, thou dost weep
Still as thou burnst, and the warm droppings creep
To measure out thy length, as if thou'dst know
What stock, and how much time were left thee now;
Nor dost thou spend one tear in vain, for still
As thou dissolvst to them, and they distill,
They're stored up in the socket, where they lie,
When all is spent, thy last, and sure supply,
And such is true repentance, every breath
We spend in sighs, is treasure after death;
Only, one point escapes thee; That thy oil
Is still out with thy flame, and so both fail;
But whensoe'er I'm out, both shall be in,
And where thou mad'st an end, there I'll begin.

MATTHEW 24:37–25:12   But as the days of Noe were, so shall also the coming of the Son of man be. . . . Then shall the kingdom of heaven be likened unto ten virgins, which took their lamps, and went forth to meet the bridegroom. And five of them were wise, and five were foolish. They that were foolish took their lamps, and took no oil with them: But the wise took oil in their vessels with their lamps. While the bridegroom tarried, they all slumbered and slept. And at midnight there was a cry made, Behold, the bridegroom cometh; go ye out to meet him. Then all those virgins arose, and trimmed their lamps. And the foolish said unto the wise, Give us of your oil; for our lamps are gone out. But the wise answered, saying, Not so; lest there be not enough for us and you: but go ye rather to them that sell, and buy for yourselves. And while they went to buy, the bridegroom came; and they that were ready went in with him to the marriage: and the door was shut. Afterward came also the other virgins, saying, Lord, Lord, open to us. But he answered and said, Verily I say unto you, I know you not.

Sonnet IX ✑ JOHN MILTON

Lady that in the prime of earliest youth,
   Wisely hast shunned the broad way and the green,
   And with those few art eminently seen
   That labor up the hill of heavenly truth,
The better part with Mary and with Ruth
   Chosen thou hast; and they that overween,
   And at thy growing virtues fret their spleen,
   No anger find in thee, but pity and ruth.
Thy care is fixed and zealously attends
   To fill thy odorous lamp with deeds of light,
   And hope that reaps not shame. Therefore be sure
Thou, when the Bridegroom with his feastful friends
   Passes to bliss at the mid-hour of night,
   Hast gained thy entrance, virgin wise and pure.

MATTHEW 25:13–25:26   Watch therefore, for ye know neither the day nor the hour wherein the Son of man cometh. For the kingdom of heaven is as a man travelling into a far country, who called his own servants, and delivered unto them his goods. And unto one he gave five talents, to another two, and to another one; to every man according to his several ability; and straightway took his journey. Then he that had received the five talents went and traded with the same, and made them other five talents. And likewise he that had received two, he also gained other two. But he that had received one went and digged in the earth, and hid his lord's money. After a long time the lord of those servants cometh, and reckoneth with them. And so he that had received five talents came and brought other five talents, saying, Lord, thou deliveredst unto me five talents: behold, I have gained beside them five talents more. His lord said unto him, Well done, thou good and faithful servant: thou hast been faithful over a few things, I will make thee ruler over many things: enter thou into the joy of thy lord. He also that had received two talents came and said, Lord, thou deliveredst unto me two talents: behold, I have gained two other talents beside them. His lord said unto him, Well done, good and faithful servant; thou hast been faithful over a few things, I will make thee ruler over many things: enter thou into the joy of thy lord. Then he which had received the one talent came and said, Lord, I knew thee that thou art an hard man, reaping where thou hast not sown, and gathering where thou hast not strawed: And I was afraid, and went and hid thy talent in the earth: lo, there thou hast that is thine. His lord answered and said unto him, Thou wicked and slothful servant, thou knewest that I reap where I sowed not, and gather where I have not strawed:

Sonnet XIX 〰 JOHN MILTON

When I consider how my light is spent,
    Ere half my days, in this dark world and wide,
    And that one talent which is death to hide,
    Lodged with me useless, though my soul more bent
To serve therewith my maker, and present
    My true account, lest he returning chide
    "Doth God exact day-labor, light denied,"
    I fondly ask; But patience to prevent
That murmur, soon replies, "God doth not need
    Either man's work or his own gifts; who best
    Bear his mild yoke, they serve him best; his state
Is kingly. Thousands at his bidding speed
    And post o'er land and ocean without rest:
    They also serve who only stand and wait."

MATTHEW 25:27–25:29   Thou oughtest therefore to have put my money to the exchangers, and then at my coming I should have received mine own with usury. Take therefore the talent from him, and give it unto him which hath ten talents. For unto every one that hath shall be given, and he shall have abundance: but from him that hath not shall be taken away even that which he hath.

On the Death of Dr. Robert Levet   ♪   SAMUEL JOHNSON

Condemned to hope's delusive mine,
    As on we toil from day to day,
By sudden blasts, or slow decline,
    Our social comforts drop away.

Well tried through many a varying year,
    See Levet to the grave descend;
Officious, innocent, sincere,
    Of every friendless name the friend.

Yet still he fills affection's eye,
    Obscurely wise, and coarsely kind;
Nor, lettered arrogance, deny
    Thy praise to merit unrefined.

When fainting nature called for aid,
    And hovering death prepared the blow
His vigorous remedy displayed
    The power of art without the show.

In misery's darkest caverns known,
    His useful care was ever nigh,
Where hopeless anguish poured his groan,
    And lonely want retired to die.

No summons mocked by chill delay,
    No petty gain disdained by pride,
The modest wants of every day
    The toil of every day supplied.

His virtues walked their narrow round,
    Nor made a pause, nor left a void;
And sure th' Eternal Master found
    The single talent well employed.

The busy day, the peaceful night,
    Unfelt, uncounted, glided by;
His frame was firm, his powers were bright,
    Though now his eightieth year was nigh.

Then with no throbbing fiery pain,
    No cold gradations of decay,
Death broke at once the vital chain,
    And forced his soul the nearest way.

MATTHEW 25:30–25:33   And cast ye the unprofitable servant into outer darkness: there shall be weeping and gnashing of teeth. When the Son of man shall come in his glory, and all the holy angels with him, then shall he sit upon the throne of his glory: And before him shall be gathered all nations: and he shall separate them one from another, as a shepherd divideth his sheep from the goats: And he shall set the sheep on his right hand, but the goats on the left.

The Tribunal ᧒ CHRIS WALLACE-CRABBE

After death, suppose we were judged by animals:
the harmless pigs and sheep,
each throat still bearing its long scar,
their eyes not meeting ours,
stand firm behind the bar of judgement
where scales flaunt their brightness
weighing us up.
'The sheep from the goats,' they would say
and laugh to themselves at the joke.

'The goats from the sheep, indeed,
that's a good one.'
Our critics chuckle away at their beastly job
separating friend from friend
and nice girl from her bloke,
sifting us finally, neatly out
with a good horse-laugh at our pride
which came to this in the end.

MATTHEW 26:26   And as they were eating, Jesus took bread, and blessed it, and brake it, and gave it to the disciples, and said, Take, eat; this is my body.

This Bread I Break ☞ DYLAN THOMAS

This bread I break was once the oat,
This wine upon a foreign tree
Plunged in its fruit;
Man in the day or wind at night
Laid the crops low, broke the grape's joy.

Once in this wine the summer blood
Knocked in the flesh that decked the vine,
Once in this bread
The oat was merry in the wind;
Man broke the sun, pulled the wind down.

This flesh you break, this blood you let
Make desolation in the vein,
Were oat and grape
Born of the sensual root and sap;
My wine you drink, my bread you snap.

JOHN 13:10–13:14   Jesus saith to him, He that is washed needeth not save to wash his feet, but is clean every whit: and ye are clean, but not all. For he knew who should betray him; therefore said he, Ye are not all clean. So after he had washed their feet, and had taken his garments, and was set down again, he said unto them, Know ye what I have done to you? Ye call me Master and Lord: and ye say well; for so I am. If I then, your Lord and Master, have washed your feet; ye also ought to wash one another's feet.

The Foot-Washing ☞ A. R. AMMONS

Now you have come,
the roads
humbling your feet with dust:

I will wash your feet
with springwater
and silver care:

the odor of your feet
is newly earthen,
honeysuckled

bloodwork in blue
raisures over the white
skinny anklebone:

if I have wronged you
cleanse me with the falling
water of forgiveness.

And woman, your flat feet
yellow, gray with dust,
your orphaned udders flat,

lift your dress
up to your knees
and I will wash your feet:

feel the serenity
cool as cool springwater
and hard to find:

if I have failed to know
the grief in your gone time,
forgive me wakened now.

JOHN 13:22–13:29   Then the disciples looked one on another, doubting of whom he spake. Now there was leaning on Jesus' bosom one of his disciples, whom Jesus loved. Simon Peter therefore beckoned to him, that he should ask who it should be of whom he spake. He then lying on Jesus' breast saith unto him, Lord, who is it? Jesus answered, He it is, to whom I shall give a sop, when I have dipped it. And when he had dipped the sop, he gave it to Judas Iscariot, the son of Simon. And after the sop Satan entered into him. Then said Jesus unto him, That thou doest, do quickly. Now no man at the table knew for what intent he spake this unto him. For some of them thought, because Judas had the bag, that Jesus had said unto him, Buy those things that we have need of against the feast; or, that he should give something to the poor.

The Bottle ✌ RALPH KNEVET

Thou bearst the bottle, I the bag (oh Lord)
Which daily I do carry at my back,
So stuffed with sin, that ready 'tis to crack:
I have no unfeigned nectar for thy gourd,
Mine eyes will no such precious drink afford:
Yet both my heart, and eyes, are deserts dry,
Even Libyan sands, where serpents crawl and fly.

Yea the two extreme zones took up my heart,
For unto good, as cold as ice, I am;
But unto evil, like an Ætna flame:
I paralytical seem in each part,
One utterly deprived of strength, and art,
When I should execute my master's will,
But active am as fire, t'accomplish ill.

I bear the bag like Judas: (Lord) do Thou,
From this unwieldy burden me dismiss,
And this bag empty, which so heavy is:
Then shall my tears into thy bottle flow;
Not only tears, which do from sorrow grow,
But cooler drops, which do from joy distill,
And to the brim, these shall thy bottle fill.

JOHN 15:12–15:13   This is my commandment, That ye love one another, as I have loved you. Greater love hath no man than this, that a man lay down his life for his friends.

At a Calvary Near the Ancre ✌ WILFRED OWEN

One ever hangs where shelled roads part.
    In this war He too lost a limb,
But His disciples hide apart;
    And now the Soldiers bear with Him.

Near Golgotha strolls many a priest,
    And in their faces there is pride

That they were flesh-marked by the Beast
    By whom the gentle Christ's denied.

The scribes on all the people shove
    And bawl allegiance to the state,
But they who love the greater love
    Lay down their life; they do not hate.

JOHN 17:13–17:26   And now come I to thee; and these things I speak in the world, that they might have my joy fulfilled in themselves. I have given them thy word; and the world hath hated them, because they are not of the world, even as I am not of the world. I pray not that thou shouldest take them out of the world, but that thou shouldest keep them from the evil. They are not of the world, even as I am not of the world. Sanctify them through thy truth: thy word is truth. As thou hast sent me into the world, even so have I also sent them into the world. And for their sakes I sanctify myself, that they also might be sanctified through the truth. Neither pray I for these alone, but for them also which shall believe on me through their word; That they all may be one; as thou, Father, art in me, and I in thee, that they also may be one in us: that the world may believe that thou hast sent me. And the glory which thou gavest me I have given them; that they may be one, even as we are one: I in them, and thou in me, that they may be made perfect in one; and that the world may know that thou hast sent me, and hast loved them, as thou hast loved me. Father, I will that they also, whom thou hast given me, be with me where I am; that they may behold my glory, which thou hast given me: for thou lovedst me before the foundation of the world. O righteous Father, the world hath not known thee: but I have known thee, and these have known that thou hast sent me. And I have declared unto them thy name, and will declare it: that the love wherewith thou hast loved me may be in them, and I in them.

I Heard Christ Sing   HUGH MACDIARMID

I heard Christ sing quhile roond him dar
The twal' disciples in a ring,
And here's the dance I saw them dance,
And the sang I heard him sing.

Ane, twa, three, and their right feet heich,
Fower, five, six, and doon wi' them,
Seevin, aucht, nine, and up wi' the left,
Ten, eleevin, twal', and doon they came.

And Christ he stude i' the middle there,
And was the thirteenth man,
And sang the bonniest sang that e'er
Was sung sin' Time began.

And Christ he was the centrepiece,
Wi' three on ilka side.
My hert stude still, and the sun stude still
But still the dancers plied.

O I wot it was a maypole,
As a man micht seek to see,
Wi' the twal' disciples dancin' roon',
While Christ sang like a lintie.

The twal' points o' the compass
Made jubilee roon' and roon',
And but for the click-click-clack o' the feet,
Christ's sang was the only soon'.

And there was nae time that could be tauld
Frae a clock wha's haun's stude still,
Quhile the figures a' gaed bizzin roon'
—I wot it was God's will.

  Wersh is the vinegar,
  And the sword is sharp.
  Wi' the tremblin' sunbeams
  Again for my harp,
  I sing to Thee.

  The spirit of man
  Is a bird in a cage,
  That beats on the bars
  Wi' a goodly rage,
  And fain 'ud be free.

Twice-caged it is,
In life and in death,
Yet it claps its wings
Wi' a restless faith,
And sings as it may.

Then fill my mouth
Wi' the needfu' words,
That sall turn its wings,
Into whirlin swords,
When it hears what I say.

Hearken my cry,
And let me speak,
That when it hears
It sall lift its beak,
And sing as it should.

Sweet is the song
That is lost in its throat,
And fain 'ud I hear
Its openin' note
As I hang on the rood.

And when I rise
Again from the dead,
Let me, I pray,
Be accompanied
By the spirit of man.

Yea, as I rise
From earth to Heaven
Fain 'ud I know
That Thou hast given
Consent to my plan—

Even as the stars
Sang here at my birth,
Let Heaven hear
The song of the earth
Then, for my sake.

The thorns are black
And callous the nails.
As a bird its bars
My hand assails
Harpstrings . . . that break!

O I wot they'll lead the warl' a dance
And I wot the sang sall be,
As a white sword loupin' at the hert
O' a' eternity.

Judas and Christ stude face to face,
And mair I couldna' see,
But I wot he did God's will wha made
Siccar o' Calvary.

LUKE 22:39   And he came out, and went, as he was wont, to the mount of
Olives; and his disciples also followed him.

A Ballad of Trees and the Master   ᔓ   SIDNEY LANIER

Into the woods my Master went,
Clean forspent, forspent.
Into the woods my Master came,
Forspent with love and shame.
But the olives they were not blind to Him,
The Little gray leaves were kind to Him:
The thorn-tree had a mind to Him
When into the woods He came.

Out of the woods my Master went,
And he was well content.
Out of the woods my Master came,
Content with death and shame.
When Death and Shame would woo Him last,
From under the trees they drew Him last:
'Twas on a tree they slew Him—last
When out of the woods He came.

MATTHEW 27:3–27:4   Then Judas, which had betrayed him, when he saw that he was condemned, repented himself, and brought again the thirty pieces of silver to the chief priests and elders, Saying, I have sinned in that I have betrayed the innocent blood. And they said, What is that to us? see thou to that.

The Hound of Heaven ༞ FRANCIS THOMPSON

I fled Him, down the nights and down the days;
   I fled Him, down the arches of the years;
I fled Him, down the labyrinthine ways
   Of my own mind; and in the midst of tears
I hid from Him, and under running laughter.
          Up vistaed hopes I sped;
          And shot, precipitated,
Adown titanic glooms of chasméd fears,
   From those strong feet that followed, followed after.
          But with unhurrying chase,
          And unperturbéd pace,
     Deliberate speed, majestic instancy,
          They beat—and a voice beat
          More instant than the feet—
   "All things betray thee, who betrayest Me."

          I pleaded, outlaw-wise,
By many a hearted casement, curtained red,
   Trellised with intertwining charities
(For, though I knew His love Who followéd,
          Yet was I sore adread
Lest, having Him, I must have naught beside);
But, if one little casement parted wide,
   The gust of His approach would clash it to.
Fear wist not to evade, as Love wist to pursue.
Across the margent of the world I fled,
   And troubled the gold gateways of the stars,
   Smiting for shelter on their clangéd bars;
          Fretted to dulcet jars
And silvern chatter the pale ports o' the moon.
I said to dawn, Be sudden; to eve, Be soon;
   With thy young skiey blossoms heap me over

From this tremendous lover!
Float thy vague veil about me, lest He see!
I tempted all His servitors, but to find
My own betrayal in their constancy,
In faith to Him their fickleness to me,
    Their traitorous trueness, and their loyal deceit.
To all swift things for swiftness did I sue;
    Clung to the whistling mane of every wind,
                But whether they swept, smoothly fleet,
        The long savannahs of the blue;
                Or whether thunder-driven
        They clanged his chariot 'thwart a heaven
Plashy with flying lightnings round the spurn o' their feet: —
    Fear wist not to evade as Love wist to pursue —
                Still with unhurrying chase,
                And unperturbéd pace,
        Deliberate speed, majestic instancy,
                Came on the following feet,
                And a voice above their beat—
    "Naught shelters thee, who wilt not shelter Me."

I sought no more that after which I strayed
                In face of man or maid;
But still within the little children's eyes
                Seems something, something that replies;
They at least are for me, surely for me!
I turned me to them very wistfully;
But, just as their young eyes grew sudden fair
        With dawning answers there,
Their angel plucked them from me by the hair.
"Come then, ye other children, Nature's—share
With me" (said I) "your delicate fellowship;
        Let me greet you lip to lip,
        Let me twine with you caresses,
                Wantoning
        With our Lady-Mother's vagrant tresses,
                Banqueting
        With her in her wind-walled palace,
        Underneath her azured daïs,
        Quaffing as your taintless way is,
                From a chalice

Lucent-weeping out of the dayspring."
                    So it was done:
I in their delicate fellowship was one—
Drew the bolts of Nature's secrecies.
I knew all the swift importings
                    On the willful face of skies;
                    I knew how the clouds arise
                    Spuméd of the wild sea-snortings;
                              All that's born or dies
                    Rose and drooped with—made them shapers
Of mine own moods, or wailful or divine—
                    With them joyed and was bereaven.
                    I was heavy with the even,
                    When she lit her glimmering tapers
                    Round the day's dead sanctities.
                    I laughed in the morning's eyes.
I triumphed and I saddened with all weather,
                    Heaven and I wept together,
And its sweet tears were salt with mortal mine;
Against the red throb of its sunset-heart
                    I laid my own to beat,
                    And share commingling heat;
But not by that, by that, was eased my human smart.
In vain my tears were wet on Heaven's grey cheek.
For ah! we know not what each other says,
                    These things and I; in sound I speak—
Their sound is but their stir, they speak by silences.
Nature, poor stepdame, cannot slake my drouth;
                    Let her, if she would owe me,
Drop yon blue bosom-veil of sky, and show me
                    The breasts o' her tenderness:
Never did any milk of hers once bless
                              My thirsting mouth.
                    Nigh and nigh draws the chase,
                    With unperturbéd pace,
          Deliberate speed, majestic instancy;
                    And past those noiséd feet
                    A voice comes yet more fleet—
    "Lo! naught contents thee, who content'st not Me."

Naked I wait Thy love's uplifted stroke!
My harness piece by piece Thou hast hewn from me,
                And smitten me to my knee;
        I am defenceless utterly.
        I slept, methinks, and woke,
And, slowly gazing, find me stripped in sleep.
In the rash lustihead of my young powers,
        I shook the pillaring hours
And pulled my life upon me; grimed with smears,
I stand amid the dust o' the mounded years—
My mangled youth lies dead beneath the heap.
My days have crackled and gone up in smoke,
Have puffed and burst as sun-starts on a stream.
                Yea, faileth now even dream
The dreamer, and the lute the lutanist;
Even the linkéd fantasies, in whose blossomy twist
I swung the earth a trinket at my wrist,
Are yielding; cords of all too weak account
For earth with heavy griefs so overplussed.
                Ah! is Thy love indeed
A weed, albeit an amaranthine weed,
Suffering no flowers except its own to mount?
                Ah! must—
                Designer infinite!—
Ah! must Thou char the wood ere Thou canst limn
My freshness spent its wavering shower i' the dust;
And now my heart is as a broken fount,
Wherein tear-droppings stagnate, spilt down ever
        From the dank thoughts that shiver
Upon the sighful branches of my mind.
        Such is; what is to be?
The pulp so bitter, how shall taste the rind?
I dimly guess what Time in mists confounds;
Yet ever and anon a trumpet sounds
From the hid battlements of Eternity;
Those shaken mists a space unsettle, then
Round the half-glimpséd turrets slowly wash again.
        But not ere him who summoneth
        I first have seen, enwound
With glooming robes purpureal, cypress-crowned;
His name I know, and what his trumpet saith.

Whether man's heart or life it be which yields
    Thee harvest, must Thy harvest fields
    Be dunged with rotten death?

        Now of that long pursuit
        Comes on at hand the bruit;
    That voice is round me like a bursting sea:
        "And is thy earth so marred,
        Shattered in shard on shard?
    Lo, all things fly thee, for thou fliest Me!
    Strange, piteous, futile thing!
Wherefore should any set thee love apart?
Seeing none but I makes much of naught"
        (He said)
"And human love needs human meriting:
        How hast thou merited—
Of all man's clotted clay the dingiest clot?
    Alack, thou knowest not
How little worthy of any love thou art!
Whom wilt thou find to love ignoble thee
    Save Me, save only Me?
All which I took from thee I did but take,
    Not for thy harms,
But just that thou might'st seek it in My arms.
    All which thy child's mistake
Fancies as lost, I have stored for thee at home;
    Rise, clasp My hand, and come!"
        Halts by me that footfall:
        Is my gloom, after all,
    Shade of His hand, outstretched caressingly?
        "Ah, fondest, blindest, weakest,
        I am He whom thou seekest!
Thou dravest love from thee, who dravest Me."

MATTHEW 27:5 And he cast down the pieces of silver in the temple, and departed, and went and hanged himself.

Judas ∽ VASSAR MILLER

Always I lay upon the brink of love,
Impotent, waiting till the waters stirred,
And no one healed my weakness with a word;
For no one healed me who lacked words to prove
My heart, which, when the kiss of Mary wove
His shroud, my tongueless anguish spurred
To cool dissent, and which, each time I heard
John whisper to Him, moaned, but could not move.

While Peter deeply drowsed within love's deep
I cramped upon its margin, glad to share
The sop Christ gave me, yet its bitter bite
Dried up my ducts. Praise Peter, who could weep
His sin away, but never see me where
I hang, huge teardrop on the cheek of night.

MARK 15:2–15:3   And Pilate asked him, Art thou the King of the Jews? And
he answering said unto them, Thou sayest it. And the chief priests accused
him of many things: but he answered nothing.

And He Answered them Nothing ∽ RICHARD CRASHAW

O Mighty *Nothing!* unto thee,
Nothing, we owe all things that be.
God spake once when he all things made,
He saved all when he *Nothing* said.
The world was made of *Nothing* then;
'Tis made by *Nothing* now again.

JOHN 19:1–19:5   Then Pilate therefore took Jesus, and scourged him. And
the soldiers platted a crown of thorns, and put it on his head, and they put
on him a purple robe, And said, Hail, King of the Jews! and they smote him
with their hands. Pilate therefore went forth again, and saith unto them,
Behold, I bring him forth to you, that ye may know that I find no fault in
him. Then came Jesus forth, wearing the crown of thorns, and the purple
robe. And Pilate saith unto them, Behold the man!

MATTHEW 27:29   And when they had platted a crown of thorns, they put it upon his head, and a reed in his right hand: and they bowed the knee before him, and mocked him, saying, Hail, King of the Jews!

One crown that no one seeks ❧ EMILY DICKINSON

One crown that no one seeks
And yet the highest head
Its isolation coveted
Its stigma deified

While Pontius Pilate lives
In whatsoever hell
That coronation pierces him
He recollects it well.

MATTHEW 27:32   And as they came out, they found a man of Cyrene, Simon by name: him they compelled to bear his cross.

Simon the Cyrenian Speaks ❧ COUNTEE CULLEN

He never spoke a word to me,
    And yet He called my name;
He never gave a sign to me,
    And yet I knew he came.

At first I said, "I will not bear
    His cross upon my back;
He only seeks to place it there
    Because my skin is black."

But He was dying for a dream,
    And He was very meek.
And in His eyes there shone a gleam
    Men journey far to seek.

It was Himself my pity bought,
   I did for Christ alone
What all of Rome could not have wrought
    With bruise of lash or stone.

LUKE 23:27   And there followed him a great company of people, and of women, which also bewailed and lamented him.

MATTHEW 27:33–27:34   And when they were come unto a place called Golgotha, that is to say, a place of a skull, They gave him vinegar to drink mingled with gall: and when he had tasted thereof, he would not drink.

Canticle for Good Friday   ᧒   GEOFFREY HILL

The cross staggered him. At the cliff-top
Thomas, beneath its burden, stood
While the dulled wood
Spat on the stones each drop
Of deliberate blood.

A clamping, cold-figured day
Thomas (not transfigured) stamped, crouched.
Watched
Smelt vinegar and blood. He,
As yet unsearched, unscratched,

And suffered to remain
At such near distance
(A slight miracle might cleanse
His brain
Of all attachments, claw-roots of sense)

In unaccountable darkness moved away,
The strange flesh untouched, carrion-sustenance
Of staunchest love, choicest defiance,
Creation's issue congealing (and one woman's).

MARK 15:25   And it was the third hour, and they crucified him.

Crucifying   ॐ   JOHN DONNE

By miracles exceeding power of man,
He faith in some, envy in some begat,
For, what weak spirits admire, ambitious, hate;
In both affections many to him ran,
But Oh! the worst are most, they will and can,
Alas, and do, unto the immaculate,
Whose creature fate is, now prescribe a fate,
Measuring self-life's infinity to'a span,
Nay to an inch. Lo, where condemned he
Bears his own cross, with pain, yet by and by
When it bears him, he must bear more and die.
Now thou art lifted up, draw me to thee,
And at thy death giving such liberal dole,
Moist, with one drop of thy blood, my dry soul.

JOHN 19:23–19:24   Then the soldiers, when they had crucified Jesus, took
his garments, and made four parts, to every soldier a part; and also his
coat: now the coat was without seam, woven from the top throughout. They
said therefore among themselves, Let us not rend it, but cast lots for it,
whose it shall be: that the scripture might be fulfilled, which saith, They
parted my raiment among them, and for my vesture they did cast lots.
These things therefore the soldiers did.

On the Cards, and Dice   ॐ   SIR WALTER RALEIGH

Before the sixth day of the next new year,
Strange wonders in this kingdom shall appear.
Four kings shall be assembled in this Isle,
Where they shall keep great tumult for a while.
Many men then shall have an end of crosses,
And many likewise shall sustain great losses.
Many that now full joyful are and glad,
Shall at that time be sorrowful and sad.
Full many a Christian's heart shall quake for fear,

The dreadful sound of trump when he shall hear.
Dead bones shall then be tumbled up and down,
In every city, and in every town.
By day or night this tumult shall not cease,
Until an herald shall proclaim a peace,
An herald strange, the like was never born
Whose very beard is flesh, and mouth is horn.[26]

MATTHEW 27:39–27:40   And they that passed by reviled him, wagging their heads, And saying, Thou that destroyest the temple, and buildest it in three days, save thyself. If thou be the Son of God, come down from the cross.

The Carpenter's Son   ᠕   A. E. HOUSMAN

'Here the hangman stops his cart:
Now the best of friends must part.
Fare you well, for ill fare I:
Live, lads, and I will die.

'Oh, at home had I but stayed
'Prenticed to my father's trade,
Had I stuck to plane and adze,
I had not been lost, my lads.

'Then I might have built perhaps
Gallows-trees for other chaps,
Never dangled on my own,
Had I but left ill alone.

'Now, you see, they hang me high,
And the people passing by
Stop to shake their fists and curse;
So 'tis come from ill to worse.

'Here hang I, and right and left
Two poor fellows hang for theft:
All the same's the luck we prove,
Though the midmost hangs for love.

26 Raleigh's poem paraphrases DAN 7:17–7:23.

'Comrades all, that stand and gaze,
Walk henceforth in other ways;
See my neck and save your own:
Comrades all, leave ill alone.

'Make some day a decent end,
Shrewder fellows than your friend.
Fare you well, for ill fare I:
Live, lads, and I will die.'

LUKE 23:39–23:43   And one of the malefactors which were hanged railed on
him, saying, If thou be Christ, save thyself and us. But the other answering
rebuked him, saying, Dost not thou fear God, seeing thou art in the same
condemnation? And we indeed justly; for we receive the due reward of our
deeds: but this man hath done nothing amiss. And he said unto Jesus,
Lord, remember me when thou comest into thy kingdom. And Jesus said
unto him, Verily I say unto thee, To day shalt thou be with me in paradise.

"Remember me" implored the Thief   ✍
EMILY DICKINSON

"Remember me" implored the Thief!
Oh Hospitality!
My Guest "Today in Paradise"
I give thee guaranty.

That Courtesy will fair remain
When the Delight is Dust
With which we cite this mightiest case
Of compensated Trust.

Of all we are allowed to hope
But Affidavit stands
That this was due where most we fear
Be unexpected Friends.

MATTHEW 27:48–27:49   And straightway one of them ran, and took a spunge, and filled it with vinegar, and put it on a reed, and gave him to drink. The rest said, Let be, let us see whether Elias will come to save him.

Christ's Passion   ABRAHAM COWLEY

Enough, my Muse, of earthly things,
And inspirations but of wind,
Take up thy lute, and to it bind
Loud and everlasting strings;
And on 'em play and to 'em sing,
The happy mournful stories,
The lamentable glories,
Of the great Crucified King.
Mountainous heap of wonders! which dost rise
   Till earth thou joinest with the skies!
Too large at bottom, and at top too high,
      To be half seen by mortal eye.
      How shall I grasp this boundless thing?
      What shall I play? what shall I sing?
I'll sing the mighty riddle of mysterious love,
Which neither wretched men below, nor blessed spirits above
      With all their comments can explain;
How all the Whole World's Life to die did not disdain.

I'll sing the searchless depths of the compassion divine,
      The depths unfathomed yet
   By reasons plummet, and the line of wit,
   Too light the plummet, and too short the line,
   How the Eternal Father did bestow
His own Eternal Son as ransom for his Foe,
      I'll sing aloud, that all the world may hear,
      The triumph of the buried conquerer.
      How hell was by its prisoner captive led,
      And the great slayer Death slain by the dead.

Me thinks I hear of murdered men the voice,
Mixed with the murderers' confused noise,
      Sound from the top of Calvary;
My greedy eyes fly up the hill, and see

Who 'tis hangs there midmost of the three;
Oh how unlike the others he!
Look how he bends head with blessings from the Tree!
His gracious hands ne'er stretched but to do good,
Are nailed to the infamous wood:
And sinful Man does fondly bind
The arms, which he extends t'embrace all human kind.

Unhappy, canst thou stand by, and see
All this as patient, as he?
Since he thy sins does bear,
Make thou his sufferings thine own,
And weep, and sigh, and groan,
And beat thy breast, and tear,
Thy garments, and thy hair,
And let thy grief, and let thy love
Through all thy bleeding bowels move.
Dost thou not see thy Prince in purple clad all o'er,
Not purple brought from the Sidonian shore,
But made at home with richer gore?
Dost thou not see the roses, which adorn
The thorny garland, by him worn?
Dost thou not see the livid traces
Of the sharp scourges rude embraces?
If yet thou feelest not the smart
Of thorns and scourges in thy heart,
If that be yet not crucified,
Look on his hands, look on his feet, look on his side.

Open, Oh! open wide the fountains of thine eyes,
And let 'em call
Their stock of moisture forth, where e'er it lies,
For this will ask it all.
'Twould all (alas) too little be,
Though thy salt tears came from a sea:
Canst thou deny him this, when he
Has opened all his vital springs for thee?
Take heed; for by his sides mysterious flood
May well be understood,
That he will still require some waters to his blood.

LUKE 23:46–23:48   And when Jesus had cried with a loud voice, he said,
Father, into thy hands I commend my spirit: and having said thus, he gave
up the ghost. . . . And all the people that came together to that sight,
beholding the things which were done, smote their breasts, and returned.

The Crucifixion of Our Blessed Lord ঙ
CHRISTOPHER SMART

The world is but a sorry scene,
Untrue, unhallowed, and unclean,
    And hardly worth a man;
The fiend upon the land prevails,
And o'er the floods in triumph sails,
    Do goodness all she can.

How many works for such a day?
How glorious? that ye scourge and slay
    Ye blind, by blinder led;
All hearts at once devising bad,
Hands, mouths against their Maker mad.
    With Satan at the head—

Are these the race of saints professed,
That for authorities contest,
    And question and debate?
Yet in so foul a deed rebel,
Beyond example, even from hell,
    To match its barbarous hate.

Behold the man! the tyrant said,
As in the robes of scoff arrayed,
    And crowned with thorns he stood;
And feigning will to let him go
He chose Barabbas, open foe
    Of human kind and good.

And was it He, whose voice divine,
Could change the water into wine,
    And first his power averred;
Which fed in Galilea's groves

The fainting thousands with the loaves
   And fishes of his word!

And was it He, whose mandate freed
The palsied suppliant, and in deed
   The sabbath-day revered;
Which bade the thankful dumb proclaim
The Lord omnipotent by name,
   Till loosened deafness heard!

And was it He, whose hand was such,
As lightened blindness at a touch,
   And made the lepers whole;
Could to the dropsy health afford,
And to the lunatic restored
   Serenity of soul!

The daughter that so long a term
By Satan's bonds had been infirm,
   Was rescued and received;
Yea, with the foes of faith and hope
His matchless charity could cope,
   When Malchus was relieved.

The woman in his garment's hem
Conceived a prevalence to stem
   The sources of her pain;
He calls—the dead from death arise,
And as their legions he defies
   The devils descend again.

His irresistable command
Conveyed the vessel to the land,
   As instant as his thought;
He caused the tempest to forget
Its rage, and into Peter's net,
   The wondrous capture brought.

The roarings of the billows cease
To hear the gospel of his peace
   Upon the still profound—

He walked the waves—and at his will,
The fish to pay th' exactor's bill
   To Judah's coast was bound.

The withered hand he saw and cured,
And health from general ail secured
   Where'er disease was rife;
And was omniscient to tell
The woman at the patriarch's well
   The story of her life.

But never since the world was known,
One so stupendous as his own,
   And rich of vast event;
From love adored, as soon as seen,
Had not his hated message been
   To bid the world repent.

Ah, still desirous of a king,
To give voluptuous vice its swing
   With passions like a brute;
By Jesus Christ came truth and grace,
But none indulgence, pension, place,
   The slaves of self to suit.

The Lord on Gabbatha they doom,
Before the delegate of Rome,
   Deserted and exposed—
They might have thought on Israel's God,
Which on the sapphire pavement trod,
   To seventy seers disclosed.

They might have thought upon the loss
Of Eden, and the dreadful cross
   That happened by a tree;
Ere yet with cursed throats they shout
To bring the dire event about,
   Though prophesied to be.

O God, the bonds of sin enlarge,
Lay not this horror to our charge,

But as we fast and weep,
Pour out the streams of love profuse,
Let all the powers of mercy loose,
    While wrath and vengeance sleep.

There were also women looking on afar off: among whom was Mary Magdalene, and Mary the mother of James the less and of Joses, and Salome;

Good Friday, 1613. Riding Westward ∿ JOHN DONNE

Let man's soul be a sphere, and then, in this,
The intelligence that moves, devotion is,
And as the other spheres, by being grown
Subject to foreign motions, lose their own,
And being by others hurried every day,
Scarce in a year their natural form obey;
Pleasure or business, so, our souls admit
For their first mover, and are whirled by it.
Hence is't, that I am carried towards the West
This day, when my soul's form bends towards the East.
There I should see a sun, by rising, set,
And by that setting endless day beget:
But that Christ on this Cross did rise and fall,
Sin had eternally benighted all.
Yet dare I almost be glad I do not see
That spectacle, of too much weight for me.
Who sees God's face, that is self life, must die;
What a death were it then to see God die?
It made his own lieutenant nature, shrink;
It made his footstool crack, and the sun wink.
Could I behold those hands which span the poles,
And tune all spheres at once, pierced with those holes?
Could I behold that endless height which is
Zenith to us, and our Antipodes,
Humbled below us? Or that blood which is
The seat of all our souls, if not of His,
Make dirt of dust, or that flesh which was worn
By God, for his apparel, ragged and torn?

If on these things I durst not look, durst I
Upon his miserable mother cast mine eye,
Who was God's partner here, and furnished thus
Half of that sacrifice which ransomed us?
Though these things, as I ride, be from mine eye,
They are present yet unto my memory,
For that looks towards them; and thou lookst towards me,
O Savior, as thou hangst upon the tree.
I turn my back to Thee but to receive
Corrections, till thy mercies bid thee leave.
O think me worth thine anger; punish me;
Burn off my rusts, and my deformity,
Restore thine Image so much, by thy grace
That thou mayst know me, and I'll turn my face.

JOHN 19:31–19:34   The Jews therefore, because it was the preparation, that the bodies should not remain upon the cross on the sabbath day, (for that sabbath day was an high day,) besought Pilate that their legs might be broken, and that they might be taken away. Then came the soldiers, and brake the legs of the first, and of the other which was crucified with him. But when they came to Jesus, and saw that he was dead already, they brake not his legs: But one of the soldiers with a spear pierced his side, and forthwith came there out blood and water.

'O, My Heart is Woe'   ✌ ANONYMOUS

'O, my heart is woe!' Mary she said so,
'For to see my dear son die, and sons I have no mo.'

'When that my sweet son was thirty winter old,
Then the traitor Judas waxed very bold:
For thirty plates of money his master he had sold.
But when I it wist, Lord, my heart was cold!

'Upon Shere Thursday then truly it was
On my son's death that Judas did compass.
Many were the false Jews that followed him by trace;
And there before them all he kissed my son's face.

'My son before Pilate brought was he,
And Peter said three times he knew him not, pardee.
Pilate said unto the Jews: 'What say ye?'
Then they cried with one voice: 'Crucify!'

'On Good Friday, at the mount of Calvary,
My son was done on the cross, nailed with nails three.
Of all the friends that he had, never one could he see
But gentle John the Evangelist, that still stood him by.

'Though I were sorrowful, no man have at it wonder;
For huge was the earthquake, horrible was the thunder.
I looked on my sweet son on the cross that I stood under;
Then came Longeus with a spear and cleft his heart in sunder.'

MARK 15:43–15:46   Joseph of Arimathæa, an honorable counselor . . .
went in boldly unto Pilate, and craved the body of Jesus. . . . And he bought
fine linen, and took him down, and wrapped him in the linen, and laid him
in a sepulchre which was hewn out of a rock, and rolled a stone unto the
door of the sepulchre.

Upon our Savior's Tomb Wherein Never Man was Laid ✍ RICHARD CRASHAW

How Life and Death in thee
                    Agree!
Thou hadst a virgin Womb
                    And Tomb.
A Joseph did betroth
                    Them both.

LUKE 23:54–23:56   And that day was the preparation, and the sabbath
drew on. And the women also, which came with him from Galilee, followed
after, and beheld the sepulchre, and how his body was laid. And they
returned, and prepared spices and ointments; and rested the sabbath day
according to the commandment.

Observation ᔐ ROBERT HERRICK

The Virgin-Mother stood at distance (there)
From her son's cross, not shedding once a tear:
Because the Law forbad to sit and cry
For those, who did as malefactors die.
So she, to keep her mighty woes in awe,
Tortured her love, not to transgress the Law.
Observe we may, how Mary Joses then,
And th'other Mary (Mary Magdalen)
Sat by the grave; and sadly sitting there,
Shed for their master many a bitter tear:
But 'twas not till their dearest Lord was dead;
And then to weep they both were licensed.

MATTHEW 27:62–27:64   Now the next day, that followed the day of the preparation, the chief priests and Pharisees came together unto Pilate, Saying, Sir, we remember that that deceiver said, while he was yet alive, After three days I will rise again. Command therefore that the sepulchre be made sure until the third day, lest his disciples come by night, and steal him away, and say unto the people, He is risen from the dead: so the last error shall be worse than the first.

Epilogue ᔐ ROBERT BROWNING

First speaker
On the first of the Feast of Feasts,
    The dedication day,
When the Levites joined the priests
    At the altar in robed array,
Gave signal to sound and say, —

When the thousands, rear and van,
    Swarming with one accord,
Became as a single man,
(Look, gesture, thought and word)
    In praising and thanking the Lord, —

When the singers lift up their voice,
   And the trumpets made endeavour,
Sounding, "In God rejoice!"
   Saying, "In Him rejoice
Whose mercy endureth for ever!"—

Then the Temple filled with a cloud,
   Even the House of the Lord;
Porch bent and pillar bowed:
   For the presence of the Lord,
In the glory of His cloud,
   Had filled the House of the Lord.[27]

Second Speaker.
Gone now! All gone across the dark so far,
   Sharpening fast, shuddering ever, shutting still,
Dwindling into the distance, dies that star
   Which came, stood, opened once! We gazed our fill
With upturned faces on as real a face
   That, stooping from grave music and mild fire,
Took in our homage, made a visible place
   Through many a depth of glory, gyre on gyre,
For the dim human tribute. Was this true?
   Could man indeed avail, mere praise of his,
To help by rapture God's own rapture too,
   Thrill with a heart's red tinge that pure pale bliss?
Why did it end? Who failed to beat the breast,
   And shriek, and throw the arms protesting wide,
When a first shadow showed the star addressed
   Itself to motion, and on either side
The rims contracted as the rays retired;
   The music, like a fountain's sickening pulse,
Subsided on itself; awhile transpired
   Some vestige of a face no pangs convulse,
No prayers retard; then even this was gone,
   Lost in the night at last. We, lone and left
Silent through centuries, ever and anon
   Venture to probe again the vault bereft

27 2 Chron 7:1–11

Of all now save the lesser lights, a mist
　　Of multitudinous points, yet suns, men say—
And this leaps ruby, this lurks amethyst,
　　But where may hide what came and loved our clay?
How shall the sage detect in yon expanse
　　The star which chose to stoop and stay for us?
Unroll the records! Hailed ye such advance
　　Indeed, and did your hope evanish thus?
Watchers of twilight, is the worst averred?
　　We shall not look up, know ourselves are seen,
Speak, and be sure that we again are heard,
　　Acting or suffering, have the disk's serene
Reflect our life, absorb an earthly flame,
　　Nor doubt that, were mankind inert and numb,
Its core had never crimsoned all the same,
　　Nor, missing ours, its music fallen dumb?
Oh, dread succession to a dizzy post,
　　Sad sway of sceptre whose mere touch appals,
Ghastly dethronement, cursed by those the most
　　On whose repugnant brow the crown next falls!

Third Speaker.
Witless alike of will and way divine,
How Heaven's high with earth's low should intertwine!
Friends, I have seen through your eyes: now use mine.

Take the least man of all mankind, as I;
Look at his head and heart, find how and why
He differs from his fellows utterly:

Then, like me, watch when nature by degrees
Grows alive round him, as in Arctic seas
(They said of old) the instinctive water flees

Toward some elected point of central rock,
As though, for its sake only, roamed the flock
Of waves about the waste: awhile they mock

With radiance caught for the occasion,—hues
Of blackest hell now, now such reds and blues
As only heaven could fitly interfuse,—

The mimic monarch of the whirlpool, king
O' the current for a minute: then they wring
Up by the roots and oversweep the thing,

And hasten off, to play again elsewhere
The same part, choose another peak as bare,
They find and flatter, feast and finish there.

When you see what I tell you,—nature dance
About each man of us, retire, advance,
As though the pageant's end were to enhance

His worth, and—once the life, his product, gained—
Roll away elsewhere, keep the strife sustained,
And show thus real, a thing the North but feigned,—

When you acknowledge that one world could do
All the diverse work, old yet ever new.
Divide us, each from other, me from you,—

Why, where's the need of Temple, when the walls
O' the world are that? What use of swells and falls
From Levites' choir, priests' cries, and trumpet-calls?

That one Face, far from vanish, rather grows,
Or decomposes but to recompose,
Become my universe that feels and knows!

MATTHEW 27:65–27:66   Pilate said unto them, Ye have a watch: go your
way, make it as sure as ye can. So they went, and made the sepulchre sure,
sealing the stone, and setting a watch.

Easter Hymn ↗ A. D. HOPE

Make no mistake; there will be no forgiveness;
No voice can harm you and no hand will save;
Fenced by the magic of deliberate darkness
You walk on the sharp edges of the wave;

Trouble with soul again the putrefaction
Where Lazarus three days rotten lies content.
Your human tears will be the seed of faction,
Murder the sequel to your sacrament.

The City of God is built like other cities:
Judas negotiates the loans you float;
You will meet Caiaphas upon committees;
You will be glad of Pilate's casting vote.

Your truest lovers still the foolish virgins,
Your heart will sicken at the marriage feasts
Knowing they watch you from the darkened gardens
Being polite to your official guests.

MATTHEW 28:1   In the end of the sabbath, as it began to dawn toward the
first day of the week, came Mary Magdalene and the other Mary to see the
sepulchre.

Resurrection, Imperfect ᴣ JOHN DONNE

Sleep sleep old sun, thou canst not have repast
As yet, the wound thou tookst on Friday last;
Sleep then, and rest; The world may bear thy stay,
A better sun rose before thee to day,
Who, not content to enlighten all that dwell
On the earth's face, as thou, enlightened hell,
And made the dark fires languish in that vale,
As, at thy presence here, our fires grow pale.
Whose body having walked on earth, and now
Hasting to Heaven, would, that he might allow
Himself unto all stations, and fill all,
For these three days become a mineral;
He was all gold when he lay down, but rose
All tincture, and doth not alone dispose
Leaden and iron wills to good, but is
Of power to make even sinful flesh like his.
Had one of those, whose credulous piety
Thought, that a soul one might discern and see

Go from a body, at this sepulcher been,
And, issuing from the sheet, this body seen,
He would have justly thought this body a soul,
If not of any man, yet of the whole.

Mary's Song ↜ SYLVIA PLATH

The Sunday lamb cracks in its fat.
The fat
Sacrifices its opacity. . . .

A window, holy gold.
The fire makes it precious,
The same fire

Melting the tallow heretics,
Ousting the Jews.
Their thick palls float

Over the cicatrix of Poland, burnt-out
Germany.
They do not die.

Grey birds obsess my heart,
Mouth-ash, ash of eye.
They settle. On the high

Precipice
That emptied one man into space
The ovens glowed like heavens, incandescent.

It is a heart,
This holocaust I walk in,
O golden child the world will kill and eat.

LUKE 24:1   Now upon the first day of the week, very early in the morning,
they came unto the sepulchre, bringing the spices which they had prepared,
and certain others with them.

MARK 16:3–16:4 And they said among themselves, Who shall roll us away the stone from the door of the sepulchre? And when they looked, they saw that the stone was rolled away: for it was very great.

To Jesus on His Birthday   ᴥ   EDNA ST. VINCENT MILLAY

For this your mother sweated in the cold,
For this you bled upon the bitter tree:
A yard of tinsel ribbon bought and sold;
A paper wreath; a day at home for me.
The merry bells ring out, the people kneel;
Up goes the man of God before the crowd;
With voice of honey and with eyes of steel
He drones your humble gospel to the proud.
Nobody listens. Less than the wind that blows
Are all your words to us you died to save.
O Prince of Peace ! O Sharon's dewy Rose !
How mute you lie within your vaulted grave.
    The stone the angel rolled away with tears
    Is back upon your mouth these thousand years.

LUKE 24:6–24:8 He is not here, but is risen: remember how he spake unto you when he was yet in Galilee, Saying, The Son of man must be delivered into the hands of sinful men, and be crucified, and the third day rise again. And they remembered his words,

Resurrection   ᴥ   JOHN DONNE

Moist with one drop of thy blood, my dry soul
Shall (though she now be in extreme degree
Too stony hard, and yet too fleshly,) be
Freed by that drop, from being starved, hard, or foul,
And life, by this death abled, shall control
Death, whom thy death slew; nor shall to me
Fear of first or last death, bring misery,
If in thy little book my name thou enrol,
Flesh in that long sleep is not putrified,
But made that there, of which, and for which 'twas;

Nor can by other means be glorified.
May then sins sleep, and deaths soon from me pass,
That waked from both, I again risen may
Salute the last, and everlasting day.

JOHN 20:1–20:2   . . .Mary Magdalene I runneth, and cometh to Simon
Peter, and to the other disciple, whom Jesus loved, and saith unto them,
They have taken away the Lord out of the sepulchre, and we know not where
they have laid him.

April Fool's Day, or, St Mary of Egypt ~

JOHN BERRYMAN

—Thass a funny title, Mr Bones.
—When down she saw her feet, sweet fish, on the threshold,
she considered her fair shoulders
and all them hundreds who have held them, all
the more who to her mime thickened & maled
from the supple stage,

and seeing her feet, in a visit, side by side
paused on the sill of The Tomb, she shrank: 'No.
They are not worthy,
fondled by many' and rushed from The Crucified
back through her followers out of the city ho
across the suburbs, plucky

to dare my desert in her late daylight
of animals and sands. She fall prone.
Only wind whistled.
And forty-seven years went by like Einstein.
We celebrate her feast with our caps on,
whom God has not visited.

JOHN 20:3–20:5   Peter therefore went forth, and that other disciple, and
came to the sepulchre. So they ran both together: and the other disciple did
outrun Peter, and came first to the sepulchre. And he stooping down, and
looking in, saw the linen clothes lying; yet went he not in.

Composed in one of the Valleys of Westmoreland, on Easter Sunday ✠ WILLIAM WORDSWORTH

With each recurrence of this glorious morn
That saw the Saviour in his human frame
Rise from the dead, erewhile the cottage-dame
Put on fresh raiment—till that hour unworn:
Domestic hand the home-bred wool had shorn,
And she who span it culled the daintiest fleece,
In thoughtful reverence to the Prince of Peace,
Whose temples bled beneath the platted thorn.
A blessed estate when piety sublime
These humble props disdained not! O green dales!
Sad may I be who heard your sabbath chime
When art's abused inventions were unknown;
Kind nature's various wealth was all your own;
And benefits were weighed in reason's scales!

JOHN 20:6–20:10   Then cometh Simon Peter following him, and went into the sepulchre, and seeth the linen clothes lie, And the napkin, that was about his head, not lying with the linen clothes, but wrapped together in a place by itself. Then went in also that other disciple, which came first to the sepulchre, and he saw, and believed. For as yet they knew not the scripture, that he must rise again from the dead. Then the disciples went away again unto their own home.

Easter 1984 ✠ LES MURRAY

When we saw human dignity
healing humans in the middle of the day

we moved in on him slowly
under the incalculable gravity

of old freedom, of our own freedom,
under atmospheres of consequence, of justice

under which no one needs to thank anyone.
If this was God, we would get even.

And in the end we nailed him,
lashed, spittled, stretched him limb from limb.

We would settle with dignity
for the anguish it had caused us,

we'd send it to be abstract again, we would set it free.

                    •

But we had raised up evolution.
It would not stop being human.

Ever afterwards, the accumulation
of freedom would end in this man

whipped, bloodied, getting the treatment.
It would look like man himself getting it.

He was freeing us, painfully, from freedom,
justice, dignity—he was discharging them

of their deadly ambiguous deposit,
remaking out of them the primal day

in which he was free not to have borne it
and we were free not to have done it,

free never to torture man again,
free to believe him risen.

                    •

Remember the day when life increased,
explainably or outright, was haloed in poignancy,

straight life, given not attained, unlurching ecstasy,
arrest of the guards for once, and ourself released,

splendour taking detail, beyond the laughter-and-tears
as if these were gateway to it, a still or moving utterness

in and all around us? Some have been this human
night and day, steadily. Flashes of it have drawn others on.

A laser of this would stand the litter-bound or Lazarus
upright, stammering, or unshroud absent Jesus

whose anguish was to be for a whole day lost to this,
making of himself the companionway of our species

up from where such love is an unreal, half-forgotten
peak, and not yet the baseline of the human.

Appearances

LUKE 24:33–24:43   And they rose up the same hour, and returned to
Jerusalem, and found the eleven gathered together, and them that were with
them, Saying, The Lord is risen indeed, and hath appeared to Simon. And
they told what things were done in the way, and how he was known of them
in breaking of bread. And as they thus spake, Jesus himself stood in the
midst of them, and saith unto them, Peace be unto you. But they were terri-
fied and affrighted, and supposed that they had seen a spirit. And he said
unto them, Why are ye troubled? and why do thoughts arise in your hearts?
Behold my hands and my feet, that it is I myself: handle me, and see; for a
spirit hath not flesh and bones, as ye see me have. And when he had thus
spoken, he shewed them his hands and his feet. And while they yet believed
not for joy, and wondered, he said unto them, Have ye here any meat? And
they gave him a piece of a broiled fish, and of an honeycomb. And he took
it, and did eat before them.

Ballad of the Goodly Fere   ᴈ   EZRA POUND
Simon Zelotes[28] speaking after the Crucifixion.
Fere = Mate, Companion

Ha' we lost the goodliest fere o' all
For the priests and the gallows tree?
Aye lover was he of brawny men,
O' ships and the open sea.

28 LUKE 6:15.

When they came wi' a host to take Our Man
His smile was good to see,
"First let these go!" quo' our Goodly Fere,
"Or I'll see ye damned," says he.

Aye he sent us out through the crossed high spears
And the scorn of his laugh rang free,
"Why took ye not me when I walked about
Alone in the town?" says he.

Oh we drank his "Hale" in the good red wine
When we last made company,
No capon priest was the Goodly Fere
But a man o' men was he.

I ha' seen him drive a hundred men
Wi' a bundle o' cords swung free,
That they took the high and holy house
For their pawn and treasury.

They'll no' get him a' in a book I think
Though they write it cunningly;
No mouse of the scrolls was the Goodly Fere
But aye loved the open sea.

If they think they ha' snared our Goodly Fere
They are fools to the last degree.
"I'll go to the feast," quo' our Goodly Fere,
"Though I go to the gallows tree."

"Ye ha' seen me heal the lame and blind,
And wake the dead," says he,
"Ye shall see one thing to master all:
'Tis how a brave man dies on the tree."

A son of God was the Goodly Fere
That bade us his brothers be.
I ha' seen him cow a thousand men.
I have seen him upon the tree.

He cried no cry when they drave the nails
And the blood gushed hot and free.
The hounds of the crimson sky gave tongue
But never a cry cried he.

I ha' seen him cow a thousand men
On the hills o' Galilee,
They whined as he walked out calm between,
Wi' his eyes like the grey o' the sea,

Like the sea that brooks no voyaging
With the winds unleashed and free,
Like the sea that he cowed at Genseret
Wi' twey words spoke' suddently.

A master of men was the Goodly Fere,
A mate of the wind and sea,
If they think they ha' slain our Goodly Fere
They are fools eternally.

I ha' seen him eat o' the honey-comb
Sin' they nailed him to the tree.

LUKE 24:44–24:51 And he said unto them, These are the words which I spake unto you, while I was yet with you, that all things must be fulfilled, which were written in the law of Moses, and in the prophets, and in the psalms, concerning me. Then opened he their understanding, that they might understand the scriptures, And said unto them, Thus it is written, and thus it behoved Christ to suffer, and to rise from the dead the third day: And that repentance and remission of sins should be preached in his name among all nations, beginning at Jerusalem. And ye are witnesses of these things. And, behold, I send the promise of my Father upon you: but tarry ye in the city of Jerusalem, until ye be endued with power from on high. And he led them out as far as to Bethany, and he lifted up his hands, and blessed them. And it came to pass, while he blessed them, he was parted from them, and carried up into heaven.

Ascention ↵ JOHN DONNE

Salute the last and everlasting day,
Joy at the uprising of this Sun, and Son,
Ye whose just tears, or tribulation
Have purely washed, or burnt your drossy clay;
Behold the Highest, parting hence away,
Lightens the dark clouds, which he treads upon,
Nor doth he by ascending, show alone,
But first he, and he first enters the way.
O strong Ram, which hast battered heaven for me,
Mild Lamb, which with thy blood, hast marked the path;
Bright Torch, which shin'st, that I the way may see,
Oh, with thy own blood quench thy own just wrath,
And if thy holy Spirit, my Muse did raise,
Deign at my hands this crown of prayer and praise.

Ascension ↵ DENIS DEVLIN

It happens through the blond window, the trees
With diverse leaves divide the light, light birds;
Aengus, the god of Love, my shoulders brushed
With birds, you could say lark or thrush or thieves

And not be right yet—or ever right—
For it was God's Son foreign to our moor:
When I looked out the window, all was white,
And what's beloved in the heart was sure,

With such a certainty ascended He,
The Son of Man who deigned Himself to be:
That when we lifted out of sleep, there was
Life with its dark, and love above the laws.

MARK 16:9–16:11   Now when Jesus was risen early the first day of the week, he appeared first to Mary Magdalene, out of whom he had cast seven devils. And she went and told them that had been with him, as they mourned and wept. And they, when they had heard that he was alive, and had been seen of her, believed not.

To St Mary Magdalen   HENRY CONSTABLE

For few nights' solace in delicious bed,
    where heat of lust, did kindle flames of hell:
    thou nak'd on naked rock in desert cell
    lay thirty years, and tears of grief did shed.
But for that time, thy heart there sorrowed,
    thou now in heaven eternally dost dwell,
    and for each tear, which from thine eyes then fell,
    a sea of pleasure now is rendered.
If short delights entice my hart to stray,
    let me by thy long penance learn to know
    how dear I should for trifling pleasures pay:
And if I virtue's rough beginning shun,
    Let thy eternal joys unto me show
    what high reward, by little pain is won.

JOHN 20:26–20:29   And after eight days again his disciples were within, and Thomas with them: then came Jesus, the doors being shut, and stood in the midst, and said, Peace be unto you. Then saith he to Thomas, Reach hither thy finger, and behold my hands; and reach hither thy hand, and thrust it into my side: and be not faithless, but believing. And Thomas answered and said unto him, My Lord and my God. Jesus saith unto him, Thomas, because thou hast seen me, thou hast believed: blessed are they that have not seen, and yet have believed.

Split the Lark – and you'll find the Music –
EMILY DICKINSON

Split the Lark – and you'll find the Music –
Bulb after Bulb, in Silver rolled –
Scantily dealt to the Summer Morning
Saved for your Ear when Lutes be old.

Loose the Flood – you shall find it patent –
Gush after Gush, reserved for you –
Scarlet Experiment! Sceptic Thomas!
Now, do you doubt that your Bird was true?

JOHN 21:18–21:19   Verily, verily, I say unto thee, When thou wast young, thou girdedst thyself, and walkedst whither thou wouldest: but when thou shalt be old, thou shalt stretch forth thy hands, and another shall gird thee, and carry thee whither thou wouldest not. This spake he, signifying by what death he should glorify God. And when he had spoken this, he saith unto him, Follow me.

The Crown ᧒ JOHN DONNE

Deign at my hands this crown of prayer and praise,
Weaved in my low devout melancholy,
Thou which of good, hast, yea art treasury,
All changing unchanged Ancient of days;
But do not, with a vile crown of frail bays,
Reward my muses white sincerity,
But what thy thorny crown gained, that give me,
A crown of glory, which doth flower always;
The ends crown our works, but thou crownst our ends,
For, at our end begins our endless rest;
The first last end, now zealously possessed,
With a strong sober thirst, my soul attends.
'Tis time that heart and voice be lifted high,
Salvation to all that will is nigh.

ACTS and EPISTLES

ACTS 1:15–1:22   And in those days Peter stood up in the midst of the disciples, and said, (the number of names together were about an hundred and twenty,) Men and brethren, this scripture must needs have been fulfilled, which the Holy Ghost by the mouth of David spake before concerning Judas, which was guide to them that took Jesus. . . . Wherefore of these men which have companied with us all the time that the Lord Jesus went in and out among us, Beginning from the baptism of John, unto that same day that he was taken up from us, must one be ordained to be a witness with us of his resurrection.

The Ballad of Joking Jesus ✄ JAMES JOYCE

—I'm the queerest young fellow that you ever heard.
My mother's a jew, my father's a bird.
With Joseph the joiner I cannot agree,
So here's to disciples and Calvary.

—If anyone thinks that I amn't divine
He'll get no free drinks when I'm making the wine
But have to drink water and wish it were plain
That I make when the wine becomes water again.

—Goodbye, now, goodbye. Write down all I said
And tell Tom, Dick and Harry I rose from the dead.
What's bred in the bone cannot fail me to fly
And Olivet's breezy . . . Goodbye, now, goodbye.

ACTS 3:2–3:9   And a certain man lame from his mother's womb was carried,
whom they laid daily at the gate of the temple which is called Beautiful, to
ask alms of them that entered into the temple; Who seeing Peter and John
about to go into the temple asked an alms. And Peter, fastening his eyes
upon him with John, said, Look on us. And he gave heed unto them, expect-
ing to receive something of them. Then Peter said, Silver and gold have I
none; but such as I have give I thee: In the name of Jesus Christ of
Nazareth rise up and walk. And he took him by the right hand, and lifted
him up: and immediately his feet and ancle bones received strength. And
he leaping up stood, and walked, and entered with them into the temple,
walking, and leaping, and praising God. And all the people saw him walking
and praising God:

Faith Healing ✄ PHILIP LARKIN

Slowly the women file to where he stands
Upright in rimless glasses, silver hair,
Dark suit, white collar. Stewards tirelessly
Persuade them onwards to his voice and hands,
Within whose warm spring rain of loving care
Each dwells some twenty seconds. Now, dear child,
What's wrong, the deep American voice demands,

And, scarcely pausing, goes into a prayer
Directing God about this eye, that knee.
Their heads are clasped abruptly; then, exiled

Like losing thoughts, they go in silence; some
Sheepishly stray, not back into their lives
Just yet; but some stay stiff, twitching and loud
With deep hoarse tears, as if a kind of dumb
And idiot child within them still survives
To re-awake at kindness, thinking a voice
At last calls them alone, that hands have come
To lift and lighten; and such joy arrives
Their thick tongues blort, their eyes squeeze grief, a crowd
Of huge unheard answers jam and rejoice –

What's wrong! Moustached in flowered frocks they shake:
By now, all's wrong. In everyone there sleeps
A sense of life lived according to love.
To some it means the difference they could make
By loving others, but across most it sweeps
As all they might have done had they been loved.
That nothing cures. An immense slackening ache,
As when, thawing, the rigid landscape weeps,
Spreads slowly through them – that, and the voice above
Saying *Dear child*, and all time has disproved.

ACTS 5:29–5:32   Then Peter and the other apostles answered and said, We ought to obey God rather than men. The God of our fathers raised up Jesus, whom ye slew and hanged on a tree. Him hath God exalted with his right hand to be a Prince and a Saviour, for to give repentance to Israel, and forgiveness of sins. And we are his witnesses of these things; and so is also the Holy Ghost, whom God hath given to them that obey him.

There was a Saviour   ⁊ DYLAN THOMAS

There was a saviour
Rarer than radium,
Commoner than water, crueller than truth;
Children kept from the sun

Assembled at his tongue
   To hear the golden note turn in a groove,
Prisoners of wishes locked their eyes
In the jails and studies of his keyless smiles.

   The voice of children says
   From a lost wilderness
There was calm to be done in his safe unrest,
      When hindering man hurt
      Man, animal, or bird
   We hid our fears in that murdering breath,
Silence, silence to do, when earth grew loud,
In lairs and asylums of the tremendous shout.

   There was glory to hear
   In the churches of his tears,
Under his downy arm you sighed as he struck,
      O you who could not cry
      On to the ground when a man died
   Put a tear for joy in the unearthly flood
And laid your cheek against a cloud-formed shell:
Now in the dark there is only yourself and myself.

   Two proud, blacked brothers cry,
   Winter-locked side by side,
To this inhospitable hollow year,
      O we who could not stir
      One lean sigh when we heard
   Greed on man beating near and fire neighbour
But wailed and nested in the sky-blue wall
Now break a giant tear for the little known fall,

   For the drooping of homes
   That did not nurse our bones,
Brave deaths of only ones but never found,
      Now see, alone in us,
      Our own true strangers' dust
   Ride through the doors of our unentered house.
Exiled in us we arouse the soft,
Unclenched, armless, silk and rough love that breaks all rocks.

ACTS *7:59–7:60*   And they stoned Stephen, calling upon God, and saying, Lord Jesus, receive my spirit. And he kneeled down, and cried with a loud voice, Lord, lay not this sin to their charge. And when he had said this, he fell asleep.

Stephen to Lazarus ᔆ C. S. LEWIS

But was I the first martyr, who
Gave up no more than life, while you,
Already free among the dead,
Your rags stripped off, your fetters shed,
Surrendered what all other men
Irrevocably keep, and when
Your battered ship at anchor lay
Seemingly safe in the dark bay
No ripple stirs, obediently
Put out a second time to sea
Well knowing that your death (in vain
Died once) must all be died again?

ACTS *9:1–9:9*   And Saul, yet breathing out threatenings and slaughter against the disciples of the Lord, went unto the high priest, And desired of him letters to Damascus to the synagogues, that if he found any of this way, whether they were men or women, he might bring them bound unto Jerusalem. And as he journeyed, he came near Damascus: and suddenly there shined round about him a light from heaven: And he fell to the earth, and heard a voice saying unto him, Saul, Saul, why persecutest thou me? And he said, Who art thou, Lord? And the Lord said, I am Jesus whom thou persecutest: it is hard for thee to kick against the pricks. And he trembling and astonished said, Lord, what wilt thou have me to do? And the Lord said unto him, Arise, and go into the city, and it shall be told thee what thou must do. And the men which journeyed with him stood speechless, hearing a voice, but seeing no man.

And Saul arose from the earth; and when his eyes were opened, he saw no man: but they led him by the hand, and brought him into Damascus. And he was three days without sight, and neither did eat nor drink.

Near Damascus ᎓ W. S. DIPIERO

The antlered scarab rolled a dungball
for its brood; a red ant, tipsy,
bulldozed a flinty wedge of chaff.
Mud slots from the recent rain,
now crusted over by the heat—
moon mountains seen close up; my mouth
plugged with road grit and surprise
just when I tried to shout *no*
to the blunt lightning spike that stopped me. . .

In the mountains of the moon I saw
a wasp dragging a grasshopper
to a frothing nest, grubs lingering
through their episode, and larvae
I'd have chewed like honeycomb
if it would have saved my sight.
Antaeus inhaled force from dirt;
he was luckier, never much
for visions, and too far gone.

In my head, I see this body
dumped flat. Painted in above,
the horse twists and straddles me,
his eyes flare, ecstatic, new,
contemptuous of the thing that fell,
while the light-shaft curries his flank
and nails me down, the unloved me,
rousted, found out, blasted, saved
down in the road's pearly filth.

ACTS 9:17–9:18   And Ananias went his way, and entered into the house;
and putting his hands on him said, Brother Saul, the Lord, even Jesus, that
appeared unto thee in the way as thou camest, hath sent me, that thou
mightest receive thy sight, and be filled with the Holy Ghost. And immedi-
ately there fell from his eyes as it had been scales: and he received sight
forthwith, and arose, and was baptized.

St. Paul ᔕ THOMAS MERTON

When I was Saul, and sat among the cloaks,
My eyes were stones, I saw no sight of heaven,
Open to take the spirit of the twisting Stephen.
When I was Saul, and sat among the rocks,
I locked my eyes, and made my brain my tomb,
Sealed with what boulders rolled across my reason!

When I was Saul and walked upon the blazing desert
My road was quiet as a trap.
I feared what word would split high noon with light
And lock my life, and try to drive me mad:
And thus I saw the Voice that struck me dead.

Tie up my breath, and wind me in white sheets of anguish,
And lay me in my three days' sepulchre
Until I find my Easter in a vision.

Oh Christ! Give back my life, go, cross Damascus,
Find out my Ananias in that other room:
Command him, as you do, in this my dream;
He knows my locks, and owns my ransom,
Waits for Your word to take his keys and come.

ACTS 17:22–17:28   Then Paul stood in the midst of Mars' hill, and said, Ye men of Athens, I perceive that in all things ye are too superstitious. For as I passed by, and beheld your devotions, I found an altar with this inscription, TO THE UNKNOWN GOD. Whom therefore ye ignorantly worship, him declare I unto you. God that made the world and all things therein, seeing that he is Lord of heaven and earth, dwelleth not in temples made with hands; Neither is worshipped with men's hands, as though he needed any thing, seeing he giveth to all life, and breath, and all things; And hath made of one blood all nations of men for to dwell on all the face of the earth, and hath determined the times before appointed, and the bounds of their habitation; That they should seek the Lord, if haply they might feel after him, and find him, though he be not far from every one of us: For in him we live, and move, and have our being; as certain also of your own poets have said, For we are also his offspring.

The Search ᘏ HENRY VAUGHAN

'Tis now clear day: I see a rose
Bud in the bright East, and disclose
The pilgrim-sun; all night have I
Spent in a roving ecstasy
To find my Savior; I have been
As far as Beth'lem, and have seen
His inn, and cradle; Being there
I met the Wise-men, asked them where
He might be found, or what star can
Now point him out, grown up a man?
To Egypt hence I fled, ran o'er
All her parched bosom to Nile's shore
Her yearly nurse; came back, enquired
Amongst the Doctors, and desired
To see the Temple, but was shown
A little dust, and for the town
A heap of ashes, where some said
A small bright sparkle was a bed,
Which would one day (beneath the pole,)
Awake, and then refine the whole.
    Tired here, I come to Sychar; thence
To Jacob's well, bequeathed since
Unto his sons, (where often they
In those calm, golden evenings lay
Watering their flocks, and having spent
Those white days, drove home to the tent
Their well-fleeced train;) And here (O fate!)
I sit, where once my Savior sat;
The angry spring in bubbles swelled
Which broke in sighs still, as they filled,
And whispered, *Jesus had been there*
But *Jacob's children would not hear.*
Loth hence to part, at last I rise
But with the fountain in my eyes,
And here a fresh search is decreed
He must be found, where he did bleed;
I walk the garden, and there see
Ideas of his agony,
And moving anguishments that set

His blest face in a bloody sweat;
I climbed the hill, perused the Cross
Hung with my gain, and his great loss,
Never did tree bear fruit like this,
Balsam of Soul, the body's bliss;
But, O his grave! where I saw lent
(For he had none,) a monument,
An undefiled, and new-hewed one,
But there was not the corner-stone;
Sure (then said I,) my quest is vain,
He'll not be found, where he was slain,
So mild a Lamb can never be
'Midst so much blood, and cruelty;
I'll to the Wilderness, and can
Find beasts more merciful than man,
He lived there safe, 'twas his retreat
From the fierce Jew, and Herod's heat,
And forty days withstood the fell,
And high temptations of hell;
With seraphims there talked he
His father's flaming ministry,
He heavened their walks, and with his eyes
Made those wild shades a Paradise,
Thus was the desert sanctified
To be the refuge of his bride;
I'll thither then; See, it is day,
The sun's broke through to guide my way.
    But as I urged thus, and writ down
What pleasures should my journey crown,
What silent paths, what shades, and cells,
Faire, virgin-flowers, and hallowed wells
I should rove in, and rest my head
Where my dear Lord did often tread,
Sugaring all dangers with success,
Me thought I heard one singing thus:

        Leave, leave, thy gadding thoughts;
            Who pores
            and spies
        Still out of doors

descries
Within them nought.

The skin, and shell of things
Though fair,
are not
Thy wish, nor prayer
but got
My mere despair
of wings.

To rack old elements,
or dust
and say
Sure here he must
needs stay
Is not the way,
nor just.

Search well another world; who studies this,
Travels in clouds, seeks manna, where none is.

ACTS 20:9–20:12   And there sat in a window a certain young man named
Eutychus, being fallen into a deep sleep: and as Paul was long preaching, he
sunk down with sleep, and fell down from the third loft, and was taken up
dead. And Paul went down, and fell on him, and embracing him said,
Trouble not yourselves; for his life is in him. When he therefore was come
up again, and had broken bread, and eaten, and talked a long while, even
till break of day, so he departed. And they brought the young man alive, and
were not a little comforted.

Eutychus ⟋ ROSEMARY DOBSON

The first day of the week he spoke to them
In Troas when they met to break their bread,
And preached till midnight. Eutychus afterwards
Could not remember anything he said.

This was an irony not easily faced:
Indeed, he kept it largely unconfessed
That after travelling many days and nights
In dangers often, and by hardships pressed,

To hear the words of Paulus and receive
Some healing comfort for his troubled mind
He could not fix his thoughts, was sorely vexed
By others pushing in the crowd behind,

Till, smarting with discomfiture and grief,
He reached a window not above his height
And climbing on the sill and looking out
Breathed in the soporific airs of night.

To saints who have received the word of God
One lifetime is too short for telling all
The joyful news. And certainly an hour
Did not suffice in Troas for Saint Paul.

His discourse lengthened. Eutychus's head
Sank on his chest (and for his sake we weep),
The saint in words that none who heard forgot
Spoke of Damascus. Eutychus was asleep.

Now they were gathered in an upper room
That rose three lofts above, as it is said,
And from his window Eutychus fell down
And those that took him up pronounced him dead.

Saint Paul went straightway to the youth and held
His body in his arms, and cried to those
Who stood about, 'Be troubled not. For see
His life is in him.' And the young man rose,

His troubled mind at peace, his body healed.
And others there were saved that else were lost.
And in the morning Paul went on afoot
To reach Jerusalem by Pentecost.

I like this story of young Eutychus
For I, like him, am troubled too, and weak,
And may, like him, be too preoccupied
To listen if a saint should come to speak.

And yet, I think, if some event befall
To bring me face to face with holiness,
I should not fail to recognize the truth
And spring to life again, like Eutychus.

ROMANS 2:1–2:3   Therefore thou art inexcusable, O man, whosoever thou
art that judgest: for wherein thou judgest another, thou condemnest thyself;
for thou that judgest doest the same things. But we are sure that the judg-
ment of God is according to truth against them which commit such things.
And thinkest thou this, O man, that judgest them which do such things,
and doest the same, that thou shalt escape the judgment of God?

Dies Iræ   ᴊ   THOMAS BABINGTON MACAULAY

On that great, that awful day,
This vain world shall pass away.
Thus the sibyl sang of old,
Thus hath holy David told.[29]
There shall be a deadly fear
When the Avenger shall appear,
And unveiled before his eye
All the works of man shall lie.
Hark I to the great trumpet's tones
Pealing o'er the place of bones:
Hark! it waketh from their bed
All the nations of the dead,—
In a countless throng to meet,
At the eternal judgment seat.
Nature sickens with dismay,
Death may not retain its prey;
And before the Maker stand
All the creatures of his hand.

29 see PSA 110

The great book shall be unfurled,
Whereby God shall judge the world:
What was distant shall be near,
What was hidden shall be clear.
To what shelter shall I fly?
To what guardian shall I cry?
Oh, in that destroying hour,
Source of goodness, Source of power,
Show thou, of thine own free grace,
Help unto a helpless race.
Though I plead not at thy throne
Aught that I for thee have done,
Do not thou unmindful be,
Of what thou hast borne for me:
Of the wandering, of the scorn,
Of the scourge, and of the thorn.
Jesus, hast thou borne the pain,
And hath all been borne in vain?
Shall thy vengeance smite the head
For whose ransom thou hast bled?
Thou, whose dying blessing gave
Glory to a guilty slave:
Thou, who from the crew unclean
Didst release the Magdalene:
Shall not mercy vast and free,
Evermore be found in thee?
Father, turn on me thine eyes,
See my blushes, hear my cries;
Faint though be the cries I make,
Save me for thy mercy's sake,
From the worm, and from the fire,
From the torments of thine ire.
Fold me with the sheep that stand
Pure and safe at thy right hand.
Hear thy guilty child implore thee,
Rolling in the dust before thee.
Oh the horrors of that day!
When this frame of sinful clay,
Starting from its burial place,
Must behold thee face to face.
Hear and pity, hear and aid,

Spare the creatures thou hast made.
Mercy, mercy, save, forgive,
Oh, who shall look on thee and live?

ROMANS 5:6–5:14   For when we were yet without strength, in due time
Christ died for the ungodly. For scarcely for a righteous man will one die:
yet peradventure for a good man some would even dare to die. But God
commendeth his love toward us, in that, while we were yet sinners, Christ
died for us. Much more then, being now justified by his blood, we shall be
saved from wrath through him. For if, when we were enemies, we were rec-
onciled to God by the death of his Son, much more, being reconciled, we
shall be saved by his life. And not only so, but we also joy in God through
our Lord Jesus Christ, by whom we have now received the atonement.
Wherefore, as by one man sin entered into the world, and death by sin;
and so death passed upon all men, for that all have sinned: (For until the
law sin was in the world: but sin is not imputed when there is no law.
Nevertheless death reigned from Adam to Moses, even over them that had
not sinned after the similitude of Adam's transgression, who is the figure
of him that was to come. . . .)

Meditation Three ᔿ EDWARD TAYLOR
Second Series

Like to the marigold, I blushing close
    My golden blossoms when thy sun goes down:
Moistening my leaves with dewy sighs, half froze
    By the nocturnal cold, that hoars my crown.
    Mine apples ashes are in apple shells
    And dirty too: strange and bewitching spells!

When Lord, mine eye doth spy thy grace to beam
    Thy mediatorial glory in the shine
Out spouted so from Adam's typic stream
    And emblemized in Noah's polished shrine
    Thine theirs outshines so far it makes their glory
    In brightest colors, seem a smoky story.

But when mine eye full of these beams, doth cast
    Its rays upon my dusty essence thin

Impregnate with a spark divine, defaced,
    All candied o'er with leprosy of sin,
    Such influences on my spirits light,
    Which them as bitter gall, or cold ice smite.

My bristled sins hence do so horrid 'pear,
    None but thyself, (and thou decked up must be
In thy transcendent glory sparkling clear)
    A mediator unto God for me.
    So high they rise, faith scarce can toss a sight
    Over their head upon thyself to light.

Is't possible such glory, Lord, e'er should
    Center its love on me sin's dunghill else?
My case up take? make it its own? Who would
    Wash with his blood my blots out? Crown his shelf
    Or dress his golden cupboard with such ware?
    This makes my pale faced hope almost despair.

Yet let my Titimouse's quill suck in
    Thy grace's milk pails some small drop: or cart
A bit, or splinter of some ray, the wing
    Of grace's sun sprindged out, into my heart:
    To build there wonders chapel where thy praise
    Shall be the Psalms sung forth in gracious lays.

ROMANS 6:8–6:9   Now if we be dead with Christ, we believe that we shall also live with him: Knowing that Christ being raised from the dead dieth no more; death hath no more dominion over him.

And death shall have no dominion   ☞   DYLAN THOMAS

And death shall have no dominion.
Dead men naked they shall be one
With the man in the wind and the west moon;
When their bones are picked clean and the clean bones gone,
They shall have stars at elbow and foot;
Though they go mad they shall be sane,
Though they sink through the sea they shall rise again;

Though lovers be lost love shall not;
And death shall have no dominion.

And death shall have no dominion.
Under the windings of the sea
They lying long shall not die windily;
Twisting on racks when sinews give way,
Strapped to a wheel, yet they shall not break;
Faith in their hands shall snap in two,
And the unicorn evils run them through;
Split all ends up they shan't crack;
And death shall have no dominion.

And death shall have no dominion.
No more may gulls cry at their ears
Or waves break loud on the seashores;
Where blew a flower may a flower no more
Lifts its head to the blows of the rain;
Though they be mad and dead as nails,
Heads of the characters hammer through daisies;
Break in the sun till the sun breaks down,
And death shall have no dominion.

ROMANS 6:21–6:23   What fruit had ye then in those things whereof ye are
now ashamed? for the end of those things is death. But now being made
free from sin, and become servants to God, ye have your fruit unto holi-
ness, and the end everlasting life. For the wages of sin is death; but the gift
of God is eternal life through Jesus Christ our Lord.

AIDS, Among Other Things   ꝫ   PETER KOCAN

The wages of sin is death. These words run
With a quiet persistence in my brain,
As though that biblical archaic phrase
Had been precisely meant to diagnose
What's bothering an unreligious man

Like me today. The blasphemy was met
By sins of silence, cowardice and doubt,

And so we muddied what clear light might thresh
The good from the bad or merely foolish
When the consequences begin to hit.

I fear that we have too glibly mocked
For too long in the word and in the act
To hope we've any second chances owed
Or plead extenuation when we're paid
The wages we knew always to expect.

We acquiesce to birth-in-bottles now,
Dissimulate on every law we knew
Was solemn in the covenants we had
With whatever we call Nature or God,
Yet we never think to reap what we sow.

The ills multiply as we unlearn
That ancient wise humility of men
Who saw, beyond the wreckage of taboos,
Despair and madness, hatred and disease
The promised payment in the promised coin.

ROMANS 7:22–7:24   For I delight in the law of God after the inward man:
But I see another law in my members, warring against the law of my mind,
and bringing me into captivity to the law of sin which is in my members. O
wretched man that I am! who shall deliver me from the body of this death?

To Heaven ᔌ BEN JONSON

Good, and great God, can I not think of thee,
    But it must, straight, my melancholy be?
Is it interpreted in me disease,
    That, laden with my sins, I seek for ease?
O, be thou witness, that the reins dost know,
    And hearts of all, if I be sad for show,
And judge me after: if I dare pretend
    To ought but grace, or aim at other end.
As thou art all, so be thou all to me,
    First, midst, and last, converted one, and three;

My faith, my hope, my love: and in this state,
   My judge, my witness, and my advocate.
Where have I been this while exiled from thee?
   And whither raped, now thou but stoopst to me?
Dwell, dwell here still O, being every-where,
   How can I doubt to find thee ever, here?
I know my state, both full of shame, and scorn,
   Conceived in sin, and unto labor born,
Standing with fear, and must with horror fall,
   And destined unto judgement, after all.
I feel my griefs too, and there scarce is ground,
   Upon my flesh t'inflict another wound.
Yet dare I not complain, or wish for death
   With holy Paul, lest it be thought the breath
Of discontent; or that these prayers be
   For weariness of life, not love of thee.

FIRST CORINTHIANS 5:6–5:8 Your glorying is not good. Know ye not that a little leaven leaveneth the whole lump? Purge out therefore the old leaven, that ye may be a new lump, as ye are unleavened. For even Christ our passover is sacrificed for us: Therefore let us keep the feast, not with old leaven, neither with the leaven of malice and wickedness; but with the unleavened bread of sincerity and truth.

On a Feast ✒ FRANCIS QUARLES

The Lord of Heaven and Earth has made a feast,
And every soul is an invited guest:
The Word's the food; the Levites are the cooks;
The Fathers' Writings are their diet-books;
But seldom used; for 'tis a fashion grown,
To recommend made dishes of their own:
What they should boil, they bake; what roast, they broil,
Their luscious salads are too sweet with oil:
In brief, 'tis nowadays too great a fault,
T'have too much pepper, and too little salt.

FIRST CORINTHIANS 13:6–13:7   Rejoiceth not in iniquity, but rejoiceth in
the truth; Beareth all things, believeth all things, hopeth all things, endureth
all things.

Forbearance ⌁   SAMUEL TAYLOR COLERIDGE

Gently I took that which ungently came,
And without scorn forgave:—Do thou the same.
A wrong done to thee think a cat's eye spark
Thou wouldst not see, were not thine own heart dark.
Thine own keen sense of wrong that thirsts for sin,
Fear that—the spark self-kindled from within,
Which blown upon will blind thee with its glare,
Or smothered stifle thee with noisome air.
Clap on the extinguisher, pull up the blinds,
And soon the ventilated spirit finds
Its natural daylight. If a foe have kenned,
Or worse than foe, an alienated friend,
A rib of dry rot in thy ship's stout side,
Think it God's message, and in humble pride
With heart of oak replace it;—thine the gains—
Give him the rotten timber for his pains!

FIRST CORINTHIANS 14:5–14:10   I would that ye all spake with tongues but
rather that ye prophesied: for greater is he that prophesieth than he that
speaketh with tongues, except he interpret, that the church may receive edi-
fying. Now, brethren, if I come unto you speaking with tongues, what shall I
profit you, except I shall speak to you either by revelation, or by knowledge,
or by prophesying, or by doctrine? And even things without life giving
sound, whether pipe or harp, except they give a distinction in the sounds,
how shall it be known what is piped or harped? For if the trumpet give an
uncertain sound, who shall prepare himself to the battle? So likewise ye,
except ye utter by the tongue words easy to be understood, how shall it
be known what is spoken? for ye shall speak into the air. There are, it may
be, so many kinds of voices in the world, and none of them is without
signification.

Revelation ﹏ ROBERT FROST

We make ourselves a place apart
   Behind light words that tease and flout,
But oh, the agitated heart
   Till someone really find us out.

'Tis pity if the case require
   (Or so we say) that in the end
We speak the literal to inspire
   The understanding of a friend.

But so with all, from babes that play
   At hide-and-seek to God afar,
So all who hide too well away
   Must speak and tell us where they are.

FIRST CORINTHIANS 15:32   If after the manner of men I have fought with beasts at Ephesus, what advantageth it me, if the dead rise not? let us eat and drink; for to morrow we die.

The Choice ﹏ DANTE GABRIEL ROSSETTI

I

Eat thou and drink; tomorrow thou shalt die.
   Surely the earth, that's wise being very old,
   Needs not our help. Then loose me, love, and hold
Thy sultry hair up from my face; that I
May pour for thee this golden wine, brim-high,
   Till round the glass thy fingers glow like gold.
   We'll drown all hours: thy song, while hours are tolled,
Shall leap, as fountains veil the changing sky.

Now kiss, and think that there are really those,
   My own high-bosomed beauty, who increase
      Vain gold, vain lore, and yet might choose our way!
      Through many years they toil; then on a day
   They die not,—for their life was death,—but cease;
And round their narrow lips the mould falls close.

II

Watch thou and fear; to-morrow thou shalt die.
   Or art thou sure thou shalt have time for death?
   Is not the day which God's word promiseth
To come man knows not when? In yonder sky
Now while we speak, the sun speeds forth: can I
   Or thou assure him of his goal? God's breath
   Even at this moment haply quickeneth
The air to a flame; till spirits, always nigh
Though screened and hid, shall walk the daylight here.
   And dost thou prate of all that men shall do?
      Canst thou, who hast but plagues, presume to be
      Glad in his gladness that comes after thee?
   Will *his* strength slay *thy* worm in Hell? Go to:
Cover thy countenance, and watch, and fear.

III

Think thou and act; to-morrow thou shalt die.
   Outstretched in the sun's warmth upon the shore,
   Thou sayst: "Man's measured path is all gone o'er:
Up all his years, steeply, with strain and sigh,
Man clomb until he touched the truth; and I,
   Even I, am he whom it was destined for."
   How should this be? Art thou then so much more
Than they who sowed, that thou shouldst reap thereby?

Nay, come up hither. From this wave-washed mound
   Unto the furthest flood-brim look with me;
Then reach on with thy thought till it be drowned.
   Miles and miles distant though the last line be,
And though thy soul sail leagues and leagues beyond, —
   Still, leagues beyond those leagues, there is more sea.

FIRST CORINTHIANS 15:46–15:55   Howbeit that was not first which is spiritual, but that which is natural; and afterward that which is spiritual. The first man is of the earth, earthy; the second man is the Lord from heaven. As is the earthy, such are they also that are earthy: and as is the heavenly, such are they also that are heavenly. And as we have borne the image of the earthy, we shall also bear the image of the heavenly. Now this I say, brethren, that flesh and blood cannot inherit the kingdom of God; neither doth corruption inherit incorruption. Behold, I shew you a mystery; We shall not all sleep, but we shall all be changed, In a moment, in the twinkling of an eye, at the last trump: for the trumpet shall sound, and the dead shall be raised incorruptible, and we shall be changed. For this corruptible must put on incorruption, and this mortal must put on immortality. So when this corruptible shall have put on incorruption, and this mortal shall have put on immortality, then shall be brought to pass the saying that is written, Death is swallowed up in victory.

O death, where is thy sting? O grave, where is thy victory?

Ode: The Dying Christian to his Soul ✌
ALEXANDER POPE

Vital spark of heavenly flame!
Quit, oh quit this mortal frame:
  Trembling, hoping, lingering, flying,
  Oh the pain, the bliss of dying!
Cease, fond nature, cease thy strife,
And let me languish into life.

Hark! they whisper; Angels say,
Sister Spirit, come away.
  What is this absorbs me quite?
  Steals my senses, shuts my sight,
Drowns my spirits, draws my breath?
Tell me, my soul, can this be death?

The world recedes; it disappears!
Heaven opens on my eyes! my ears
  With sounds seraphic ring:
Lend, lend your wings! I mount! I fly!
O grave! where is thy victory?
  O death! where is thy sting?

SECOND CORINTHIANS 5:10   For we must all appear before the judgment seat of Christ; that every one may receive the things done in his body, according to that he hath done, whether it be good or bad.

Sonnet XIV ◇ JOHN MILTON
On the Religious Memory of Mrs. Catharine Thomason,
My Christian Friend, Deceased 16 December, 1646

When faith and love which parted from thee never,
    Had ripened thy just soul to dwell with God,
    Meekly thou didst resign this earthy load
    Of death, called life; which us from life doth sever.
Thy works and alms and all thy good endeavor
    Stayed not behind, nor in the grave were trod;
    But, as faith pointed with her golden rod,
    Followed thee up to joy and bliss for ever.
Love led them on, and faith who knew them best
    Thy handmaids, clad them o'er with purple beams
    And azure wings, that up they flew so dressed,
And spake the truth of thee in glorious themes
    Before the Judge? who thenceforth bid thee rest
    And drink thy fill of pure immortal stream.

EPHESIANS 4:4–4:10   There is one body, and one Spirit, even as ye are called in one hope of your calling; One Lord, one faith, one baptism, One God and Father of all, who is above all, and through all, and in you all. But unto every one of us is given grace according to the measure of the gift of Christ. Wherefore he saith, When he ascended up on high, he led captivity captive, and gave gifts unto men. (Now that he ascended, what is it but that he also descended first into the lower parts of the earth? He that descended is the same also that ascended up far above all heavens, that he might fill all things.)

Adam Lay I-bounden ◇ ANONYMOUS

Adam lay i-bounden, bounden in a bond;
Four thousand winter thought he not too long.
And all was for an apple, an apple that he took,
As clerks finden written in their book.

Ne had the apple taken been, the apple taken been,
Ne had never our Lady aye been Heaven's queen.
Blessed be the time that apple taken was,
Therefore may we singen, *"Deo gracias!"*

Amoretti. Sonnet LXVIII ✌ EDMUND SPENSER

Most glorious Lord of life, that on this day
Didst make thy triumph over death and sin,
And having harrowed hell, didst bring away
Captivity thence captive, us to win:
This joyous day, dear Lord, with joy begin,
And grant that we, for whom thou diddest die,
Being with thy dear blood clean washed from sin,
May live for ever in felicity:
And that thy love we weighing worthily,
May likewise love thee for the same again;
And for thy sake, that all like dear didst buy,
May love with one another entertain.
So let us love, dear love, like as we ought:
Love is the lesson which the Lord us taught.

PHILIPPIANS 3:8–3:11   Yea doubtless, and I count all things but loss for the excellency of the knowledge of Christ Jesus my Lord: for whom I have suffered the loss of all things, and do count them but dung, that I may win Christ, And be found in him, not having mine own righteousness, which is of the law, but that which is through the faith of Christ, the righteousness which is of God by faith: That I may know him, and the power of his resurrection, and the fellowship of his sufferings, being made conformable unto his death; If by any means I might attain unto the resurrection of the dead.

The Litany of the Dark People ✌ COUNTEE CULLEN

Our flesh that was a battle-ground
Shows now the morning-break;
The ancient deities are drowned
For thy eternal sake.
Now that the past is left behind,
Fling wide thy garment's hem
To keep us one with Thee in mind,
Thou Christ of Bethlehem.

The thorny wreath may ridge our brow,
The spear may mar our side,

And on white wood from a scented bough
We may be crucified;
Yet no assaults the old gods make
Upon our agony
Shall swerve our footsteps from the wake
Of Thine toward Calvary.

And if we hunger now and thirst,
Grant our withholders may,
When heaven's constellations burst
Upon Thy crowning day,
Be fed by us, and given to see
Thy mercy in our eyes,
When Bethlehem and Calvary
Are merged in Paradise.

PHILIPPIANS 4:9–4:12   Those things, which ye have both learned, and received, and heard, and seen in me, do: and the God of peace shall be with you. But I rejoiced in the Lord greatly, that now at the last your care of me hath flourished again; wherein ye were also careful, but ye lacked opportunity. Not that I speak in respect of want: for I have learned, in whatsoever state I am, therewith to be content. I know both how to be abased, and I know how to abound: every where and in all things I am instructed both to be full and to be hungry, both to abound and to suffer need.

Contentment ᧵ WILLIAM COWPER

Fierce passions discompose the mind,
    As tempests vex the sea:
But calm content and peace we find,
    When, Lord, we turn to thee.

In vain by reason and by rule
    We try to bend the will;
For none but in the Savior's school
    Can learn the heavenly skill.

Since at his feet my soul has sat,
    His gracious words to hear,

Contented with my present state,
   I cast on him my care.

"Art thou a sinner, soul?" he said,
   "Then how canst thou complain?
How light thy troubles here, if weighed
   With everlasting pain!

"If thou of murmuring wouldst be cured,
   Compare thy griefs with mine;
Think what my love for thee endured,
   And thou wilt not repine.

" 'tis I appoint thy daily lot,
   And I do all things well;
Thou soon shalt leave this wretched spot,
   And rise with me to dwell.

"In life my grace shall strength supply,
   Proportioned to thy day;
At death thou still shalt find me nigh,
   To wipe thy tears away."

Thus I, who once my wretched day
   In vain repinings spent,
Taught in my Savior's school of grace,
   Have learnt to be content.

FIRST TIMOTHY 6:11–6:16   But thou, O man of God, flee these things; and follow after righteousness, godliness, faith, love, patience, meekness. Fight the good fight of faith, lay hold on eternal life, whereunto thou art also called, and hast professed a good profession before many witnesses. I give thee charge in the sight of God, who quickeneth all things, and before Christ Jesus, who before Pontius Pilate witnessed a good confession; That thou keep this commandment without spot, unrebukeable, until the appearing of our Lord Jesus Christ: Which in his times he shall show, who is the blessed and only Potentate, the King of kings, and Lord of lords; Who only hath immortality, dwelling in the light which no man can approach unto; whom no man hath seen, nor can see: to whom be honour and power everlasting. Amen.

Pilate Remembers ✥ WILLIAM E. BROOKS

I wonder why that scene comes back tonight,
That long-forgotten scene of years ago.
Perhaps this touch of spring, that full white moon,
For it was spring, and spring's white moon hung low
Above my garden on the night He died.
I still remember how I felt disturbed
That I must send Him to a felon's cross
On such a day when spring was in the air,
And in His life, for He was young to die.
How tall and strong He stood, how calm His eyes,
Fronting me straight and while I questioned Him;
His fearless heart spoke to me through His eyes.
Could I have won Him as my follower,
And a hundred more beside, my way had led
To Cæsar's palace and I'd wear today
The imperial purple. But He would not move
One little bit from His wild madcap dream
Of seeking truth. What wants a man with "truth"
When He is young and spring is at the door?
He would not listen, so He had to go.
One mad Jew less meant little to the state,
And pleasing Annas made my task the less.
And yet for me He spoiled that silver night,—
Remembering it was spring and he was young.

SECOND TIMOTHY 4:6–4:8   For I am now ready to be offered, and the time of my departure is at hand. I have fought a good fight, I have finished my course, I have kept the faith: Henceforth there is laid up for me a crown of righteousness, which the Lord, the righteous judge, shall give me at that day: and not to me only, but unto all them also that love his appearing.

Crossing the Bar ✥ ALFRED, LORD TENNYSON

Sunset and evening star,
    And one clear call for me!
And may there be no moaning of the bar,
    When I put out to sea,

But such a tide as moving seems asleep,
    Too full for sound and foam,
When that which drew from out the boundless deep
    Turns again home.

Twilight and evening bell,
    And after that the dark!
And may there be no sadness of farewell,
    When I embark;

For though from out our bourn of Time and Place
    The flood may bear me far,
I hope to see my Pilot face to face
    When I have crossed the bar.

TITUS 1:10–1:12   For there are many unruly and vain talkers and deceivers, specially they of the circumcision: Whose mouths must be stopped, who subvert whole houses, teaching things which they ought not, for filthy lucre's sake. One of themselves, even a prophet of their own, said, The Cretians are alway liars, evil beasts, slow bellies.

For a Poet   ↲   GEORGE WITHER

Poets are prophets, not only in the vulgar acception, among human authors, but so called by St. Paul, Tit. i. 12. By this hymn, therefore, such poets as are not past grace may be remembered to exercise their faculty to that end for which it was given unto them by God.

By art a poet is not made;
For though by art some bettered be,
Immediately his gift he had
From thee, O God, from none but thee.
    And fitted in the womb he was
To be, by what thou didst inspire,
In extraordinary place,
A chaplain of this lower choir.
    Most poets future things declare,
    And prophets, true or false, they are.
They who with meekness entertain,

And with a humble soul admit
Those raptures which thy grace doth deign,
Become for thy true service fit.
 And though the scapes which we condemn
In these may otherwhile be found,
Thy secrets thou revealest by them,
And mak'st their tongues thy praise to sound.
  Such Moses was, such David proved,
  Men famous, holy, and beloved.
And such, though lower in degree,
Are some who live among us yet;
And they with truth inspirëd be,
By musing on thy holy writ.
 In ordinary, some of those
Upon thy service do attend;
Divulging forth in holy prose
The messages which thou dost send;
  And some of these thy truths display,
  Not in an ordinary way.
But where this gift puffs up with pride,
The devil enters in thereby,
And through the same doth means provide
To raise his own inventions high;
  Blasphemous fancies are infused,
  All holy new things are expelled.
He that hath most profanely mused
Is famed as having most excelled;
  And those are priests and prophets made
  To him from whom their strains they had.
Such were those poets who of old
To heathen gods their hymns did frame;
Or have blasphemous fables told,
To truth's abuse and virtue's blame.
 Such are these poets in these days
Who vent the fumes of lust and wine,
Then crown each others' heads with bays,
As if their poems were divine.
  And such, though they some truths foresee,
  False-hearted and false prophets be.
Therefore, since I reputed am
Among these few on whom the times

Imposëd have a poet's name,
Lord, give me grace to shun their crimes;
    My precious gift let me employ
Not, as imprudent poets use,
That grace and virtue to destroy
Which I should strengthen by my muse;
    But help to free them of the wrongs
    Sustained by drunkards' rhymes and songs.
Yea, whilst thou shalt prolong my days,
Lord, all the musings of my heart,
To be advancements of thy praise,
And to the public weal convert;
    That when to dust I must return,
It may not justly be my thought
That to a blessing I was born,
Which, by abuse, a curse hath brought.
    But let my conscience truly say,
    My soul in peace departs away.

HEBREWS 6:16–6:19   For men verily swear by the greater: and an oath for
confirmation is to them an end of all strife. Wherein God, willing more
abundantly to shew unto the heirs of promise the immutability of his coun-
sel, confirmed it by an oath: That by two immutable things, in which it was
impossible for God to lie, we might have a strong consolation, who have
fled for refuge to lay hold upon the hope set before us: Which hope we have
as an anchor of the soul, both sure and stedfast, and which entereth into
that within the veil;

Hope ♈ GEORGE HERBERT

I gave to Hope a watch of mine: but he
    An anchor gave to me.
Then an old prayer-book I did present:
    And he an optic sent.
With that I gave a vial full of tears:
    But he a few green ears:
Ah Loiterer! I'll no more, no more I'll bring:
    I did expect a ring.

HEBREWS 10:28–10:31   He that despised Moses' law died without mercy under two or three witnesses: Of how much sorer punishment, suppose ye, shall he be thought worthy, who hath trodden under foot the Son of God, and hath counted the blood of the covenant, wherewith he was sanctified, an unholy thing, and hath done despite unto the Spirit of grace? For we know him that hath said, Vengeance belongeth unto me, I will recompense, saith the Lord. And again, The Lord shall judge his people. It is a fearful thing to fall into the hands of the living God.

The Hands of God   ⤳   D. H. LAWRENCE

It is a fearful thing to fall into the hands of the living God.
But it is a much more fearful thing to fall out of them.

Did Lucifer fall through knowledge?
oh then, pity him, pity him that plunge!

Save me, O God, from falling into the ungodly knowledge
of myself as I am without God.
Let me never know, O God
let me never know what I am or should be
when I have fallen out of your hands, the hands of the living God.

That awful and sickening endless sinking, sinking
through the slow, corruptive levels of disintegrative knowledge
when the self has fallen from the hands of God,
and sinks, seething and sinking, corrupt
and sinking still, in depth after depth of disintegrative consciousness
sinking in the endless undoing, the awful katabolism into the abyss!
Even of the soul, fallen from the hands of God!

Save me from that, O God!
Let me never know myself apart from the living God!

JAMES 1:4–1:11   But let patience have her perfect work, that ye may be perfect and entire, wanting nothing. If any of you lack wisdom, let him ask of God, that giveth to all men liberally, and upbraideth not; and it shall be given him. But let him ask in faith, nothing wavering. For he that wavereth is like a wave of the sea driven with the wind and tossed. For let not that man think that he shall receive any thing of the Lord. A double minded man is unstable in all his ways. Let the brother of low degree rejoice in that he is exalted: But the rich, in that he is made low: because as the flower of the grass he shall pass away. For the sun is no sooner risen with a burning heat, but it withereth the grass, and the flower thereof falleth, and the grace of the fashion of it perisheth: so also shall the rich man fade away in his ways.

from *Jubilate Agno* ↝ CHRISTOPHER SMART

For the doubling of flowers is the improvement of the gardener's
    talent.
For the flowers are great blessings.
For the Lord made a nosegay in the meadow with his disciples and
    preached upon the lily.
For the angels of God took it out of his hand and carried it to
    the Height.
For a man cannot have public spirit, who is void of private
    benevolence.
For there is no Height in which there are not flowers.
For flowers have great virtues for all the senses.
For the flower glorifies God and the root parries the adversary.
For the flowers have their angels even the words of God's
    Creation.
For the warp and woof of flowers are worked by perpetual
    moving spirits.
For flowers are good both for the living and the dead.
For there is a language of flowers.
For there is a sound reasoning upon all flowers.
For elegant phrases are nothing but flowers.
For flowers are peculiarly the poetry of Christ.
For flowers are medicinal.
For flowers are musical in ocular harmony.
For the right names of flowers are yet in heaven. God make gardeners
    better nomenclators.
For the poor man's nosegay is an introduction to a Prince.

SECOND PETER 3:9–3:12   The Lord is not slack concerning his promise, as some men count slackness; but is longsuffering to us-ward, not willing that any should perish, but that all should come to repentance. But the day of the Lord will come as a thief in the night; in the which the heavens shall pass away with a great noise, and the elements shall melt with fervent heat, the earth also and the works that are therein shall be burned up. Seeing then that all these things shall be dissolved, what manner of persons ought ye to be in all holy conversation and godliness, Looking for and hasting unto the coming of the day of God, wherein the heavens being on fire shall be dissolved, and the elements shall melt with fervent heat?

A Dream ☙ SIR JOHN SUCKLING

Scarce had I slept my wonted round
But that methoughts I heard the last Trump sound:
And in a moment Earth's fair frame did pass,
The heavens did melt, and all confusion was.
My thoughts straight gave me, Earth's great day was come,
And that I was now to receive my doom.
'Twixt hope and fear, whilst I thus trembling stood
Fearing the bad, and yet expecting good:
Summoned I was, to show how I had spent,
That span-long time which God on earth me lent.
Cold fears possessed me; for I knew no lies
(Though gilded o'er) could blind th' Eternal's eyes.
Besides my bosom friend my conscience me accused,
That I too much this little time abused.
And now no sums of gold, no bribes (alas)
Could me reprieve, sentence must straightway pass.
Great friends could nothing do, no lustful peer,
No smooth-faced Buckingham, was favorite here.
These helps were vain; what could I then say more?
I had done ill, and death lay at the door.
But yet methoughts it was too much to die,
To die a while, much less eternally:
And therefore straight I did my sins unmask
And in Christ's name, a pardon there did ask
Which God then granted; and God grant he may
Make this my dream prove true i'th' latter day.

FIRST JOHN 2:15–2:17   Love not the world, neither the things that are in the world. If any man love the world, the love of the Father is not in him. For all that is in the world, the lust of the flesh, and the lust of the eyes, and the pride of life, is not of the Father, but is of the world. And the world passeth away, and the lust thereof: but he that doeth the will of God abideth for ever.

The World ~ HENRY VAUGHAN

I saw Eternity the other night
Like a great ring of pure and endless light,
    All calm, as it was bright,
And round beneath it, time in hours, days, years
        Driven by the spheres
Like a vast shadow moved, in which the world
    And all her train were hurled;
The doting lover in his quaintest strain
        Did there complain,
Near him, his lute, his fancy, and his flights,
        Wit's sour delights,
With gloves, and knots the silly snares of pleasure
        Yet his dear treasure
All scattered lay, while he his eyes did pour
        Upon a flower.

The darksome statesman hung with weights and woe
Like a thick midnight-fog moved there so slow
    He did nor stay, nor go;
Condemning thoughts (like sad eclipses) scowl
        Upon his soul,
And clouds of crying witnesses without
    Pursued him with one shout.
Yet digged the mole, and lest his ways be found
        Worked under ground,
Where he did clutch his prey, but one did see
        That policy,
Churches and altars fed him, perjuries
        Were gnats and flies,
It rained about him blood and tears, but he
        Drank them as free.

The fearful miser on a heap of rust
Sat pining all his life there, did scarce trust
      His own hands with the dust,
Yet would not place one piece above, but lives
            In fear of thieves.
Thousands there were as frantic as himself
      And hugged each one his pelf,
The down-right epicure placed heaven in sense
            And scorned pretence
While others slipped into a wide excess
            Said little less;
The weaker sort slight, trivial wares enslave
            Who think them brave,
And poor, despised truth sat counting by
            Their victory.

Yet some, who all this while did weep and sing,
And sing, and weep, soared up into the ring,
      But most would use no wing.
O fools (said I,) thus to prefer dark night
            Before true light,
To live in grots, and caves, and hate the day
      Because it shows the way,
The way which from this dead and dark abode
            Leads up to God,
A way where you might tread the sun, and be
            More bright than he.
But as I did their madness so discuss
            One whispered thus,
This ring the Bride-groom did for none provide
            But for his bride.

REVELATION

1:1–1:19   . . . I John, who also am your brother, and companion in tribula-
tion, and in the kingdom and patience of Jesus Christ, was in the isle that is
called Patmos, for the word of God, and for the testimony of Jesus Christ. I
was in the Spirit on the Lord's day, and heard behind me a great voice, as of
a trumpet, Saying, I am Alpha and Omega, the first and the last: and, What

thou seest, write in a book, and send it unto the seven churches which are in Asia; unto Ephesus, and unto Smyrna, and unto Pergamos, and unto Thyatira, and unto Sardis, and unto Philadelphia, and unto Laodicea. And I turned to see the voice that spake with me. . . . And when I saw him, I fell at his feet as dead. And he laid his right hand upon me, saying unto me, Fear not; I am the first and the last: I am he that liveth, and was dead; and, behold, I am alive for evermore, Amen; and have the keys of hell and of death. Write the things which thou hast seen, and the things which are, and the things which shall be hereafter;

To God ❧ ROBERT HERRICK

Do with me, God! as Thou didst deal with John,
(Who writ that heavenly *Revelation*)
Let me (like him) first cracks of thunder hear;
Then let the harp's enchantments strike mine ear;
Here give me thorns; there, in thy Kingdom, set
Upon my head the golden coronet;
There give me day; but here my dreadful night:
My sackcloth here; but there my stole of white.

3:1–3:6   And unto the angel of the church in Sardis write; These things saith he that hath the seven Spirits of God, and the seven stars; I know thy works, that thou hast a name that thou livest, and art dead. Be watchful, and strengthen the things which remain, that are ready to die: for I have not found thy works perfect before God. Remember therefore how thou hast received and heard, and hold fast, and repent. If therefore thou shalt not watch, I will come on thee as a thief, and thou shalt not know what hour I will come upon thee. Thou hast a few names even in Sardis which have not defiled their garments; and they shall walk with me in white: for they are worthy. He that overcometh, the same shall be clothed in white raiment; and I will not blot out his name out of the book of life, but I will confess his name before my Father, and before his angels. He that hath an ear, let him hear what the Spirit saith unto the churches.

Sardis ↝ WILLIAM COWPER

"Write to Sardis," saith the Lord,
    And write what he declares,
He whose Spirit and whose word,
    Upholds the seven stars:
"All thy works and ways I search,
    Find thy zeal and love decayed:
Thou art called a living church,
    But thou art cold and dead.

"Watch, remember, seek, and strive,
    Exert thy former pains;
Let thy timely care revive,
    And strengthen what remains:
Cleanse thine heart, thy works amend,
    Former times to mind recall,
Lest my sudden stroke descend,
    And smite thee once for all.

"Yet I number now in thee
    A few that are upright:
These my Father's face shall see,
    And walk with me in white,
When in judgment I appear,
    They for mine shall be confessed;
Let my faithful servants hear,
    And woe be to the rest!"

7:1–7:3   And after these things I saw four angels standing on the four cor-
ners of the earth, holding the four winds of the earth, that the wind should
not blow on the earth, nor on the sea, nor on any tree. And I saw another
angel ascending from the east, having the seal of the living God: and he
cried with a loud voice to the four angels, to whom it was given to hurt the
earth and the sea, Saying, Hurt not the earth, neither the sea, nor the trees,
till we have sealed the servants of our God in their foreheads.

The Trees are Down ✣ CHARLOTTE MEW

They are cutting down the great plane-trees at the end of the gardens.
For days there has been the grate of the saw, the swish of the branches
       as they fall,
The crash of trunks, the rustle of trodden leaves,
With the "Whoops" and the "Whoas," the loud common talk, the
       loud common laughs of the men, above it all.

I remember one evening of a long past Spring
Turning in at a gate, getting out of a cart, and finding a large dead rat
       in the mud of the drive.
I remember thinking: alive or dead, a rat was a god-forsaken thing,
But at least, in May, that even a rat should be alive.

The week's work here is as good as done. There is just one bough
    On the roped bole, in the fine gray rain,
        Green and high
        And lonely against the sky.
            (Down now!)
        And but for that,
        If an old dead rat
Did once, for a moment, unmake the Spring, I might never have
       thought of him again.

It is not for a moment the Spring is unmade today;
These were great trees, it was in them from root to stem:
When the men with the "Whoops" and the "Whoas" have carted the
       whole of the whispering loveliness away,
Half the Spring, for me, will have gone with them.

It is going now, and my heart has been struck with the hearts of the
       planes;
Half my life it has beat with these, in the sun, in the rains,
        In the March wind, the May breeze,
In the great gales that came over to them across the roofs from the
       great seas.
        There was only a quiet rain when they were dying;
        They must have heard the sparrows flying,
And the small creeping creatures in the earth where they were lying—
        But I, all day, I heard an angel crying:
        "Hurt not the trees."

8:1–8:6   And when he had opened the seventh seal, there was silence in heaven about the space of half an hour. And I saw the seven angels which stood before God; and to them were given seven trumpets. And another angel came and stood at the altar, having a golden censer; and there was given unto him much incense, that he should offer it with the prayers of all saints upon the golden altar which was before the throne. And the smoke of the incense, which came with the prayers of the saints, ascended up before God out of the angel's hand. And the angel took the censer, and filled it with fire of the altar, and cast it into the earth: and there were voices, and thunderings, and lightnings, and an earthquake. And the seven angels which had the seven trumpets prepared themselves to sound.

Holy Sonnet VII   ᔓ   JOHN DONNE

At the round Earth's imagined corners, blow
Your trumpets, Angels, and arise, arise
From death, you numberless infinities
Of souls, and to your scattered bodies go,
All whom the flood did, and fire shall o'erthrow,
All whom war, dearth, age, agues, tyrannies,
Despair, law, chance, hath slain, and you whose eyes,
Shall behold God, and never taste death's woe.
But let them sleep, Lord, and me mourn a space,
For, if above all these, my sins abound,
'Tis late to ask abundance of thy grace,
When we are there; here on this lowly ground,
Teach me how to repent; for that's as good
As if thou hadst sealed my pardon, with thy blood.

12:1–12:6   And there appeared a great wonder in heaven; a woman clothed with the sun, and the moon under her feet, and upon her head a crown of twelve stars: And she being with child cried, travailing in birth, and pained to be delivered. And there appeared another wonder in heaven; and behold a great red dragon, having seven heads and ten horns, and seven crowns upon his heads. And his tail drew the third part of the stars of heaven, and did cast them to the earth: and the dragon stood before the woman which was ready to be delivered, for to devour her child as soon as it was born. And she brought forth a man child, who was to rule all nations with a rod of iron: and her child was caught up unto God, and to his throne. And

the woman fled into the wilderness, where she hath a place prepared of
God, that they should feed her there a thousand two hundred and
threescore days.

The Mental Traveller ᴣ WILLIAM BLAKE

I travelled through a Land of Men,
A Land of Men and Women too,
And heard and saw such dreadful things
As cold Earth wanderers never knew.

For there the Babe is born in joy
That was begotten in dire woe;
Just as we Reap in joy the fruit
Which we in bitter tears did sow.

And if the Babe is born a Boy
He's given to a Woman Old,
Who nails him down upon a rock,
Catches his shrieks in cups of gold.

She binds iron thorns around his head,
She pierces both his hands and feet,
She cuts his heart out at his side
To make it feel both cold and heat.

Her fingers number every Nerve,
Just as a Miser counts his gold;
She lives upon his shrieks and cries,
And she grows young as he grows old.

Till he becomes a bleeding youth,
And she becomes a Virgin bright;
Then he rends up his Manacles
And binds her down for his delight.

He plants himself in all her Nerves,
Just as a Husbandman his mould;
And she becomes his dwelling place
And Garden fruitful seventy fold.

An aged Shadow, soon he fades,
Wand'ring round an Earthly Cot,
Full filled all with gems and gold
Which he by industry had got.

And these are the gems of the Human Soul,
The rubies and pearls of a lovesick eye,
The countless gold of the aching heart,
The martyr's groan and the lover's sigh.

They are his meat, they are his drink;
He feeds the Beggar and the Poor
And the wayfaring Traveller:
For ever open is his door.

His grief is their eternal joy;
They make the roofs and walls to ring;
Till from the fire on the hearth
A little Female Babe does spring.

And she is all of solid fire
And gems and gold, that none his hand
Dares stretch to touch her Baby form
Or wrap her in his swaddling-band.

But She comes to the Man she loves,
If young or old, or rich or poor;
They soon drive out the aged Host,
A Beggar at another's door.

He wanders weeping far away,
Until some other take him in;
Oft blind and age-bent, sore distrest,
Until he can a Maiden win.

And to allay his freezing Age
The Poor Man takes her in his arms;
The Cottage fades before his sight,
The Garden and its lovely Charms.

The Guests are scattered through the land,
For the Eye altering alters all;
The Senses roll themselves in fear,
And the flat Earth becomes a Ball;

The stars, sun, Moon, all shrink away,
A desart vast without a bound,
And nothing left to eat or drink,
And a dark desart all around.

The honey of her Infant lips,
The bread and wine of her sweet smile,
The wild game of her roving Eye,
Does him to Infancy beguile;

For as he eats and drinks he grows
Younger and younger every day;
And on the desart wild they both
Wander in terror and dismay.

Like the wild Stag she flees away,
Her fear plants many a thicket wild;
While he pursues her night and day,
By various arts of Love beguiled,

By various arts of Love and Hate,
Till the wide desart planted o'er
With Labyrinths of wayward Love,
Where roam the Lion, Wolf and Boar,

Till he becomes a wayward Babe,
And she a weeping Woman Old.
Then many a Lover wanders here;
The Sun and Stars are nearer rolled.

The trees bring forth sweet Extacy
To all who in the desart roam;
Till many a City there is Built,
And many a pleasant Shepherd's home.

But when they find the frowning Babe,
Terror strikes through the region wide:
They cry "The Babe! the Babe is Born!"
And flee away on Every side.

For who dare touch the frowning form,
His arm is withered to its root;
Lions, Boars, Wolves, all howling flee,
And every Tree does shed its fruit.

And none can touch that frowning form,
Except it be a Woman Old;
She nails him down upon the Rock,
And all is done as I have told.

13:1–13:3   And I stood upon the sand of the sea, and saw a beast rise up out of the sea, having seven heads and ten horns, and upon his horns ten crowns, and upon his heads the name of blasphemy. And the beast which I saw was like unto a leopard, and his feet were as the feet of a bear, and his mouth as the mouth of a lion: and the dragon gave him his power, and his seat, and great authority. And I saw one of his heads as it were wounded to death; and his deadly wound was healed: and all the world wondered after the beast.

Sonnet XII   ᒎ   EDMUND SPENSER

I saw an ugly beast come from the sea,
That seven heads, ten crowns, ten horns did bear,
Having thereon the vile blaspheming name.
The cruel leopard she resembled much:
Feet of a bear, a lion's throat she had.
The mighty dragon gave to her his power.
One of her heads yet there I did espy,
Still freshly bleeding of a grievous wound.
One cried aloud. What one is like (quoth he)
This honored dragon, or may him withstand?
And then came from the sea a savage beast,
With dragon's speech, and showed his force by fire,
With wondrous signs to make all wights adore
The beast, in setting of her image up.

16:1–16:18   And I heard a great voice out of the temple saying to the seven angels, Go your ways, and pour out the vials of the wrath of God upon the earth. And the first went, and poured out his vial upon the earth; and there fell a noisome and grievous sore upon the men which had the mark of the beast, and upon them which worshipped his image. And the second angel poured out his vial upon the sea; and it became as the blood of a dead man: and every living soul died in the sea. And the third angel poured out his vial upon the rivers and fountains of waters; and they became blood. And I heard the angel of the waters say, Thou art righteous, O Lord, which art, and wast, and shalt be, because thou hast judged thus. For they have shed the blood of saints and prophets, and thou hast given them blood to drink; for they are worthy. And I heard another out of the altar say, Even so, Lord God Almighty, true and righteous are thy judgments. And the fourth angel poured out his vial upon the sun; and power was given unto him to scorch men with fire. And men were scorched with great heat, and blasphemed the name of God, which hath power over these plagues: and they repented not to give him glory. And the fifth angel poured out his vial upon the seat of the beast; and his kingdom was full of darkness; and they gnawed their tongues for pain, And blasphemed the God of heaven because of their pains and their sores, and repented not of their deeds. And the sixth angel poured out his vial upon the great river Euphrates; and the water thereof was dried up, that the way of the kings of the east might be prepared.

And I saw three unclean spirits like frogs come out of the mouth of the dragon, and out of the mouth of the beast, and out of the mouth of the false prophet. For they are the spirits of devils, working miracles, which go forth unto the kings of the earth and of the whole world, to gather them to the battle of that great day of God Almighty. Behold, I come as a thief. Blessed is he that watcheth, and keepeth his garments, lest he walk naked, and they see his shame. And he gathered them together into a place called in the Hebrew tongue Armageddon. And the seventh angel poured out his vial into the air; and there came a great voice out of the temple of heaven, from the throne, saying, It is done. And there were voices, and thunders, and lightnings; and there was a great earthquake, such as was not since men were upon the earth, so mighty an earthquake, and so great.

Armageddon   ॐ   JOHN CROWE RANSOM

Antichrist, playing his lissome flute and merry
As was his wont, debouched upon the plain;
Then came a swirl of dust, and Christ drew rein,
Brooding upon his frugal breviary.

Now which shall die, the roundel, rose, and hall,
Or else the tonsured beadsman's monkery?
For Christ and Antichrist arm cap-a-pie,
The prospect charms the soul of the lean jackal.

But Antichrist got down from the Barbary beast
And doffed his plume in courteous prostration;
Christ left his jennet's back in deprecation
And raised him, his own hand about the waist.

Then next they fingered chivalry's quaint page,
Of precedence discoursing by the letter.
The oratory of Antichrist was better,
He invested Christ with the elder lineage.

He set Christ on his own Mahomet's back
Where Christ sat fortressed up like Diomede;
The cynical hairy jennet was his steed.
Obtuse, and most indifferent to attack.

The lordings measured lances and stood still,
And each was loath to let the other's blood;
Originally they were one brotherhood;
There stood the white pavilion on the hill.

To the pavilion went then the hierarchs,
If they might truce their honorable dispute;
Firm was the Christian's chin and he was mute,
And Antichrist ejected scant remarks.

Antichrist tendered a spray of rosemary
To serve his brother for a buttonhole;
Then Christ about his adversary's poll
Wrapped a dry palm that grew on Calvary.

Christ wore a dusty cassock, and the knight
Did him the honors of his tiring-hall,
Whence Christ did not come forth too finical,
But his egregious beauty richly dight.

With feasting they concluded every day,
And when the other shaped his phrases thicker
Christ, introducing water in the liquor,
Made wine of more ethereal bouquet.

At wassail Antichrist would pitch the strain
For unison of all the retinue;
Christ beat the time, and hummed a stave or two,
But did not say the words, which were profane.

Perruquiers were privily presented,
Till, knowing his need extreme and his heart pure,
Christ let them dress him his thick chevelure,
And soon his beard was glozed and sweetly scented.

And so the Wolf said Brother to the Lamb,
The True Heir keeping with the poor Impostor,
The rubric and the holy paternoster
Were jangled strangely with the dithyramb.

It could not be. There was a patriarch,
A godly liege of old malignant brood,
Who could not fathom the new brotherhood
Between the children of the light and dark.

He sought the ear of Christ on these strange things,
But in the white pavilion when he stood,
And saw them favored and dressed like twins at food,
Profound and mad became his misgivings.

The voices, and their burdens, he must hear,
But equal between the pleasant Princes flew
Theology, the arts, the old customs and the new;
Hoarsely he ran and hissed in the wrong ear.

He was discomfited, but Christ much more.
Christ sheds unmannerly his devil's pelf,
Takes ashes from the hearth and smears himself,
Calls for his smock and jennet as before.

His trump recalls his own to right opinions,
With scourge they mortify their carnal selves,
With stone they whet the ax-heads on the helves
And seek the Prince Beelzebub and minions.

Christ and his myrmidons, Christ at the head,
Chanted of death and glory and no complaisance;
Antichrist and the armies of malfeasance
Made songs of innocence and no bloodshed.

The immortal Adversary shook his head:
If now they fought too long, then he would famish;
And if much blood was shed, why, he was squeamish:
"These Armageddons weary me much," he said.

17:1–17:5   And there came one of the seven angels which had the seven
vials, and talked with me, saying unto me, Come hither; I will shew unto
thee the judgment of the great whore that sitteth upon many waters: With
whom the kings of the earth have committed fornication, and the inhabi-
tants of the earth have been made drunk with the wine of her fornication.
So he carried me away in the spirit into the wilderness: and I saw a woman
sit upon a scarlet coloured beast, full of names of blasphemy, having seven
heads and ten horns. And the woman was arrayed in purple and scarlet
colour, and decked with gold and precious stones and pearls, having a gold-
en cup in her hand full of abominations and filthiness of her fornication:
And upon her forehead was a name written, MYSTERY, BABYLON THE
GREAT, THE MOTHER OF HARLOTS AND ABOMINATIONS OF THE
EARTH.

Sonnet XIII   ❧   EDMUND SPENSER

I saw a woman sitting on a beast
Before mine eyes, of orange color hue:
Horror and dreadful name of blasphemy
Filled her with pride. And seven heads I saw,
Ten horns also the stately beast did bear.
She seemed with glory of the scarlet fair,
And with fine pearl and gold puffed up in heart.
The wine of whoredom in a cup she bare.

The name of Mystery writ in her face.
The blood of martyrs dear were her delight.
Most fierce and fell this woman seemed to me.
An angel then descending down from Heaven,
With thundering voice cried out aloud, and said,
Now for a truth great Babylon is fallen.

18:1–18:2   And after these things I saw another angel come down from heaven, having great power; and the earth was lightened with his glory. And he cried mightily with a strong voice, saying, Babylon the great is fallen, is fallen, and is become the habitation of devils, and the hold of every foul spirit, and a cage of every unclean and hateful bird.

Let go the Whore of Babylon   ⁊   MILES COVERDALE

Let go the whore of Babylon,
   Her kingdom falleth sore
Her merchants begin to make their moan
   The Lord be praised therefore.
Their ware is naught / it will not be bought
Great falsehood is found therein.
Let go the whore of Babylon
   The mother of all sin.

No man will drink her wine any more
   The poison is come to light,
That maketh her merchants to weep so sore
   The blind have gotten their sight
For now we see / gods grace seely
Is Christ offered us so fair
Let go the whore of Babylon
   And buy no more her ware.

Of Christian blood so much she shed
   That she was drunken withal
But now God's word hath broken her head
   And she hath gotten a fall
God hath raised / some men in deed
To utter her great wickedness

Let go the whore of Babylon
   And her ungodliness.

Ye hypocrites what can ye say?
   Woe be unto you all
Ye have beguiled us many a day
   Heretics ye did us call
For loving the word / of Christ the Lord
Whom ye do always resist
Let go the whore of Babylon
   That rideth upon the beast.

Ye proud and cruel Egyptians
   That did us so great wrong
The lord hath sent us deliverance
   Though ye have troubled us long
Your Pharaoh / with other mo
He drowned in the Reed Sea
Let go the whore of Babylon
   With her captivity.

Ye Canaanites ye enemies all
   Though ye were many in deed
Yet hath the lord given you a fall
   And us delivered
Even in your land / do we now stand
Our lord god hath brought us in
Let go the whore of Babylon
   And flee from all her sin.

Dagon Dagon that false idol
   The Philistine's god
Which hath deceived many a soul
   In such honor he stood
But now the lord / with his sweet word
   Hath broken him down before the ark
Let go the whore of Babylon
   And forsake the beastës mark.

Balaam Balaam thou false prophet
   Thou hast cursed us right sore

Yet into a blessing hath God turned it
　　No thank to thee therefore
For thy belly / thou wouldest lie
　　Though God make thee to say the sooth
Let go the whore of Babylon
　　And turn you to the truth.

Thy God be praised o Daniel
　　For his goodness so great
The greedy priests of the Idol Bel
　　Were wont too much to eat
And that privily / no man did see
But now the king hath spied their cast
Let go the whore of Babylon
　　For Bel is destroyed at the last.

O glorious God full of mercy
　　We thank thee evermore
Thou hast showed us thy verity
　　Thy name be praised therefore
For thy sweet word / O gracious Lord
Let us be ever thankful to thee
And send the whore of Babylon
　　Into captivity.

Rejoice with me thou heaven above
　　And ye Apostles all
Be glad ye people for Christ's love
　　That the whore hath gotten a fall
Be thankful now / I require you
Amend your lives while ye have space
Let go the whore of Babylon
　　And thank God of his grace.

19:11–19:13　　And I saw heaven opened, and behold a white horse; and he
that sat upon him was called Faithful and True, and in righteousness he
doth judge and make war. His eyes were as a flame of fire, and on his head
were many crowns; and he had a name written, that no man knew, but he
himself. And he was clothed with a vesture dipped in blood: and his name
is called The Word of God.

Sonnet XIV ᷤ EDMUND SPENSER

Then might I see upon a white horse set
The faithful man with flaming countenance,
His head did shine with crowns set thereupon.
The word of God made him a noble name.
His precious robe I saw embrewed with blood.
Then saw I from the heaven on horses white,
A puissant army come the self-same way.
Then cried a shining angel as me thought,
That birds from air descending down on earth
Should war upon the kings, and eat their flesh.
Then did I see the beast and kings also
Joining their force to slay the faithful man.
But this fierce hateful beast and all her train,
Is pitiless thrown down in pit of fire.

20:5–20:6   But the rest of the dead lived not again until the thousand years were finished. This is the first resurrection. Blessed and holy is he that hath part in the first resurrection: on such the second death hath no power, but they shall be priests of God and of Christ, and shall reign with him a thousand years.

'Woefully Arrayed' ᷤ JOHN SKELTON

Woefully arrayed,
My blood, man,
For thee ran,
It may not be nayed:
My body blue and wan,
Woefully arrayed.

Behold me, I pray thee, with all thine whole reason,
And be not hard-hearted for this encheason,
That I for thy soul's sake was slain in good season,
Beguiled and betrayed by Judas' false treason,
Unkindly entreated,
With sharp cords sore fretted,
The Jewës me threated,

They mowed, they spitted and despised me
Condemned to death, as thou mayst see.

Thus naked am I nailed, O man, for thy sake.
I love thee, then love me. Why sleepest thou? Awake!
Remember my tender heart-root for thee brake,
With pains my veins constrained to crack.
      Thus was I defaced,
      Thus was my flesh rased,
      And I to death chased,
Like a lamb led unto sacrifice,
Slain I was in most cruel wise.

Of sharp thorn I have worn a crown on my head
So rubbed, so bobbed, so rueful, so red;
Sore pained, sore strained, and for thy love dead,
Unfeigned, not deemed, my blood for thee shed;
      My feet and hands sore
      With sturdy nails bore.
      What might I suffer more
Than I have suffered, man, for thee.
Come when thou wilt and welcome to me!

Dear brother, none other thing I desire
But give me thy heart free, to reward mine hire.
I am he that made the earth, water and fire.
Sathanas, that sloven, and right loathly sire,
      Him have I overcast
      In hell-prison bound fast,
      Where aye his woe shall last.
I have purveyed a place full clear
For mankind, whom I have bought dear.

20:12–20:13   And I saw the dead, small and great, stand before God; and
the books were opened: and another book was opened, which is the book of
life: and the dead were judged out of those things which were written in the
books, according to their works. And the sea gave up the dead which were
in it; and death and hell delivered up the dead which were in them: and they
were judged every man according to their works.

The Resurrection ✍ ABRAHAM COWLEY

Not winds to voyagers at sea,
Not showers to earth more necessary be,
(Heavens vital seed cast on the womb of earth
        To give the fruitful year a birth)
        Than verse to virtue, which can do
The midwife's office, and the nurse's too;
It feeds it strongly, and it clothes it gay,
        And when it dies, with comely pride
Embalms it, and erects a pyramid
        That never will decay
    Till Heaven itself shall melt away,
And nought behind it stay.

Begin the song, and strike the living lyre;
Lo how the years to come, a numerous and well-fitted choir,
All hand in hand do decently advance,
And to my song with smooth and equal measures dance.
Whilst the dance lasts, how long so e'er it be,
My music's voice shall bear it company.
        Till all gentle notes be drowned
        In the last Trumpet's dreadful sound.[30]
That to the spheres themselves shall silence bring,
        Untune the universal string.
        Then all the wide extended sky,
        And all th'harmonious worlds on high,
        And Virgil's sacred work shall die.
And he himself shall see in one fire shine
Rich nature's ancient Troy, though built by hands divine.

    Whom thunders dismal noise,
And all that Prophets and Apostles louder spake,
And all the creatures plain conspiring voice,
        Could not whilst they lived, awake,
        This mightier sound shall make
            When dead t'arise,
        And open tombs, and open eyes
To the long sluggards of five thousand years.

30 1 COR 15:51–53

This mightier sound shall make its hearers ears.
Then shall the scattered atoms crowding come
       Back to their ancient home,
       Some from birds, from fishes some,
       Some from earth, and some from seas,
       Some from beasts, and some from trees.
       Some descend from clouds on high,
       Some from metals upwards fly,
And where th'attending soul naked, and shivering stands,
       Meet, salute, and join their hands.
As dispersed soldiers at the trumpet's call,
       Haste to their colors all.
   Unhappy most, like tortured men,
Their joints new set, to be new racked again.
   To mountains they for shelter pray,
The mountains shake, and run about no less confused than they.

Stop, stop, my Muse, allay thy vigorous heat,
       Kindled at a hint so great.
Hold thy Pindaric Pegasus closely in,
       Which does to rage begin,
And this steep hill would gallop up with violent course,
'Tis an unruly, and a hard-mouthed horse,
       Fierce, and unbroken yet,
       Impatient of the spur or bit.
Now prances stately, and anon flies o'er the place,
Disdains the servile law of any settled pace,
Conscious and proud of his own natural force.
       'Twill no unskillful touch endure,
But flings writer, and reader too, that sits not sure.

21:1–21:3   And I saw a new heaven and a new earth: for the first heaven
and the first earth were passed away; and there was no more sea. And I
John saw the holy city, new Jerusalem, coming down from God out of heav-
en, prepared as a bride adorned for her husband. And I heard a great voice
out of heaven saying, Behold, the tabernacle of God is with men, and he will
dwell with them, and they shall be his people, and God himself shall be with
them, and be their God.

A Vision of Sunday in Heaven ⨍ VICTOR DALEY

At a meeting of the Presbyterian General Assembly, the Rev. Mr. Meiklejohn
made a statement to the effect that 'It was a matter upon which every right-
minded man should congratulate himself that recent attempts to throw open
the Museum and Libraries on Sunday had not been successful.'

Methought, one night, I saw, in trance sublime,
    With wonder, and with terror, and with awe,
Builded beyond the bounds of Space and Time,
    The glorious city John in Patmos saw.

Mighty and high it shone, a living glow,
    A splendid sun of suns in azure pendent:
Not all the wealth of all this world below
    Would make a string-course for its walls resplendent.

For every brick therein was solid gold
    (Of diamond were the turrets and pilasters)
For one of them you might have bought, behold,
    The Presbyterian Church with all its pastors!

Even in my trance, though a good Catholic,
    I could not at this sight my envy smother:
I could pay all my debts with half-a-brick
    I saw one little saint throw at another.

Too much, mayhap, of democratic leaven
    Remains in me; but, on its bright outside, as
I gazed, this city looked to me like Heaven
    According to the gospel of St. Midas.

So dazzling-new it seemed hung in the skies!
    It would have pleased me more had it been duller
In tone; its dreadful splendour scorched mine eyes
    Accustomed to the cult of quiet colour.

Ah, purblind eyes! It was God's Golden Rose
    To music grand unfolding every petal,
Flooding all space with solemn overflows—
    The Choir Invisible was on its mettle.

But suddenly there came before my view
   A Shape lugubrious: 'twas another mortal,
Attired in garments of funereal hue,
   A-knocking sadly at the Heavenly Portal.

His face was sour to see, with lips down-drawn,
   And bilious eyes. A foe to all jocoseness
He seemed; a victim to a woe-begone,
   Incurable, inherited moroseness.

The Portal opened with melodious clang,
   And forth came Peter, in a style theatric,
And down the gulfs of space his laughter rang—
   'Twas at a joke, he said, made by St. Patrick.

The Shape frowned gloomily, and said, 'I am
   The Reverend Meiklejohn.' Then, very slyly,
Winking at one inside the Gate, 'Salaam!
   I've often heard of you,' quoth Peter, dryly.

'We've no free passes here, but if you stand
   Beside me, you may look.' At this grown bolder
I also ranged up on his other hand—
   I think the good saint saw me o'er his shoulder.

Then soared into the crystal air above
   A song seraphic, pulsing, glowing, thrilling
With heavenly heart-notes of immortal love,
   The infinite blue dome with rapture filling.

Ah, hymn divine, I ne'er may hear again!
   Song of the full-voiced soul, freed from the yearning
Known here on earth! I listened to the strain,
   And mine own soul I felt within me burning.

St. Peter spake; with pride his visage shone:
   'What think you, reverend sir, of our intoning?'
He shook his head, the Reverend Meiklejohn—
   He missed the good old Presbyterian droning.

But now the inner glory of the place
    Was visible, and, desperately folding
His hands, the trembling pastor hid his face.
    His grief was terrible, such sights beholding

Upon a Sabbath-day. For, lo, he saw
    Angels and saints—confessor, martyr, virgin—
Holding high sport, and—spectacle of awe!—
    Leading the revels the late Reverend Spurgeon!

'Have sense! You're now too good for us by half,'
    Said Peter. 'take a hint from yonder trio!
The red-faced saint is Luther—hear him laugh!—
    Huss has some jest told to the Tenth Pope Leo.'

The pastor lost what sense he had to lose,
    When, down a jasper-kerbed celestial strada,
Came, chatting pleasantly with Moors and Jews,
    His Eminence the General, Torquemada.

And then passed by, linked arm in arm, a pair:
    ' 'tis Cyril and Hypatia, talking sweet as
Two seraphs. In the alley over there
    Is Calvin, playing skittles with Servetus.'

Thus Peter. Beatrice and Dante then
    We saw; the Poet's brow no more was wrinkled.
He looked the mirthfullest of sainted men—
    The very laurels on his forehead twinkled.

And, on a slope abloom with asphodel,
    Grandly aloof from all amusements petty,
We saw Rossetti's Blessed Damozel,
    And, at her feet, reciting verse, Rossetti.

A ring of dancing angels next we spied—
    To tell the truth I liked their style extremely—
But Reverend Meiklejohn was shocked, and cried,
    'Oh, Peter, Peter, mon—it's maist onseemly.'

St. Peter smiled—'Judge not of anything
   In haste; all things are pure unto the pure,' he
Remarked: 'Observe John Knox outside the ring
   Clapping his hands with corybantic fury!'

There was a spice of malice, nowise lost,
   In that last sentence by St. Peter spoken;
He would have stood a jest at his own cost,
   But Reverend Meiklejohn was too heart-broken.

'And whaur's the Scarlet Woman—she of Rome?'
   The pastor cried, his temper tried severely.
St. Peter frowned: 'Sir, this is not a Home
   For Presbyterian myths,' he said, austerely.

Just as the pastor's hand was raised on high
   In act to pass on all he saw stern stricture,
He caught Fra Lippo Lippi's merry eye,
   And saw him slyly sketching out his picture.

Then Peter kindly said, 'Laugh more; groan less;
   That Heaven is dull is simply Satan's rumour;
The ways of God are ways of pleasantness,
   And well He loves a saint with wit and humour.'

'I've neither,' sighed the Reverend Meiklejohn.
   And with these words the conversation ended—
'I doot that God's nae a richt-thinkin' mon!'
   He said, and sadly to the earth descended.

21:21   And the twelve gates were twelve pearls: every several gate
was of one pearl: and the street of the city was pure gold, as it were
transparent glass.

Sonnet XV ❧ EDMUND SPENSER

I saw new Earth, new Heaven, said Saint John.
And lo, the sea (quoth he) is now no more.
The holy City of the Lord, from high

Descendeth garnished as a loved spouse.
A voice then said, behold the bright abode
Of God and men. For he shall be their God.
And all their tears he shall wipe clean away.
Her brightness greater was than can be found.
Square was this city, and twelve gates it had.
Each gate was of an orient perfect pearl,
The houses gold, the pavement precious stone.
A lively stream, more clear than crystal is,
Ran through the mid, sprung from triumphant seat.
There grows life's fruit unto the Churches good.

22:10–22:11   And he saith unto me, Seal not the sayings of the prophecy
of this book: for the time is at hand. He that is unjust, let him be unjust
still: and he which is filthy, let him be filthy still: and he that is righteous, let
him be righteous still: and he that is holy, let him be holy still.

A Commination   ᔛ   A. D. HOPE

Like John on Patmos, brooding on the Four
Last Things, I meditate the ruin of friends
Whose loss, Lord, brings this grand new Curse to mind.
Now send me foes worth cursing, or send more
—Since means should be proportionate to ends—
For mine are few and of the piddling kind:

Drivellers, snivellers, writers of bad verse,
Backbiting bitches, snipers from a pew,
Small turds from the great arse of self-esteem;
On such as these I would not waste my curse.
God send me soon the enemy or two
Fit for the wrath of God, of whom I dream:

Some Caliban of Culture, some absurd
Messiah of the Paranoiac State,
Some Educator wallowing in his slime,
Some Prophet of the Uncreating Word
Monsters and man might reasonably hate,
Masters of Progress, Leaders of our Time;

But chiefly the Suborners: Common Tout
And Punk, the Advertiser, him I mean
And his smooth hatchet-man, the Technocrat,
Them let my malediction single out,
These modern Dives with their talking screen
Who lick the sores of Lazarus and grow fat,

Licensed to pimp, solicit and procure
Here in my house, to foul my feast, to bawl
Their wares while I am talking with my friend,
To pour into my ears a public sewer
Of all the Strumpet Muses sell and all
That prostituted science has to vend.

In this great Sodom of a world, which turns
The Treasure of the Intellect to dust
And every gift to some perverted use,
What wonder if the human spirit learns
Recourses of despair or of disgust,
Abortion, suicide and self-abuse.

But let me laugh, Lord; let me crack and strain
The belly of this derision till it burst;
For I have seen too much, have lived too long
A citizen of Sodom to refrain,
And in the stye of Science, from the first,
Have watched the pearls of Circe drop on dung.

Let me not curse my children, nor in rage
Mock at the just, the helpless and the poor,
Foot-fast in Sodom's rat-trap; make me bold
To turn on the Despoilers all their age
Invents: damnations never felt before
And hells more horrible than hot and cold.

And, since in Heaven creatures purified,
Rational, free, perfected in their kinds
Contemplate God and see Him face to face,
In Hell, for sure, spirits transmogrified,
Paralysed wills and parasitic minds
Mirror their own corruption and disgrace.

Now let this curse fall on my enemies,
My enemies, Lord, but all mankind's as well,
Prophets and panders of their golden calf;
Let Justice fit them all in their degrees;
Let them, still living, know that state of hell,
And let me see them perish, Lord, and laugh.

Let them be glued to television screens
Till their minds fester and the trash they see
Worm their dry hearts away to crackling shells;
Let ends be so revenged upon their means
That all that once was human grows to be
A flaccid mass of phototropic cells;

Let the dog love his vomit still, the swine
Squelch in the slough; and let their only speech
Be Babel; let the specious lies they bred
Taste on their tongues like intellectual wine;
Let sung commercials surfeit them, till each
Goggles with nausea in his nauseous bed.

And, lest with them I learn to gibber and gloat,
Lead me, for Sodom is my city still,
To seek those hills in which the heart finds ease;
Give Lot his leave; let Noah build his boat,
And me and mine, when each has laughed his fill,
View thy damnation and depart in peace.

22:17   And the Spirit and the bride say, Come. And let him that heareth
say, Come. And let him that is athirst come. And whosoever will, let him
take the water of life freely.

Paradise Re-entered   ᔥ   D. H. LAWRENCE

Through the strait gate of passion,
Between the bickering fire
Where flames of fierce love tremble
On the body of fierce desire:

To the intoxication,
The mind, fused down like a bead,
Flees in its agitation
The flames' stiff speed:

At last to calm incandescence,
Burned clean by remorseless hate,
Now, at the day's renascence
We approach the gate.

Now, from the darkened spaces
Of fear, and of frightened faces,
Death, in our awed embraces
Approached and passed by;

We near the flame-burnt porches
Where the brands of the angels, like torches,
Whirl,—in these perilous marches
Pausing to sigh;

We look back on the withering roses,
The stars, in their sun-dimmed closes,
Where 'twas given us to repose us
Sure on our sanctity;

Beautiful, candid lovers,
Burnt out of our earthly covers,
We might have nestled like plovers
In the fields of eternity.

There, sure in sinless being,
All-seen, and then all-seeing,
In us life unto death agreeing,
We might have lain.

But we storm the angel-guarded
Gates of the long discarded
Garden, which God has hoarded
Against our pain.

The Lord of Hosts and the Devil
Are left on Eternity's level
Field, and as victors we travel
To Eden home.

Back beyond good and evil
Return we. Eve dishevel
Your hair for the bliss-drenched revel
On our primal loam.

22:18–22:20 For I testify unto every man that heareth the words of the prophecy of this book, If any man shall add unto these things, God shall add unto him the plagues that are written in this book: And if any man shall take away from the words of the book of this prophecy, God shall take away his part out of the book of life, and out of the holy city, and from the things which are written in this book.

He which testifieth these things saith, Surely I come quickly. Amen. . . .

The Second Coming ❧ WILLIAM BUTLER YEATS

Turning and turning in the widening gyre
The falcon cannot hear the falconer;
Things fall apart; the centre cannot hold;
Mere anarchy is loosed upon the world,
The blood-dimmed tide is loosed, and everywhere
The ceremony of innocence is drowned;
The best lack all conviction, while the worst
Are full of passionate intensity.

Surely some revelation is at hand;
Surely the Second Coming is at hand.
The Second Coming! Hardly are those words out
When a vast image out of *Spiritus Mundi*
Troubles my sight: somewhere in sands of the desert
A shape with lion body and the head of a man,
A gaze blank and pitiless as the sun,
Is moving its slow thighs, while all about it
Reel shadows of the indignant desert birds.

The darkness drops again; but now I know
That twenty centuries of stony sleep
Were vexed to nightmare by a rocking cradle,
And what rough beast, its hour come round at last,
Slouches towards Bethlehem to be born?

INDEX OF TITLES

INDEX OF FIRST LINES

INDEX OF POETS

CREDITS